Attachment

The Family Therapy and Counseling Series
Series Editor
Jon Carlson, Psy.D., Ed.D.

Attachment

Edited by

Phyllis Erdman
and Kok-Mun Ng

Expanding the Cultural Connections

Routledge
Taylor & Francis Group
New York   London

This book is part of the Family Therapy and Counseling Series, edited by Jon Carlson.

Routledge
Taylor & Francis Group
270 Madison Avenue
New York, NY 10016

Routledge
Taylor & Francis Group
27 Church Road
Hove, East Sussex BN3 2FA

© 2010 by Taylor and Francis Group, LLC
Routledge is an imprint of Taylor & Francis Group, an Informa business

Printed in the United States of America on acid-free paper
10 9 8 7 6 5 4 3 2 1

International Standard Book Number: 978-0-415-99059-2 (Hardback)

Library of Congress Cataloging-in-Publication Data

Attachment : expanding the cultural connections / edited by Phyllis Erdman and Kok-Mun Ng.
    p. cm.
    ISBN 978-0-415-99059-2 (hardback : alk. paper)
    1. Attachment behavior--Cross-cultural studies. 2. Intimacy (Psychology)--Cross-cultural studies. I. Erdman, Phyllis, 1949- II. Ng, Kok-Mun.

BF575.A86A777 2010
155.9'2--dc22
                                        2009045290

Visit the Taylor & Francis Web site at
http://www.taylorandfrancis.com

and the Routledge Web site at
http://www.routledgementalhealth.com

Contents

SECTION V   CLINICAL APPLICATIONS

Series Editor's Foreword

"What cannot be communicated to the (m) other cannot be communicated to the self."

John Bowlby, 1991

Attachment theory is concerned with the relationships between people. Its fundamental premise seems to be that children need to have *attached* to at least one of their primary love objects or parents in order to develop normally. The theory is attributed to psychiatrist John Bowlby.

There has been extensive research showing how attachment correlates with children's functioning as well as adult behavior. The level or style of attachment seems to explain adult relationships as to whether relationships are insecure or secure. Securely attached adults have positive views of themselves and partners and feel comfortable with intimacy. Insecure styles tend to be less trusting and have more difficulty connecting with their partners and their own children.

In an earlier volume in this series Phyllis Erdman and Tom Caffrey showed how family systems theory and attachment theory are complimentary and can be combined to deepen therapeutic effect. In this volume she combines with Kok-Mun Ng to explore the universality of attachment theory. They bring together professionals from around the globe—Spain, United Kingdom, Turkey, Korea, India, Israel, South Africa, and several locations in the United States. These authors from various cultural backgrounds provide a new, cross-cultural perspective to attachment theory.

This book provides the foundation to effectively use attachment theory with today's multi-cultural clients. This volume provides the research and knowledge to help therapists to effectively understand their clients and develop attachment-centered interventions. The profession is indebted to the work of Drs. Erdman, Ng and their collaborators.

Jon Carlson, PsyD, EdD
Series Editor

Acknowledgments

We want to thank all of our authors who contributed to this project. We feel honored to have had the opportunity to work with so many accomplished individuals from different parts of the world. We believe this project has further advanced the understanding of attachment and culture. Without your hard work and dedication, this project would not have materialized. We also want to especially thank Sue Metzger, Keith Hill, Jared Lau, and Arika Garner for providing extra pairs of eyes to review and proofread for APA (American Psychological Association) elements when our eyes were tired and crossed after reading the manuscripts for hours.

I (Phyllis Erdman) would like to give special thanks to my coeditor and former student, Dr. Kok-Mun Ng. His help in conceptualizing the book from the beginning, and his commitment and support throughout the many drafts have been priceless to the success of this book.

I (Kok-Mun Ng) want to also thank Mayron, my spouse, for her support and understanding when I had to spend evenings and weekends working on this project instead of spending time with her. I appreciate her understanding of how much this project means to me.

Contributors

Itziar Alonso-Arbiol, PhD
Associate Professor
Psychology Department
University of the Basque Country
Donostia, Spain

Kazuko Y. Behrens, PhD
Assistant Professor
Human Development and Family
    Studies
Texas Tech University
Lubbock, Texas

Peter Cooper, PhD
Research Professor and Codirector
Winnicott Research Unit
University of Reading
Reading, United Kingdom

Phyllis Erdman, PhD
Professor and Interim Dean
College of Education
Washington State University
Pullman, Washington

Miriam Firpo-Jimenez, MA
Treatment Director
Broward County (Florida) Sexual
    Assault Treatment Center
and
Adjunct Instructor
Florida Atlantic University
Boca Raton, Florida

Elizabeth A. Gassin, PhD
Associate Professor of Psychology
Department of Behavioral Sciences
Olivet Nazarene University
Bourbonnais, Illinois

Elaine Hatfield, PhD
Professor of Psychology
University of Hawaii
Honolulu, Hawaii

Nancy Hazen, PhD
Associate Professor
Human Development and Family
    Sciences
University of Texas at Austin
Austin, Texas

E. Olcay Imamoğlu, PhD
Professor of Social Psychology
Department of Psychology
Middle East Technical University
Ankara, Turkey

Selen Imamoğlu, PhD
Assistant Professor
Department of Psychology
Bahçeşehir University
Istanbul, Turkey

Deborah Jacobvitz, PhD
Professor
Human Development and Family
    Sciences
University of Texas at Austin
Austin, Texas

Mi Kyoung Jin, PhD
Assistant Professor
Child Welfare
Namseoul University
Cheonan, Korea

Rachana Johri, PhD
Department of Psychology
Lady Shri Ram College for Women
University of Delhi
Delhi, India

Nilüfer Kafescioğlu, PhD
Assistant Professor
Psychology
Dogus University
Istanbul, Turkey

Çiğdem Kağıtçıbaşı, PhD
Professor
Psychology
Koc University
Istanbul, Turkey

Günnur Karakurt, PhD
Assistant Professor
Department of Applied and
    Professional Studies
Marriage and Family Therapy
    Program
Texas Tech University
Lubbock, Texas

Margaret K. Keiley, EdD
Associate Professor and Director of
    Clinical Research
Marriage and Family Therapy
    Program
Department of Human Development
    and Family Studies
Auburn University
Auburn, Alabama

Shiri Lavy, PhD
Lecturer
Psychology Department
Ariel University Center and Bar Ilan
    University
Israel

Carol M. Magai, PhD
Founding Director
Intercultural Institute on Human
    Development and Aging
and
Dean of Research
Long Island University Brooklyn
    Campus
Brooklyn, New York

Kathleen Malley-Morrison, EdD
Director
Group on International Perspectives
    on Governmental Aggression and
    Peace (GIPGAP)
and
Professor of Psychology
Boston University
Boston, Massachusetts

Suzanne Metzger, MA, NCC
Director and Owner
Focus Counseling Services
Spokane, Washington

Mario Mikulincer, PhD
Professor of Psychology
Interdisciplinary Center (IDC)
Herzliya, Israel

Alexis O. Miranda, PhD
Past Chair and Dean of Research
Florida Atlantic University
Tallahassee, Florida

Amy Morgenstern, PhD
Staff Psychologist
Jewish Child Care Association
Bronx, New York

Lynne Murray, PhD
Research Professor and Codirector
Winnicott Research Unit
University of Reading
Reading, United Kingdom

Kok-Mun Ng, PhD
Associate Professor
Department of Counseling
University of North
    Carolina–Charlotte
Charlotte, North Carolina

Paul R. Peluso, PhD
Assistant Professor
Mental Health Counseling
Florida Atlantic University
Boca Raton, Florida

Mylinh T. Pham
Doctoral Student
Counseling
Florida Atlantic University
Tallahassee, Florida

Kimberly Rapoza, PhD
Assistant Professor
School of Social and Behavioral
    Sciences
Mercy College
Dobbs Ferry, New York

Richard L. Rapson, PhD
Professor of History
University of Hawaii
Honolulu, Hawaii

David P. Schmitt, PhD
Chair and Caterpillar Professor of
    Psychology
Department of Psychology
Bradley University
Peoria, Illinois

Phillip R. Shaver, PhD
Distinguished Professor of Psychology
Department of Psychology
University of California, Davis
Davis, California

Lin Shi, PhD
Associate Professor and Master's
    Program Director
Marriage and Family Therapy
Northern Illinois University
Chicago, Illinois

Young S. Song, PhD
Doctoral Student
Counseling Psychology
University of Missouri–Kansas City
Kansas City, Missouri

Nebi Sümer, PhD
Chair and Professor
Department of Psychology
Middle East Technical University
Ankara, Turkey

Mark Tomlinson, PhD
Associate Professor
Department of Psychology
Stellenbosch University
Stellenbosch, South Africa

Chia-Chih DC Wang, PhD
Assistant Professor
Division of Counseling and
    Educational Psychology
University of Missouri–Kansas City
Kansas City, Missouri

Alev Yalçınkaya, PhD
Assistant Professor
Yeditepe University
Istanbul, Turkey

Section *I*

Introduction

1

Attachment in Cultural Contexts

SUZANNE METZGER, PHYLLIS ERDMAN, and KOK-MUN NG

CONTENTS

> The repertoire of attachment behaviors is similar across countries, but the selection of these behaviors is culturally specific.
>
> **—Abraham Sagi (1990, p. 19)**

BRIEF HISTORY OF ATTACHMENT THEORY

Attachment research has grown steadily since its inception in the 1950s and has flourished in the past few decades (Bretherton, 1992; Cassidy & Shaver, 1999; Rholes & Simpson, 2004). The scope of attachment theory and its clinical applications has expanded from its initial focus on infant–caregiver relationships (Bowlby, 1969, 1973, 1980) to adult intimate relationships (Bartholomew & Horowitz, 1991; George, Kaplan, & Main, 1985; Hazan & Shaver, 1987), and, more recently, to family relationships (Erdman & Caffery, 2003). Since Bowlby's

(1969, 1973, 1980) trilogy on attachment and loss, the tenets of attachment theory have been developed, refined, tested, and applied to a broad spectrum of human functioning across the life span. Historically, the appeal of attachment theory lies in its rich theoretical structure that combines ethological, psychoanalytic, cognitive, and systemic perspectives (Harwood, Miller, & Irizarry, 1995). It is a theory that provides a comprehensive understanding of how individuals relate to one another that encompasses worldviews of self and others (Bartholomew & Horowitz, 1991), the evolutionary adaptation of needs for survival and security (Ainsworth, 1963), and developmental processes that drive exploration and individuation (Ainsworth, Bell, & Stayton, 1971; Main & Solomon, 1986).

OVERVIEW OF ATTACHMENT THEORY

Attachment theory was first introduced by John Bowlby (1969, 1973, 1980) and was based on the supposition that there is an innate biological behavioral control system in all of us, referred to as an attachment system that contributes to individual survival. As humans, we are strongly inclined to seek proximity to and contact with a clearly identified attachment figure and do so particularly in times of stress (Bowlby, 1988; Bretherton, 1985). The psychological goal of physical closeness for the attached person is security in the presence of the attachment figure (Ainsworth, Blehar, Waters, & Wall, 1978; Bretherton, 1985), and the physiological goal of the system is survival. Additionally, our ability to form intimate bonds with others is considered an essential component of an individual's mental health and social adaptation (Bowlby, 1988).

Although the development of attachments in human infants was thought to be usually activated within the first 9 months of life (Bowlby, 1977; Mace & Margison, 1997), Bowlby (1988) suggested that attachment continues across the life span of humans. As individuals develop attachment patterns in infancy, they internalize these patterns into working models of self and others, which result in the cognitive structural properties applied to later intimate relationships.

Attachment behavior refers to any form of behavior that results in a person achieving or maintaining a desired proximity to an indentified individual whom the person sees as better able to cope with the world (Bowlby, 1988). The activation of attachment behavior is most obvious when the attached person is in a vulnerable state, such as being frightened, fatigued, or sick, and is deactivated when the attachment figure provides protection, help, and soothing (Bretherton, 1985). In adults, attachment is reciprocal, which means that two adults involved in the attachment relationship mutually act as attachment figures to each other (Bowlby, 1982).

Feeney and Noller (1996) identified four functions of attachment behavior: (a) proximity maintenance, to establish and maintain contact with the attachment figure; (b) separation protest, to resist separations from the attachment figure; (c) secure base, to use the attachment figure as a base from which to explore and master the environment; and (d) safe haven, to return to the attachment figure for comfort and support. Ainsworth et al. (1978) first described three principal patterns of attachment in their assessment of infant–mother attachment: anxious avoidance, secure, and anxious resistant. They described anxious avoidant infants as willing to explore independently but actively avoiding their caregiver upon reunion after a period of separation. These infants respond less positively to being held, but more negatively to being put down. Secure infants use their caregivers as a secure base for exploration, and actively seek contact or interaction with the caregiver upon reunion after a period of separation. These infants exhibit minimal resistant and avoidant behavior, and although they become somewhat upset when their caregiver leaves, they become calm upon their return. Anxious resistant infants experience difficulty separating from the caregiver in order to explore, but also find it difficult to settle down upon reunion after a period of separation. They concurrently seek contact with their caregivers as well as resist them.

Subsequent researchers (Main & Solomon, 1986) proposed a fourth attachment pattern, a disorganized/disoriented category of insecure attachment. Infants in this group tend to exhibit conflicting reunion behavior, demonstrated by confusion or apprehension, when the attachment figure returns, and often show depressed affect.

Initial adult attachment research adopted the infant attachment style typology to describe adult attachment styles (Hazan & Shaver, 1987). In 1990, Bartholomew proposed four categories of adult attachment: *secure, dismissing, preoccupied,* and *fearful.* In contrast to infant attachment styles, Bartholomew distinguished between dismissing individuals from fearful ones in that the former avoid attachment because they do not value it, whereas the latter do so because they fear rejection. The preoccupied individuals are analogous to the anxious-resistant/ ambivalent type.

Recent research has indicated that adult attachment styles are best conceptualized as spaces defined by two orthogonal dimensions: attachment-related anxiety and attachment-related avoidance (Shaver & Mikulincer, 2002). The secure type is defined by the space where both anxiety and avoidance are low. The preoccupied type is when anxiety is high and avoidance is low. The fearful type is when anxiety and avoidance are both high, and the dismissing type is when anxiety is low and avoidance is high. Despite the popularity of the four-category attachment style typology in the literature, researchers have recently advocated for the conceptualization of attachment dimensionally rather than categorically (Shaver & Mikulincer, 2002).

ATTACHMENT WITHIN CULTURAL CONTEXTS

Despite Ainsworth's (1963) initial application of the Strange Situation to a population in Uganda, attempts to categorize attachment styles have been largely limited to White United States and European populations (Ainsworth, Blehar, & Waters, 1978; Mizuta, Zahn-Waxler, Cole, & Hiruma, 1996). Attachment assessment measures were developed and normed based on similar populations, often using convenience samples, such as college students in introductory psychology and human development courses, and only rarely did these samples even include minority university populations within the United States. As a result, the associations between attachment and cultural variables remained largely unexplored. Researchers in recent years have begun attempts to rectify this gap by discussing and investigating the subject (e.g., Rothbaum, Rosen, Ujiie, & Uchilda, 2002; Schmitt et al., 2004). Although evidence documenting the universality of the basic constructs underlying attachment theory has been accumulating (Schmitt et al., 2004; van IJzendoorn & Sagi, 1999), culture has been shown to play an important role in the formation of attachment quality and to impact its relationship with other psychological correlates (Bretherton, 1992; Rothbaum et al., 2002).

As time evolved and practitioners sought information on clinical applications for attachment theory in broader settings, the conceptualization of the theory began to expand (Dozier, Stovall, & Albus, 1999; Greenberg, 1999; Johnson, 2004; Kobak, Cassidy, & Ziv, 2004; Lieberman & Zeanah, 1999). Consequently, cross-cultural comparison studies in non-Western settings began to increase, resulting in the development of certain assumptions about cultural similarities and differences in attachment relationships. For example, distinct patterns of what had been labeled insecure attachment were found to be especially prevalent in certain cultures, whereas other forms of insecure attachment were entirely absent (van IJzendoorn & Kroonenberg, 1988; van IJzendoorn & Sagi, 1999). Assumptions were made that secure attachment is adaptive. Additionally, some researchers suggested that observed patterns of attachment follow cultural approaches of collectivism and individualism (Bretherton, 1992; Grossmann, Grossmann, Spangler, Suess, & Unzner, 1985; Miyake, Chen, & Campos, 1985; Rothbaum, Weisz, Pott, Miyake, & Morelli, 2000; Sagi et al., 1985). Schmitt et al.'s (2004) and Schmitt's (2005) cross-cultural studies of global attachment relationships showed more patterns of secure and insecure attachment, further questioning the universality of attachment theory. Slowly, a shift occurred that challenged the categorizations of attachment styles themselves, particularly addressing the validity and reliability of the attachment measures that were being used cross-culturally.

The sphere of inquiry widened, and the scrutiny applied to cultural differences in attachment classification patterns was also applied to socioeconomic differences and interventions in high-risk populations (Carlson, Cicchetti, Barnett, & Braunwald, 1989; Lyons-Ruth, Connell, & Grunebaum, 1990; Olds, Kitzman, Cole, & Robinson, 1997). Counterintuitively, some researchers found that in situations of extreme depravity, poverty, illness, and associated high incidents of infant and childhood mortality that secure attachment still prevailed (Tomlinson, Cooper, & Murray, 2005). Differences in patterns of attachment by gender and in subpopulations within the same culture further complicated assumptions about the universality of attachment.

PURPOSE OF THE BOOK

It is our belief the time has come for attachment research to further expand its scope to explore the connections between attachment and culture. Technological advances and mass communications have mollified international borders, hence, making it even more important to understand how relational connections are viewed around the world. The United States, as well as many other countries, is becoming increasingly globalized; we are a people on the move. As such, scientists, practitioners, students, and teachers must be prepared to interact with people of diverse cultural backgrounds both in their countries of origin, as well as when traveling to other countries to live, work, and study. In general terms, this book is designed to illustrate how attachment theory, when viewed through a cultural context, can deepen our understanding of relational connections across the globe, broaden our perspectives of various cultures, and increase our knowledge base to expand cultural connections. In specific terms, these questions begged to be answered: What is universal about attachment and what is context specific? Are we, as researchers and clinicians, assigning similar meanings about attachment styles and their predictions toward mental health without considering cultural contexts?

This book is the first attempt to bring together in one volume the scholarly works from various parts of the world to critically examine the connections that exist between culture and attachment. In doing so, we hope to contribute to filling the gap in the attachment literature and further advance the development of attachment theory and its practice across cultural lines.

We embarked on this project with great excitement and saw it as a wonderful opportunity to assemble international experts in this burgeoning field. The contributors in this book are highly qualified researchers and clinicians from a multitude of cultural backgrounds. What they provide to the reader is solid, real, and what they live in their own culture; hence, much of it is *emic* in nature. Each of the contributors provides a strong argument for the cultural expansion of attachment theory.

This book has multiple purposes: (a) to offer empirically based analyses of the current theory and application of cross-cultural attachment, (b) to illustrate through clinical applications how attachment and culture may be interconnected, and (c) to provide directions for future research. We have provided the reader with some tentative conclusions, but also with many more new questions. Our hope is that as you peruse the chapters your understanding of the role of culture in attachment will expand as ours did throughout the preparation of this book. We also hope you experience the same enthusiasm that our contributors did in writing about this topic and that you recognize the abundant possibilities for new ideas and new research in this area. This book is only the beginning and by no means conclusive. We invite you, the reader, to continue the work of these dedicated researchers and clinicians and hope this book inspires you to join us in our effort to expand cultural connections.

ORGANIZATION OF THE BOOK

Several chapters include a brief overview of attachment theory; however for those interested in reviewing some of the seminal works in attachment theory we recommend the following: John Bowlby's trilogy of *Attachment and Loss* (1969/1982, 1973, 1980); Ainsworth (1963), Ainsworth et al. (1971, 1978); Sroufe and Waters (1977); and Main and Weston (1981). In addition, we recommend the *Handbook of Attachment* (Cassidy & Shaver, 1999, 2008); and *Adult Attachment: Theory, Research, and Clinical Implications* (Rholes & Simpson, 2004).

The major tenets of attachment theory, as described earlier, underlie the focus of all of the chapters in this book. They include the following: (a) attachment involves healthy dependency and is an internal driving force; (b) this dependency encourages secure development involving confident interdependence as well as autonomy; (c) attachment is related to survival, and secure attachment offers a safe haven or secure base from which to explore both inner and outer worlds;

(d) emotional availability and sensitivity to communicational cues enhance connectedness with others; (e) attachment responses are activated in situations that invoke fear and uncertainty; (f) behavioral expression of emotional discomfort associated with separation follows a predictable pattern; (g) insecure attachment behavior is organized and strategies expressed along a limited number of pathways; (h) expressions of attachment is associated with world and self views that are based on previous interpersonal experiences; (i) attachment involves working models of self and other; and (j) isolation and loss are inherently traumatic (Johnson, 2004). The four hypotheses developed by van IJzendoorn and Sagi (1999)—universality, normativity, sensitivity, and competency—are also addressed throughout the chapters, as they are either supported or challenged in relation to cultural contexts.

The book is divided into four parts that follow this introduction: "Conceptual Extensions and Measurement Issues," "Child–Caregiver Attachment," "Adult Attachment," and "Clinical Applications." As we selected the focus for each section and chapter, we chose to include both empirical work and practice-based clinical applications. We also selected work that included cultures where previous work in attachment has been particularly lacking (e.g., Africa, India, Turkey, Latin America). Because this area of research may still be considered in its neophyte phase, we considered it important to validate the theoretical work with empirical findings. We found it equally important to provide examples of clinical applications within various cultural frameworks so that the reader may better understand how it looks when the constructs of attachment theory are applied to culture-related issues. Hence, most chapters include either a brief case study or a sample of dialogue that illustrates the author's concepts and brings them to life for the reader. We hope that the research presented in this book will provide a foundation for practitioners to justify their use of attachment within cultural contexts. Readers do not need to read this book linearly. Each chapter stands alone and is rich in its own content.

Part II: Conceptual Extensions and Measurement Issues

Part II includes chapters that extend the conceptual framework for attachment theory across various cultural contexts and address the applicability of various assessment measures across cultures.

In Chapter 2, Wang and Song describe a Chinese adult attachment model. In Chapter 3, Imamoğlu and Imamoğlu explore the connections of attachment and exploration and its association with the relatedness–individual linkage using the balanced integration–differentiation (BID) model. The Japanese concept of *amae* and its relation to attachment theory is described by Behrens in Chapter 4. Gassin addresses bereavement as it applies across cultures in Chapter 5. In Chapter 6 Shaver, Mikulincer, Alonso-Arbiol, and Lavy review the conceptual and methodological considerations across cultures. Karakurt, Kafescioğlu, and Keiley (Chapter 7) present the issues concerning cross-cultural studies on adult attachment, specifically the Adult Attachment Interview, the Adult Attachment Q-sort, and various self-report and narrative measures. In the last chapter in this part, Chapter 8, Morgenstern and Magai provide a brief history of the Adult Attachment Interview and discuss their research in determining the applicability and validity of the instrument with Caucasian, African American, and African Caribbean populations in the United States.

Part III: Child–Caregiver Attachment

Part III includes chapters that focus on the child–caregiver relationships in various cultures. In Chapter 9, Jin, Jacobvitz, and Hazen present a cross-cultural comparison between the United States and Korea. Sümer and Kağıtçıbaşi, in Chapter 10, discuss parenting styles in Turkey. In Chapter 11, Tomlinson, Murray, and Cooper present a review of attachment styles in Africa.

Part IV: Adult Attachment

Part IV includes chapters that compare adult attachment concepts across cultures. In Chapter 12, Yalçınkaya, Rapoza, and Malley-Morrison present the debate over the universality of attachment theory and the cross-cultural generalizability of research findings associated with theories of adult attachment. In Chapter 13, Schmitt reviews romantic attachment across cultures focusing on findings from the International Sexuality Description Projects. Hatfield and Rapson, in Chapter 14, describe love schemas and how they impact adult romantic relationships across cultures. In Chapter 15, Johri discusses the mother–daughter relationship in India, and finally, in Chapter 16, Shi compares the differences between romantic relationships as they exist in China and the United States.

Part V: Clinical Applications

In Chapter 17, Peluso, Miranda, Firpo-Jimenez, and Pham present the attachment dynamics in Latino cultures, illustrated by a case study. Shi in Chapter 18 describes implications for the clinical assessment of Chinese families.

RECOMMENDATIONS FOR FUTURE WORK

As you read through the chapters in this book, it is obvious that there is still much work to be done, particularly for clinicians who wish to use attachment theory as a conceptual framework within various cultural contexts. Using the metaphor of a *secure base*, it is time for clinicians to venture into uncharted territory. However, to do so they must feel secure that their interventions are well grounded and supported. As we learn more about the various cultural meanings that are assigned to attachment concepts such as secure, dismissing, and avoidant, we will become more tolerant of the uniqueness of a culture's norms and less willing to make generalizations.

The time is ripe for a variety of studies. Specifically, we call for the following: investigation of variables within a culture (e.g., religion, spirituality, gender role socialization, marital practices, bereavement, and language) that may act as mediating factors between attachment and its psychological correlates; examinations of attachment in developing countries and in areas where urbanization and global influences (often media based) are causing a shift in parental and gender roles; continued development and refinement of culturally specific assessment methods and tools; an increase in interdisciplinary attachment dialogue and research; expansion of culturally specific emic studies; exploration of countries and populations within countries that are not currently represented or are underrepresented in attachment research (e.g., South American countries); further examination of attachment in high-risk populations both in developed and underdeveloped countries; practitioner-based publication of cross-cultural attachment techniques, methods, and interventions; in-depth studies of attachment-related worldviews and how those impact responses to traumatic events such as war and abuse; attachment-based preventative measures to build resilience and mitigate anticipated trauma (such as with those sent into combat); and, finally, integration of outcome efficacy measures to clinical interventions. This list is by no means exhaustive, but we hope it provides some direction for future research.

We are grateful to have had this opportunity to further the research on cross-cultural attachment. It is our hope that you enjoy this book as much as we enjoyed working with the authors. We look forward to increased depth and breadth of study in the years to come.

REFERENCES

Ainsworth, M. D. S. (1963). The development of infant-mother interaction among the Ganda. In B. M. Foss (Ed.), *Determinants of infant behavior* (Vol. 2, pp. 67–112). New York: Wiley.

Ainsworth, M. D. S., Bell, S. M., & Stayton, D. J. (1971). Individual differences in strange-situation behavior of one-year-olds. In J. R. Schaffer (Ed.), *The origins of human social relations* (pp. 17–52). New York: Academic Press.

Ainsworth, M. D. S., Blehar, M., Waters, E., & Wall, S. (1978). *Patterns of attachment: A psychological study of the strange situation.* Hillsdale, NJ: Lawrence Erlbaum Associates.

Bartholomew, K. (1990). Avoidance of intimacy: An attachment perspective. *Journal of Social and Personal Relationships, 7,* 147–178.

Bartholomew, K., & Horowitz, L. M. (1991). Attachment styles among young adults: A test of a four-category model. *Journal of Personality and Social Psychology, 61*(2), 226–244.

Bowlby, J. (1969). *Attachment and loss (Vol. 1).* New York: Basic Books.

Bowlby, J. (1973). *Attachment and loss: Vol. 2. Separation.* New York: Basic Books.

Bowlby, J. (1977). The making and breaking of affectional bonds: Aetiology and psychopathology in the light of attachment theory. *The British Journal of Psychiatry, 130,* pp. 201–210.

Bowlby, J. (1980). *Attachment and loss: Vol. 3. Loss.* New York: Basic Books.

Bowlby, J. (1982). *Attachment and loss: Vol. 1. Attachment.* New York: Basic Books. (Original work published 1969)

Bowlby, J. (1988). A secure base: Parent-child attachment and healthy human development. New York: Basic Books.

Bretherton, I. (1985). Attachment theory: Retrospect and prospect. In I. Bretherton & E. Waters (Eds.), Growing points of attachment theory and research, *Monographs of the Society for Research in Child Development, 50*(1–2, Serial No. 209), 3–35.

Bretherton, I. (1992). The origins of attachment theory. *Developmental Psychology, 28,* 759–775.

Carlson, V., Cicchetti, D., Barnett, D., & Braunwald, K. (1989). Disorganized/disoriented attachment relationships in maltreated infants. *Developmental Psychology*, 25, 525–531.

Cassidy, J., & Shaver, P. (Eds.). (1999). *Handbook of attachment*. New York: Guilford Press.

Cassidy, J., & Shaver, P. (Eds.). (2008). *Handbook of attachment* (2nd ed.). New York: Guilford Press.

Dozier, M., Stovall, K. C., & Albus, K. (1999). Attachment and psychopathology in adulthood. In J. Cassidy & P. R. Shaver (Eds.), *Handbook of attachment, theory, research, and clinical applications* (pp. 497–519). New York: Guilford Press.

Erdman, P., & Caffery, T. (Eds.). (2003). *Attachment and family systems: Conceptual, empirical, and therapeutic relatedness*. New York: Brunner-Routledge.

Feeney, J. A., & Noller, P. (1996). *Adult attachment*. Thousand Oaks: Sage.

George, C., Kaplan, N., & Main, M. (1985). *The adult attachment interview* (2nd ed.). Unpublished manuscript, University of California, Berkeley.

Greenberg, M. (1999). Attachment and psychopathology in childhood. In J. Cassidy & P. R. Shaver (Eds.), *Handbook of attachment, theory, research, and clinical applications* (pp. 469–496). New York: Guilford Press.

Grossmann, K., Grossmann, K. E., Spangler, G., Suess, G., & Unzner, L. (1985). Maternal sensitivity and newborns' orientation responses as related to quality of attachment in Northern Germany. In I. Bretherton & E. Waters (Eds.), Growing points of attachment theory and research, *Monographs of the Society for Research in Child Development*, 50(1–2, Serial No. 209), 233–256.

Harwood, R. L., Miller, J. G., & Irizzary, N. L. (1995). *Culture and attachment: Perceptions of the child in context*. New York: Guilford Press.

Hazan, C., & Shaver, P. (1987). Romantic love conceptualized as an attachment process. *Journal of Personality and Social Psychology*, 52, 511–524.

Johnson, S. M. (2004). *The practice of emotionally focused couples therapy* (2nd ed.). New York: Brunner-Routledge.

Kobak, R., Cassidy, J., & Ziv, Y. (2004). Attachment-related trauma and posttraumatic stress disorder. Implications for adult adaptation. In J. A. Simpson & W. S. Rholes (Eds.), *Adult attachment: Theory, research, and clinical implications* (pp. 388–407). New York: Guilford Press.

Lieberman, A., & Zeanah, C. (1999). Contribution of attachment theory to infant-parent psychotherapy and other interventions with infants and young children. In J. Cassidy & P. R. Shaver (Eds.), *Handbook of attachment, theory, research, and clinical applications* (pp. 555–574). New York: Guilford Press.

Lyons-Ruth, K., Connell, D. B., & Grunebaum, H. U. (1990). Infants at social risk: Maternal depression and family support services as mediators of infant development and security of attachment. *Child Development*, 61, 85–98.

Mace, C., & Margison, F. (1997). Attachment and psychotherapy: An overview. *British Journal of Medical Psychology*, 70, 209–215.

Main, M., & Solomon, J. (1986). Discovery of an insecure-disorganized/disoriented attachment pattern. In T. B. Brazelton & M. W. Yogman (Eds.), *Affective development in infancy* (pp. 95–124). Norwood, NJ: Ablex.

Main, M., & Weston, D. (1981). The quality of the toddler's relationship to mother and to father: Related to conflict behavior and readiness to establish new relationships. *Child Development*, 52, 932–940.

Miyake, K., Chen, S. J., & Campos, J. J. (1985). Infant temperament, mother's mode of interaction, and attachment in Japan: An interim report. In I. Bretherton & E. Waters (Eds.), Growing points of attachment theory and research, *Monographs of the Society for Research in Child Development*, 50(1–2, Serial No. 209), 276–297.

Mizuta, I., Zahn-Waxler, C., Cole, P. M., & Hiruma, N. (1996). A cross-cultural study of pre-schoolers' attachment: Security and sensitivity in Japanese and US dyads. *International Journal of Behavioral Development, 19*, 141–159.

Olds, D., Kitzman, H., Cole, R., & Robinson, J. (1997). Theoretical foundations of a program of home visitation for pregnant women and parents of young children. *Journal of Community Psychology, 25*(1), 9–25.

Rholes, W. S., & Simpson, J. A. (Eds.). (2004). *Adult attachment: Theory, research, and clinical implications.* New York: Guilford Press.

Rothbaum, F., Rosen, K., Ujiie, T., & Uchilda, N. (2002). Family systems theory, attachment theory, and culture. *Family Process, 41*, 328–350.

Rothbaum, F., Weisz, J., Pott, M., Miyake, K., & Morelli, G. (2000). Attachment and culture: Security in the United States and Japan. *American Psychologist, 55*, 1093–1104.

Sagi, A. (1990). Attachment theory and research from a cross-cultural perspective. *Human Development, 33*, 10–22.

Sagi, A., Lamb, M. E., Lewkowicz, K. S., Shoham, R., Dvir, R., & Estes, D. (1985). Security of infant-mother, -father, and -metapelet attachments among kibbutz-reared Israeli children. In I. Bretherton & E. Waters (Eds.), Growing points of attachment theory and research. *Monographs of the Society for Research in Child Development, 50*(1–2, Serial No. 209, pp. 257–275).

Schmitt, D. P. (2005). Sociosexuality from Argentina to Zimbabwe: A 48-nation study of sex, culture, and strategies of human mating. *Behavioral and Brain Sciences, 28*, 247–275.

Schmitt, D. P., Alcalay, L., Allensworth, M., Allik, J., Ault, L., Austers, I., … Zupanèiè, A. (2004). Patterns and universals of adult romantic attachment across 62 cultural regions: Are models of self and of other pancultural constructs? *Journal of Cross-Cultural Psychology, 35*, 367–402.

Shaver, P. R., & Mikulincer, M. (2002). Attachment-related psychodynamics. *Attachment and Human Development, 4*, 133–161.

Sroufe, L. A., & Waters, E. (1977). Attachment as an organizational construct. *Child Development, 48*, 1184–1199.

Tomlinson, M., Cooper, P., & Murray, L. (2005). The mother-infant relationship and infant attachment in a South African peri-urban settlement. *Child Development, 76*, 1044–1054.

van IJzendoorn, M. H., & Kroonenberg, P. M. (1988). Cross-cultural patterns of attachment: A meta-analysis of the strange situation. *Child Development, 50*, 971–975.

van IJzendoorn, M. H., & Sagi, A. (1999). Cross cultural patterns of attachment: Universal and contextual determinants. In J. Cassidy & P. R. Shaver (Eds.), *Handbook of attachment: Theory, research, and clinical applications* (pp. 713–734). New York: Guilford Press.

Section *II*

Conceptual Extensions and Measurement Issues

2

Adult Attachment Reconceptualized
A *Chinese Perspective*

CHIA-CHIH DC WANG and YOUNG S. SONG

CONTENTS

After the application of attachment perspectives was expanded from parent–child relationships to adult attachment in the 1980s, a rapidly growing body of empirical literature has used attachment theory as an organizational framework to conceptualize a wide range of psychosocial and relational issues in adulthood (Simpson & Rholes, 1998). Recently, the concept of adult attachment security has been promoted as a basis for understanding adult development of the "healthy and effective self" (Lopez & Brennan, 2000). As the theory quickly gains popularity, however, awareness of the limitations on the theory's cross-cultural validity and potential overgeneralization of the Western-based attachment perspectives to non-Western adult populations has grown among adult attachment researchers (Wang & Mallinckrodt, 2006). We believe that culture plays a critical role in the manifestation of attachment styles and behaviors in adults and that an accurate understanding of the guiding attachment system of non-Western individuals can only be obtained through considerations of relevant cultural contexts. In this chapter, we use Chinese culture to illustrate how cultural factors may affect adult attachment with an aim to offer an alternative attachment model consistent with indigenous Chinese cultural context. We begin with a brief review of basic attachment constructs and cross-cultural adult attachment research findings and then follow with introductions of some important cultural factors to provide readers the necessary understanding of the cultural context. Then, the proposed adult attachment model and its implications are presented and discussed.

ADULT ATTACHMENT AND CROSS-CULTURAL RESEARCH FINDINGS

According to attachment theory (Bowlby, 1969), the attachment system is an innate, goal-corrected control system, regulating behavior of both children and their caregivers to maintain a balance between exploring the environment and maintaining proximity between the child and the attachment figure(s). Children gradually develop different attachment styles based on perceived availability and responsiveness from their primary caretakers during childhood. It is believed that the attachment styles, once developed, remain relatively stable throughout the span of life and function as internal working models guiding a person's interactions in all significant relationships (Bowlby, 1969).

The extension of attachment perspectives to adulthood began when adult romantic relationships were reconceptualized in terms of attachment theory (Hazan & Shaver, 1987). Contemporary adult attachment perspectives conceptualize individuals' attachment based on two orthogonal dimensions: *anxiety* and *avoidance*. This two-dimensional adult attachment model is consistent with the internal working models of self and of others as proposed by the theory and has received clear empirical support (Brennan, Clark, & Shaver, 1998). Attachment security refers to those low on both dimensions. Adults with high attachment anxiety are likely to present characteristics such as lower sense of self-worth, fear of rejection and abandonment in relationships, emotional dependence, less social self-confidence, and obsessive/dependent love styles (Collins & Read, 1990). On the other hand, individuals high on attachment avoidance tend to demonstrate mistrust toward others, discomfort with social closeness, low intensity of love experiences, and excessive need for self-reliance (Feeney & Noller, 1990). Based on one's scores on these two dimensions, researchers may classify individuals into four categorical attachment styles: *secure* (low on both dimensions), *preoccupied* (high on anxiety but low on avoidance), *dismissing* (low on anxiety but high on avoidance), and *fearful* (high on both dimensions).

Cross-Cultural Validity of Adult Attachment

Bowlby (1969) contended that key elements of attachment theory are culturally universal because they apply to all members of the human species. This contention was given a strong initial impetus because early empirical attachment studies were replicated with mother–infant dyads in both Uganda and the United States (Ainsworth, 1967; Ainsworth, Blehar, Waters, & Wall, 1978). Many leading attachment researchers have also supported this notion (e.g., Main, 1990; van IJzendoorn & Sagi, 1999). Nevertheless, critics (e.g., Rothbaum, Weisz, Pott, Miyake, & Morelli, 2000; Takahashi, 1990) have pointed out that the fundamental assumptions and philosophies underlying attachment concepts are deeply rooted in Western cultures and that the bulk of empirical studies supporting the theory were conducted in North America with White middle-class subjects. Therefore, they argue that attachment theory concepts are not cultural universals as proponents claim.

Empirical studies examining the universal applicability of attachment theory on non-Western adults are sparse as most cross-cultural attachment studies were found to focus on attachment in infancy and early childhood. We conducted a search for all adult attachment empirical studies in the PsycINFO database published before July 2008 that involve cross-cultural comparisons of adult attachment between Asian (or Asian American) and Western samples, and only seven studies were identified. These seven studies examined various cultural variations and functions of East Asian adult attachment styles, and are grouped into the following two sections based on the shared themes.

Comparison of Attachment Styles Between Eastern and Western Groups

In a study that examined the associations of attachment styles and social intimacy with friends, You and Malley-Morrison (2000) found that Korean students scored higher on preoccupied attachment, and lower on intimacy and expectations in friendships compared to their White American counterparts. The authors suspected that these findings may be related to cultural norms that are reflective of Korean practices. Koreans were identified to have stronger ties with families than with friends, when compared to White Americans. In another study, Malley-Morrison, You, and Mills (2000) investigated how attachment styles were associated with college students' perceptions on abusive behaviors toward elders. They found that Korean students reported higher preoccupied attachment scores than White American college students and that among those who endorsed a preoccupied attachment style, Korean and White participants differed significantly in their perceptions' of abusive behaviors toward the elderly. Authors concluded that the interaction of culture and attachment styles accounted for the differences between the two groups. Findings from a large-scale cross-cultural study consisting of samples from 62 cultures conducted by Schmitt et al. (2004) indicated that preoccupied attachment styles were found to be particularly more prevalent in East Asian cultures (i.e., samples from Hong Kong, Taiwan, South Korea, and Japan), and that participants from the East Asian region reported higher scores on the Internal

Working Model of Others. Researchers speculated that collectivistic orientation appeared to be associated with higher levels of preoccupied romantic attachment.

DiTommaso, Brannen, and Burgess (2005) also studied the relationships between attachment (including attachment with parents, romantic partners, and peers) and loneliness in a comparative study between Caucasian Canadian and Chinese international students. Chinese participants reported significantly lower attachment security in both romantic and peer relationships, but not attachment with parents, than their Canadian counterparts. In another study, Wang and Mallinckrodt (2006) found that the perception of optimal secure adult attachment held by Taiwanese college students contained significantly higher levels of attachment anxiety and avoidance than the ideal attachment security pictured by American college students, and that attachment anxiety was positively associated with interdependent (collectivistic) beliefs. The authors concluded that beliefs held in the Taiwanese culture included behavioral norms suggestive of Western-based attachment anxiety and avoidance.

Influences of Adult Attachment on Individuals' Well-Being

Several studies have examined cultural differences in how attachment styles are manifested among Asian American adults and the associations between adult attachment and factors contributing to psychosocial functioning. Wei, Russell, Mallinckrodt, and Zakalik (2004) investigated the associations between negative mood and insecure adult attachment across four ethnic samples. The results indicated that Asian Americans reported higher attachment anxiety and higher attachment avoidance than their Caucasian peers. Furthermore, significant associations between insecure attachment and negative mood were found for all ethnic groups, but a significantly stronger association was found in the Asian American sample. Kim and Zane (2004) conducted a study with samples of Korean American and European American male batterers and found that higher attachment anxiety and attachment avoidance, along with the emotion of anger, were risk factors for marital violence. In addition, the authors found that Korean batterers endorsed higher levels of attachment avoidance when compared to their European counterparts, who endorsed higher levels of attachment anxiety, and that independent self-construal was found to mediate the influence of ethnicity on attachment avoidance. In another comparative study, Wang (2007) found a significant moderator effect of cultural group on the links of anxiety-depressive symptoms and anxiety-emotional expression. Specifically, attachment anxiety was found to be a significant predictor for Taiwanese emotional expression but not for the U.S. participants. The association between anxiety and depression for Taiwanese samples was also significantly greater than the one of the U.S. sample.

Based on the limited empirical literature available, two tentative conclusions can be drawn. First, Asian adults generally endorse higher attachment anxiety and avoidance when compared to individuals in Western societies. Second, the associations of adult attachment with some indicators of individuals' psychosocial functioning appear to differ between Asian and Western samples.

In observing human behaviors and cultural phenomena across cultures, scholars have used the *emic* and *etic* methods. The emic methods describe behavior by using concepts endorsed only in that culture (Davidson, Jaccard, Triandis, Morales, & Diaz-Guerrero, 1976) where observations are described and understood primarily from an indigenous standpoint and considered culturally and historically bound (Morris, Leung, Ames, & Lickel, 1999). In contrast, the etic methodology uses universal categories or external criteria imposed by the researcher, such as theories, to explain human behavior (Davidson et al., 1976). Brislin (1976) stated that the goal of cross-cultural studies is twofold. They describe behaviors or interpret observed phenomena in any one culture taking into account what members of that particular group value as meaningful and important. Second, they aim to make generalizations across cultures and generate theories to best explain all human behavior. Researchers have argued that studies using only etic methods are not considered to be true cross-cultural research because information sensitive to a particular culture may be lost (Davidson et al., 1976). In review of the adult attachment literature, it is unfortunately evident that current literature of adult attachment studies almost exclusively take an etic approach, relying on Western-based attachment perspectives and instruments developed and validated in the United States to investigate Asian adult attachment.

CULTURAL CONTEXT AND ADULT ATTACHMENT

Attachment is described as mental representation of self, others, and the world (Main, Kaplan, & Cassidy, 1985). Adult attachment styles are distinctly developed patterns of relating to significant others and maintaining relationships that involve different strategies of affect regulation and interpersonal behaviors in response to actual or potential attachment threats. Although infant–caregiver attachment behaviors appear fundamentally similar in all members of the human species (van IJzendoorn & Sagi, 1999), the much greater scope for cultural influence and societal norms on adult attachment dramatically increases the likelihood that these constructs will diverge across cultures. Because Chinese styles of relatedness distinctly differ from those of Western cultures in many important aspects, taking an emic approach to create a culturally sensitive conceptual framework appears imperative for an accurate understanding of Chinese adults' attachment.

In the following section, we will introduce five cultural concepts identified from the literature, which particularly pertain to Chinese ways of relatedness, based on our understanding of Chinese cultural characteristics. The five cultural concepts are interdependent self-construals, yuan, filial piety, romantic love, and dialectical thinking. We propose that these five constructs encompass key cultural contexts for understanding the Chinese adult attachment model, which will then be further discussed in the chapter's later section.

Self-Construals

Self-construal was conceptualized as a trait-like disposition involving beliefs, feelings, attitudes, and actions regarding one's relationship to others, especially the degree of separation or connectedness between the self and others (Triandis,

1996). In a comprehensive review of cultural influences on self-concept, Markus and Kitayama (1991) proposed two distinct types of self-construal: *independent* and *interdependent*. They suggested that individuals develop and define their self-construal based on cultural norms. For example, because Western culture generally values individualism, in which independence, uniqueness, and distinction of each individual are emphasized, in keeping with the general cultural norm, individuals from Western cultures develop a stronger independent self-construal. These individuals are characterized as having distinct self–others boundaries, emphasizing identifiable inner attributes, abilities, and characteristics; pursuing goals of individual self-interest; and being direct in self-expression. When considering interpersonal relationships, people with an independent self-construal tend to consider the self and others as separate units (Markus & Kitayama, 1991).

In contrast, many Asian cultures tend to endorse a collectivistic orientation, with emphasis on interdependence and connectedness among individuals. These cultural values strongly favor the development of an interdependent self-construal, in which the self is defined as inseparable from one's relational context (Markus & Kitayama, 1991). Those with strong interdependent self-construal value harmonious interpersonal relationships, meeting one's social obligation, fitting in, and maintaining esteem and status as viewed by other members of one's social group. People with an interdependent self-construal define themselves by multiple relationships with significant others, and they believe that fulfillment of life comes mostly through seeking a harmonious integration between self and the surrounding social context (Markus & Kitayama, 1991; Triandis, 1996).

The central tenets of Markus and Kitayama's (1991) proposed self-construals may have important implications for adult attachment. Conceptually, the Western attachment model consists of two orthogonal dimensions, with the underlying assumptions that the self is an independent entity from others and that the internal working model of self functions separately from the working model of others (Bartholomew & Horowitz, 1991). This model is clearly rooted in Western individualistic philosophies. In other words, although the attachment framework may appear to be an effective framework for those with strong independent self-construals, it may not provide an accurate depiction of adult attachment in Asians who are likely to have stronger interdependent self-construals.

Yuan

Another concept featuring Chinese culture is *yuan* (緣). Yuan can be understood as the predestined connection between two persons or the opportunity presented by fate for an upcoming event (Yang & Ho, 1988). The concept of yuan originates from a foreign religion (i.e., Buddhism), but it has been adopted by Chinese culture with profound influences onto almost all aspects of day-to-day interpersonal interactions (Chang & Holt, 1991). Although texts written in English sometimes use yuan and karma interchangeably, usage of these two concepts by native Chinese has some subtle yet noteworthy distinctions. Karma (業 or 因果) focuses on the cause and effect, emphasizing how previous committed actions will affect one's fate in later life. On the other hand, yuan refers to the predestined relationship with a foundation on fatalistic perspectives. Chinese people believe that the onset and development of significant interpersonal relationships is never a random formation; it is a relational fate that brings two individuals together from among millions to form a particular relationship. The concept of *yuan* applies to all important social relationships, including parent–child, spousal, friendship, teacher–student, sibling, and boss–employee. It is very common to hear one say, "We have the yuan to become friends with each other." Based on this philosophy, every important relationship occurs for a reason and significant interpersonal relationships in life cannot be unilaterally abandoned even in the face of lasting discord, conflict, or mistreatment. Relationships serve as an opportunity to complete what was left undone in previous lifetimes, so the yuan (and karma) will be completed and fulfilled. With the philosophy of "it is meant to be," the concept of "following the yuan" refers to a distinctive Chinese worldview in which one strives for acceptance of the destination and occurring events in life with a peaceful mind (Chang & Holt, 1991; Hsu, 1981).

Attachment mostly pertains to significant relationships. According to the Western-based attachment model, *distrust* is a fundamental element of negative internal working models and a salient characteristic of developed insecurity, in which an individual generally perceives that others are not trustworthy (Wang & Mallinckrodt, 2006). In mainstream Western philosophies, each person is considered an independent individual and one may decide to terminate the relationship if the sense of trust no longer exists or has been violated. However, this often is not the case for intimate relationships among Chinese adults. In reflection of how the concept of yuan plays a critical role on Chinese behaviors and values of relatedness, we believe that the prevalent acceptance of predestined connections in significant relationships seen in Chinese individuals has significant implications for understanding Chinese adult attachment. This will be further elaborated later in the proposed model.

Filial Piety

Many Chinese cultural norms are relation-based involving definitions and interaction guidelines for desirable social behaviors and attitudes. Among them, filial piety (孝) is perhaps the most prominent one. Filial piety is a cultural value that essentially outlines individual loyalty and obligated practice to the family, especially with regard to respect and care for the elderly. Originating from Confucius thought, classic forms of filial piety focus on children's loyalty to their parents. For instance, a filial son is to respect, obey, please, and take the best possible care of his parents when they are aging. A daughter's filial conduct is to faithfully serve her in-laws and become part of her husband's family, and by fulfilling these duties, the woman gains prestige for her own family. Children are required to perform rituals to express their continued devotion and respect even after their parents' death, which is called ancestral worship (Ikels, 2004). Yeh (1997) identified two distinct practices of filial piety: *reciprocity* and *authoritarianism*. Reciprocity includes emotional and spiritual attention to one's family, especially parents, as they age. An example of this is when East Asian adults experience a role reversal with their parents as they become increasingly responsible for their parents' well-being. Authoritarianism, on the other hand, encompasses the suppression of one's own desires by complying with parents' wishes. Both practices accentuate individual submission to those older or with higher social status, and one must take these into account when interacting with others. That is, the practices of filial piety not only influence parent–child relationships within the family, but also impact important aspects of behavior observed in Chinese adults in their everyday lifestyle (Ikels, 2004).

The core tenet of adult attachment is the relatedness of self and others, which we believe overlaps with the Chinese cultural practice and value of filial piety. In Chinese culture, the adult self is defined in reference to relationships established with others; and filial piety, a practice that specifically identifies the individual self in reference to the family and others, is an important framework to understanding Chinese ways of self and relatedness. Hierarchical roles within the family and the society are established according to generational status, age, and gender, and corresponding responsibilities associated with different roles are identified. For example, the eldest son is expected to carry the family business and marry a wife suitable to support his parents when he is of age to support his family. These roles and responsibilities are highly endorsed by people in East Asian cultures and often considered as defining factors for individuals' identity in society (Ikels, 2004). Because both the Chinese self and interpersonal relationships are heavily influenced by practices of filial piety, we believe filial piety is a critical factor in understanding Chinese adult attachment.

Romantic Love

Although anthropologists suggest that romantic love is a universal phenomenon, cross-cultural researchers have found strong evidence indicating how love is experienced and expressed among in-love individuals and the degree to which people believe in the significance of love as the basis of marriage vary substantially in different cultures (Hatfield & Rapson, 1996). A number of researchers have compared the differences of romantic love and relationship between Chinese and Western (mainly North American) cultures. For instance, after analyzing American and Chinese societal norms and cultural beliefs related to love and romantic relationships, Hsu (1981) contended that there are some significant differences in romantic relationship between American and Chinese cultures. He concluded that the Western ideals of romantic love characterized by intensive emotional experience, direct affective expression, and exclusive commitment to romantic partners fit well with the cultural orientation in North America, but not in the context of the Chinese cultural orientation. This orientation where collectivist characteristics, such as emotional restraint and obligation to the parents, extended family, and social network, are emphasized is not conducive to love as characterized by Western ideals. Such a sharp contrast could be depicted through Hsu's words for love being considered in the two cultures: "An American asks, 'How does my heart feel?' A Chinese asks, 'What will other people say?'" (Hsu, 1981, p. 50).

Another study examined love attitudes of 99 Taiwanese college students (Cho & Cross, 1995). The authors identified two prevailing love styles with unique Chinese flavor, which distinctly differ from those recognized in Western societies. "Obligatory love" reflects traditional Chinese beliefs related to romantic love (e.g., willing to sacrifice and selecting partners for the best fit with the family of origin), whereas "calculated love" tends to be more orientated toward personal benefits in one's career or future. The authors concluded that the differences of love styles between Taiwanese and Americans are mainly due to differing values, beliefs, and societal norms existing in the two cultures (Cho & Cross, 1995). Moore (1998) also conducted a study in China using a sample of 230-plus university students to investigate Chinese romantic love. The author identified "conservatism" as an essential element differentiating Chinese dating/courtship behavior and romantic beliefs from those of Western cultures. This conservatism involves a set of standards for courtship and romantic love among Chinese students, including caution, slow pacing, limited experiences, seriousness, and parental approval. Moore also suggested that the culturally prescribed parent–child relationship, which emphasizes emotional closeness between mothers and their children, may play a significant role in shaping romantic behavior of young Chinese.

Dion and Dion (1996) have provided a theoretical framework explaining reasons for this difference among cultures. They proposed that passionate romantic love is an opportunity to explore the individual self and, therefore, is more likely to be prompted in individualistic societies. They also suggested that romantic love could be best understood and studied only when fundamental cultural values and beliefs in a given culture are taken into account (Dion & Dion, 1993, 1996). After Hazan and Shaver (1987) made the first attempt to conceptualize romantic relationships in adulthood as an attachment process, a large volume of adult attachment research with nonclinical samples investigated adult romantic relationships (e.g., Feeney, 1994; Simpson, 1990). But as previously indicated, the manner in which romantic love is experienced, expressed, and considered by Chinese and Western people differs, which leads to the question of whether the findings and conceptualizations based on American samples' romantic attachment is applicable to Chinese adults.

Dialectical Thinking Pattern

More recently, cross-cultural researchers have identified another important concept—dialectical thinking pattern—to help understand behavioral differences observed in individuals from East Asian and Western cultures. Dialectical thinking involves the embodiment and comprehension of contradictory and inconsistent elements and accepting their coexistence in one entity (Peng & Nisbett, 1999). The well-known Chinese symbol of Taoism in which *yin* and *yang* coreside and intertwine to form a circle exemplifies this dialectical thinking. Researchers suggest that dialectical thinking is a salient pattern in the Chinese cognitive process (and among many East Asians) and that it is deeply rooted in traditional Eastern philosophical beliefs such as *the principle of contradiction*, *the principle of change*, and *the principle of holism* (Spencer-Rodgers, Peng, Wang, & Hou, 2004). Western cultures, on the other hand, place high values on an analytical and logical approach, which tends to polarize contradictory/opposing elements, and to compare and contrast found similarities and differences. This pattern of thinking naturally promotes a stronger tendency to identify the most accurate element (and exclude others) among all elements or to synthesize a new, better cohesive whole by integrating inconsistent parts.

The dialectical thinking pattern has been found to have direct effects on expression of self-concept and psychological well-being demonstrated by Easterners and Westerners (Spencer-Rodgers et al., 2004). We believe it may also have significant implications on adult attachment. Based on the Western attachment perspective, individuals with attachment security are likely to develop self-acceptance, which based on a linear model will lead to a positive self-appraisal with decreased negative self-image. The dialectical nature of cognitive processing and self-appraisal for a psychologically healthy Chinese may mean she or he further adapts to the principle of contradiction and is more readily to attend to the possession of negative characteristics and endorse negative indicators. Therefore, the dichotomous, linear dimension of anxiety (with positive and negative internal working model of self as the two ends) may not be an effective conceptual framework in understanding Chinese adult attachment.

CHINESE ADULT ATTACHMENT MODEL

As discussed in the previous section, we believe that the Western-based adult attachment model does not fit well with many principle elements of the Chinese cultural context. As an initial attempt, we propose a model with two interactive strata that we believe are critically pertinent to the psychosocial dynamics of interpersonal relatedness (i.e., adult attachment) in the Chinese cultural context. The first layer is the perception of one's relational status and the second one is the fulfillment of one's relational obligations.

Perception of One's Relational Status

The concepts of self, significant others, and relationships are inseparable entities in Chinese culture, and therefore, an accurate understanding of internal working models for Chinese adult attachment should be cast within a relation-based context. With this in mind, the first stratum in our proposed model for Chinese attachment is understanding one's perception of her or his position in a relationship, interpersonal situation, or social network. The nature and importance of this layer can be elaborated from two aspects. First, the fatalistic perspective is a fundamental component in Chinese viewpoint about the formation of self–other relations. As described earlier, the development of significant relationships (parent–child, spousal, close friendship, etc.) is, to a large extent, believed to be predestined. Because an essential part of life for the Chinese is to complete the destined yuan with significant others, disowning a conflicting significant relationship is generally not considered an option. Affected by the fatalistic beliefs, when experiencing lasting relational conflicts many Chinese individuals may attribute the engagement in

a less desirable relationship to their fate and consider the discontentment a natural part of the attachment with this significant other. This frame of mind (i.e., acceptance of one's fate) shifts people's attention to focus on relational needs (e.g., what needs to be done to maintain the relationship) and obligation fulfillment according to the perceptions of their relational status and roles. It also provides a basis for the hope in reaching an ultimate resolution (e.g., negative yuan will be eventually completed after I pay off all of my relational debts). This fatalistic perspective, although seemingly philosophic, represents a unique element of Chinese attachment.

The second important aspect in understanding the perception of one's relational status dimension relates to the social structure and interpersonal norms. As described in the previous sections, Chinese society tends to be a hierarchical social system with sets of clearly defined behavioral guidelines for how to interact with others according to relative social and relational statuses. The system of ethics established by Confucius, also known as the *Five Cardinal Relationships* (i.e., ruler–subject, parent–child, husband–wife, siblings, and friend–friend), has been deeply embedded in the Chinese societal norms and people's day-to-day interpersonal interactions (Tamura, Mention, Lush, Tsui, & Cohen, 1997). Striving to fit into the social context, Chinese are likely to deliberately adjust their behaviors according to prescribed cultural rules and expectations associated with one's relational status in a particular social context. Within this framework, the manifestation of adult attachment behaviors is also likely to be more consistent with external cultural norms. That is, we believe that Chinese attachment involves a more complicated cognitive appraising process to identify what is a person's appropriate role and associated status so she or he can act properly, in contrast to spontaneity and authenticity of attachment behaviors reflecting on or guided by one's attachment styles/ needs as emphasized in the Western adult attachment model. For instance, after an unexpected stressful situation occurs (e.g., spouse's sudden illness) a Westerner with secure attachment style is likely to spontaneously share the news with her or his coworkers or supervisors, and seek emotional support or advice from them. However, a "secure" Chinese adult who faces a similar situation is more likely to deliberately assess the nature of their relationships with different coworkers and supervisors before deciding on who to and how to disclose the information.

The Western attachment model posits that a person who has developed a negative internal working model of others will tend to distrust others, experience higher degrees of discomfort for interpersonal closeness, and have excessive needs for self-reliance (Collins & Read, 1990). Observable behaviors, such as unwillingness to ask others for help when needed, reluctance to express internal feelings, and discomfort with interpersonal closeness, are considered signs for insecure attachment (Brennan et al., 1998). Because of the strong endorsement of the interdependent self-construal, fatalistic perspective, and filial piety and other interpersonal norms, the internal sense of trust (toward significant others) may not be the most prominent factor affecting Chinese adults' attachment styles and behaviors in the face of threats. Instead, we believe that how a person perceives her or his relative status in a relationship (e.g., to be a good wife, I need to always be supportive to my husband; I am the head of the family and I need to protect my wife and children; I am in a better situation than my best friend John and I should not bother him with my own problems; I am a child to my parents and I should obey them) is more fundamental for Chinese ways of relatedness (attachment and attachment behaviors). For instance, if a Chinese man perceives that he is in a position with higher social/relational status (e.g., the head of a family), when encountering attachment threats this individual is likely to continue acting as an authority figure and may refuse to seek help or support from his wife and adult children (who are perceived by the person to be in lower social/relational status).

In addition, because Chinese culture in general prescribes a more reserved norm for interpersonal interactions, valuing indirect communications to reduce risks of damaging interpersonal harmony (Tamura et al., 1997), behaviors such as overtly expressing intense emotions (especially negative emotions) and directly asking others to provide help (even within an intimate adult relationship like husband and wife) are considered immature, self-centered, and therefore discouraged. Within this context, this individual would likely employ "deactivating" strategies (e.g., suppressing threat-related thoughts, keeping the distressing feelings to themselves, reluctance of asking for help) to cope with the distressing situations. Although many of these behaviors are referred to as "avoidant behaviors" based on concepts and definitions of Western attachment, the same set of avoidant behaviors observed from this Chinese adult is likely to be compliant to cultural norms and should not be considered as demonstrations of insecure attachment.

Fulfillment of One's Relational Obligations

The second branch of the proposed model is the fulfillment of one's responsibility and obligations. This layer parallels the internal working model of self in the contemporary Western attachment model. The Western-based attachment perspectives posit that individuals who have developed negative internal working models of self tend to worry about being abandoned in relationships, possess low self-worthiness, and have strong needs for reassurance and approval from others (Brennan et al., 1998). A Westerner with insecure attachment associated with the developed negative internal working model of self is likely to employ "hyperactivating" strategies of affect regulation that involve being constantly alert and vigilant to potential threats or relevant information and excessive attempts of seeking attention (Florian, Mikulincer, & Bucholtz, 1995). However, the higher degree of observed attachment anxiety may not be necessarily equal to the developed negative internal working model of self for Chinese adults. Reflecting on the collectivistic cultural norms and dialectical thinking pattern, the frequency and magnitude of worry and distress for not belonging to or maintaining a relationship, the need to seek approval from significant others, and endorsement of negative traits observed on Chinese individuals are likely to be significantly higher than those seen on Westerners (Wang & Mallinckrodt, 2006). Thus, the characteristics of the Western-based "insecure self," although having received much empirical support with White middle-class samples, may not be effective indicators for many critical elements of internal security of self experienced by Chinese adults.

In contrast to the Western-based sense of self-security, which is mainly constituted of internal self-acceptance and positive self-appraisal, the evaluation of self-worthiness for Chinese people is largely based on the assessment of whether one is fulfilling important responsibilities and obligations associated with her or his social roles (Tamura et al., 1997). Hence, we believe that fulfillment of one's relational obligations is the most prominent source contributing to the sense of attachment security experienced by Chinese adults with regard to the self. This reasoning is also consistent with the psychosocial dynamics and needs likely experienced by individuals in a collectivist society. Chinese culture emphasizes interdependent, collectivist social norms in which group identity is often considered as more important than individual identity (Markus & Kitayama, 1991). Within this cultural norm, people tend to have greater needs in gaining acceptance and approval from significant others as well as striving to maintain a strong sense of belongingness to one's social groups than those in individualist cultures. Fulfillment of one's relational obligations helps to address these psychosocial needs, which will then lead to the development of positive self-identity and a sense of security. Along the same reasoning, because attachment insecurity of self for a Chinese adult is related to incompletion or underperformance of one's social duties and obligations, the main feeling associated with it is shame, and the most likely strategy in response to this insecure feeling is withdrawal from seeking any social attention.

The following brief case demonstrates the counseling application of the proposed model. A 26-year-old Chinese male client was experiencing a great deal of distress because his parents did not accept his girlfriend. He stated that he had tried to communicate with his parents on two different occasions about his romantic feelings toward this girl, which always led to augments and further escalated his stress level. The client reported that he was not mad at his parents because he understood their concerns and valued their advice; however, he was angry at himself for not being able to convince his parents and for feeling sad about hurting his girlfriend. The client was reluctant to discuss his distress and struggles with his girlfriend because he believed that would only cause her more harm. He mentioned that his parents had introduced another girl to him few weeks later who they described as a good candidate for marriage. The client decided to terminate the relationship with his current girlfriend to "prevent everyone from suffering further" in this situation, and stated, "Maybe, this is the end of our yuan!"

Using the proposed model to conceptualize this case, a counselor/therapist will not only reduce the potential danger of overpathologizing the client's ways of handling the situation (e.g., avoidance of conflicts, overt submissiveness to parents, and lack of responsibility) but also acquire an accurate understanding on the underlying cultural factors and psychosocial needs of the client associated with this distressing event and his decision. The ability to comprehend the situation via a similar worldview will enable the counselor/therapist to better empathize with the client regarding his experienced attachment threat and to process observed attachment behaviors in a nonjudgmental manner. The counselor/therapist can also use the proposed model to identify client's strengths such as ability of tolerating internal distress, fulfillment of relational obligations, acceptance of yuan, and willingness to take actions to ease others' pains and to assist the client in gaining awareness on the decision-making process with a goal of developing a positive perspective and healthy coping strategies.

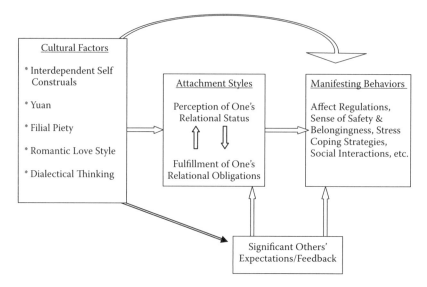

Figure 2.1   The relationships of cultural factors, attachment styles, and attachment behaviors.

Cultural Context and Chinese Attachment Model

Figure 2.1 illustrates the relationships among various cultural factors, Chinese adult attachment, and manifesting attachment behaviors. There are several noticeable characteristics regarding the nature of the proposed Chinese attachment model. Because the orthogonal two-dimensional structure organized in the Western attachment model may conflict with some factors in Chinese cultural contexts such as dialectical thinking and the relation-based self-concept, the Chinese attachment model is conceptualized as a bilayer, circular configuration. One's appraisal on each layer as well as the external factors linked to the model will have reciprocal influences on Chinese adult attachment. Based on this model, individuals demonstrating healthy attachment style are those who have unambiguous perceptions (and acceptance) of their relational roles/statuses that are mostly in harmony with social expectations, as well as a clear sense of fulfillment from the obligations/responsibilities related to their relational roles.

For East Asians, self is deeply embedded in relationships and this relation-based self is likely to be context specific (Choi & Choi, 2002). We believe that the concept of contextual specificity has an important implication in understanding the manifestation of Chinese attachment. Rather than having a unifying, single attachment style consistently manifesting across various contexts, Chinese people may possess multiple attachment patterns with each being context or relationship specific. This is because the relational roles and statuses a Chinese person perceives for each of the five major relationships may vary significantly from one another. The contextualized attachment changes according to the encountered social situations and some of them may even seem contradictory to one another's. For instance, when activating by potential attachment threats (e.g., loss of a significant other), which link to different relationships (e.g., parent–adult child vs. spousal), Chinese individuals with secure attachment may demonstrate distinctively different behavioral patterns in response to the perceived attachment threats. In a situation where one's aged parent is severely ill, an adult child may openly express her or his feeling of sadness and seek help and input from close family members of same generation with regard to how to best handle the situations. In contrast, when the same person encounters a situation in which her or his spouse is ill, she or he may withhold expressing feelings to others, be reluctant to openly ask close friends for help, and try to deal with the adversity on her or his own.

Another important facet of this model is the influential role of significant others' feedback. Although a person's self-appraisals of her or his degree of responsibility fulfillment and social/rational status are the deciding blocks of one's attachment, the internal evaluations as well as the manifesting attachment behaviors are susceptible to external standards and feedback (both criticisms and praises) given by significant others. Based on this model, we believe that the measurement of Chinese adult attachment of a particular person may demonstrate greater fluctuation at different times compared to Western attachment. This strong influence of others reflects the interdependent nature and close interpersonal ties of Chinese culture. It is also consistent with the notion that Chinese individuals' adult attachment is best understood in the relation-based context.

Although the proposed Chinese adult attachment model provides an indigenous perspective to understand Chinese (and possibly other East Asian) adult attachment, relevant behaviors, and interpersonal interactions within relevant cultural contexts, the contextualized perspective of attachment proposed in this chapter is not a new invention. The evolutionary root of attachment theory and the reciprocal determinism between the infant and the environment on the development of one's attachment style emphasized by Bowlby (1969) clearly mark the notion that attachment development and manifestation are likely context sensitive. Other attachment researchers (e.g., Feeney, 1994; Fraley, 2007; Hinde & Stevenson-Hinde, 1990) have also talked about attachment being context based, although they did not necessarily refer to cultural contexts.

FUTURE RESEARCH DIRECTIONS AND CONCLUSION

Although the aforementioned Chinese cultural characteristics and logical reasoning have provided a rather solid conceptual basis for the proposed Chinese adult attachment model, evidence drawn from empirical studies is necessary in validating the accuracy and usefulness of this model. We suggest that future studies examine the influences of the two proposed Chinese attachment components (i.e., perception of one's relational status and fulfillment of one's relational obligation) on Chinese adults' self-appraisal, perceived relationship quality, life satisfaction, reactions to interpersonal conflicts, coping strategies for stress and interpersonal conflicts, emotional stability, psychological distress/symptoms, or other relevant psychological or behavioral outcome variables. Another fruitful direction for future research is to further pinpoint specific underlying factors that account for the attachment mechanism. For instance, adult attachment is considered a cognitive appraisal system and its functioning will presumably be filtered by learned societal norms or cultural norms. Therefore, researchers could explore various cultural beliefs as potential mediators (e.g., filial piety and familism) to clarify the specific psychosocial dynamics of Chinese adult attachment influence. Given the possible cultural difference and the strong Western influence on many Asian countries, researchers may also explore possible moderator effects of gender role beliefs and other important cultural factors such as acceptance of fatalistic perspective, endorsement of filial piety, and interdependent self-construals for the Chinese adult attachment model. In addition, the possession of multiple relationship-specific attachment styles by an individual, rather than having a single, consistent adult attachment, posited by the model is another possible direction for future research.

It is important to note the influences of Western cultures and social–political–economic systems on Asian cultural and values, commonly referred to as the Westernization or modernization of Asia (Islam & Chowdhury, 2000) and how they may have altered, in part, cultural practices in Asian societies. Some Western values such as liberty, individual-centered perspectives, and individual rights have emerged in many East Asian nations; and as a result, Chinese societies in Hong Kong, Singapore, Taiwan, and even mainland China have begun to adopt some Western cultural values or interpersonal norms, which have also led to changes in some traditional forms of relationships (Compton, 2000). For instance, filial piety is considered a critical factor in understanding the cultural context of the proposed model; yet researchers have described that modernization in contemporary Chinese societies has lowered the status of the elderly in their families and weakened the traditional values and practice of filial piety (Ikels, 2004). With the emergence of Western values in a variety of social, political and governmental, religious, and educational systems, it is likely that the modification of cultural norms may also lead to changes in one's perception of self and others as well as the desirable ways of relatedness in respect to intimate relationships or attachments. Because of these changes, it appears necessary to assess both enculturation (i.e., acceptance of native Chinese cultural values and beliefs) and Westernization/acculturation (i.e., exposure and endorsement of Western cultural norms) held by Chinese individuals, especially those residing in highly Westernized cities or regions, in order to obtain an accurate picture of their attachment styles.

We believe that the Western attachment model remains to be a useful framework if researchers are mindful of cultural issues and avoid overgeneralizations of research findings. When an adult attachment study with non-Western populations is done based on the Western model, we believe it is important to explicitly state the etic approach taken in the study, rather than automatically assuming the universality of Western attachment perspectives. Findings of these studies need to be understood in the proper cultural contexts, instead of being interpreted with Western behavioral norms. Researchers should also be cautious of errors produced due to measurement issues. For instance, the assessment accuracy of adult attachment interview methods may be interfered by the effect of filial piety. Many of the self-report adult attachment scales developed in the United States focus on romantic relationships and their results may not be applicable to other relational domains. In addition, due to the dialectical thinking pattern prevalent in Chinese populations, researchers should also pay attention to Chinese participants' response differences between positively and negatively worded items when using self-report adult attachment measures.

In this chapter, we offer a Chinese adult attachment model as an alternative framework to conceptualize Chinese adult attachment behaviors and relevant phenomena. The proposed model, with considerations of cultural contexts, in our belief is more accurately representative of Chinese ways of relatedness, self, and sense of attachment security. We hope this model will aspire and stimulate more cross-cultural adult attachment research using emic methods and proposals of other indigenous perspectives. If so, the joint effort would likely further advance the adult attachment perspectives by adding a multicultural layer to the theory.

REFERENCES

Ainsworth, M. D. S. (1967). *Infancy in Uganda: Infant care and the growth of love.* Baltimore: Johns Hopkins University Press.

Ainsworth, M. S., Blehar, M., Waters, E., & Wall, S. (1978). *Patterns of attachment.* Hillsdale, NJ: Erlbaum.

Bartholomew, K., & Horowitz, L. M. (1991). Attachment styles among young adults: A test of a four-category model. *Journal of Personality and Social Psychology, 61,* 226–244.

Bowlby, J. (1969). *Attachment and loss: Vol. I. Attachment.* New York: Basic Books.

Brennan, K. A., Clark, C. L., & Shaver, P. R. (1998). Self-report measurement of adult attachment: An integrative overview. In J. A. Simpson & W. S. Rholes (Eds.), *Attachment theory and close relationships* (pp. 46–76). New York: Guilford Press.

Brislin, R. W. (1976). Comparative research methodology: Cross-cultural studies. *International Journal of Psychology, 11,* 215–229.

Chang, H.-C., & Holt, G. R. (1991). The concept of yuan and Chinese interpersonal relationships. In S. Ting-Toomey & F. Korzenny (Eds.), *Cross-cultural interpersonal communication* (pp. 25–57). Newbury Park, CA: Sage.

Cho, W., & Cross, S. E. (1995). Taiwanese love styles and their association with self-esteem and relationship quality. *Genetic, Social, and General Psychology Monographs, 121,* 283–309.

Choi, I., & Choi, Y. (2002). Culture and self-concept flexibility. *Personality & Social Psychology Bulletin, 28,* 1508–1517.

Collins, N. L., & Read, S. J. (1990). Adult attachment working models and relationship quality in dating couples. *Journal of Personality and Social Psychology, 58,* 644–663.

Compton, R. W. (2000). *East Asian democratization: Impact of globalism, culture, and economy.* London: Praeger.

Davidson, A. R., Jaccard, J. J., Triandis, H. C., Morales, M. L., & Diaz-Guerrero, R. (1976). Cross-cultural model testing: Toward a solution of the etic-emic dilemma. *International Journal of Psychology, 11,* 1–13.

Dion, K. K., & Dion, K. L. (1996). Cultural perspectives on romantic love. *Personal Relationships, 3,* 5–17.

Dion, K. L., & Dion, K. K. (1993). Individualistic and collectivistic perspectives on gender and the cultural concept of love and intimacy. *Journal of Social Issues, 49,* 53–69.

DiTommaso, E., Brannen, C., & Burgess, M. (2005). The universality of relationship characteristics: A cross-cultural comparison of different types of attachment and loneliness in Canadian and visiting Chinese students. *Social Behavior and Personality, 33,* 57–67.

Feeney, J. A. (1994). Attachment style, communication patterns and satisfaction across the life cycle of marriage. *Personal Relationships, 1*, 333–348.

Feeney, J. A., & Noller, P. (1990). Attachment style as a predictor of adult romantic relationships. *Journal of Personality and Social Psychology, 58*, 281–291.

Florian, V., Mikulincer, M., & Bucholtz, L. (1995). Effects of adult attachment style on the perceptions and search for social support. *The Journal of Psychology, 129*, 665–676.

Fraley, A. C. (2007). A connectionist approach to organization and continuity of working models of attachment. *Journal of Personality, 75*, 1157–1180.

Hatfield, E., & Rapson, R. L. (1996). Love and sex: Cross-cultural perspectives. Boston: Allyn & Bacon.

Hazan, C., & Shaver, P. (1987). Romantic love conceptualized as an attachment process. *Journal of Personality and Social Psychology, 52*, 511–524.

Hinde, R. A., & Stevenson-Hinde, J. (1990) Attachment: Biological cultural and individual desiderata. *Human Development, 33*, 62–72.

Hsu, F. L. K. (1981). *Americans and Chinese: Passage to differences* (3rd ed.). Honolulu: University Press of Hawaii.

Ikels, C. (2004). Introduction. In C. Ikels (Ed.), *Filial piety, practice and discourse in contemporary East Asia* (pp. 1–15). Stanford, CA: Stanford University Press.

Islam, I., & Chowdhury, A. (2000). *The political economy of East Asia: Post-crisis debates*. New York: Oxford University Press.

Kim, I. J., & Zane, N. W. S. (2004). Ethnic and cultural variations in anger regulation and attachment patterns among Korean American and European American male batterers. *Cultural Diversity and Ethnic Minority Psychology, 10*, 151–168.

Lopez, F. G., & Brennan, K. A. (2000). Dynamic processes underlying adult attachment organization: Toward an attachment theoretical perspective on the health and effective self. *Journal of Counseling Psychology, 47*, 283–300.

Main, M. (1990). Cross-cultural studies of attachment organization: Recent studies, changing methodologies, and the concept of conditional strategies. *Human Development, 33*, 48–61.

Main, M., Kaplan, N., & Cassidy, J. (1985). Security in infancy childhood and adulthood: A move to the level of representation. *Monographs of The Society for Research in Child Development, 50*(1–2), 66–104.

Malley-Morrison, K., You, H. S., & Mills, R. B. (2000). Young adult attachment styles and perceptions of elder abuse: A cross-cultural study. *Journal of Cross-Cultural Gerontology, 15*, 163–184.

Markus, H. R., & Kitayama, S. (1991). Culture and the self: Implications for cognition emotion and motivation. *Psychological Review, 98*(2), 224–253.

Moore, R. L. (1998). Love and limerence with Chinese characteristics: Student romantic in the PRC. In V. C. de Munck (Ed.), *Romantic love and sexual behavior: Perspectives from the social science* (pp. 251–284). Westport, CT: Praeger.

Morris, M. W., Leung, K., Ames, D., & Lickel, B. (1999). Views from inside and outside: Integrating emic and etic insights about culture and justice judgment. *The Academy of Management Review, 24*, 781–796.

Peng, K., & Nisbett, R. E. (1999). Culture, dialectics, and reasoning about contradiction. *American Psychologist, 54*, 741–754.

Rothbaum, F., Weisz, J., Pott, M., Miyake, K., & Morelli, G. (2000). Attachment and culture: Security in the United States and Japan. *American Psychologist, 55*, 1093–1104.

Schmitt, D. P., Alcalay, L., Allensworth, M., Allik, J., Ault, L., Austers, L., … Zupanèiè, A. (2004). Patterns and universals of adult romantic attachment across 62 cultural regions: Are models of self and of other pancultural constructs? *Journal of Cross-Cultural Psychology, 35*, 367–402.

Simpson, J. A. (1990). Influence of attachment styles on romantic relationships. *Journal of Personality and Social Psychology, 59*, 971–980.

Simpson J. A., & Rholes, W. S. (1998). Attachment theory: A glance at the past, a look to the future. In J. A. Simpson & W. S. Rholes (Eds.), *Attachment theory and close relationships* (pp. 3–21). New York: Guilford Press.

Spencer-Rodgers, J., Peng, K., Wang, L., & Hou, Y. (2004). Dialectical self-esteem and East-West differences in psychological well-being. *Personality and Social Psychology Bulletin, 30*, 1416–1432.

Takahashi, K. (1990). Are the key assumptions of the Strange Situation procedure universal? A view from Japanese research. *Human Development, 33*, 23–30.

Tamura, E. H., Mention, L. K., Lush, N. W., Tsui, K. C., & Cohen, W. (1997). *China: Understanding its past.* Honolulu: University Press of Hawaii.

Triandis, H. C. (1996). The psychological measurement of cultural syndromes. *American Psychologist, 51*, 407–415.

van IJzendoorn, M. H., & Sagi, A. (1999). Cross-cultural patterns of attachment: Universal and contextual dimensions. In J. Cassidy & P. R. Shaver (Eds.), *Handbook of attachment: Theory, research, and clinical application* (pp. 713–734). New York: Guilford Press.

Wang, C. D. (2007, August). *A cross-cultural comparison of adult attachment function.* Poster presentation at the 2007 American Psychological Association Annual Convention in San Francisco, CA.

Wang, C. D., & Mallinckrodt, B. S. (2006). Differences between Taiwanese and U.S. cultural beliefs about ideal adult attachment. *Journal of Counseling Psychology, 53*, 192–204.

Wei, M., Russell, D. W., Mallinckrodt, B., & Zakalik, R. A. (2004). Cultural equivalence of adult attachment across four ethnic groups: Factor structure, structured means, and associations with negative mood. *Journal of Counseling Psychology, 51*, 408–417.

Yang, K.-S., & Ho, D. Y. F. (1988). The role of yuan in Chinese social life: A conceptual and empirical analysis. In A. C. Paranjpe, D. Y.-F. Ho, & R. W. Rieber (Eds.), *Asian contributions to psychology* (pp. 263–281). New York: Praeger.

Yeh, K. H. (1997). Changes in the Taiwanese people's concept of filial piety. In L. Y. Cheng, Y. H. Lu, & F. C. Wang (Eds.), *Taiwanese society in the 1990s* (pp. 171–214). Taipei, Taiwan: Institute of Sociology, Academic Sinica.

You, H., & Malley-Morrison, K. (2000). Young adult attachment styles and intimate relationships with close friends: A cross-cultural study of Koreans and Caucasian Americans. *Journal of Cross-Cultural Psychology, 31*, 528–534.

3

Attachment Within a Cultural Perspective
Relationships With Exploration and Self-Orientations

E. OLCAY IMAMOĞLU and SELEN IMAMOĞLU

CONTENTS

An important problem in attachment literature concerns the cross-cultural valid-ity of attachment theory. Whereas some question its universality by arguing that it reflects an individualistic bias (e.g., Rothbaum, Weisz, Pott, Miyake, & Morelli, 2000), van IJzendoorn and Sagi (1999) in their review of the related literature concluded that attachment theory might claim cross-cultural validity but that "data on attachment in India and the Islamic world are still completely lacking" (p. 731).

In this chapter, we aim to contribute to filling that lag by considering some aspects of attachment theory within a cultural perspective with particular reference to findings from Turkey, where Islam is the predominant religion in a traditionally collectivistic context (Hofstede, 2001). In accordance with the collectivist and religious traditions, the Turkish context is characterized by an emphasis on interpersonal relationships and close ties with family and relatives encouraging higher levels of relatedness than, for instance, the more individualistic Swedes (E. O. Imamoğlu & Imamoğlu, 1992; E. O. Imamoğlu, Küller, Imamoğlu, & Küller, 1993) or Americans (E. O. Imamoğlu & Karakitapoğlu-Aygün, 2006; Uleman, Rhee, Bardoliwalla, Semin, & Toyama, 2000). Furthermore, when asked about their desired levels of relatedness, Turkish people consistently report favoring even more relatedness with family members and neighbors (E. O. Imamoğlu, 1987; E. O. Imamoğlu & Imamoğlu, 1996). Thus, in spite of the rapid socioeconomic change Turkey has been going through especially since the last five decades, and the trends toward individuation in self-development and values (E. O. Imamoğlu, 1987; E. O. Imamoğlu & Karakitapoğlu-Aygün, 1999; Karakitapoğlu-Aygün & Imamoğlu, 2002), there has not been a parallel decrease in relatedness trends.

Those findings question the individualist tradition in psychology, which assumes relatedness and individuation are mutually exclusive (E. O. Imamoğlu, 1987, 2003). The issues we consider in this chapter are related to the problem of such unwarranted theoretical assumptions, which may hinder or limit the generalizability of those outlooks to different environmental contexts. That is, in psychology there seems to be a tendency to explicitly or implicitly assume that some basic human (or cultural) orientations are mutually exclusive (e.g., individuation versus relatedness, individualism versus collectivism, independence versus interdependence) or that they are inexorably linked (e.g., individuation with separateness, attachment security with exploration). In this chapter, we aim to tackle this issue by exploring the attachment–exploration linkage and its association with the relatedness–individuation linkage, using the conceptual framework provided by the balanced integration–differentiation (BID) model (E. O. Imamoğlu, 1998, 2003). Specifically, we consider the issue of the attachment–exploration linkage, first indirectly, by examining the association of attachment security with self-orientations of relatedness and individuation (the latter considered as an exploration of one's inner world). Next, we present findings from our more recent research in which we measured attachment and exploration as separate orientations to investigate their interrelationship with each other and with other self-orientations. In doing so, we try to show that other alternative combinations of the attachment-exploration linkage may be possible than that assumed by attachment theory. Next, the theoretical base provided by the BID model is briefly explained.

AN OVERVIEW OF THE BID MODEL: RELATEDNESS AND INDIVIDUATION AS DISTINCT AND COMPLEMENTARY SELF-ORIENTATIONS

The individualistic tradition in mainstream psychology generally has valued gaining independence from others over relatedness with them in self-development. As noted by E. O. Imamoğlu (2003), that tradition has been characterized by two tacit assumptions. First, the *developmental gain* assumption regards learning to overcome one's social bonds to become more independent from others as a developmental achievement. Second, the *bipolar dichotomy* assumption considers independence and/or individuation and relatedness as opposites; accordingly, it suggests that separation from others should be regarded as an inevitable component of individuation and autonomous functioning. Both of those tacit assumptions are contrary to the attachment outlook within which relationality plays a pivotal role in life-span human development (Ainsworth, 1972; Ainsworth, Bell, & Stayton, 1971; Bowlby, 1982, 1988).

In a similar vein, the BID model (E. O. Imamoğlu, 1995, 1998, 2003) considers individuation and relatedness as not opposite but distinct and complementary orientations. The BID model is based on the assumption that

> the natural order involves a balanced system resulting from the interdependent integration of differentiated components. In other words, differentiation and integration do not represent opposing forces but distinct and complementary processes of a balanced order ... They are distinct in that differentiation refers to an intraorganismic process, whereas integration involves an interorganismic process. (E. O. Imamoğlu, 2003, pp. 371–372)

Accordingly, human beings, as parts of this natural system, are assumed to have basic psychological needs for both *interpersonal integration* (i.e., a genuine interrelational tendency to be connected to others) and for *intrapersonal differentiation* (i.e., a genuine self-developmental tendency to explore or actualize one's unique potentials and be effective; coined as intrapersonal to highlight that it is not a process that happens from others, as is usually understood, but one that involves an intrinsic exploration orientation). The low and high ends of the former orientation are referred to as *separatedness* and *relatedness*, respectively. The high end of the latter orientation is labeled as *individuation* (i.e., becoming differentiated as a unique person with genuine intrinsic referents, such as personal capabilities, genuine inclinations, free will or willful consent), while the low end is labeled as *normative patterning* (i.e., becoming patterned in accordance with extrinsic referents, such as normative expectations and social control). It is proposed that when relatedness and individuation can find mutual satisfaction in a balanced state, they tend to complement one another.

Related studies, involving Turkish, American, and Canadian samples, have supported the model by indicating that individuation and relatedness are distinct orientations, and that they tend to be associated with qualitatively distinct and complementary domains of variables. Individuation is associated with intrinsic motivational variables (involving an authentic tendency to explore and cognize), such as the need for cognition, need for exploration, curiosity, tolerance for ambiguity, low materialism, perceived autonomy, and identity. Relatedness is associated with affective-relational variables such as parental love–acceptance; satisfaction with one's self, family, marriage, work, and life in general; emotional closeness with parents; trust for self; positive future expectations; positive affectivity; low trait anxiety; positive self–other models; and attachment security (Beydoğan, 2008; Güler-Edwards, 2008; Gündoğdu, 2007; E. O. Imamoğlu, 1998, 2003, 2008, 2009; E. O. Imamoğlu &

Güler-Edwards, 2007; E. O. Imamoğlu & Imamoğlu, 2007; E. O. Imamoğlu & Karakitapoğlu-Aygün, 2006, 2007; S. Imamoğlu, 2005; Karakitapoğlu-Aygün & Imamoğlu, 2008; Kurt, 2002a, 2002b; Turan, 2007).

Four Self-Types Proposed

Considering the intrapersonal differentiation and interpersonal integration orienta-tions as distinct, the BID model maintains that one can be either high or low on both. Thus, combinations of being high or low on each orientation are suggested to give rise to four types of prototypical self-constructions: *separated-individuated, related-patterned* (representing the most *differentiated* and the *integrated* types, respectively), *separated-patterned,* and *related-individuated* (representing the most *unbalanced* and *balanced* types, respectively). Accordingly, only being high on both orientations (i.e., the *related-individuated* self-type) represents a balanced being because for opti-mal psychological functioning the basic needs for both integration and differentiation should be satisfied. It should be noted that the usage of the word *balanced* here is congruent with the definition of balance as "a harmonious or satisfying arrangement of parts or elements" (*Webster's II New Riverside University Dictionary*, 1984, p. 148).

BID-related studies, referred to earlier, provided systematic differences between those self-types and supported the basic assertion that balanced rela-tional and individuational self-orientations serve complementary functions in the self-system. Accordingly, a balanced self-construction was perceived as an ideal state of being by a sample of Turkish adults and was associated with psychological well-being (E. O. Imamoğlu, 2008, 2009). It is also important to note that pat-terns of relatedness with parents associated with the BID-related self-types were found to be similar across individualist and collectivist contexts (E. O. Imamoğlu & Karakitapoğlu-Aygün, 2006, 2007), which would not be expected from the bipolar formulation of the individualism–collectivism (I–C) framework (e.g., Markus & Kitayama, 1991; Triandis, 1995).

Four Contexts (or Family Types) Proposed

Contexts proposed to be conducive for the development of the four self-types (E. O. Imamoğlu, 2003) are briefly described next.

Differentiative (Family) Contexts   Differentiative contexts, conducive for the development of separated-individuated (or differentiated) persons, tend to be low in both nurturance–relatedness, as well as in restrictive psychological control. Persons raised in those contexts tend to be encouraged to differentiate *away* from their fami-lies or others; that is, they would be granted autonomy to be detached individuals. They may either experience their families' efforts toward detachment as rejection (Ryan & Lynch, 1989), or may in fact be rejected, so that they may experience nega-tive affectivity toward their parents (E. O. Imamoğlu, 2003) and they try to be self-sufficient individuals. However, such individuals, though insecure in their attachment orientations, may try to engage in exploratory acts as a part of their efforts toward individuation or, perhaps, to prove that they are worthy of the love–acceptance they

feel they lack. Thus, in such contexts, although one's need for individuation (or explo-ration) tends to be emphasized, that for relatedness (or attachment) may be seen as an impediment to individuation and, hence, neglected or deemphasized.

Integrative (Family) Contexts   In contexts conducive for the development of related-patterned (or integrated) persons, interpersonal integration seems to be favored over intrapersonal differentiation, which tends to be seen as a threat to family or group harmony; that is, such persons would be expected to be integrated to their families, or groups, not only in terms of affective attachments, but also in terms of cognitive or ideational similarities. Accordingly, ideal children in those settings may be conceived of as obedient, respectful, and well-mannered (E. O. Imamoğlu, 1987). Those contexts may be likely to be characterized by nurturance and sacrifice, as well as strict, intrusive, overprotective control, so that children learn to develop and act in accordance with external referents, ready to accommo-date and fulfill their obligations toward their supportive parents or close others to whom they have learned to be grateful. Such persons may be characterized by pos-itive bonds toward their families (E. O. Imamoğlu, 2003) but, to the degree that they feel psychologically restrained, they may feel anxious about meeting external expectations, and insecure or restrained in exploring on their own. Rather than an intrinsic motivation for exploration, they may be more likely to have an accommo-dative orientation to preserve social harmony.

Unbalanced (Family) Contexts   Such contexts, conducive for the develop-ment of separated-patterned (or unbalanced) persons, are considered as fully unbal-anced because they tend to be suitable for the satisfaction of neither interpersonal integration nor intrapersonal differentiation needs. Persons who develop in such contexts, which are high in restrictive control and low in nurturance-acceptance, are likely to be emotionally detached, but cognitively bonded or patterned; hence they might be characterized by both negative affectivity and stereotyped thinking. This family type may resemble Baumrind's (1991) authoritarian parents, who tend to be highly demanding but not responsive. The resulting unbalanced self-type is proposed to be associated with insecurity in both attachment and exploration, and hence, as supported by the studies noted earlier, it may represent the worst state in terms of psychological functioning.

Balanced (Family) Contexts   Balanced contexts, conducive for the develop-ment of related-individuated (or balanced) persons, tend to enable the satisfaction of the basic needs for both interpersonal integration and intrapersonal differentia-tion; that is, they tend to be both relatedness-supportive and exploration-individ-uation-supportive in a complementary manner. Consistent with studies conducted in the United States (e.g., Anderson, Manoogian, & Reznick, 1976; Ryan & Grolnick, 1986), research findings from Turkey indicated that love–acceptance and autonomy–supportiveness dimensions of parenting seem to complement each other in producing contexts conducive for the satisfaction of both relational and individuational needs. Accordingly, related-individuated respondents were found to characterize their families as both more loving–accepting and less restrictively controlling than the other self-types (E. O. Imamoğlu, 2003). Interestingly, low restrictive (psychological) control was found to predict individuation not directly but indirectly, through the mediation of the need for cognition (E. O. Imamoğlu, 2003). Thus, people raised in contexts characterized by low restrictive control and high mutual love–acceptance and nurturant–involvement, may be expected to perceive their parents as having a genuine love for and interest in them as unique persons. They may be more likely to develop a genuine exploratory, intrinsic orientation toward both themselves and the outer world, while maintaining their secure attachments and social bonds; that is, they tend to individuate, not *from* others, but *with* others. In such balanced contexts, parents tend to be responsive both affectively and cognitively, and differences between family members are regarded as something not to be "tolerated" or curbed, but to be explored in a context of mutual perspective taking.

Those contexts that enable both secure attachment and secure exploration are considered optimal for the balanced satisfaction of one's needs for both interpersonal integration (i.e., relatedness) and intrapersonal differentiation (i.e., individuation), asserted and found to be associated with optimal psychological functioning and well-being (E. O. Imamoğlu, 2008, 2009). In congruity with this proposition, related studies indicate the development of intrinsic motivation to be positively associated with self-satisfaction, which tends to be associated also with family satisfaction (E. O. Imamoğlu, 2003; Osberg, 1987; Pretty & Seligman, 1984). In a similar vein, self-determination theorists reject the outlook in developmental psychology that during the process of individuation adolescents need to become detached from their parents and develop emotional autonomy. For example, Ryan and Lynch (1989) found that compared to the detached American adolescents, those having more emotional ties and feeling accepted were more likely to develop a positive view of themselves and they argued that

> growth in independence and autonomy does not necessarily require severing emotional ties with parents or nonutilization of the emotional support parents can afford. More likely it requires that parents provide support for the developmental tasks of adolescence in a context of family cohesion and love. Insofar as one conceives of attachment as both an emotional bond and sensitivity to developmental needs, then it would seem that it is attachment rather than detachment that optimizes individuation and the capacities for relatedness to self and others during adolescence and early adulthood. (p. 355)

Thus, the BID model, in congruence with the aforementioned assertions of self-determination theorists, attachment theory, and other somewhat related formulations (e.g., Bell et al., 2007; Guisinger & Blatt, 1994; Helgeson, 1994; Kağıtçıbaşı, 2005; Raeff, 1997), differs from the bipolar self-construal formulations within the I–C framework (e.g., Markus & Kitayama, 1991; Triandis, 1995), which seem to confound the relational and individuational orientations of individuals (e.g., by assuming that individuation necessarily implies separation), and seem to refer to highly global constructs, encompassing multiple components (Oyserman, Coon, & Kemmelmeier, 2002). Furthermore, independently of idiocentric and allocentric (referring to I–C at the personal level) orientations, individuation and relatedness, as considered by the BID model, were found to be consistent predictors of authenticity (E. O. Imamoğlu, Günaydın, & Selçuk, 2009). Accordingly, in line with Kernis and Goldman's (2006) definition of authenticity as "the unobstructed operation of one's true- or core-self in one's daily enterprises" (p. 294), a balanced self-construction appears to be associated with awareness of one's characteristics, unbiased processing of self-relevant information, behaving in accordance with one's true self, and being sincere in one's close relationships. Thus, the prediction of the BID model, that both relatedness and individuation are important for an optimal authentic functioning, has been supported.

THE NATURE OF THE ATTACHMENT AND EXPLORATION LINKAGE: ARE THEY INEXORABLY LINKED OR DISTINCT ORIENTATIONS?

Attachment theorists maintain that an important function of secure attachment is to provide a *secure base* from which to explore. Such exploration may involve not just the external world, but the internal world as well (Ainsworth, 1972; Ainsworth et al., 1971; Bowlby, 1982, 1988). For instance, Grosmann, Grossmann, and Zimmermann (1999) note that "freedom to explore the external and internal world is an important attachment-related issue throughout the lifespan" (p. 767). In a similar vein, Posada et al. (1995) stated that Bowlby and Ainsworth "placed the secure base phenomenon at the center of their analysis and defined an attachment figure as a person whom the child uses as a secure base across time and situations" (p. 27).

Support has been found for secure attachment to be associated with exploratory tendencies in both childhood and adulthood (e.g., S. Imamoğlu, 2005; Magai & McFadden, 1995; Mikulincer, 1997). As suggested by Mikulincer and Sheffi (2000), securely attached individuals may interpret their positive affect as a positive signal about their performance and enjoyment of the task at hand, and, hence, may be more likely to engage in playful–creative exploration. In general, secure children seem to engage in more concentrated exploration of novel stimuli and show more focused attention as they engage in particular tasks (Grossmann et al., 1999). When they cannot readily adapt to a particular situation, secure children can respond flexibly to challenges while maintaining a secure feeling during exploration, and if their competence ceases to be sufficient, they can turn to their social resources. Grossmann et al. (1999) called this a "wider view of attachment," in which the freedom to explore against difficulties and the freedom to seek help are both viewed as "necessary and important aspects of security" (p. 781). In their words:

> A secure parental base provides a child with the confidence needed for meeting challenges of exploration … Exploratory interest and enthusiasm are based on a feeling of security that reflects an anticipated positive evaluation of the environment. We propose to use the concept of "security of exploration" as an integral part of the concept of "security of attachment." (p. 761)

Thus, attachment theorists have assumed the attachment system to be linked with the exploration system in an inexorable manner via the secure base concept.

However, Aspelmeier and Kerns (2003) noted that "none of the investigations of attachment exploration dynamics to date ... clearly identify the mechanism(s) that mediates the association between attachment and exploration" (p. 27). Furthermore, in recent years, basic assertions of attachment theory involving exploration and the secure base notion have been challenged from a cross-cultural perspective (Harwood, Miller, & Irizarry, 1995; Rothbaum, Pott, Azuma, Miyake, & Weisz, 2000; Rothbaum, Weisz, et al., 2000). Those critics note that the theory is built on the values of autonomy, individuation, and exploration, which are emphasized in the Western outlook, whereas in countries such as Japan, caregiver sensitivity, social competence, and secure base are understood quite differently. Questionning the universality claim of attachment theory, Rothbaum, Pott, et al. (2000) suggest that development follows different paths in different cultures. For example, whereas the U.S. path may be one of *generative tension*, characterized by a conflict between the desires for closeness and separation–exploration, the Japanese one may be referred to as a path of *symbiotic harmony*, emphasizing union, others' expectations, stability, and assurance of relationships. Regarding the relationship between attachment and exploration, Rothbaum, Weisz, et al. (2000) argue that the link between attachment and exploration systems may not be primary and universal as it is claimed; instead, in Japan, the primary link may be between attachment and dependence systems. That is, whereas sensitive caregivers in the United States may be promoting their children's exploration of the environment, the Japanese caregivers may be promoting their dependence on attachment figures. Hence, they argue that caregivers' sensitivity may be responsive to the infants' need for social engagement in the Japanese context and to that of individuation and autonomy in the U.S. context. Other psychologists also have provided similar arguments and supportive data (see Harwood et al., 1995, for a review). For example, Anglo-American mothers' representation of the desirable Strange Situation behavior involved an optimal balance of autonomy and relatedness, whereas that of Puerto Rican mothers' involved a balance of proper conduct (i.e., obedient, quiet, respectful, well-mannered, etc.) and positive engagement (Harwood et al., 1995).

The criticisms raised especially by Rothbaum and his associates have been the target of extensive dialogue among attachment theorists (e.g., Chao, 2001; Gjerde, 2001; Kondo-Ikemura, 2001; Posada & Jacobs, 2001; van IJzendoorn & Sagi, 2001). Within the limits of this chapter we will not consider them, but just note that there seems to be a controversy regarding the exact nature of the relationship between attachment and exploration systems, and that both groups seem to agree that the role of possible cultural or within-culture contextual differences needs to be specified empirically. In the following, we consider the attachment–exploration linkage from the perspective of the BID model and the related studies.

Association of Attachment Security With Relational and Individuational Self-Orientations

Within the conceptualization of the BID model, which regards individuation as the exploration and development of one's inner qualities and inclinations, attachment and exploration orientations are considered to represent the foundations of the basic relational and individuational self-orientations, and hence as distinct and complementary. We believe that the general conceptualization of the BID model is compatible with attachment theory. For instance, regarding attachment and exploratory systems, Ainsworth (1972) stated, "The dynamic equilibrium between these two behavioral systems is of even more significance for development (and for survival) than either in isolation" (p. 118). However, we argue that the inter-relationship between attachment and exploration, as distinct orientations (parallel to relational and individuational self-orientations), should not be considered as an inexorable one. Accordingly, as noted earlier, we argue that the nature of their relationship may vary depending on environmental influences because caregivers may or may not respond to infants' exploratory attempts in the same way that they do to their attachment signals. Thus, attachment security, though important, may not be sufficient for the activation of exploration if the environmental conditions discourage or inhibit it.

In our line of research, we first considered the association between attachment security and self-orientations of relatedness and individuation (E. O. Imamoğlu & Imamoğlu, 2007). Our earlier findings from Turkish respondents had suggested that attachment could be conceptualized in both general (as specified by Bartholomew & Horowitz, 1991) and relationship-specific terms (S. Imamoğlu & Imamoğlu, 2006b), in congruence with the related literature (Baldwin, Keelan, Fehr, Enns, & Koh-Rangarajoo, 1996; Bartholomew, 1993; Cozzarelli, Hoesktra, & Bylsma, 2000; Kobak, 1994; Lewis, 1994). Accordingly, assuming that individuation involves an exploration of one's inner world, we inquired whether attachment security (i.e., both general and specific security in relationships with one's family, friends, and romantic partners) tends to be consistently associated with individuation, as with relatedness. Based on the assertion that attachment is an "affectional bond" (Ainsworth, 1989, p. 711) and on findings that associate secure attachment with positive affectivity regarding self and others (e.g., Bylsma, Cozzarelli, & Sümer, 1997; Collins & Read, 1990; Feeney & Noller, 1990; Griffin & Bartholomew, 1994; Hazan & Shaver, 1987; Kafetsios & Nezlek, 2002; Mikulincer, 1998; Mikulincer, Florian, & Tolmacz, 1990; Simpson, 1990), we expected attachment security to be associated mainly with the relational self-orientation. The same prediction was made on the basis of studies involving the BID model, which also suggest relatedness to be associated with having a positive affective orientation. On the other hand, based on the inexorable linkage assumption between secure attachment and exploration, attachment security may be expected to be also associated with individuation, as with relatedness. However, in view of the distinctness assumption of the BID model, we expected individuation to be either distinct or somewhat positively associated with attachment security by way of its complementary association with relatedness.

In consistency with the predictions of both attachment theory and the BID model, we found attachment security to be associated basically with the relational self-orientation (E. O. Imamoğlu & Imamoğlu, 2007): A related self-construction significantly and consistently predicted both general and relationship-specific attachment security, hence supporting the association of attachment security with positive affectivity regarding self and others. However, unlike relatedness, individuation did not appear to be a significant predictor of general attachment security, hence implying that it tends to be independent of attachment considered as a trait-like characteristic. Our results also suggested that in specific relationship contexts, such as with peers or the family, individuation may be positively but weakly associated with attachment security (E. O. Imamoğlu & Imamoğlu, 2007). Thus, findings supported our BID-based expectation by suggesting that, due to the complementary nature of the basic self-orientations, a related *and* individuated self-construction tends to be associated with enhanced attachment security in some relationships. However, to the degree that individuation reflects one's exploration orientation, our findings also question the inexorable attachment–exploration linkage assumption by suggesting that they need to be conceptualized as distinct orientations (E. O. Imamoğlu & Imamoğlu, 2007; S. Imamoğlu, 2005).

Attachment and Exploration as Distinct and Complementary Orientations

As part of our second line of research, we first suggested a new model of exploration (S. Imamoğlu, 2005; S. Imamoğlu & Imamoğlu, 2006a) involving positive or negative internal models of self (trust or mistrust) and the unknown (approach or avoidance), parallel to the attachment model proposed by Bartholomew and Horowitz (1991). Accordingly, a secure exploration style is assumed to involve being trustful of self in approaching the unknown, whereas the insecure types are assumed to have at least one negative model concerning either the self or the unknown. Factor analyses of the data based on separately measured attachment and exploration orientations obtained from Bartholomew and Horowitz's (1991) Relationship Questionnaire and the parallel Exploration Questionnaire (S. Imamoğlu & Imamoğlu, 2006a), respectively, provided support to the expectation that attachment and exploration represent distinct orientations. Congruent with earlier cross-cultural findings involving Turkey (Schmitt et al., 2004), our results supported conceptualization of attachment in terms of self and other models. Our findings also provided support to the conceptualization of exploration in terms of trust for self and approaching the unknown; thereby suggesting that secure attachment may make exploration more likely by strengthening the former but seemed to be generally independent of the latter dimension of exploration. Furthermore, our research (S. Imamoğlu & Imamoğlu, 2006a) suggested that exploration can be conceptualized both as a general and domain-specific (i.e., cognitive, relational, self-related, spatial, and time-related) orientation with which attachment security tends to be positively but weakly associated (correlations ranging between .18 and .24), except for the relational–exploration (for which correlation is .40), where the "unknown" involves other people. Thus, our results support the contention regarding the distinct but complementary nature of the relationship between attachment and exploration orientations.

We further examined the nature of the relationship between attachment and exploration in terms of their associations with other related variables. Consistent with earlier findings involving the BID model (e.g., E. O. Imamoğlu, 2003), results of exploratory and confirmatory factor analyses indicated that attachment security tends to be associated mainly with the affective-relational domain, involving such variables as self-satisfaction, a related self-construction, positive future expectations, and low trait anxiety, whereas exploration security tends to belong to the intrinsic motivational domain, involving such variables as the need for cognition, tolerance for ambiguity, and an individuated self-construction (S. Imamoğlu, 2005). In fact, using structural equation modeling analysis, we found evidence that attachment security tends to be a predictor of relatedness, whereas exploration security tends to be a predictor for individuation (S. Imamoğlu & Imamoğlu, 2008). Thus, our findings support the idea of the distinct but complementary nature of the relationship between attachment and exploration as well as between relatedness and individuation.

A Four-Category Model Associated With Secure/Insecure Combinations of Attachment and Exploration Orientations

Assuming that attachment and exploration represent conceptually distinct orientations, it is possible for secure or insecure attachment to be associated with either secure or insecure exploration. Accordingly, we proposed four types of combinations by crossing the low and high ends of attachment and exploration security; that is, *secure–safe* (high in both attachment security and exploration security), *secure–unsafe* (high in attachment security, low in exploration security), *insecure–safe* (low in attachment security, high in exploration security), and *insecure–unsafe* (low in both attachment and exploration security). Our research (S. Imamoğlu & Imamoğlu, 2008) involving Turkish university students representing those four attachment–exploration types yielded systematic results and supported the present assertion that the association between attachment and exploration, though positive, may not be regarded as inexorable. However, the importance of the complementarity of secure attachment and exploration was clearly implied in that the secure–safe type was found to represent an optimal state of psychological functioning in terms of both the affective–relational and the intrinsic–motivational variable domains, noted earlier (particularly as compared to the insecure–unsafe type).

Furthermore, our research demonstrated striking parallels between the four attachment–exploration types and the four self-construction types proposed by the BID model in psychological functioning. As expected, of the self-types proposed by the BID model, the related-individuated, or the balanced self-type, appears to be secure in both attachment and exploration orientations; the related-patterned, or the most integrated self-type, seems to represent being secure in attachment but unsafe in exploration; the separated-individuated, or the most differentiated self-type seems to be insecure in attachment but safe in exploration; and finally, the separated-patterned, representing the most unbalanced self-type, tends to be characterized by insecurity in both attachment and exploration orientations (S. Imamoğlu & Imamoğlu, 2008).

The parallel trends we have identified between different combinations of attachment–exploration orientations with those of relatedness–individuation orientations provide converging evidence for the validity of our present conceptualization, which, we believe, enables attachment to be better integrated with other self-related variables beyond relationality. However, more research is needed to further clarify the present conceptualization.

CONCLUSIONS AND SUGGESTIONS

Using the conceptual framework of the BID model, we first presented evidence to indicate that relatedness and individuation are not opposing, as often assumed, but distinct and complementary orientations of a balanced self-system, associated with optimal psychological functioning, and that other less balanced self-constructions may also be possible. Following a similar line of logic, we suggested that the linkage between attachment and exploration need not necessarily be inexorable, as assumed by attachment theory, but that they can be viewed as distinct but complementary orientations parallel to the relational and individuational self-orientations. We then proposed that by considering them as distinct orientations, theoretically, it becomes possible to conceptualize four different combinations of secure or insecure attachment and exploration orientations, and noted that those combinations tend to parallel the self-types suggested by the BID model in psychological functioning. Our studies provided converging evidence for the aforementioned proposals.

Thus, we suggest that the nature of the linkage between attachment and exploration may be affected by external influences. Secure attachment, though important for effectively meeting the challenges of exploration, may not be a sufficient condition for its activation: The exploration–fostering or inhibiting nature of the familial context may enhance or hinder the organismic tendency to explore. As proposed in the BID model, family contexts may differ in the degree to which they may be conducive for the development not only of attachment (and relatedness) but also of exploration (and individuation) security. For instance, Rothbaum, Pott, et al. (2000) note that in the U.S. context, children generally tend to be encouraged to explore, and more space and stimulation are available in U.S. homes. In such contexts, securely attached children may be more likely to use the attachment figure as a secure base from which to explore; that is, they may be more likely to develop differentiation security, which may orient them toward exploration of the unknown (and individuation). On the other hand, in other contexts, for example, integrative contexts, children may be more restrained from exploration but be oriented toward a symbiotic union with the attachment figure and may feel more anxious during separations. For example, although the percentage of secure babies seems to be the same in the United States and Japan, Japanese babies seem to show less exploration, to be more upset by separations, to display greater anxiety toward strangers, and to prefer to maintain close contact with their mothers (Miyake, Chen, & Campos, 1985; Takahashi, 1990). Whereas those Japanese mothers may be more likely to orient the child inward and to encourage accommodation to each other, some American mothers may be more likely to encourage exploration by directing the child's attention outward to toys, events, or strangers in the environment (Bornstein, Azuma, Tamis-LeMonda, & Ogina, 1990; Bornstein, Toda, Azuma, Tamis-LeMonda, & Ogina, 1990; Takahashi, 1990).

The findings support our contention regarding the possibility of alternative combinations of attachment and exploration in different contexts; however, in assessing such cross-cultural findings, we believe that one needs to be cautious against the bipolarity fallacy of assuming that individualist and collectivist cultures represent the opposite ends of a continuum. On the contrary, our studies involving the BID model suggest that there seems to be more within-culture variation (e.g., in perceived relatedness with parents) associated with self-types (as well as with idiocentric or allocentric value orientations, or socioeconomic status) than across cultures such as in the United States and Turkey (E. O. Imamoğlu & Karakitapoğlu-Aygün, 2007). Although the individualist or collectivist cultures tend to differ in terms of their differentiative or integrative *expectations* (E. O. Imamoğlu & Karakitapoğlu-Aygün, 2006), those normative outlooks may be influential only to the degree that individuals internalize them. However, because individuals living in a particular culture come to internalize such cultural claims through social interactions, they may vary in the degree to which they do so. As Geertz (1973a, 1973b) suggested, those social relations depend on the interaction of cultural, social structural, and personality or self-systems. Therefore, rather than talking about culture abstractly as a property of some social groups, psychologists need "to delineate a more explicitly psychological picture of culture processes" (Shore, 1996, p. 311) because behind any apparent differences across cultures, some universal aspects of psychological functioning may be possible. For example, studies involving the BID model demonstrated that similar trends can be observed in individualist and collectivist contexts in perceived parent–child relations (Karakitapoğlu-Aygün & Imamoğlu, 2008) and psychological functioning (E. O. Imamoğlu & Karakitapoğlu-Aygün, 2004, 2006, 2007), pointing to the importance of parental acceptance and psychological control as well as of the BID-related self-types across cultures. In a similar vein, we suggest to focus on delineating those contextual factors that may be involved in the specific type of attachment–exploration linkages across or within cultures.

In this regard, we propose that in view of the similar trends noted involving attachment–exploration and self-orientations, the four types of contexts proposed by the BID model to be conducive for the self-types may also be relevant to conceptualizing the contextual influences on different attachment–exploration combinations suggested. Accordingly, assuming that attachment and exploration form the foundations of relational and individuational self-orientations, we propose that in balanced contexts, where parents tend to be responsive to the needs for both attachment and exploration, development of attachment *and* exploration security (as well as related-individuated self-constructions) may be more likely, as exemplified in the hypothetical case of Lucky: She was brought up in an intrinsically stimulating environment with genuine affection and acceptance. Her parents were not only warm and loving but were also sensitive to her developmental needs and enabled her to have opportunities for self-growth. As an authentic person, Lucky has a positive outlook toward herself, people, and life in general. Having a basic trust in life and a genuine need for cognition, she enjoys exploring the wonders of even daily life. She believes that the meaning of life resides in genuine personal relationships and growth.

In contrast, unbalanced contexts, where parents are responsive to the needs for neither attachment nor exploration, may be more conducive for the development of both attachment and exploration insecurity (as well as separated-patterned self-constructions), as exemplified in the hypothetical case of Darky: Her parents were distant, at times even rejecting-punitive, and exerted strict psychological control as if wanting to mold her into something other than herself. Having a generally negative outlook toward herself, people and life in general, Darky feels lonely and separated from people. She has a low tolerance for ambiguity and often functions stereotypically as if on an automatic pilot controlled by external forces.

On the other hand, integrative family contexts may be expected to be conducive for the development of secure–unsafe (as well as related-patterned) individuals, who, though secure in attachment, may be likely to feel constrained and unsafe in exploration, as exemplified in the hypothetical case of Nicey: Nicey's parents were loving but also strictly controlling and overprotective. So she has grown up feeling loved but anxious to explore on her own with a low tolerance for ambiguity. Nicey maintains good relations with people, and often accommodates in accordance with external expectations. In general, she has a positive outlook and feels content with her life but sometimes wishes she could have more confidence for exploration and personal growth.

Finally, differentiative contexts may be more conducive for the development of insecure–safe (as well as separated-individuated) persons, who, though insecure in attachment, may be likely to engage in exploration in response to stimulating environmental conditions, or perhaps in an effort to gain the love and attention that the parents fail to provide; but, once engaged, may learn to trust themselves in approaching the unknown, as exemplified in the hypothetical case of Loney: Loney's parents, who valued independence, were quite distant and uninvolved so that she, at times, even suspected that they did not really love her. She grew up not only being free to explore on her own but also feeling pressured to be self-sufficient. She has problems relating to people and often presumes a negatively critical and skeptical outlook toward people and life in general. Loney seems quite self-confident but down deep in her heart she feels she is not worthy. She often imagines herself as a lonesome adventurer who engages in daring missions and proves to the world that she is a worthy and self-sufficient individual. In a similar vein, Bloland (1999, as cited in Nakamura & Csikszentmihalyi, 2004), the late Erik Erikson's daughter, proposed that a strong pursuit of fame and recognition may be based on an unsatisfied need for human connection.

Thus, we propose that the two-dimensional attachment–exploration model, yielding four secure–insecure attachment–exploration types and the contexts proposed to be conducive for their development, may enable a more specific characterization in understanding the related within and cross-cultural differences. However, the research findings we have referred to were derived mainly from adolescents or young adults; therefore, more research is needed in different contexts, especially with children, to test our proposals, and to have a better understanding of the dynamics involved in the development of the basic attachment-relatedness and exploration–individuation orientations. Based on existing evidence, we conclude that our research involving Turkish respondents provides general support to the universality claim of attachment theory and suggests how it can incorporate alternative attachment–exploration linkages to better handle the criticisms regarding its universality.

REFERENCES

Ainsworth, M. D. S. (1972). Attachment and dependency. In J. L. Gewirtz (Ed.), *Attachment and dependency* (pp. 97–137). Washington, DC: V. H. Winston & Sons.

Ainsworth, M. D. S. (1989). Attachments beyond infancy. *American Psychologist, 44, 4,* 709–716.

Ainsworth, M. D. S., Bell, S. M., & Stayton, D. (1971). Individual differences in Strange Situation behavior of one-year-olds. In H. R. Schaffer (Ed.), *The origins of human social relations* (pp. 17–57). London: Academic Press.

Anderson, R., Manoogian, S. T., & Reznick, J. S. (1976). The undermining and enhancing of intrinsic motivation in preschool children. *Journal of Personality and Social Psychology, 34,* 915–922.

Aspelmeier, J. E., & Kerns, K. A. (2003). Love and school: Attachment/exploration dynamics in college. *Journal of Social and Personal Relationships, 20*(1), 5–30.

Baldwin, M. W., Keelan, J. P. R., Fehr, B., Enns, V., & Koh-Rangarajoo, E. (1996). Social-cognitive conceptualization of attachment working models: Availability and accessibility effects. *Journal of Personality and Social Psychology, 71,* 94–109.

Bartholomew, K. (1993). From childhood to adult relationships: Attachment theory and research. In S. Duck (Ed.), *Learning about relationships* (pp. 30–62). London: Sage.

Bartholomew, K., & Horowitz, L. M. (1991). Attachment styles among young adults: A test of a four-category model. *Journal of Personality and Social Psychology, 61*(2), 226–244.

Baumrind, D. (1991). Effective parenting during the early adolescent transition. In P. A. Cowan & M. H. Hetherington (Eds.), *Family transitions* (pp. 111–163). Hillsdale, NJ: Lawrence Erlbaum Associates.

Bell, L. G., Meyer, J., Rehal, D., Swope, C., Martin, D. R., & Lakhani, A. (2007). Connection and individuation as separate and independent processes: A qualitative analysis. *Journal of Family Psychotherapy, 18,* 43–59.

Beydoğan, B. (2008). *Self-construal differences in perceived work situation and well-being* (Unpublished doctoral dissertation). Middle East Technical University, Ankara, Turkey.

Bornstein, M. H., Azuma, H., Tamis-LeMonda, C., & Ogina, M. (1990). Mother and infant activity and interaction in Japan and in the United States: I. A comparative macro-analysis of naturalistic exchanges. *International Journal of Behavioral Development, 13,* 267–287.

Bornstein, M. H., Toda, S., Azuma, H., Tamis-LeMonda, C., & Ogina, M. (1990). Mother and infant activity and interaction in Japan and in the United States: II. A comparative microanalysis of naturalistic exchanges focused on the organization of infant attention. *International Journal of Behavioral Development, 13,* 289–308.

Bowlby, J. (1982). *Attachment and loss: Vol. 1. Attachment* (2nd ed.). New York: Basic Books.

Bowlby, J. (1988). *A secure base.* New York: Basic Books.

Bylsma, W. H., Cozzarelli, C., & Sümer, N. (1997). Relation between adult attachment styles and global self-esteem. *Basic and Applied Social Psychology, 19*(1), 1–16.

Chao, R. (2001). Integrating culture and attachment. *American Psychologist, 56,* 822–823.

Collins, N. L., & Read, S. J. (1990). Adult attachment, working models, and relationship quality in dating couples. *Journal of Personality and Social Psychology, 58,* 644–663.

Cozzarelli, C., Hoekstra, S. J., & Bylsma, W. H. (2000). General versus specific mental models of attachment: Are they associated with different outcomes? *Personality and Social Psychology Bulletin, 26*(5), 605–618.

Feeney, J., & Noller, P. (1990). Attachment style as a predictor of adult romantic relationships. *Journal of Personality and Social Psychology, 58*, 281–291.

Geertz, C. (1973a). Religion as a cultural system. In *The interpretation of cultures: Selected essays by Clifford Geertz* (pp. 87–125). New York: Basic Books.

Geertz, C. (1973b). Ritual and social change: A Javanese example. In *The interpretation of cultures: Selected essays by Clifford Geertz* (pp. 142–169). New York: Basic Books.

Gjerde, P. F. (2001). Attachment, culture, and *amae*. *American Psychologist, 56*, 826–827.

Griffin, D., & Bartholomew, K. (1994). Models of the self and other: Fundamental dimensions underlying measures of adult attachment. *Journal of Personality and Social Psychology, 67*, 430–445.

Grossmann, K. E., Grossmann, K., & Zimmermann, P. (1999). A wider view of attachment and exploration: Stability and change during the years of immaturity. In J. Cassidy & P. R. Shaver (Eds.), *Handbook of attachment: Theory, research, and clinical applications* (pp. 760–786). New York: Guilford Press.

Guisinger, S., & Blatt, S. J. (1994). Individuality and relatedness: Evolution of a fundamental dialectic. *American Psychologist, 49*, 104–111.

Güler-Edwards, A. (2008). *Relationship between future time orientation, adaptive self-regulation, and well-being: Self-type and age related differences* (Unpublished doctoral dissertation). Middle East Technical University, Ankara, Turkey.

Gündoğdu, A. (2007). *Relationship between self-construals and marital quality* (Unpublished master's thesis). Middle East Technical University, Ankara, Turkey.

Harwood, R. L., Miller, J. G., & Irizarry, N. L. (1995). *Culture and attachment: Perceptions of the child in context*. New York: Guilford Press.

Hazan, C., & Shaver, P. R. (1987). Romantic love conceptualized as an attachment process. *Journal of Personality and Social Psychology, 52*(3), 511–524.

Helgeson, V. S. (1994). Relation of agency and communion to well-being: Evidence and potential explanations. *Psychological Bulletin, 116*, 412–428.

Hofstede, G. (2001). *Culture's consequences: Comparing values, behaviors, institutions, and organizations* (2nd ed.). Thousand Oaks, CA: Sage.

Imamoğlu, E. O. (1987). An interdependence model of human development. In Ç. Kağıtçıbaşı (Ed.), *Growth and progress in cross-cultural psychology* (pp. 138–145). Lisse, The Netherlands: Swets & Zeitlinger.

Imamoğlu, E. O. (1995). *Değişim sürecinde aile: Evlilik ilişkileri, bireysel gelişim ve demokratik değerler* [Family in the process of change: Marital relations, self-development, and democratic values]. *Aile Kurultayı: Değişim sürecinde aile: Toplumsal katılım ve demokratik değerler* (pp. 33–51). Ankara: T.C. Başbakanlık Aile Araştırma Kurumu.

Imamoğlu, E. O. (1998). Individualism and collectivism in a model and scale of balanced differentiation and integration. *Journal of Psychology, 132*(1), 95–105.

Imamoğlu, E. O. (2003). Individuation and relatedness: Not opposing but distinct and complementary. *Genetic, Social, and General Psychology Monographs, 129*(4), 367–402.

Imamoğlu, E. O. (2008, September). *Dengeli benlik modeli çalışmaları ve düşündürdükleri* [Studies on the balanced self model and their implications]. Invited speech, 15th Turkish Psychology Congress, Istanbul.

Imamoğlu, E. O. (2009, November). Towards a balanced construction of selves and relationships. Invited paper presented at the Mini-Conference of the International Association for Relationship Research (IARR) on New Directions in Research on Close Relationships: Integrating Across Disciplines and Theoretical Approaches. Lawrence, Kansas, U.S.A.

Imamoğlu, E. O., & Güler-Edwards, A. (2007). Geleceğe ilişkin yönelimlerde benlik tipine bağlı farklılıklar [Self-related differences in future time orientations]. *Turkish Journal of Psychology, 22*, 115–138.

Imamoğlu, E. O., Günaydın, G., & Selçuk, E. (2009). Individuation and relatedness as predictors of the authentic self: Beyond individualism, collectivism, and gender. Unpublished manuscript, Middle East Technical University, Ankara, Turkey.

Imamoğlu, E. O., & Imamoğlu, S. (2007). Relationships between attachment security and self-construal orientations. *The Journal of Psychology, 141*(5), 539–558.

Imamoğlu, E. O., & Imamoğlu, V. (1992). Life situations and attitudes of the Turkish elderly toward institutional living within a cross-cultural perspective. *Journal of Gerontology: Psychological Sciences, 47*(2), 102–108.

Imamoğlu, E. O., & Imamoğlu, V. (1996). *Insan, evi ve çevresi [Individuals, their homes, and environments]*. Ankara: Başbakanlık Toplu Konut Idaresi Yayını.

Imamoğlu, E. O., & Karakitapoğlu-Aygün, Z. (1999). 1970lerden 1990lara değerler: Üniversite düzeyinde gözlenen zaman, kuşak ve cinsiyet farklılıkları [Value preferences from 1970s to 1990s: Cohort, generation and gender differences at a Turkish university]. *Turkish Journal of Psychology, 14*(44), 1–22.

Imamoğlu, E. O., & Karakitapoğlu-Aygün, Z. (2004). Self-construals and values across different cultural and socioeconomic contexts. *Genetic, Social, and General Psychology Monographs, 130*, 277–306.

Imamoğlu, E. O., & Karakitapoğlu-Aygün, Z. (2006). Actual, ideal, and expected relatedness with parents across and within cultures. *European Journal of Social Psychology, 36*, 721–745.

Imamoğlu, E. O., & Karakitapoğlu-Aygün, Z. (2007). Relatedness of identities and emotional closeness with parents across and within cultures. *Asian Journal of Social Psychology, 10*, 145–161.

Imamoğlu, E. O., Küller, R., Imamoğlu, V., & Küller, M. (1993). The social psychological worlds of Swedes and Turks in and around retirement. *Journal of Cross-Cultural Psychology, 24*, 26–41.

Imamoğlu, S. (2005). *Secure exploration: Conceptualization, types, and relationships with secure attachment, self-construals, and other self-related variables* (Unpublished doctoral dissertation). Middle East Technical University, Ankara, Turkey.

Imamoğlu, S., & Imamoğlu, E. O. (2006a, September). *Güvenli keşif yönelimi: Iki boyutlu bir model önerisi, tipleri ve güvenli bağlanma ile ilişkisi [Secure exploration orientation: A two-dimensional model proposal, types, and relationships with attachment security]*. 14th Turkish Psychology Congress, Ankara, Turkey.

Imamoğlu, S., & Imamoğlu, E. O. (2006b). Relationship between general and context specific attachment orientations in a Turkish sample. *Journal of Social Psychology, 146*, 261–274.

Imamoğlu, S., & Imamoğlu, E. O. (2008, September). *Beş alanda dengeli benlik: Bağlanma-keşif ve benlik yönelimleri arasındaki ilişkiler [Balanced self in five domains: Relationships between attachment-exploration and self orientations]*. 15th Turkish Psychology Congress, Istanbul, Turkey.

Kafetsios, K., & Nezlek, J. B. (2002). Attachment styles in everyday social interaction. *European Journal of Social Psychology, 32*, 719–735.

Kağıtçıbaşı, Ç. (2005). Autonomy and relatedness in cultural context: Implications for self and family. *Journal of Cross-Cultural Psychology, 36*, 403–422.

Karakitapoğlu-Aygün, Z., & Imamoğlu, E. O. (2002). Value domains of Turkish adults and university students. *The Journal of Social Psychology, 142*, 333–351.

Karakitapoğlu-Aygün, Z., & Imamoğlu, E. O. (2008, September). *Beş alanda dengeli benlik: Farklı kültür ve aile ortamlarında benlik kurguları ve iyi olma hali ile ilişkileri [Balanced self in five domains: Relationships between self-construals and well-being at different cultural and familial contexts]*. 15th Turkish Psychology Congress, Istanbul, Turkey.

Kernis, M. H., & Goldman, B. M. (2006). A multicomponent conceptualization of authenticity: Theory and research. *Advances in Experimental Social Psychology, 38*, 283–357.

Kobak, R. (1994). Adult attachment: A personality or relationship construct? *Psychological Inquiry, 5*, 42–44.

Kondo-Ikemura, K. (2001). Insufficient evidence. *American Psychologist, 56*, 825–826.

Kurt, A. (2002a, February). *A comparison of three self-construal conceptualizations with respect to issues of culture and gender.* Poster presented at the Annual Convention of the Society for Personality and Social Psychology, Savannah, Georgia.

Kurt, A. (2002b, June). *Autonomy and relatedness: A comparison of Canadians and Turks.* Paper presented at the Annual Convention of Canadian Psychological Association, Vancouver, British Columbia.

Lewis, M. (1994). Does attachment imply a relationship or multiple relationships? *Psychological Inquiry, 5*, 47–51.

Magai, C., & McFadden, S. (1995). *The role of emotions in social and personality development: History, theory, and research.* New York: Plenum Press.

Markus, H. R., & Kitayama, S. (1991). Culture and the self: Implications for cognition, emotion and motivation. *Psychological Review, 98*, 224–253.

Mikulincer, M. (1997). Adult attachment style and information processing: Individual differences in curiosity and cognitive closure. *Journal of Personality and Social Psychology, 72*(5), 1217–1230.

Mikulincer, M. (1998). Attachment working models and the sense of trust: An exploration of interaction goals and affect regulation. *Journal of Personality and Social Psychology, 74*, 1209–1224.

Mikulincer, M., Florian, V., & Tolmacz, R. (1990). Attachment styles and fear of personal death: A case study of affect regulation. *Journal of Personality and Social Psychology, 58*, 273–280.

Mikulincer, M., & Sheffi, E. (2000). Adult attachment style and cognitive reactions to positive affect: A test of mental categorization and creative problem solving. *Motivation and Emotion, 24*(3), 149–174.

Miyake, K., Chen, S., & Campos, J. (1985). Infant temperament, mother's mode of interaction, and attachment in Japan: An interim report. In I. Bretherton & E. Waters (Eds.), Growing points of attachment theory and research. *Monographs of the Society for Research in Child Development, 50*(1–2, Serial No. 209), 276–297.

Nakamura, J., & Csikszentmihalyi, M. (2004). The motivational sources of creativity as viewed from the paradigm of positive psychology. In L. G. Aspinwall & U. M. Staudinger (Eds.), *A psychology of human strengths: Fundamental questions and future directions for a positive psychology* (pp. 257–269). Washington, DC: APA.

Osberg, T. (1987). The convergent and discriminant validity of the Need for Cognition Scale. *Journal of Personality Assessment, 51*, 441–450.

Oyserman, D., Coon, H. M., & Kemmelmeier, M. (2002). Rethinking individualism and collectivism: Evaluation of theoretical assumptions and meta-analyses. *Psychological Bulletin, 128*, 3–72.

Posada, G., Gao, Y., Wu, F., Posada, R., Tascon, M., Schöelmerich, A., … Synnevaag, B. (1995). The secure-base phenomenon across cultures: Children's behavior, mother's references, and experts' concepts. *Monographs of the Society for Research in Child Development, 60*(2–3, Serial No. 244), 27–48.

Posada, G., & Jacobs, A. (2001). Child-mother attachment relationships and culture. *American Psychologist, 56*, 821–822.

Pretty, G. H., & Seligman, C. (1984). Affect and overjustification effect. *Journal of Personality and Social Psychology, 46*, 1241–1253.

Raeff, C. (1997). Individuals in relationships: Cultural values, children's social interactions, and the development of an American individualistic self. *Developmental Review, 17,* 205–238.

Rothbaum, F., Pott, M., Azuma, H., Miyake, K., & Weisz, J. (2000). The development of close relationships in Japan and the United States: Paths of symbiotic harmony and generative tension. *Child Development, 71*(5), 1121–1142.

Rothbaum, F., Weisz, J., Pott, M. L., Miyake, K., & Morelli, G. (2000). Attachment and culture: Security in the United States and Japan. *American Psychologist, 55*(10), 1093–1104.

Ryan, R. M., & Grolnick, W. S. (1986). Origins and pawns in the classroom: Self-report and projective assessments of individual differences in children's perceptions. *Journal of Personality and Social Psychology, 50,* 550–558.

Ryan, R. M., & Lynch, J. H. (1989). Emotional autonomy versus detachment: Revisiting the vicissitudes of adolescence and young adulthood. *Child Development, 60,* 340–356.

Schmitt, D. P., Alcalay, L., Allensworth, M., Allik, J., Ault, L., & Austers, I., … Zupanèiè, A. (2004). Patterns and universals of adult romantic attachment across 62 cultural regions. *Journal of Cross-Cultural Psychology, 35,* 367–402.

Shore, B. (1996). *Culture in mind: Cognition, culture, and the problem of meaning.* Oxford: Oxford University Press.

Simpson, J. A. (1990). Influence of attachment styles on romantic relationships. *Journal of Personality and Social Psychology, 59,* 971–980.

Takahashi, K. (1990). Are the key assumptions of the "Strange Situation" procedure universal? A view from Japanese research. *Human Development, 33,* 23–30.

Triandis, H. C. (1995). *Individualism and collectivism.* Boulder, CO: Westview Press.

Turan, G. (2007). *Relationship between materialism and self-construals* (Unpublished master's thesis). Middle East Technical University, Ankara, Turkey.

Uleman, J., Rhee, E., Bardoliwalla, N., Semin, G., & Toyama, M. (2000). The relational self: Closeness to ingroups depends on who they are, culture, and the type of closeness. *Asian Journal of Social Psychology, 3,* 1–17.

van IJzendoorn, M. H., & Sagi, A. (1999). Cross-cultural patterns of attachment: Universal and contextual dimensions. In J. Cassidy & P. R. Shaver (Eds.), *Handbook of attachment: Theory, research, and clinical applications* (pp. 713–734). New York: Guilford Press.

van IJzendoorn, M. H., & Sagi, A. (2001). Cultural blindness or selective inattention? *American Psychologist, 56,* 824–825.

Webster's II new Riverside university dictionary. (1984). Boston: Riverside Publishing.

4

Amae Through the Eyes of Japanese Mothers
Refining Differences and Similarities Between Attachment and Amae

KAZUKO Y. BEHRENS

CONTENTS

*B*owlby's (1982) attachment theory explains that attachment is a species-wide, in-built behavioral system in the young for survival based on the evolutionary and ethological perspectives. From those perspectives attachment formation is considered to be a universal phenomenon. Rothbaum, Weisz, Pott, Miyake, and Morelli (2000) voiced their concern that attachment theory would not accurately explain parent–child relationships in some non-Western cultures, specifically Japan. They argued in part that the indigenous Japanese concept of *amae*, which is sometimes translated simply as "dependence," would better depict preferred Japanese parent–child relationships. In contrast, traditional attachment security is often associated with autonomy. It is predicted that attachment research in Japan would not yield fruitful results because the security of Japanese parent–child dyads would mean something different. Security in Japan would be based on the concept of *amae* rather than on the attachment paradigm. Recently, Behrens, Hesse, and Main (2007) countered this opinion showing that Japanese mothers' attachment status strongly predicts their 6-year-olds' attachment security. These measures were based on categorical assessments utilizing the Adult Attachment Interview (AAI; protocol: George, Kaplan, & Main, 1996; scoring and classification system: Main, Goldwyn, & Hesse, 2002) and Main and Cassidy's (1988) 6th-year reunion procedures. This was previously reported in the United States (George & Solomon, 1996). In addition, Kazui, Endo, Tanaka, and Sakagami (2000), who administered the first AAI in Japan, indicated a link in the expected direction between Japanese mothers' AAI status and their children's attachment security measured on the Attachment Q-sort (Waters & Deane, 1985). These empirical findings do appear to support Bowlby's universal assumption with regard to attachment formation as well as the applicability of certain attachment measures developed in the United States in populations with diverse cultural and language bases such as Japan.

Theoretical confusion regarding *amae* in relation to attachment still remains. Behrens (2004) has attempted to clarify the concept of *amae* by presenting a multifaceted view of *amae*. Based on her analyses of *amae* in various contexts, Behrens identified five categories of *amae*° in three developmental phases. She shows that *amae* has many functions and meanings and can be fully understood only when viewed in context (Behrens, 2004). Therefore, *amae* cannot be given a single, global definition as Rothbaum et al. (2000) assumed in their attempt to claim that *amae* would override attachment in Japan. More recently, Rothbaum and his colleagues presented a much more comprehensive view and definition of *amae* (Rothbaum & Kakinuma, 2004; Rothbaum, Kakinuma, Nagoka, & Azuma, 2007). These appear to be primarily derived from discussions on *amae* that Behrens (2004) and Yamaguchi (2004) presented. Consolidation of these studies lead to a definition of *amae* as the presumption or expectation in others for indulgence and acceptance even when the request is inappropriate.

Although Behrens (2004) provided a much broader view of *amae* than what was previously available, discussion on similarities and differences of *amae* in relation to attachment has been less extensive partly due to lack of empirical evidence. In light of growing attachment research in Japan (Behrens et al., 2007; Kazui et al., 2000) a common and better understanding of similarities and differences between attachment and *amae* from both the conceptual and behavioral perspectives should be established. A given behavior exhibited by Japanese children can be seen as attachment behavior, *amae* behavior, or both. If not taken in context, an erroneous assessment could result. For example, when observing older children, as opposed to infants, it is generally more challenging to detect attachment behaviors. The array of behaviors that older children exhibit is much wider and

---

° *Amae* I–Affective, present in infancy, childhood, and adulthood; *Amae* II–Manipulative, present in childhood and adulthood; *Amae* III–Reciprocal, present in childhood and adulthood; *Amae* IV–Obligatory, present only in adulthood; *Amae* V–Presumptive, present only in adulthood.

more complex (Solomon & George, 1999). It is likely to be even more challenging to observe Japanese children when behavioral similarities between attachment and *amae* have been already identified (Behrens, 2004; Rothbaum et al., 2007; Yamaguchi, 2004). It is perhaps more beneficial to focus on functional differences to distinguish between attachment and *amae*. Previously, Mizuta, Zahn-Waxler, Cole, and Hiruma (1996) were able to distinguish certain *amae* behaviors during the Crowell's (Crowell, Feldman, & Ginsberg, 1988) separation/reunion procedures when they compared Japanese and U.S. children. Mizuta et al. (1996) defined *amae* behaviors of preschoolers as "seeking close physical contact, such as clambering up and sitting on mothers' lap, and burying face against mother's chest" (p. 144). They found that Japanese children did show more *amae* behaviors than did U.S. children, but overall attachment behaviors did not differ even if Japanese children's *amae* behaviors may have appeared as more insecure-ambivalent than the behaviors of U.S. children (Mizuta et al., 1996). It appears reasonable to assume then that *amae* behaviors are observable and distinguishable from attachment behaviors once *amae* behaviors are clearly defined as to function and within context (Mizuta et al., 1996).

In the first part of this chapter I will revisit *amae* with an attempt to further refine similarities and differences between attachment and *amae*. Specifically, two of Behrens' (2004) categories of *amae* (i.e., *Amae* I–Affective and *Amae* II–Manipulative) are compared with two patterns of attachment (i.e., secure attachment and insecure-ambivalent attachment) for behavioral similarities and functional differences. *Amae* phenomena in *Amae* I–Affective category refer to behaviors exhibited by children and adults, primarily to enhance or renew emotional closeness without instrumental motives, assuming their cues will be understood and wishes will be fulfilled. *Amae* phenomena in the *Amae* II–Manipulative category refer to behaviors exhibited by children and adults, primarily to push their demand even when the request is unreasonable, expecting their demand will be granted. These two categories of *amae* appear to be most often confused with attachment for apparent similarities in their behaviors. For example, species-wide attachment behaviors such as calling, following, crying, or clinging are displayed to induce caregiving behaviors and thus to increase a chance of survival (Bowlby, 1982; Main, Hesse, & Kaplan, 2005). These exact behaviors can be also viewed in certain contexts as categories I and II *amae* behaviors by Japanese observers. The remaining categories that Behrens (2004) presented (*Amae* III–Reciprocal, *Amae* IV–Obligatory, and *Amae* V–Presumptive) can be observed in relationships less intimate than parent–child relationships. They are not considered to be as relevant to attachment phenomena and will not be discussed here.

In the second part, I will present some empirical evidence of *amae* within the attachment context. Mizuta et al. (1996) teased out children's *amae* behaviors in the attachment context. Here I present *amae* by presenting excerpts from the AAI to show how the term *amae* was spontaneously used to describe childhood relationships during the AAI with Japanese mothers. I will examine how *amae* experience, or lack of it, affects the way they perceive their childhood attachment relationships. This chapter is exploratory and I intend to demonstrate how attachment and *amae* are indeed intricately linked theoretically and empirically, yet seemingly through fundamentally different mechanisms. This endeavor is far from complete. Any causal link or prediction with regard to attachment and *amae* should be avoided until a systematic approach to investigate these concepts together is established.

REFINING SIMILARITIES AND DIFFERENCES BETWEEN ATTACHMENT AND *AMAE*

Amae I–Affective Amae and Attachment

Doi (1973) describes *amae* as "an emotion felt by the baby at the breast towards its mother" (p. 20) and "an attempt psychologically to deny the fact of separation from the mother" (p. 75), thus naturally seeking closeness to the mother while not being in distress or without any instrumental motive. Such behaviors are included in Behrens' (2004) categorization of *Amae* I–Affective. However, if the same infant engages in the same behavior when in distress such behavior would be considered an attachment behavior.

Behavioral Similarities   The following can be either *amae* or attachment behaviors: showing a desire to be picked up, clambering up, grasping hold of the mother, molding or sinking into the mother's body, or burying the face on the mother's chest. Likewise for older children, desires to be cuddled, sitting on mother's lap, or wanting a hug can be either *amae* behaviors or attachment behaviors (Ainsworth, Blehar, Waters, & Wall, 1978; Mizuta et al., 1996).

Functional Differences   According to the Strange Situation classification system (Ainsworth et al., 1978), if a child is distressed and wants to be picked up, this can be regarded as "proximity and contact seeking behavior" (p. 343). High scores often indicate a sign of secure attachment behaviors. The child is able to use the mother as a haven of safety and a secure base from which to explore, indicating the child's relational experiences with the mother has given the child confidence to approach the mother, with the belief that their cue will be accurately read and they will be comforted. Similarly, if a child is distressed and is put down before soothed, the fuss or the protest can be regarded as "contact maintenance behavior" (p. 347): another indication of secure attachment behaviors. The child is signaling the mother that more contact is needed before exploration resumes. If a highly distressed child approaches and establishes contact with the mother but never settles, even after being held for a long period, it is an indication that the child is unable to use the mother as a secure base to return to exploration. This suggests attachment insecurity: specifically insecure-ambivalent attachment. In contrast, if a child shows a desire to be picked up or buries the face on the mother's chest when the child is not distressed, then the child would be doing *amae*, perhaps to enjoy the pleasurable feeling of the warmth of the mother or of basking in the mother's arms. From the attachment perspective, the mother should serve both as a haven of safety to comfort the child in distress and as a secure base, from which the child can explore. From the *amae* interpretation, the mother can be an *amae* grantor, providing the pleasurable feelings to encourage the child to remain in contact. As

Rothbaum et al. (2007) found, contemporary Japanese mothers value autonomy in children as do American mothers. Nevertheless, it can be speculated that Japanese mothers' degree of tolerance for accepting children's prolonged desire for contact may exceed the American counterpart, particularly if they value *amae* as defined by Rothbaum & Kakinuma (2004): harmony in relationships.

For toddlers and older children, the attachment system is believed to operate similarly although behaviors become subtler with increasing age (Main & Cassidy, 1988; Main, Kaplan, & Cassidy, 1985). For example, when children are ill, upset, or frightened they are likely to seek attachment figures to be cuddled or hugged, so that they can be comforted and gain a sense of safety and assurance. Feeling secure, they can go out and explore again, thus increasing a chance of success in mastering the environment in the social world. When children are not distressed, yet approach their attachment figures for physical contact, they are likely to be doing *Amae* I to renew intimacy, and being playful for fun without an instrumental motive (Taketomo, 1986).

Amae II–Manipulative and Attachment

Behavioral Similarities   Any children, regardless of the quality of their relationships with their caregivers, may engage in behaviors that look insecure. This is especially true when they are ill or extremely tired, as these physiological states lead to an increase in clingy or whiny behavior. Typically, however, children in the insecure-ambivalent group are described as immature, or show preoccupation with their mothers by being clingy or acting helpless, which compromises exploration (Ainsworth, 1984; Ainsworth & Wittig, 1969). Preschoolers who were judged insecure-ambivalent as infants were found to spend longer time with their mothers than with peers during free play and explored the environment much less than did their secure counterparts (Jacobson & Wille, 1986). These rather nonautonomous behaviors of preschool children resemble what some Japanese mothers have described as unwelcomed *amae*. For example, they described how their children would demand the mothers' help in getting dressed in the morning when they ordinarily could dress themselves, or would claim they could not get up until they got the mother's hug when the mother is busy, attending to the younger sibling (Behrens, 2004).

Functional Differences   Children who exhibit insecure-ambivalent behaviors are believed to engage in such behaviors to maximize their chances of gaining their inconsistent caregivers' attention and care (e.g., Cassidy & Berlin, 1994). From the evolutionary perspective, this is adaptive if children are unsure when their attachment needs will be met. On the other hand, children may engage in manipulative *amae* behaviors to demand their caregivers' attention even when there is no cue of danger or distress. For example, in addition to acting helpless or immature as some Japanese mothers described earlier, a child may throw a tantrum in a public place when wanting a toy in a store and the request is denied. Such an act can be also regarded as *amae* and viewed highly negatively. When children show prolonged immature or preoccupied behaviors toward caregivers in stressful situations, the children are likely to be demonstrating an insecure-ambivalent strategy to maximize chances their attachment needs will be met. The goal of children in this attachment group is believed to be to organize their behaviors to accommodate rather inconsistent or unpredictable care from their caregivers. They often exaggerate the expressions of their needs when they experience stressful situations (e.g., Ainsworth et al., 1978; Cassidy & Berlin, 1994). In contrast, when children engage in similar behaviors of being excessively needy when there is no apparent reason to be distressed, the goal is to manipulate their caregivers to grant the unreasonable request. The testing of wills and pushing of demands is considered *Amae* II behavior. This is contrary to Rothbaum and Kakinuma's (2004) proposed definition of *amae*, as Japanese mothers are not likely to give in and welcome such behaviors. Refer to Behrens (2004) for specific examples.

Maternal Behaviors   Cassidy and Berlin (1994), in their discussion of maternal strategies of insecure-ambivalent children, describe the child's mother as one who "(consciously or nonconsciously) wants to be particularly assured of her importance to the infant, of his dependence on her, and of his availability to meet her own attachment needs" (p. 984). Such maternal behaviors resemble what Watanabe (1992) describes as behaviors that promote *amae* to fulfill mothers' egoistic needs. Watanabe regards this as problematic from the mental health point of view. A link between attachment and *amae* can be observed in maternal behaviors. For example, mothers who engage in excessive *amayakasu* behaviors (i.e., allow or let the child do *amae*) may do so out of guilt for being insensitive to the child's needs at other times. They demonstrate inconsistent maternal behaviors by mixing insensitivity with excessively indulgent behaviors. This results in inconsistent maternal behaviors similar to Ainsworth et al.'s (1978) description of mothers of ambivalently attached children. Japanese children, like children from elsewhere in the world, may develop ambivalent attachment if they are met with mothers' inconsistent behaviors at the time of distress. However, Japanese children may engage in *Amae* II behaviors, hoping to get their *amae* granted, without necessarily developing ambivalent attachment if mothers provide frequent *amayakasu* behaviors but otherwise meet the child's needs at the time of distress. As Sroufe, Egeland, Carlson, and Collins (2005) argue, sensitive and responsive parenting is crucial for children to develop attachment security. Yet parents do more than that. They also instill necessary social skills in children to successfully meet social expectations. If the mother always responds to meet the child's attachment needs, that would be highly plausible to warrant a secure pattern of mother–child attachment relationship. If she gives in too easily and always allow the child's *amae* in any situation, the child may not learn optimal socialization skills such as cooperation with peers, even though the quality of mother–child attachment relationship may be secure.

Amae Under the Attachment Framework

Conceptual Similarities   Bowlby (1982) argues that an infant, based on only months of interactive experiences with the caregiver, begins to form an internal working model (IWM) of the mother, the self, and the mother and the self in interaction by the end of the first year. If a baby has plentiful experiences of being cuddled and held, basked in the warmth of the mother, as Doi (1973) describes *amae*, the baby is likely to continue to do so or show the desire to do so simply because it feels pleasurable to the baby. However, if a baby was rarely cuddled or held, the baby may show little *amae* behaviors simply because of lacking the experience of the pleasurable feelings of *amae* or uncertainty of the mother's willingness to let the child do *amae*. In other words, a child forms some expectation or assumption based on experiences that the child's *amae* desire can or cannot be fulfilled, according to the child's IWM of *amae* relationships, drawn from the theoretical framework of IWM of attachment relationships. Furthermore, as Bowlby (1982) argues, a child's IWM of attachment relationships can change when the child's environment changes. A once sensitive mother may become unavailable physically or emotionally upon encountering marital disruption or economic hardship. This may lead to a change in the child's IWM of the attachment relationship. The change can go in either direction of course. Similarly, a child's IWM of *amae* relationship can also change. For example, upon arrival of a sibling, the youngest in the family becomes the older child and thus must assume a big brother or sister role. This often comes with the expectation of decreased engagement in *amae*.

Conceptual Differences   Following Bowlby's concept of IWM (1982), infants who have experiences of loving and trusting relationships with their mothers (i.e., they can use the mothers as a haven of safety and secure base from which to explore) are likely to develop a secure attachment strategy: a balance of attachment and exploration. Infants who have experienced repeated rejections from their mothers are believed to develop an avoidant strategy. This emphasizes premature independence and exploration without adequate use of attachment when in need. Infants who have experiences of inconsistent caregiving may develop an ambivalent strategy as discussed earlier.

For *amae*, Japanese infants, based on their experiences, are likely to simply learn that they can exhibit *amae* a lot, a little, or not at all. They do not seem to develop different strategies for different *amae* relationships. Japanese infants may learn early on to discriminate to whom they can do *amae*. Unlike built-in attachment behavioral systems that are expected to be formed in all children (except for in extremely anomalous conditions) and that are closely tied to survival as Bowlby claimed, not all Japanese children engage in *amae*. Instead, the degree to which a child's demonstration of *amae* has been accepted or rejected leads to trait-like qualities of interaction and socialization. Children who had little *amae* experiences early on may later encounter difficulties giving and receiving *amae*. On the other hand, a child exhibiting a high quantity of *amae*, either *Amae* I or *Amae* II, may gain a title such as *amaekko* (or *amaenbo*) that indicates a child who is prone to do *amae* a lot. Although amaekko typically describes a "spoiled child," it can be expected and accepted if the child is the youngest, thus assuming the "baby of the family" role. On the contrary, a child who does not do *amae* at all may be perceived as a "not-cuddly" or "not-lovable" child. The child can be praised, however, if assuming a big brother or sister's role and thus refraining with effort from engaging in *amae*.

Despite the extended theoretical discussions presented here, empirical evidence can truly show how attachment and *amae* are linked. *Amae* is an everyday word for Japanese people and every Japanese person should know what *amae* is, yet his or her own definition of *amae* is likely to vary (Behrens, 2004). Next I present how some Japanese mothers referred to *amae* while discussing their attachment experiences during the AAI: that is, *amae* in the attachment context at the mental level.

AMAE THROUGH THE EYES OF JAPANESE MOTHERS

Source of Evidence

The AAI data of mothers in Sapporo, Japan, were analyzed in a study reported by Behrens et al. (2007) are the source for the current report of the contextual analyses of *amae*. In this study an intergenerational transmission of attachment between Japanese mothers and their 6-year-olds was explored and a series of statistical analyses was conducted to report the findings. No specific analysis on *amae* based on the AAI data was reported. Out of 49 participants, one was excluded from all analyses due to procedural errors (see Behrens et al., 2007), leaving 48 AAI transcripts as the base for the current analysis. This report examines how Japanese mothers may or may not bring up *amae* spontaneously either as a concept or a particular behavior during the AAI. The results are presented descriptively through selected excerpts.

Analysis   In the Japanese Microsoft Word program, the Find command was executed on *amae* as well as its conjugated forms (e.g., *amaeru, amaerareru, amaeta, amaerareta, amayakasu, amayakasareta*) for each of 48 transcripts in their entirety. Every page that contained the word *amae* or its conjugated forms was reviewed for its usage and context.

Amae in the AAI   During the AAI, nearly half of Japanese mothers (46%) voluntarily discussed their relationships with their attachment figures in their childhood, casually referring to *amae*, indicating that *amae* is assumed to be understood within the family context. Some even used the word *amae* repeatedly to describe different attachment relationships. Readers should be reminded that the AAI contains no *amae* question and thus the Japanese mothers' reference to or usage of *amae* is strictly spontaneous in their attempt to describe their childhood relationships with their attachment figures. A number of different usages of *amae* with different functions were identified and are summarized in the following.

Different Usages of Amae in the AAI

Amae as a General Descriptor of Childhood Relationships   Some
mothers use *amae* in a very general sense when describing their relationships with

their parents as children. The first example is from a response to a question, asking the mother to describe her relationship with her parents in early childhood.

1. Let's see ... I would say it wasn't a bad [parent-child] relationship but um (um, hmm), honestly, I don't think I did *amae* much at all (umm).

The second example is from a response to a question, asking the mother why there wasn't the same feeling of closeness with her mother in early childhood.

2. Hmm, maybe [I] was just thinking my father was the one for *amae*, [I] wonder.

The third example is from a response to a question, asking the mother to come up with five adjectives that reflect her relationship with her mother in early childhood

3. Uhh, [I] wo, wonder, hmm. Uhm, [it] wasn't *amae* relationship ...

The fourth example is from a response to a question asking another mother to describe her relationship with her parents in early childhood.

4. Hmm, uhm, like, [I] don't think (um) [I]'ve ever interacted with my father much at all (um hmm), you know? ... So, [I] don't think [he] ever did dakko (let [a child] sit on lap/hug) me or anything like that, you know? (Oh, you mean your dad?) Yeah, [I] mean, [I] never did *amae* [on him].

This speaker appears to believe that *amae* should involve some affective and physical interactions. The fifth example is from a response to a question, asking the mother to support one of five adjectives to describe her relationship with her mother as a child, which was *"amaeta toki wa yasashikatta"* ("[my mother was] kind/generous when [I] did *amae*").

5. Oh, well, rather than the time when [I] did *amae* (um, hmm), actually, uhm, it's not emotional/mental *amae*, how should I say, ... so, [I] think that the fact that [I] have to call that *amae* is sad, but.

This example illustrates how this thoughtful mother, who went on to say that her mother did buy her a variety of things when she asked for them, in fact, referred to *amae* by distinguishing *amae* of an affective nature from *amae* of materialistic type. The sixth example is from a response to a question, asking another mother to support one of five adjectives to describe her relationship with her mother as a child, which was *"okaasan wa otoosan o tateteta"* ("[my] mom was deferential toward [my] dad").

6. ... so, it's rather strange to say but [I] couldn't do *amae* (umm), um, yeah, like, ... and also, I had never seen my mother did *amae* on my father at all either, so ...

This example presented an atmosphere of this mother's family in which *amae* was not that common. She also demonstrated her view that *amae* should exist not only for a child toward a parent but also between a wife and a husband.

Amae **Grantor as a Haven of Safety**   Some mothers described those who let them do *amae* as a haven of safety where they could get comfort when they were upset. The first example is from a response to a question, asking the mother to describe what she would do when she was upset as a child.

1. … [I] used to take it out (um, hmm) on my mother (oh, I see), yes, then, uhm, um, then, [I] would go and do *amae* [on my mother].

The second example is from a response to a question, asking the mother about her grandfather, to whom she felt close, like a parent, when she was a child.

2. Right, a parent, yeah, let's see (umm). [He] was someone whom [I] could really do *amae* a lot (uh). … At night too, [I] would sleep with my grandpa (oh, is that right).

This example shows how her grandfather was the one with whom she could do *amae* and sleep next to at night, indicating that her grandfather was likely to be her haven of safety. The third example is from a response to a question, asking the mother whether her grandmother's death had an effect on her.

3. My grandmother was like … I mean, really, um, whatever I say, [she] would do it for me (umm), that kind of person (uh, huh), you know? Well, uhm, [I] guess [she] was just *amayakasu*-ing (let me do *amae*), too but (uh, huh). It was like that, that's why, in that aspect, I feel I was saved by it, you know?

This mother had described her rejecting mother and her chaotic family but because her grandmother let her do *amae* a lot, she felt she was saved by that, indicating the importance of her grandmother as a haven of safety with whom she could do *amae*.

Amae **With a Trait-Like Quality**   Some mothers refer to *amae* as something of a trait or personal characteristic. The first example is from a response to a question, asking the mother whether she felt rejected as a young child.

1. It wasn't like any particular time but like, [I] was a type [of child] who couldn't do *amae*, you know? So.

The second example is from a response to a question, asking the mother to describe her relationship with her father but her relationship with her mother came up, referring to *amae*.

2. … Well, uhm, yeah, it's like, [I] didn't depend on [her] (uh, huh, umm). Hmm, [I] think [I] wasn't skilled at doing *amae* (umm), you know?

This example shows how this mother believes that *amae* requires some skills or experiences to be successfully carried out, which she lacked.

Amae **With a Role or Status**   *Amae* is often status or role oriented not only in a societal level but also within a family (Behrens, 2004). There is a commonly expected *amae* phenomenon for each relationship with each role or status, as in much *amae* from the youngest child but not much from the older child as discussed earlier. The first example is from a response to a question asking the mother whether she felt rejected as a child.

1. Rejection or, umm, not sure, but my mother (yes, uh, huh) wouldn't let me do *amae* (um, hmm), this could be rather one-sided view but (um, hmm), … my little sister was (uh, huh) doing *amae* (umm), but I was, um, being a big sister, … umm, [she/they] didn't let me do *amae* or, [it/there was] something like that, (um, hmm).

The second example is from a response to a question, asking the mother how overall experiences with her parents had affected her.

2. Uhm, yes, well, um, [I] was raised as a big sister (uh, huh), so [I] couldn't do *amae* (umm). Uhm, well, rather than [I] couldn't [do *amae*], more like [I] couldn't show weakness, it's kind of strange to say but (hmm).

This example shows her view of *amae* as something that represents some weakness. The third example is from a response to a question asking another mother how overall experiences with her parents had affected her.

3. I think I said this before (uh, huh), I don't think I did *amae* when I was a child (right) … so instead, now, [to make up for that] I feel I'm doing a lot of *amae* (I see), uhm, how shall [I] say, or depending on my mother (uh, huh), or things like that (um), you know?

Interestingly, this particular mother described how she did not do much *amae* as a child and thus she is doing a lot of *amae* now to her mother, indicating that the status-oriented *amae* may remain the same (i.e., mother–child), and also showing her view of *amae* involving dependence.

DISCUSSION

This chapter began with an attempt to further articulate associations between attachment and *amae*, following the previous discussion on the topic (Behrens, 2004). Specifically, particular *amae* categories, *Amae* I and *Amae* II, were reviewed and compared to two attachment patterns, secure and insecure-ambivalent. Similarities and differences were examined, as well as additional exploration of the conceptual link.

Next, Japanese mothers' spontaneous usages of *amae* were presented. Different usages of *amae* were identified while describing these mothers' childhood experiences with their parents during the AAI. For example, *amae* was used as a key concept to describe general relationships with their parents (e.g., "Mom is for *amae*, but not Dad") or to describe their own characteristics as a child (e.g., "I was a type of child who was not good at doing *amae*"). With regard to their childhood period, many mothers appear to regard *amae* as childlike phenomenon that should naturally be expected and mostly accepted, referring to *amae* in Behrens' (2004) *Amae*

I category. Thus, a lack of *amae* relationship with parents was described as either something regrettable, such as a rather cold mother or unapproachable father, or something for which the speaker was to be blamed because of her inability to do *amae* as being her trait-like quality. *Amae* was also described to be associated with a particular role or status that the speaker was expected to assume in her family. Younger siblings were expected and thus allowed to engage in more *amae*, whereas a big sister was expected to control her desire to engage in *amae*. Rivalry with siblings for *amae* or even some resentment was apparent in some statements such as how their younger siblings were always doing *amae* to their parents, leaving little room for the big sisters to do *amae*.

When *amae* is viewed through the eyes of Japanese mothers, *amae* does appear to represent a part of their childhood attachment relationships. Thus a link between attachment and *amae* is empirically supported. Careful examination also supports a claim that attachment and *amae* are fundamentally different in their goals and functions even though certain behaviors may appear similar (Behrens, 2004; Behrens et al., 2007). Readers should be also reminded that more than half of Japanese mothers in the current sample never referred to *amae* during the AAI, indicating that not all Japanese people consider *amae* something that represents childhood attachment relationships or that it is necessary in the family context. This could be interpreted to mean that attachment is an overarching construct in family relationships that is evolutionary in nature. This applies to all individuals regardless of whether the quality of relationship is secure and whether the family is American or Japanese. On the other hand, *amae* is a construct that is not limited to or even necessary to explain attachment relationships. It is specific to Japanese people. *Amae* presents a larger construct for Japanese people that explains certain phenomena or relationships other than family relationships. Different usages of *amae* identified even within the same category of *amae* (e.g., *Amae* I) do indeed demonstrate the complex nature of *amae* as Behrens (2004) claims. Precisely because of the complexity or multiplicity of *amae*, for Japanese people, the single word *amae* (including its conjugated forms) takes the place of many words that would otherwise be required for more explicit description of certain behaviors or phenomena. Reference to *amae* when describing a relationship can immediately transmit a vivid imagery of a particular relationship among Japanese people.

Amae can be considered a tool for describing attachment relationships. Childhood *amae* may describe only a part of attachment relationships. Certain categories of *amae* can emerge later in life as one's social network expands. These categories are more closely related to societal roles and expectations than to attachment phenomena (Behrens, 2004). In sum, it is my hope that readers can now get a sense how Japanese people may view *amae* in the attachment context, but *amae* per se should not be assumed to always be linked to attachment. What is necessary now is to find a way to utilize the *amae* concept as a possible predictor for individual differences in the quality of attachment relationships for Japanese populations. For example, once we compile enough data, we may find that those Japanese who voluntarily discuss the import of *amae* relationships in their childhood tend to have secure or some type of insecure states of mind. Rothbaum et al.'s (2007) recent study was an attempt to integrate and understand a link between attachment and *amae*. Although their attempt is plausible and their research design incorporating *amae* components is highly creative, it is rather difficult to interpret their findings, as they themselves recognized (Rothbaum et al., 2007). Without observation of actual behaviors or mental representations with respect to attachment, the validity of their findings as attachment data is rather questionable. Nevertheless, the cultural differences that they found in mothers' attributions in *amae* situations are informative and should be incorporated or expanded in future research. It is imperative in attachment research to explore individual differences within a group or culture. For example, mothers who are judged secure, compared to mothers who are judged insecure, are likely to perceive a child's secure behavior differently. Harwood, Miller, and Irizarry (1995), whose method Rothbaum et al. (2007) have utilized, also emphasize that their findings of cultural differences do not invalidate the significance of individual differences in attachment behavior. They suggest it is important to be culturally sensitive and to seek the different contextual meanings. It will be of great interest to compare Japanese mothers' views of their child's *amae* behaviors from different attachment categories.

Future Research

Behrens (2004) previously argued it would be logical to incorporate *amae* study into attachment research due to the availability of several established attachment measures. For behavioral assessment an *Amae* Q-sort might be the ideal tool to be developed (M. van IJzendoorn, personal communication, July 2003). This could be simultaneously administered with a well-established Attachment Q-sort (Waters & Deane, 1985) through systematic observation in a home environment to compare and explore a link between the behaviors: Do certain *amae* behaviors overlap with certain attachment behaviors? If so, how would these be paired with attachment classifications? Such research will provide empirical evidence to theoretical claims presented in the first part of this chapter.

When administering the AAI to Japanese participants, several questions on *amae* can be added at the end of the AAI protocol to explore this link without obstructing the AAI coding scheme. For example, unless already described voluntarily the following questions can be added:

> How would you define *amae* in your own words?
> Did you or could you do *amae* to your mother and father when you were little?
> > If they answer yes: Do you think she/he let you do *amae* a lot or not much when you were little?
> > If they answer no: Did you have anybody else let you do *amae*?
>
> How or what kind of *amae* did you typically do when you were little?
> Does your child engage in *amae* similarly to or differently from the way you did (or did not do) *amae* when you were little?

These basic *amae* questions can possibly tap a link between their own conceptualization of *amae* and attachment security assessed on the AAI. Based on these questions, it is possible to create an *amae* scale and assign scores for Japanese participants. These could be compared separately with other AAI scales or a final AAI classification. Such questions in AAI's with Japanese people would add empirical evidence to the understanding of attachment and *amae*. Short interviews in response to *amae* situation scenarios as Rothbaum et al. (2007) presented, after the standard attachment measures, can be useful to explore the link. Such additions to attachment measures would offer a much needed systematic investigation of a link between attachment and *amae*.

REFERENCES

Ainsworth, M. D. S. (1984). Attachment. In N. S. Endler & J. McVicker Hunt (Eds.), *Personality and the behavioral disorders* (Vol. 1, pp. 559–602). New York: Wiley.

Ainsworth, M. D. S., Blehar, M. C., Waters, E., & Wall, S. (1978). *Patterns of attachment*. Hillsdale, NJ: Erlbaum.

Ainsworth, M. D. S., & Wittig, B. A. (1969). Attachment and exploratory behavior of one-year-olds in a strange situation. In B. M. Foss (Ed.), *Determinants of infant behaviour* (Vol. 4, pp. 129–173). London: Methuen.

Behrens, K. Y. (2004). A multifaceted view of the concept of *amae*: Reconsidering the indigenous Japanese concept of relatedness. *Human Development, 47,* 1–27.

Behrens, K. Y., Hesse, E., & Main, M. (2007). Mothers' attachment status as determined by the Adult Attachment Interview predicts their 6-year-olds' reunion responses: A study conducted in Japan. *Developmental Psychology, 43,* 1553–1567.

Bowlby, J. (1982). *Attachment and loss: Vol. I. Attachment* (2nd ed.). New York: Basic Books.

Cassidy, J., & Berlin, L. J. (1994). The insecure/ambivalent pattern of attachment: Theory and research. *Child Development, 65,* 971–991.

Crowell, J. A., Feldman, S. S., & Ginsberg, N. (1988). Assessment of mother-child interaction in preschoolers with behavior problems. *Journal of U.S. Academy of Child and Adolescent Psychiatry, 27,* 303–311.

Doi, T. (1973). *The anatomy of dependence*. New York: Kodansha.

George, C., Kaplan, N., & Main, M. (1996). *Adult Attachment Interview*. Unpublished protocol, University of California, Berkeley.

George, C., & Solomon, J. (1996). Representational models of relationships: Links between caregiving and attachment. *Infant Mental Health Journal, 17,* 198–216.

Harwood, R. L., Miller, J. G., & Irizarry, N. L. (1995). *Culture and attachment: Perceptions of the child in context*. New York: Guilford Press.

Jacobson, J. L., & Wille, D. E. (1986). The influence of attachment patterns on developmental changes in peer interaction from the toddler to the preschool period. *Child Development, 57,* 338–347.

Kazui, M., Endo, T., Tanaka, A., & Sakagami, H. (2000). Intergenerational transmission of attachment: Japanese mother-child dyads. *Japanese Journal of Educational Psychology, 48,* 323–332.

Main, M., & Cassidy, J. (1988). Categories of response to reunion with the parent at age 6: Predictable from infant attachment classifications and stable over a 1-month period. *Developmental Psychology, 24,* 415–426.

Main, M., Goldwyn, R., & Hesse, E. (2002). *Adult attachment scoring and classification system*. Unpublished manuscript, University of California, Berkeley.

Main, M., Hesse, E., & Kaplan, N. (2005). Predictability of attachment behavior and representational processes at 1, 6, and 19 years of age: The Berkeley longitudinal study. In K. E. Grossmann, K. Grossmann, & E. Waters (Eds.), *Attachment from infancy to adulthood: The major longitudinal studies* (pp. 245–304). New York: Guildford Press.

Main, M., Kaplan, N., & Cassidy, J. (1985). Security in infancy, childhood, and adulthood: A move to the level of representation. *Monographs of the Society for Research in Child Development, 50*, 66–104.

Mizuta, I., Zahn-Waxler, C., Cole, P. M., & Hiruma, N. (1996). A cross cultural study of preschoolers' attachment: Security and sensitivity in Japanese and U.S. dyads. *International Journal of Behavioral Development, 19*, 141–159.

Rothbaum, F., & Kakinuma, M. (2004). Amae and attachment: Security in cultural context. *Human Development, 47*, 34–39.

Rothbaum, F., Kakinuma, M., Nagaoka, R., & Azuma, H. (2007). Attachment and amae: Parent-child closeness in the United States and Japan. *Journal of Cross-Cultural Psychology, 38*, 465–486.

Rothbaum, F., Weisz, J., Pott, M., Miyake, K., & Morelli, G. (2000). Attachment and culture: Security in the United States and Japan. *American Psychologist, 55*, 1093–1104.

Solomon, J., & George, C. (1999). The measurement of attachment security in infancy and childhood. In J. Cassidy & P. R. Shaver (Eds.), *Handbook of attachment: Theory, research, and clinical applications* (pp. 287–316). New York: Guilford Press.

Sroufe, L. A., Egeland, B., Carlson, E., & Collins, A. (2005). *The development of the person: The Minnesota study of risk and adaptation from birth to adulthood*. New York: Guilford Press.

Taketomo, Y. (1986). Amae as metalanguage: A critique of Doi's theory of *amae*. *Journal of the American Academy of Psychoanalysis, 14*, 525–544.

Watanabe, E. (1992). Difficulties in amae: A clinical perspective. *Infant Mental Health Journal, 13*, 26–33.

Waters, E., & Deane, K. E. (1985). Defining and assessing individual differences in attachment relationships: Q-sort methodology and the organization of behavior in infancy and early childhood. *Monographs of the Society for Research in Child Development, 50*, 41–65.

Yamaguchi, S. (2004). Further clarifications of the concept of amae in relation to dependence and attachment. *Human Development, 47*, 28–33.

5

Cultural Variations in the Link Between Attachment and Bereavement

ELIZABETH A. GASSIN

CONTENTS

*F*ew experiences are as universal as the death of a loved one. In this respect, it is not surprising that researchers have connected another presumed universal experience— attachment—to coping with another's death. However, given discussion in the scholarly literature about cultural variations in attachment and bereavement patterns, it would be premature to assume that attachment is related to bereavement in the same way in all cultures. My purpose in this chapter is to review work conducted in the West on the attachment–bereavement link and initiate a discussion of cultural variations in this link. Because the topic of cultural variations in the link between attachment style and bereavement is relatively unexplored, the content of this chapter is by necessity interdisciplinary, drawing not only on psychology but on anthropology and history as well. In addition, because attachment theory and research identifies relationships with parents and romantic partners as the main venue for bonding, I am limiting the discussion in this chapter to the discussion of bereavement in these contexts. Therefore, the tentative conclusions reached in this chapter may not apply to processes of mourning the death of persons who play roles other than these in an individual's life.

ATTACHMENT–BEREAVEMENT CONNECTIONS IN WESTERN CULTURE

Although a person's reaction to another's death is determined by many factors, the link between attachment and bereavement has received special attention in the psychological literature almost since the beginning of modern psychology's history. Although empirical work on large samples is a relatively recent and rare phenomenon, early psychoanalytic writers contributed greatly to theorizing about how these two constructs might be connected. Within their work, we find development in the understanding of whether and how a person may remain attached to one who has died.

Early Psychoanalytic Work

The father of psychoanalysis, Sigmund Freud, was not ignorant of the role attachment might play in mourning the loss of a loved one. In his classic essay, "Mourning and Melancholia" (1957), Freud compared and contrasted the experiences of depression and bereavement. He noted that during bereavement, the ego is charged with the task of reality testing or coming to terms with the fact that the dead person no longer exists. This, in turn, allows the libido to decathect from the love object. Problems in the relationship with the deceased prior to his or her death may interrupt this process. For example, Freud wrote:

> The loss of a love-object constitutes an excellent opportunity for the ambivalence in love-relationships to make itself felt and come to the fore. Consequently where there is a disposition to obsessional neurosis the conflict of ambivalence casts a pathological shade on the grief. … These obsessional states of depression following upon the death of loved persons show us what the conflict of ambivalence by itself can achieve, when there is no regressive withdrawal of libido as well. (p. 132)

Clearly, at least in his classic statement on the problem, Freud maintained that healthy grieving mandated that the ego "sever its attachment" (p. 137) to the deceased and that problems in the prebereavement relationship with the dead person could interfere with this process.

By far, the most well-known writer on attachment and bereavement is John Bowlby, whose classic work on the topic is *Loss: Sadness and Depression* (1980). Bowlby worked mostly within psychoanalytic, ethological, and cognitive frameworks. Based on theory, clinical case studies, and the occasional early research project on bereavement, he proposed that there are two main forms of disordered bereavement: one involving chronic mourning and the other involving a prolonged absence of conscious mourning (in some cases accompanied by compulsive caregiving for others). Chronic mourners suffer from persistent yearning for the deceased and from depression and unremitting anger directly traceable to the loss. Survivors who experience prolonged absence of conscious mourning are those who do not experience any significant grief even after an expected brief period of numbness after the loss. Such persons may appear to be paragons of self-control who have quickly "gotten over" their loss but still display behaviors that betray subconscious suffering: physical illness, irritableness, and discomfort at mention of the loss. Those who engage in compulsive caregiving after bereavement may be projecting their suffering onto others. Bowlby briefly discussed a third, unusual type of disordered mourning, *euphoria*, which he maintained can either represent complete denial of the death or a staunch claim that the death is actually to one's advantage.

Bowlby (1980) acknowledged that a variety of etiological factors may underlie the development of disordered grieving. Not surprisingly, however, he gave special attention to the role of the quality of the attachment between the survivor and his or her parents in childhood and of the attachment between spouses prior to the death of one of them. (Both factors are relevant in the cases of adult spousal bereavement; the former is relevant in the case of a child's loss of a parent.) In general, Bowlby associated traits of anxious attachment with chronic mourning. Characteristics suggesting an avoidant attachment style are linked with absence of grief, although Bowlby clearly stated that some who maintain an emotional distance from mourning do actually seem to be coping well (a claim that foreshadowed the empirical work of Fraley & Bonanno, 2004).

There has been some disagreement as to whether Bowlby viewed healthy grieving as a process of detachment from the deceased attachment figure (Fraley & Shaver, 1999; Klass, Silverman, & Nickman, 1996). In his early work, Bowlby (1969) used the term *detachment* to describe the last step of adaption to separation from the attachment figure. It seems he intended this to be the reversal of attachment, for at least in one place, he noted that he has chosen the word because it is "a natural counterpart to 'attachment'" (1969, p. 29). However, by the time his 1980 volume on bereavement was published, it was clear that Bowlby believed that the bereaved individual could maintain some kind of connection with the deceased. In that volume, Bowlby noted that a bereaved individual who is grieving in a healthy fashion must "reorganize" or "reorient" (p. 18) attachment behavior and that detachment was a defensive reaction that was relevant only in cases where a separation from an attachment figure ended in the reunion with the same. In Bowlby's (1980) final formulation, this reorganized bond to a deceased person continued to play a role in the survivor's life, although if the mourning process is to remain healthy, the bond must change over time in an adaptive manner.

Recent Theoretical Work

Recent theoretical work extends the ideas Bowlby presented in his seminal work. In this section I will review one model that links attachment style to general bereavement outcomes. Later, we will look at models that specifically address how attachment before the death of a significant other relates to continuing attachment to that person after her death.

Stroebe, Schut, and Stroebe (2005) proposed the main extant model linking attachment styles to general coping after the passing of a loved one. These authors maintained that adaptive bereavement involves oscillation between the tasks that are loss oriented (e.g., coping with grief, reframing bonds) and those that are restoration oriented (e.g., adapting to new roles postloss, establishing new relationships). A bereaved person may have both positive and negative interpretations of tasks in each category. For most persons facing a loss, negative interpretations cannot be completely avoided, and therefore within the categories of loss-oriented and restoration-oriented tasks, healthy grieving also involves oscillation between assigning positive and negative meanings to the experiences. Based on further theoretical analysis and a review of relevant research, the authors proposed that upon loss of an attachment figure, a person with a secure attachment will oscillate appropriately between the tasks mentioned and therefore cope well. Persons with a preoccupied attachment style may focus more than others on loss-oriented experiences and less on restoration, while those with an avoidant style may be more inclined than others to attend to restoration-oriented issues and evade loss-oriented experiences. Persons with disorganized attachment patterns may exhibit poor coping marked by lack of control over oscillation, inability to articulate grief-related experience, and inability to construct a coherent grieving process. Although Stroebe et al. (2005) did not offer an empirical test of their model, they reviewed existing research that supports the claims they made about the connections between attachment style and coping in the face of loss.

Recent Empirical Work

Most of the extant research on the connection between attachment styles and bereavement has been completed in the United Kingdom and United States. First I will address work demonstrating a connection between childhood attachment and bereavement reactions later in life; then we will turn to a discussion of research linking attachment to spouse or other significant person and bereavement outcomes in adulthood.

Childhood Attachment and Adult Bereavement   Although many have contributed to research on the attachment–bereavement link, perhaps no one has been as prolific as Parkes, a colleague of Bowlby (e.g., Parkes, 2001, 2006; Parkes & Weiss, 1983). Theoretical analysis and case studies from the longitudinal Harvard Bereavement Study (Parkes & Weiss, 1983) of spousal bereavement suggested that nonsecure attachment in childhood is linked with poorer bereavement outcomes in adulthood. Here I will draw mostly on Parkes 2006 book, in which he summarized the results of a major study on attachment and bereavement in London. Parkes studied bereaved adults, most of whom had lost a family member. Attachment in childhood and relationship quality in adulthood were assessed. Secure childhood attachment was a strong negative predictor of overall distress during adulthood bereavement, both directly and indirectly through mediator variables. Anxious attachment in childhood predicted higher scores in grief/loneliness and clinging

after the death of a loved one. Early avoidant bonds with a parent predicted higher scores in grief/loneliness, difficulty expressing grief, and feelings of regret, whereas disorganized style in childhood predicted feeling that one was at the end of his rope, anxiety, depression, and alcohol abuse. These findings echoed conclusions from the earlier works of Parkes and colleagues.

Although Parkes's work is ubiquitous in the field, other researchers have reached conclusions similar to his. For example, a series of studies by Sable (1989, 1992) suggested that anxiety-related themes in participants' accounts of childhood attachment predicted anxiety after the death of a spouse, whereas secure child-hood attachment predicted lower grief-related symptomatology.

Adult Attachment and Bereavement   In general and not surprisingly, empirical work demonstrates a positive correlation between secure adult attachment status and adaptive bereavement to the loss of a spouse or other person close to survivors (Waskowic & Chartier, 2003; Wayment & Vierthaler, 2002). Typical bereavement outcomes for securely attached adults include less anger, isolation, depression, guilt, somatization, and rumination. Field and Sundin (2001) reported that response patterns indicative of an anxious attachment to a spouse were cor-related with feeling unable to cope, having positive thoughts about one's spouse, feeling emotionally numb, reported health problems, and global severity of psycho-logical distress; those patterns indicative of avoidant attachment predicted nega-tive thoughts about the spouse and intrusion of unwanted thoughts and feeling related to bereavement. In the same study, angry withdrawal (which can be cor-related with both anxious and avoidant attachment) predicted global severity of psychological distress in the first 14 months postloss. In a study of persons who had lost someone relatively close to them, Wayment and Vierthaler (2002) found that anxious attachment predicts overall levels of grief and level of depression, whereas avoidant attachment is positively correlated with level of somatization.

A crucial study by Fraley and Bonnano (2004) demonstrated that Bartholomew's (Bartholomew & Horowitz, 1991) distinction between dismissing-avoidant and fearful-avoidant attachment styles is important when predicting grief-related reac-tions. These authors found that over time, dismissing adults demonstrated few signs of complications in bereavement and looked very similar in their adaption to securely attached persons. Fearful-avoidant and preoccupied individuals fared the worst, over time demonstrating elevated levels of anxiety, depression, grief-related symptoms, and posttraumatic stress disorder (PTSD) symptoms. Fearfully avoidant adults were especially likely to exhibit PTSD symptomatology early in the bereavement process. Importantly, ratings that friends made of participants' adaption paralleled those of the participants themselves. Considering these results, it seems the main ingredi-ent of the link between insecure attachment and poor bereavement outcomes is relationship-related anxiety common to preoccupied and fearful attachment styles.

General Themes in Western Literature

This brief overview of theory and research from Anglo and Germanic cultures suggests that some link exists between attachment and individuals' adaption in the face of loss. Those who report secure attachments to the deceased, and perhaps those who had a dismissing attachment style with the deceased, demonstrate less symptomatology in the wake of the death of a loved one. Those with attachment styles to the deceased involving some level of anxiety seem to fare the worst. There is less evidence connecting attachment in childhood with adaption to loss in adulthood, but the evidence that does exist suggests a similar pattern—those whose childhood attachments were anxious in nature demonstrate poorer adjustment during bereavement in adulthood.

Having looked at the link between attachment and individual outcomes in bereavement, we now turn to a discussion of attachment to living persons and how that might predict the existence and style of a continuing relationship with one who is deceased.

CONTINUING BONDS: ATTACHMENT TO THE DECEASED?

Most of the work on attachment and bereavement assesses whether child and adult attachment styles predict various mourning-related outcomes for the bereaved as an individual, such as depression or anxiety. A crucial question, however, is whether attachment styles contribute to the way in which survivors reconstruct their *relationship* with the deceased. In their 1996 volume, Klass, Silverman, and Nickman described in detail how people indeed often maintain some kind of connection with deceased loved ones. This phenomenon, which was widely observed but at best was only implicit in most of the Western work on grief to date, has been referred to as *continuing bonds* (CB). In the 1996 volume and a variety of other publications, Klass and colleagues (e.g., Klass, 2001; Klass & Goss, 2003) documented CB and its function in various cultural contexts. Examples of the manner in which survivors maintain CB include ancient Confucian rituals designed to elicit the dead person's assistance (Klass & Goss, 2003); Buddhist rituals including items representing the deceased and serving to comfort the living, express gratitude and respect to the deceased, and ask for favors from the same (Klass, 1996); and more informally, persons having conversations with the dead designed to elicit guidance and solace (Marwit & Klass, 1996). In one study done in Israel, the intensity of adult children's self-reported affective bonds with deceased parents did not differ from those with living parents (Shmotkin, 1999). Even in certain Islamic cultures, in which religious tenets and rituals tend to promote acceptance of a loved one's death and the bereaved person's quick return to society, people sometimes maintain a connection to the dead through actions undertaken in memory of the deceased and private, internal experience of the lost loved one (Rubin & Yasien-Esmael, 2004). A recent review of literature (Boerner & Heckhausen, 2003) demonstrated that experiencing CB with the deceased is quite common, even in Western cultures.

Does CB with a deceased person qualify as an attachment in the strictest sense of the term? The most basic function of interpersonal attachment is to develop a bond that provides security. This leads to behavior on the part of the person that has the goal of (a) generally maintaining proximity to the attachment target, and

felt more peaceful. He experienced rare pangs of sadness, regret, and anxiety in connection with his mother's death, but such feelings were often assuaged by his continued practice of ancestor veneration rituals at home and at her burial site.

Although there is less evidence regarding the case of interpersonal bonding and mourning in German cultures, the information that does exist tentatively supports the conclusion that there are culturally relevant parallels between attachment styles and bereavement patterns. An early meta-analysis of children's attachment patterns (van IJzendoorn & Kroonenberg, 1988) demonstrated that when grouped together, samples from Germany significantly deviated from expected patterns of secure attachment toward avoidance. Considering that two of the three studies reported from Germany were completed by researchers who report fine-tuning scoring methods to account for "the German manner of conversation, which tends to understate the intensity of emotions" (Grossmann, Grossmann, & Kindler, 2005, p. 106), finding a tendency toward avoidance is even more remarkable. More recent work from Germany (Pauli-Pott, Haverkock, Pott, & Beckmann, 2007) reported a sample in which 36% of classifiable infants studied were labeled as avoidant, the same overall percentage found in studies from Germany reported in van IJzendoorn and Kroonenberg's meta-analysis.

Similar trends can be seen in patterns of adult attachment. Broemer and Blümle (2003), classifying adults into one of four attachment styles, reported that 25% of their German sample was labeled dismissing. Grossmann (personal communication, September 16, 2007) reported that in two major longitudinal studies of attachment conducted in Germany, between 30% and 39% of samples in adolescence and young adulthood were classified as dismissing via the AAI. The prevalence of dismissing attachment in nonclinical, Western samples tends to run about 20% (Bartholomew & Horowitz, 1991; Brennan, Clark, & Shaver, 1998; van IJzendoorn & Bakermans-Kranenburg, 1996). Although he used continuous scales rather than a classification scheme, Banse's (2005) recent work in Germany on relationship satisfaction and attachment in married couples provided more data supporting a tendency toward what seems to be a greater likelihood of dismissing attachment. In the study, on average, both persons in couples received the second highest score on the dismissing scale; this average score was typically half of a point higher (on a 5-point scale) than the average scores on the other nonsecure styles of attachment.

Is there a parallel between the apparent prevalence of avoidant/dismissing attachment styles among Germanic peoples and bonds between the living and the dead in the same culture? Koslofsky's (2000) historical analysis of death rituals in early modern Germany provides a very tentative positive answer to this question. Koslofsky reviewed evidence that breaking the bond between the living and the dead was part and parcel of the Protestant Reformation. Given that the Reformation emphasized one's personal, internal spiritual experience over communal and ritualistic avenues to religious development, it is probably not coincidental that concrete rituals signifying a continuing relationship with the dead began to fall out of favor around the same era. Before this movement, rites existed that "marked the presence of the dead in daily life" (p. 22). The living prayed for the dead and relied on the prayers of saints who had already passed away. Relics of saints were venerated as a means of obtaining grace. The Reformation changed all this, abolishing prayers for deceased individuals and veneration of the bones and possessions of saints. This religious movement also furthered the new tradition of burying the dead outside city walls, away from the daily life of survivors. It is interesting to note that the figures who consolidated this religious movement and sometimes went as far as to label the bond between the living and dead as "diabolical" (p. 34) were almost all of Germanic descent or from geographic areas such as England or the Baltic states that are historically and linguistically connected to Germany.

Clearly, the apparent parallel between (a) interpersonal attachment measured in the 20th and 21st centuries and (b) changes in death ritual that occurred in a similar geographic region hundreds of years before hardly qualifies as hard evidence to back the claims made in this chapter. However, considering various lines of evidence from Japanese and Germanic cultures, a similar pattern emerges—in two cultures with relative tendencies toward one extreme or the other in attachment dependence, there are also bereavement rituals that parallel those attachment styles. This bolsters the cross-cultural validity of research results obtained in Western cultures that show a general correspondence between style of attachment to a living person and patterns of bereavement.

Another question regarding the cross-cultural generalizability of the attachment–bereavement link is whether specific types of CB linked with indicators of an insecure attachment in Western cultures are necessarily indicators of such an attachment style in other contexts. Recall from the discussion earlier that in Western cultures, CB experiences that involve sensing the dead person's presence or holding on to tangible reminders of the deceased tend to be empirically linked with poorer adaption. Based on such evidence, Field (2006; Field et al., 2005) proposed that such CB strategies develop in part from an insecure attachment to the deceased, represent a long-lasting inability to acknowledge the boundary between the living and the dead, and are not part of a cohesive system of meaning (such as a religious belief system) that assist in reorganizing one's relationship to the dead. In other words, long-lasting patterns of behavior and experiences that (a) suggest that a bereaved individual is still searching for and expecting to find a concrete manifestation of the person who died and (b) are not of a cultural belief system may well be rooted in ambivalent/preoccupied or disorganized attachment styles. Field (2006) demonstrated how certain Japanese rituals of ancestor worship, although they involve concrete reminders of the deceased, need not be classified as arising from insecure attachment style because they demonstrate a clear understanding that there is a boundary between the living and the dead and are part of rites embedded in a cultural and religious tradition.

Field's (2006; Field et al., 2005) criteria for identifying healthy forms of CB flow logically from the extant work on attachment, bereavement, and culture. However, it is also important to ascertain whether there are exceptions to the principles he has identified. One possible exception may be the case of children. There is some evidence that maintaining concrete mementos connected with a dead parent may be particularly characteristic of children's grieving processes (Normand, Silverman, & Nickman, 1996; Silverman & Nickman, 1996). Although such a focus on concrete reminders may be linked with insecure attachment to the deceased in adulthood, it may not necessarily be so in childhood, at least for a time. Inability to engage in abstract thinking may prohibit children from restructuring the relationship with a dead parent to a more spiritual or psychological connection. Interestingly, and in congruence with adult data, it seems that those children who rely on past memories and concrete mementos long term (rather than restructuring the relationship to a more interactive and internal plane) demonstrate signs of negative adjustment such as never crying about the dead parent or feeling even more pain years after the death (Normand et al., 1996). Quite possibly unresolved attachment issues to either the deceased or living parent accompany such a constellation of experiences.

Another possible exception may be the case of mortuary cannibalism, also referred to as funerary cannibalism or endocannibalism. In some cultures, it was or is customary to eat part of the remains of a deceased loved one. This is perhaps physical union with the dead par excellence and has been interpreted by some anthropologists as attempts to negate the death of an individual and keep him or her alive within oneself (Engel, 2000). If conclusions from scholarly work conducted in Western cultures hold, this striving to be physically united to a deceased loved one should be linked to ambivalent or preoccupied attachment; however, it is hard to imagine preoccupied attachment would be so widespread among a people that it would underlie a tradition practiced by most or all individuals in a particular society. In all fairness, it seems many cases of endocannibalism are explained by its practitioners as a way of respecting the dead and transforming one's relationship with them by ensuring their energy (not their physical bodies) is left behind (e.g., Conklin, 1995; Sanday, 1986). In such cases, mortuary cannibalism fits Field's (2006; Field et al., 2005) criterion of a CB strategy that, from an attachment perspective, is healthy: a culturally coherent strategy that assists in transforming the relationship with a dead person to a more spiritual plane. Another implication of these findings is that culture's greatest influence may be over the manner in which a bereaved individual maintains and expresses a healthy attachment to the deceased, rather than over the objective nature and function of that attachment.

In fact, it may be Field's (2006; Field et al., 2005) emphasis on bereavement strategies reflecting coherent cultural and personal belief systems that proves to be crucial in identifying those approaches to CB that represent secure versus insecure attachments to the deceased. The ability to offer a coherent narrative about relationships and secure attachment has been linked in the literature (Hesse, 1999). If this link holds after the death of one of the persons in a relationship, it should not matter if CB strategies involve perceived physical connection with the deceased: if the strategies exist within the context of a coherent cultural or personal narrative, in all likelihood they represent the continuation of a secure bond.

FUTURE WORK

Clearly, work on the attachment–bereavement link is well underway in Western cultures. However, certain questions remain unanswered. First, although there are retrospective data linking attachment to a person and bereavement patterns after that person's death, it would be most helpful to have prospective studies that assessed attachment styles before bereavement (and in the case of death by illness, before diagnosis). Second, experimental work that assesses the impact of interventions designed to restructure attachment between persons before death and restructure the bonds bereaved individuals have with those who have died may help clarify cause-and-effect relationships between attachment and the process of mourning.

Regarding cross-cultural work, it seems the following areas of exploration are important. First, it is important to continue exploration of how people in various cultures maintain attachment-like relationships with the deceased. Much information on this topic exists in anthropology, but the unfortunate fact is that psychologists and anthropologists are quite unaware of each others' work. Another important second step is to determine if and how patterns of attachment in childhood and adulthood are related to expressions of CB in various cultures. Are there exceptions to the model Field (2006; Field et al., 2005) so ably put forth? Another interesting question concerns if and how various rituals and cultural belief systems help or hinder the process of reworking the bond with the deceased after her death.

As is always the case in cross-cultural work, researchers must be aware of certain caveats. Equivalence of measures is a major confounding issue in cross-cultural work and therefore an important initial step in exploring the questions discussed earlier is establishing the cross-cultural validity of all measures used. Although this has been discussed among scholars of attachment, there must be evidence of cross-cultural validity of all measures of all constructs under study in all cultures in which research is being conducted if the scientific community is to be confident in the results. This is no small task. In addition, researchers must assess laypersons' views of how (a) practices aimed at and (b) experiences with the deceased represent continuing bonds, rather than relying only on scholarly elaborations of formal religious and philosophical explanations of rituals and experiences. Lay understanding of a philosophical or religious system may be somewhat different than it is presented in sacred texts or scholars' analyses thereof. Quite possibly, laypersons' understandings of why certain rituals are undertaken will be better predictors of how attachment and bereavement are related than will official statements of rituals' purposes.

CONCLUSION

Thanks to the foundation of empirical work in the West that links attachment and bereavement patterns and to the theoretical integration of scholars like Field, cross-cultural study of attachment and bereavement seems poised to make great empirical strides. The evidence to date suggests that in those cultures where evidence exists, there is a predictable relationship between (a) attachment in both childhood and adulthood, and (b) strategies and experiences in maintaining or breaking connections to the deceased. However, it is clear that these connections must be seen in the light of relevant cultural worldviews that impart meaning to interpersonal bonds in life and beyond the grave. Further interdisciplinary research by psychologists, anthropologists, and scholars from other areas of the social sciences is needed to test the tentative conclusions offered by existing scholarship on culture's effect on the attachment–bereavement link.

REFERENCES

Banse, R. B. (2005). Adult attachment and marital satisfaction: Evidence for dyadic configuration effects. *Journal of Social and Personal Relationships, 21,* 273–282.

Bartholomew, K., & Horowitz, L. M. (1991). Attachment styles among young adults: A test of a four-category model. *Journal of Personality and Social Psychology, 61,* 226–244.

Behrens, K. Y. (2004). A multifaceted view of the concept of *amae*: Reconsidering the indigenous Japanese concept of relatedness. *Human Development, 47,* 1–27.

Boerner, K., & Heckhausen, J. (2003). To have and have not: Adaptive bereavement by transforming mental ties to the deceased. *Death Studies, 27,* 199–226.

Bonanno, G. A., Papa, A., Lalande, K., Zhang, N., & Noll, J. (2005). Grief processing and deliberate grief avoidance: A prospective comparison of bereaved spouses and parents in the United States and the People's Republic of China. *Journal of Consulting and Clinical Psychology, 73,* 86–98.

Bowlby, J. (1969). *Attachment and loss: Vol. I. Attachment.* New York: Basic Books.

Bowlby, J. (1980). *Attachment and loss: Vol. III. Loss: Sadness and depression.* New York: Basic Books.

Brennan, K. A., Clark, C. L., & Shaver, P. R. (1998). Self-report measurement of adult attachment: An integrative overview. In J. A. Simpson & W. S. Rholes (Eds.), *Attachment theory and close relationships* (pp. 46–76). New York: Guilford Press.

Broemer, P., & Blümle, M. (2003). Self-views in close relationships: The influence of attachment styles. *British Journal of Social Psychology, 42,* 445–460.

Choi, H. H. (1998). A study on agreement between child attachment classification and adult representational level of attachment. *Korean Journal of Developmental Psychology, 11,* 131–142. Abstract retrieved from PsycINFO.

Conant, R. D. (1996). Memories of the death and life of a spouse: The role of images and sense of presence in grief. In D. Klass, P. R. Silverman, & S. L. Nickman (Eds.), *Continuing bonds: New understandings of grief* (pp. 179–196). Washington, DC: Taylor & Francis.

Conklin, B. A. (1995). "Thus are our bodies, thus was our custom": Mortuary cannibalism in an Amazonian society. *American Ethnologist, 22,* 75–101.

Engel, S. (Producer). (2000). *Cannibals* [Television series]. New York: The History Channel.

Epstein, R., Kalus, C., & Berger, M. (2006). The continuing bond of the bereaved towards the deceased and adjustment to loss. *Mortality, 11,* 253–269.

Field, N. P. (2006). Unresolved grief and continuing bonds: An attachment perspective. *Death Studies, 30,* 739–756.

Field, N. P., Gao, B., & Paderna, L. (2005). Continuing bonds in bereavement: An attachment theory based perspective. *Death Studies, 29,* 277–299.

Field, N. P., Nichols, C., Holen, A., & Horowitz, M. J. (1999). The relation of continuing attachment to adjustment in conjugal bereavement. *Journal of Consulting and Clinical Psychology, 67,* 212–218.

Field, N. P., & Sundin, E. C. (2001). Attachment style in adjustment to conjugal bereavement. *Journal of Social and Personal Relationships, 18,* 347–361.

Fraley, R. C., & Bonanno, G. A. (2004). Attachment and loss: A test of three competing models on the association between attachment-related avoidance and adaption to bereavement. *Personality and Social Psychology Bulletin, 30,* 878–890.

Fraley, R. C., & Shaver, P. R. (1999). Loss and bereavement: Attachment theory and recent controversies concerning "grief work" and the nature of detachment. In J. Cassidy & P. R. Shaver (Eds.), *Handbook of attachment: Theory, research, and clinical applications* (pp. 735–759). New York: Guilford Press.

Freud, S. (1957). Mourning and melancholia. In J. Rickman (Ed.), *A general selection from the works of Sigmund Freud* (pp. 124–140). New York: Liveright Publishing.

Gorer, G. (1965). *Death, grief, and mourning.* New York: Doubleday.

Grossmann, K., Grossmann, K., & Kindler, H. (2005). Early care and the roots of attachment and partner representations: The Bielefeld and Regensburg longitudinal studies. In K. E. Grossmann, K. Grossmann, & E. Waters (Eds.), *Attachment from infancy to adulthood: The major longitudinal studies* (pp. 98–136). New York: Guilford Press.

Hesse, E. (1999). The Adult Attachment Interview: Historical and current perspectives. In J. Cassidy & P. R. Shaver (Eds.), *Handbook of attachment: Theory, research, and clinical applications* (pp. 395-433). New York: Guilford Press.

Klass, D. (1996). Grief in an Eastern culture: Japanese ancestor worship. In D. Klass, P. R. Silverman, & S. L. Nickman (Eds.), *Continuing bonds: New understandings of grief* (pp. 59–70). Washington, DC: Taylor & Francis.

Klass, D. (2001). Continuing bonds in the resolution of grief in Japan and North America. *American Behavioral Scientist, 44*, 742–763.

Klass, D., & Goss, R. (1999). Spiritual bonds to the dead in cross-cultural and historical perspective: Comparative religion and modern grief. *Death Studies, 23*, 547–567.

Klass, D., & Goss, R. (2003). The politics of grief and continuing bonds with the dead: The cases of Maoist China and Wahhabi Islam. *Death Studies, 27*, 787–811.

Klass, D., Silverman, P. R., & Nickman, S. L. (Eds.). (1996). *Continuing bonds: New understandings of grief*. Washington, DC: Taylor & Francis.

Koslofsky, C. M. (2000). *The reformation of the dead: Death and ritual in early modern Germany, 1450–1700*. New York: St. Martin's Press.

Lalande, K. M., & Bonanno, G. A. (2006). Culture and continuing bonds: A prospective comparison of bereavement in the United States and People's Republic of China. *Death Studies, 30*, 303–324.

Lindstrom, T. C. (1995). Experiencing the presence of the dead: Discrepancies in "the sensing experience" and their psychological concomitants. *Omega, 31*, 11–21.

Malley-Morrison, K., You, H. S., & Mills, R. B. (2000). Young adult attachment styles and perceptions of elder abuse: A cross-cultural study. *Journal of Cross-Cultural Gerontology, 15*, 163–184.

Marwit, S. J., & Klass, D. (1996). Grief and the inner role of the representation of the deceased. In D. Klass, P. R. Silverman, & S. L. Nickman (Eds.), *Continuing bonds: New understandings of grief* (pp. 297–309). Washington, DC: Taylor & Francis.

Mizuta, I., Zahn-Waxler, C., Cole, P. M., & Hiruma, N. (1996). A cross-cultural study of preschoolers' attachment: Security and sensitivity in Japanese and US dyads. *International Journal of Behavioral Development, 19*, 141–159.

Neimeyer, R. A., Baldwin, S. A., & Gillies, J. (2006). Continuing bonds and reconstructing meaning: Mitigating complications in bereavement. *Death Studies, 30*, 715–738.

Normand, C. L., Silverman, P. R., & Nickman, S. L. (1996). Bereaved children's changing relationship with the deceased. In D. Klass, P. R. Silverman, & S. L. Nickman (Eds.), *Continuing bonds: New understandings of grief* (pp. 87–111). Washington, DC: Taylor & Francis.

Parkes, C. M. (2001). *Bereavement: Studies of grief in adult life*. Philadelphia: Taylor & Francis.

Parkes, C. M. (2006). *Love and loss: The roots of grief and its complications*. New York: Routledge.

Parkes, C. M., & Weiss, R. S. (1983). *Recovery from bereavement*. New York: Basic Books.

Pauli-Pott, U., Haverkock, A., Pott, W., & Beckmann, D. (2007). Negative emotionality, attachment quality, and behavior problems in early childhood. *Infant Mental Health Journal, 28*, 39–53.

Rubin, S. S., & Yasien-Esmael, H. (2004). Loss and bereavement among Israel's Muslims: Acceptance of God's will, grief, and the relationship to the deceased. *Omega, 49*, 149–162.

Sable, P. (1989). Attachment, anxiety, and loss of a husband. *American Journal of Orthopsychiatry, 59*, 550–556.

Sable, P. (1992). Attachment, loss of spouse, and disordered mourning. *Families in Society, 73*, 266–273.

Sanday, P. R. (1986). *Divine hunger: Cannibalism as a cultural system.* New York: Cambridge University Press.

Schmitt, D. P., Alcalay, L., Allensworth, M., Allik, J., Ault, L., Austers, I., … Zupanèiè, A. (2004). Patterns and universals of adult romantic attachment across 62 cultural regions: Are models of self and of other pancultural constructs? *Journal of Cross-Cultural Psychology, 35*, 367–402.

Shmotkin, D. (1999). Affective bonds of adult children with living versus deceased parents. *Psychology and Aging, 14*, 473–482.

Silverman, P. R., & Nickman, S. L. (1996). Children's construction of their dead parent. In D. Klass, P. R. Silverman, & S. L. Nickman (Eds.), *Continuing bonds: New understandings of grief* (pp. 73–86). Washington, DC: Taylor & Francis.

Stroebe, M., Schut, H., & Stroebe, W. (2005). Attachment in coping with bereavement: A theoretical integration. *Review of General Psychology, 9*, 48–66.

van IJzendoorn, M. H., & Bakermans-Kranenburg, M. J. (1996). Attachment representations in mothers, fathers, adolescents, and clinical groups: A meta-analytic search for normative data. *Journal of Consulting and Clinical Psychology, 64*, 8–21.

van IJzendoorn, M. H., & Kroonenberg, P. M. (1988). Cross-cultural patterns of attachment: A meta-analysis of the strange situation. *Child Development, 59*, 147–156.

Waskowic, T. D., & Chartier, B. M. (2003). Attachment and the experience of grief following the loss of a spouse. *Omega, 47*, 77–91.

Wayment, H. A., & Vierthaler, J. (2002). Attachment style and bereavement reactions. *Journal of Loss and Trauma, 7*, 129–149.

6

Assessment of Adult Attachment Across Cultures
Conceptual and Methodological Considerations

PHILLIP R. SHAVER, MARIO MIKULINCER,
ITZIAR ALONSO-ARBIOL, and SHIRI LAVY

CONTENTS

*A*ttachment theory (Bowlby, 1973, 1980, 1982) was developed in England and tested mainly in the United States, beginning with Ainsworth and her students (Ainsworth, Blehar, Waters, & Wall, 1978). Its strong roots in Anglo-American culture, despite Ainsworth's (1967) preliminary work in Uganda, might have rendered it far from culturally universal. Moreover, when attachment researchers turned their attention to attachment processes in adulthood (e.g., Hazan & Shaver, 1987; Main, Kaplan, & Cassidy, 1985), the initial work was conducted in the United States, and when it began to spread abroad, it appeared first in European countries (e.g., Grossmann, Grossmann, Huber, & Wartner, 1981; van IJzendoorn, Goosens, Kroonenberg, & Tavecchio, 1985; van IJzendoorn & Kroonenberg, 1988), Australia (e.g., Feeney & Noller, 1990), and Israel (e.g., Mikulincer, Florian, & Tolmacz, 1990), which has strong cultural connections with Europe and the United States.

Despite attachment theory's potentially culture-specific foundations, a cross-culturally oriented literature review by van IJzendoorn and Sagi-Schwartz (2008) indicates that infant–caregiver attachment processes are similar everywhere. This is not surprising given that many of Bowlby's (1982) ideas came from studies of nonhuman primates, with whom humans in all cultures share more than 95% of their genes as well as many genetically based motives and behavior patterns.

Studies of adult attachment are based mainly on two kinds of measures, the Adult Attachment Interview (AAI; Main et al., 1985) and self-report questionnaires (e.g., Brennan, Clark, & Shaver, 1998). So far, the results of studies using these measures in different cultures also seem to be generally similar (see the review of AAI studies by Hesse, 2008, and of self-report studies by Mikulincer & Shaver, 2007). With regard to the self-report adult-attachment measures, Schmitt et al. (2003, 2004) used Bartholomew and Horowitz's (1991) Relationship Questionnaire, finding that it had similar correlates in 62 different cultures. Moreover, people worldwide seem to view secure attachment as the ideal for both infants (van IJzendoorn & Sagi-Schwartz, 2008) and adults (Schmitt et al., 2003, 2004), and security seems to be more common than the different kinds of attachment insecurity in many different societies, except under unusual circumstances (e.g., adults in some Third-World countries or children being subjected to aversive child-rearing techniques; Schmitt et al., 2004; van IJzendoorn & Sagi-Schwartz, 2008).

In the present chapter we focus mainly on self-report measures of adult attachment patterns or of the underlying dimensions of attachment insecurity. We begin with a brief summary of attachment theory and a description of the major dimensions of attachment insecurity. We then present a model of attachment-related processes in adulthood, based on an extensive review of hundreds of studies (Mikulincer & Shaver, 2007). Next, we consider how attachment processes addressed by the model might be affected by cultural and sociodemographic factors. After presenting these ideas, we outline a number of important considerations when conducting cross-cultural studies of adult attachment using self-report measures.

OVERVIEW OF ADULT ATTACHMENT THEORY

According to Bowlby (1982), proximity-seeking behavior is the result of an innate, adaptive behavioral system (the *attachment behavioral system*). This system emerged over the course of evolution because it increased the survival chances of human infants, who are born with immature capacities for locomotion, feeding, and defense. Because human (and other primate) infants require a long period of care and protection, they are born with a repertoire of behaviors that maintain proximity to others who are able to protect them and help regulate their emotions (Coan, 2008). Although the attachment system is most critical during the early years of life, Bowlby (1988) assumed that it is active over the entire life span and is manifested in thoughts and behaviors related to seeking protection and emotional support.

Bowlby (1982) also specified the provisions that a relationship partner should supply, or the functions this person should serve, if he or she is to become an *attachment figure* (see also Hazan & Shaver, 1994; Hazan & Zeifman, 1994). First, attachment figures are targets of *proximity maintenance*. Humans of all ages tend to seek and enjoy proximity to their attachment figures in times of need and to experience distress upon separation from these figures. Second, attachment figures provide a physical and emotional *safe haven*; they facilitate distress alleviation and are a source of support and comfort. Third, attachment figures provide a *secure base* from which people can explore and learn about the world and develop their own capacities and personality. By accomplishing these functions, a relationship partner becomes a source of attachment security.

Beyond describing universal aspects of the attachment system, Bowlby (1973) described individual differences in the system's functioning. Interactions with significant others who are available in times of need, sensitive to one's attachment needs, and responsive to one's bids for proximity (*attachment-figure availability*) facilitate the optimal functioning of the system and promote the formation of a sense of attachment security. As a result, positive expectations about others' availability and positive views of the self as competent and valued are formed throughout early development, and major affect-regulation strategies are organized around these positive beliefs. However, when significant others are unavailable or unresponsive to one's needs, proximity seeking fails to relieve distress and a sense of attachment security is not attained. As a result, negative representations of self and others are formed (e.g., worries about others' good will and doubts about self-worth), and strategies of affect regulation other than proximity seeking (*secondary attachment strategies*) are developed. In other words, attachment-figure availability is one of the major sources of individual differences in strategies of affect regulation.

Most empirical tests of these theoretical ideas have focused on a person's *attachment style*—the systematic pattern of relational expectations, emotions, and behavior that results from internalization of a particular history of attachment experiences and consequent reliance on a particular attachment-related strategy of affect regulation (Fraley & Shaver, 2000; Shaver & Mikulincer, 2002). Initially, research was based on Ainsworth et al.'s (1978) typology of attachment styles in infancy—secure, anxious, and avoidant—and Hazan and Shaver's (1987) conceptualization of parallel adult styles in the romantic relationship (adult pair-bonding) domain. However, subsequent studies (e.g., Bartholomew & Horowitz, 1991; Brennan et al., 1998) revealed that attachment styles are best conceptualized as regions in a two-dimensional space. The dimensions defining this space, *attachment anxiety* and *avoidance,* can be measured with reliable and valid self-report scales and are, in line with Bowlby's theory, associated with relationship functioning and affect regulation (see Mikulincer & Shaver, 2007, for a review).

In this two-dimensional space, low scores on both anxiety and avoidance indicate a secure attachment style or orientation. This region is characterized by a sense of attachment security, comfort with closeness and interdependence, and reliance on support seeking and other constructive means of coping with stress. The region that parallels Ainsworth et al.'s (1978) anxious attachment orientation is defined by a relatively high score on the anxiety dimension and a relatively low score on the avoidance dimension. This region is characterized by a lack of attachment security, a strong need for closeness, worries about relationships, and fear of being rejected. The attachment pattern that Ainsworth et al. called "avoidant" corresponds to the region of the two-dimensional space where avoidance is high and anxiety is relatively low. This region is also characterized by a lack of attachment security, but people with scores in this region of the space are also compulsively self-reliant and prefer to remain emotionally distant from others. The fourth region of the space, where scores on both dimensions are high, corresponds to what Bartholomew and Horowitz (1991) called "fearful avoidance," which is, in some respects, similar to the fourth infant attachment pattern, disorganized/disoriented, described by Main and Solomon (1990) subsequent to the work of Ainsworth et al. (1978). People in this region of the space are especially low in trust and may have been abused or neglected by parents (Shaver & Clark, 1994).

A MODEL OF ATTACHMENT-SYSTEM FUNCTIONING IN ADULTHOOD AND ITS IMPLICATIONS FOR CROSS-CULTURAL RESEARCH

In summarizing the hundreds of empirical studies of adult attachment processes, Mikulincer and Shaver (2007) created a flowchart model of the activation and dynamics of the attachment system. This model integrates research findings with previous theoretical proposals offered by Bowlby (1973, 1982), Ainsworth (1991), Cassidy and Berlin (1994), Cassidy and Kobak (1988), and Fraley and Shaver (2000). The model (Figure 6.1) includes three major components. The first involves the monitoring and appraisal of threatening events; it is responsible for activation of the primary attachment strategy—proximity seeking. The second component involves monitoring and appraisal of the availability of external or internalized attachment figures; it is responsible for individual differences in the sense of attachment security and the development of what we call *security-based strategies*. The third component involves monitoring and appraisal of the viability of proximity seeking as a means of coping with attachment insecurity and distress. This component is responsible for individual differences in the development of specific secondary attachment strategies (*anxious hyperactivating* versus *avoidant deactivating strategies*). The new model includes excitatory and inhibitory pathways that result from recurrent use of secondary attachment strategies; these pathways in turn affect the monitoring of threatening events and attachment figures' availability.

Attachment-System Activation and the Primary Attachment Strategy

Mikulincer and Shaver (2007) assumed that the monitoring of mental and environmental events results in activation of the attachment system whenever a potential

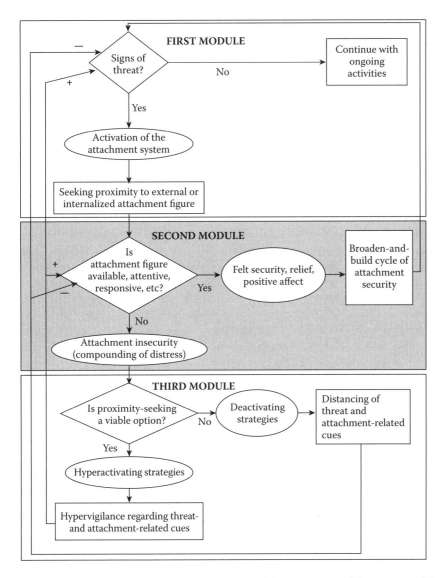

Figure 6.1   Mikulincer and Shaver's (2007) model of the activation and functioning of the attachment system in adulthood.

or actual threat is encountered. This idea follows Bowlby's (1982) statement that "a child seeks his attachment-figure when he is tired, hungry, ill, or alarmed and also when he is uncertain of that figure's whereabouts" (p. 307). That is, during encounters with physical or psychological threats, the attachment system is activated and the primary attachment strategy is set in motion. This strategy leads adults to turn to internalized representations of attachment figures or to actual supportive others, and to maintain symbolic or actual proximity to these figures. We assume that age and development result in an increased ability to gain comfort from symbolic representations of attachment figures, but like Bowlby (1982, 1988) we also assume that no one of any age is completely free of actual reliance on others.

As has been well documented in studies of infants and young children, activation of the attachment system generally results in seeking proximity to a reliable attachment figure and an attempt to obtain comfort, reassurance, and support (e.g., Ainsworth, 1973, 1991; Heinicke & Westheimer, 1966). Conceptually parallel research with adults indicates that the departure of a relationship partner heightens proximity seeking (Fraley & Shaver, 1998; Medway, Davis, Cafferty, Chappell, & O'Hearn, 1995; Vormbrock, 1993). Recent studies have also shown that thoughts related to proximity seeking, as well as mental representations of internalized attachment figures, tend to be activated even in minimally threatening situations (Mikulincer, Birnbaum, Woddis, & Nachmias, 2000; Mikulincer, Gillath, & Shaver, 2002).

Although few studies have compared people from different cultures with respect to attachment-system activation, we can make some testable predictions about it. To the extent that people from different cultures, subcultures, or geographical areas encounter different degrees of threat (e.g., epidemics, warfare, tsunamis, or earthquakes), they may have different thresholds for attachment-system activation. The ones who more often encounter serious threats may exhibit chronic hyperaccessibility of attachment-related goals and representations, which could be studied with methods used in studies of individual differences by Baldwin, Fehr, Keedian, Seidel, and Thompson (1993), Gillath et al. (2006), and Mikulincer et al. (2002). Moreover, people in cultures and geographical locations where serious threats occur relatively often may generally seek, or be pre-prepared to seek, safe-haven support (protection) rather than secure-base support (encouragement and admiration for achievements). Even within a particular society (such as the United States), poorer people, who encounter more threats and challenges of many kinds, may be more oriented toward safe-haven support from attachment figures, whereas their wealthier, safer counterparts may be more oriented toward seeking a secure base for exploration and achievement (Schmitt et al., 2004).

Attachment-Figure Availability and the Sense of Security

Once the attachment system is activated, an affirmative answer to the question "Is the attachment figure literally or symbolically available?" results in a sense of attachment security and what we, following Fredrickson (2001), call a "broaden and build" cycle of attachment security. This cycle bolsters a person's resources for maintaining mental health in times of stress and broadens his or her perspectives and capacities. As a person gains experience and develops cognitively, more of the role of a security-enhancing attachment figure can be internalized and become part of personal strength and resilience. In adulthood, the question about literal attachment-figure availability becomes transformed into a question about the adequacy of internal as well as external attachment-related resources for coping with stress. In many cases, internal resources, which were created originally with the help of security-providing attachment figures, are likely to be sufficient, but when they are not, the person with a secure attachment history is willing and able to depend on actual attachment figures for support.

The sense of attachment security is a foundation for the optimal functioning of the other behavioral systems discussed by Bowlby (1982), such as exploration, affiliation, caregiving, and sex. According to attachment theory, insecure individuals, or anyone suffering from a period of insecurity, are occupied or preoccupied with confronting the distress-eliciting situation and thus have fewer resources available for exploring the environment, having fun with others, attending to others' needs, or having mutually satisfying sex in a supportive relational context. Only when relief is attained and security is restored can people direct energy to activities that broaden their perspectives and skills. Moreover, with confidence that support is available when needed, people can take risks and engage in autonomy-promoting activities. Many studies have shown that lower scores on the attachment anxiety and avoidance dimensions, as well as priming (stimulating or activating) the sense of attachment security in experimental settings, are associated with more positive representations of self and others, more effective strategies for coping with stress, more considerate provision of care to relationship partners, and more mutually satisfying sexual relationships (Mikulincer & Shaver, 2007).

Few studies have addressed these issues in multiple cultures (for an exception see Schmitt et al., 2004), but we can make some predictions for future research. First, it seems likely that people living in dangerous, unstable situations (because of warfare; natural disasters; unhealthy, disease-ridden environments; or extreme poverty) will generally seek external, instrumental support and have less opportunity to develop internal, symbolic sources of security. Moreover, repeated reliance, in emergencies, on external support may increase both a person's sense of dependency and outside observers' perception of the person's chronic dependency or helplessness (Shnabel & Nadler, 2010). Second, even if a person has an internalized safe haven or secure base, the identity of the represented person, persons, or agency (e.g., mother, spouse, the Dear Leader, Allah, Jesus, the Virgin Mary) will depend on cultural, political, and religious socialization. Third, when and if a person attains a sense of security within a particular life period or set of circumstances, it may not be possible to say, without knowledge of the person's culture and religion, which alternative behavioral system (exploration, caregiving, or sex) will be activated. There will likely be an interaction between attachment security and a cultural or subcultural value system that determines whether individual exploration and self-actualization or benevolent service and self-transcendence will be favored (Schwartz, 2009). As explained previously (Mikulincer & Shaver, 2007), attachment security should not be equated with openness and creativity, at least in the usual Western sense, because among people who value tradition and conformity, security may lead to deeper participation in a traditional culture. It is even possible that security might be associated with violence or self-destruction in a cultural or religious context that make these activities a primary route to self-expression, contribution to others, and self-transcendence (Stern, 2003).

Proximity-Seeking Viability and Secondary Attachment Strategies

Attachment-figure unavailability results in attachment insecurity, which compounds the distress anyone might experience when encountering a threat. Shaver and Mikulincer (2002) claimed that this state of insecurity forces a decision—conscious or unconscious—about the viability of proximity seeking as a means of self-regulation, which in turn leads to activation of a specific secondary attachment strategy. The appraisal of proximity seeking as a viable option can result in very energetic, insistent attempts to attain proximity, support, and love. In the literature on attachment, these active, intense secondary strategies are called *anxious hyperactivating strategies* (Cassidy & Berlin, 1994); they require constant vigilance, concern, and effort until an attachment figure is perceived to be available and a sense of security is attained. Hyperactivating strategies include a strong approach orientation toward relationship partners; attempts to elicit their involvement, care, and support through clinging and controlling responses; and cognitive and behavioral efforts aimed at minimizing distance from them (Shaver & Hazan, 1993). These strategies are also indicated by overdependence on relationship partners as a source of protection (Shaver & Hazan, 1993) and perception of oneself as helpless and incompetent at affect regulation (Mikulincer & Florian, 1998). Hyperactivating strategies are characteristic of people who score relatively high on the attachment anxiety dimension (Mikulincer & Shaver, 2007), although the expression of hyperactivation also depends on a person's location on the avoidance dimension.

Individuals who use hyperactivation strategies in their personal lives tend to use them in clinical settings as well. For example, in a chapter of a recent book about clinical applications of attachment research, we (Mikulincer, Shaver, Cassidy, & Berant, 2009) described the case of Ruth, a 40-year-old married woman who became extremely angry whenever she felt that her husband was not being sufficiently attentive or appreciative. She was hurt and upset, for example, when he failed to meet her exaggerated expectations (e.g., when he did not hold her hand when they attended a lecture together, especially when she noticed that the lecturer was an attractive woman). Ruth continually doubted her husband's love. No matter what he did, she found it difficult to believe that he was really attracted to her and sincerely cared for her. She expressed her protest with rage and her disappointments with sorrow, which made her husband feel discouraged and helpless. This case shows how anxious, hyperactivated attachment strategies can often destroy a relationship that the anxious person claims to need and value.

The problems are quite different when a person appraises proximity seeking and intimacy to be a dangerous or nonviable option. This kind of appraisal promotes deactivation of proximity seeking, inhibition of desires for comfort and support, and determination to handle distress alone. These coping mechanisms are called *avoidant deactivating strategies* (Cassidy & Kobak, 1988), because their primary goal is to keep the attachment system deactivated so as to avoid frustration and further distress caused by attachment-figure unavailability. This goal leads to the denial of attachment needs; avoidance of closeness, intimacy, and dependence in close relationships; maximization of cognitive, emotional, and physical distance from others; and strivings for self-reliance and independence. With practice and experience, these deactivating strategies often broaden to include literal and symbolic distancing of oneself from distress whether it is directly attachment related or not. Deactivating strategies are characteristic of people scoring relatively high on the attachment avoidance dimension (Mikulincer & Shaver, 2007).

Thirty-year-old Sam is a clinical example of the use of deactivating attachment strategies in relationships (Mikulincer et al., 2009). Sam tended to dismiss and devalue others (including his therapist), especially when he most needed help. On one occasion while he was in therapy, Sam learned that he had not won a short-story competition. When his therapist asked him how he felt about it, he first claimed he did not "feel anything." He said his story had not fit the criteria for the competition in the first place, so it was bound to be rejected. He then abruptly changed the subject and said that he would not tell the therapist about his dreams anymore, because she was more interested in his dreams than she was in him. These reactions revealed Sam's difficulties in confronting feelings of rejection, which he tried to minimize by using deactivating emotion-regulation strategies (suppressing and denying his feelings, devaluing the therapist's efforts to provide support).

People who score high on both insecurity dimensions (anxiety and avoidance), who were labeled fearfully avoidant by Bartholomew and Horowitz (1991) and disorganized/disoriented by Main and Solomon (1990), adopt conflicting strategies. The details of this pattern are beyond the scope of the present chapter, but it will suffice for present purposes to say that they feel anxious and uncertain but often behave avoidantly.

Cross-cultural research on infants and young children has already documented cross-cultural differences in the relative frequencies of different attachment patterns (van IJzendoorn & Sagi-Schwartz, 2008). There are fewer studies of different self-reported adult attachment patterns, but the few that exist already indicate that average degrees of attachment anxiety and avoidance in adults differ across countries and cultures. For example, avoidance scores are especially high in certain central African countries. According to Schmitt et al. (2003, 2004), this may be an effect of high parental mortality, frequent warfare and violence, and AIDS (the spread of which may also be a function of low-investment, relatively avoidant, short-term sex). In addition, it seems likely that if a culture tends to socialize its children to be relatively self-reliant (as may be the case in northern Germany; Grossmann et al., 1981), the adult score on avoidant attachment will be higher. In cultures that socialize children to be highly reliant on others for comfort and support (as may be the case in Japan; Rothbaum, Weisz, Pott, Miyake, & Morelli, 2000), the average adult score on the attachment anxiety dimension is likely to be relatively high.

METHODOLOGICAL ISSUES IN CROSS-CULTURAL RESEARCH ON ADULT ATTACHMENT

Although the Mikulincer–Shaver model and self-report measures of adult attachment have begun to be explored in different countries (e.g., Alonso-Arbiol, Shaver, & Yárnoz, 2002; Gillath et al., 2005), little attention has been paid to the issues raised by translating and transporting measures from one culture or language to others. In fact, the optimal procedures for translating and adapting measures from one culture or language to another are not widely known and are not commonly taught in psychology departments (Hambleton, 1993, 1994, 2005; Hui & Triandis,

1985; van de Vijver & Hambleton, 1996). Even when careful procedures are followed, they are often not described in sufficient detail for readers to evaluate their adequacy (as discussed by Mallinckrodt & Wang, 2004). In the remainder of this chapter we consider the major problems and issues that arise when transferring measures from one culture or language to another. We also provide examples to illustrate our points.

As several authors have observed (Balluerka, Gorostiaga, Alonso-Arbiol, & Haranburu, 2007; Hambleton, 2005; Muñiz, 2000; Muñiz & Hambleton, 1996; Sireci, Patsula, & Hambleton, 2005; van de Vijver & Hambleton, 1996; van de Vijver & Poortinga, 2005), the adaptation of measures for use in new cultures is complex and controversial. Nevertheless, the International Test Commission (ITC), enlisting the advice of an international group of assessment experts, created the ITC Guidelines for Test Adaptation, which is still the gold standard for test adaptations (Hambleton, 1994; van de Vijver & Hambleton, 1996). Based on these guidelines, we will consider the kinds of issues and problems that arise when one translates self-report attachment measures from English to other languages. These difficulties include lack of conceptual, content, and semantic equivalence; insufficient empirical analyses; inadequate use of short forms of a questionnaire; and inadequate consideration of different forms or dialects of a particular language.

Lack of Conceptual, Content, and Semantic Equivalence

One important issue is the possibility that a construct measured by a particular instrument in one culture or language will not have the same meaning in different cultures. An example is the term *romantic partners* used in Brennan et al.'s (1998) Experiences in Close Relationships measure (often referred to as the ECR). We have received e-mail messages from people in various countries asking what, precisely, the term *romantic* means. Other such issues, beyond the specific wording of a measure, include "romantic attachment" researchers' emphasis on emotional intimacy and fear of rejection, which may or may not be relevant to adult couple relationships in all cultures (such as India, Pakistan, and Thailand; Gupta, 1992; Levine, Sato, Hashimoto, & Verma, 1995; Mace & Mace, 1960). There are two ways to deal with such problems, one having to do with theory and the other having to do with empirical evidence.

The first step in the translation process should be conducted by bilingual researchers in the target culture. They are likely to notice concepts in the original measure (e.g., avoidance of intimacy) that may not make sense, or transfer easily, from the original measure to the translation. In the case of adults' attachment figures, these figures may not always, or even usually, include romantic partners. In some cultures, partners in a marriage may rely on other people (e.g., parents, sisters/brothers, in-laws, close friends) as primary attachment figures rather than relying on their spouse (e.g., Gore, 1965; see D'Cruz & Bharat, 2001, for a description of the joint family). In such cases, even if the attachment system were activated when threats to safety or security arose, the marital partner might not be the primary safe haven or secure base.

A second step, after researchers in the target culture provide a preliminary estimate about the relevance of a construct to their culture, is to collect empirical evidence about the attachment issues and relationships to be studied. In-depth interviews, open-ended questionnaires, and other measures might allow research participants to help researchers map, and perhaps revise, a particular construct in their culture. Another empirical procedure might then be useful: factor-analyzing preliminary items used on a reasonable sample of people from the target culture to see if subconstructs in the original measure (e.g., attachment anxiety and avoidance in the ECR) are distinct in the target culture. An example is the study by Alonso-Arbiol, Balluerka, and Shaver (2007; see also Alonso-Arbiol, Balluerka, Shaver, & Gillath, 2008), in which the factor structure and item loadings for ECR items were compared across American and Spanish samples. Another example is a study by Wei, Russell, Mallinckrodt, and Zakalik (2004) that included four American ethnic groups—African American, Asian American, Hispanic American, and Caucasian—to test whether the latent variables of adult attachment anxiety and avoidance appeared equally clearly in the four groups, which in fact they did.

A related but slightly different problem is that particular items in the original instrument may not represent the intended construct as well in the target culture. For example, Feeney, Noller, and Hanrahan (1994) used an achievement-oriented item, "Achieving things is more important than building relationships," to measure avoidant attachment in Australia. However, a person in a different culture might be avoidant in several senses (e.g., avoiding self-disclosure, not seeking a partner's support) but not value achievement over relationships—perhaps not even value individual achievement at all. This may be the case in collectivist cultures in which relationships and tradition are more important than individual achievement or self-enhancement (Hofstede, 2001; Schwartz, 2009).

Once one is fairly certain that the proposed measure has conceptual and content equivalence across the original and target cultures, it becomes important to look in greater detail at the semantic equivalence of parallel items in the two versions of the measure. Basically, this means that it is important to go beyond a literal translation of each item to make sure the words in the items convey the same meaning to people in the two cultures (van de Vijver & Poortinga, 2005). This can be done by various methods (back-translation, forward-translation, a combination of both) and by relying on both linguistic and psychological criteria.

For instance, in creating the Spanish version of the Experiences in Close Relationships measure (ECR-S) Alonso-Arbiol et al. (2007) relied on both researchers familiar with attachment theory and Spanish linguists. Two bilingual attachment researchers who were fluent in both English and Spanish evaluated the content equivalence of each item. Also, to increase the semantic equivalence of the English and Spanish items, a back-translation method was used. The same two bilingual researchers translated each English item into Spanish independently, and the two translations were compared, discussed, and reduced to a single mutually agreeable form. A bilingual linguist who was unfamiliar with attachment theory then translated the proposed Spanish-language items back into English. Finally, the authors examined this back-translation to determine whether the items seemed to be essentially the same as the English-language originals.

Some changes were made during this process to adapt the items to fit with contemporary Spanish. The translators used the wording *pareja* (partner) when *romantic partner* was used in English, because the word *romantic* would not have had the appropriate meaning in Spanish. Similarly, they decided to use only the singular form of the word for *partner*, even though some of the English items (generalizing across a person's history of "romantic" relationships) used the plural form, because the plural form in Spanish was potentially misleading, perhaps implying that the respondent was involved in several couple relationships at the same time.

Another example in which small but necessary changes in the final version of items might need to be made concerns the treatment of gender in certain languages. For instance, Moreira et al. (2006) designed two separate versions of the Portuguese ECR to measure attachment in male and female samples because there were several words that differed slightly depending on gender (e.g., *Fico ressentido quando a minha parceira passa tempo longe de mim* and *Fico ressentida quando a meu parceiro passa tempo longe de mim*—masculine and feminine versions of the English item "I resent it when my partner spends time away from me"). Mikulincer and Florian (2000) confronted a similar problem when creating the Hebrew version of the ECR.

Insufficient Empirical Analyses of the Adequacy of the Adapted Measure

The empirical testing of the adapted measure is as important as establishing conceptual, content, and semantic equivalence. Nevertheless, it is still common to hear at professional meetings and conferences that an instrument was adapted or translated into French, Spanish, or Chinese without testing its psychometric properties in the target culture. Ideally, researchers should conduct pilot studies to test participants' understanding of items (e.g., Tsagarakis, Kafetsios, & Stalikas, 2007, took this step when adapting and translating the ECR into Greek). Then, in subsequent uses of the adapted questionnaire, the following features should be examined: (a) construct validity, (b) criterion-related validity, (c) convergent validity, (d) discriminant validity, and (e) internal consistency and test–retest reliability. To check the measure's intended structure, one could use exploratory or confirmatory factor analysis.

Another issue worth considering is the age and relationship status of one's respondents. A great deal of adult attachment research in English-speaking countries has been conducted on college students, some of whom were and some of whom were not involved in "romantic" or couple relationships at the time. But there have also been studies of nationally representative samples in the United States (e.g., Mickelson, Kessler, & Shaver, 1997) and of special groups, such as cohabiting French Canadians (Brassard, Shaver, & Lussier, 2007) and elderly Americans (e.g., Zhang & Labouvie-Vief, 2004). When attachment measures are translated into different languages, it is important to test their appropriateness in samples of different ages and relationship statuses. This has recently been done, for example, with both college students and coupled adults from community samples (e.g., regarding the Dutch ECR, see Conradi, Gerlsma, van Duijn, & de Jonge, 2006; regarding the Spanish ECR, see Alonso-Arbiol et al., 2007).

Inadequate Use of Short Forms of a Questionnaire

At times, when conducting self-report studies in a new culture, it may be desirable for practical reasons (e.g., to avoid an overly long questionnaire), not only to translate an existing measure from another language but also to shorten the measure in the process. In selecting items to be retained, two empirical criteria are used: choosing the items with the highest factor loadings on a particular subscale or choosing items with the highest item-total correlations. Wei, Russell, Mallinckrodt, and Vogel (2007) mentioned additional considerations when creating a short form of the ECR in both English and Chinese. They made sure to retain some items that were reverse-scaled, to avoid response bias, and to retain some diversity of item content so as not to reduce the breadth of a particular construct. For example, the ECR attachment anxiety scale mentions not only fear of rejection, abandonment, and being insufficiently loved, but also anger about a partner's absences or lack of attention. This anger component was included in the original ECR to capture important aspects of anxious attachment in infancy (e.g., anger at mother following a separation in Ainsworth et al.'s, 1978, Strange Situation test). If only the highest-loading items on a factor analysis of the ECR were retained in a short form of the scale, the construct would be narrowed from the full range of what Bowlby (1982) called separation anxiety and "protest" to something more like fear of rejection.

Inadequate Use of Versions of a Language

Adapting a measure for use in another culture requires more than just a linguistic translation and more than the mainly statistical considerations we have discussed so far. In some cultures there are several subcultures, even though all of them may use the same, or approximately the same, language. For example, Spanish is spoken in several different countries, on different continents, and in subcultures of English-speaking societies. It cannot be assumed that a single translation of a measure like the ECR can be used equivalently in different regions of Spain, or different Latin American countries, or different American cities (some of which have a high proportion of Mexican Americans and some of which have a high proportion of Cuban Americans or people from Puerto Rico).

Cognitive and Behavioral Measures

Adult attachment research uses many different kinds of measures, not only self-report questionnaires. For example, Fraley and Shaver (1998) observed couple members' separations in a California airport, as one member prepared to board a plane and the other prepared to return home alone. The researchers designed a standardized observational coding system containing the following categories: contact maintenance, contact seeking, avoidance, resistance, sadness, caregiving, and sexuality. The specific behaviors included such things as crying, intimately kissing, and petting or caressing a partner's head. Even though some of these behaviors and categories would be applicable to airport behavior in other countries, open expressions of intimacy such as kissing in public are not accepted by all cultures and subcultures (e.g., Indian Hindus, ultra-Orthodox Jews, and many Arab Muslims). Another example: In the cognitive studies by Mikulincer et al. (2000) and Mikulincer and Shaver (2001), certain words and pictures were used to prime a sense of security (e.g., love, hug, a Picasso drawing of a mother and baby). Stimuli such as these might or might not work in other cultures. For each study, it will be necessary to pilot test procedures to make sure they have similar effects in different cultures.

CONCLUDING REMARKS

Although the core of attachment theory—regarding the activation of proximity and support seeking during times of threat and stress, the process of becoming emotionally attached to another person, and the existence of different patterns of attachment—has been empirically supported in many cultures, differences have also been found, especially with regard to the relative frequencies of the different patterns of attachment. As researchers begin to examine adult attachment in different cultures, it will be important to expand the theoretical framework and identify cross-cultural differences, where they exist, in the details of attachment, the forms of threat that matter most in a particular society or cultural context, the choice of primary attachment figures (e.g., spouse, parents, relatives, close friends), and the specific forms of secure and insecure adult attachment.

One of the most important challenges in cross-cultural research on adult attachment is to find the *reasons* for particular differences. It is worth considering that some of the differences may be due to genetic factors. Preliminary research has already provided evidence for genetic influences on attachment patterns, even within a particular culture (e.g., Crawford et al., 2007; Donnellan, Burt, Levendosky, & Klump, 2008; Gillath, Shaver, Baek, & Chun, 2008). But most of the cross-cultural variance is likely to be due to the kinds of differences between cultures and countries identified by Hofstede (2001) and Schwartz (2009)—differences in individualism versus collectivism, distributed versus concentrated power, gender roles, acceptance versus avoidance of uncertainty and ambiguity, and short- versus long-term temporal orientation. Variations in family structure and marriage, including methods of choosing mates, are also likely to matter.

Because attachment theory views patterns of attachment as outcomes of actual social experiences within the family of origin and within romantic/marital relationships, it will be worthwhile to consider whether particular attachment patterns are especially adaptive in certain cultures or subcultures. It seems likely that avoidant attachment is more adaptive in highly individualistic cultures, for example, whereas anxious attachment may be more compatible with a highly collectivist culture in which tight interdependence is regarded favorably. Simpson and Belsky (2008) summarized research suggesting that insecure attachment in childhood is a precursor to early engagement in sexual behavior and early pregnancy, which may make biological sense under conditions (e.g., war, extreme poverty) in which waiting for a secure relationship may mean failing to have children.

Understanding how different attachment patterns do or do not fit in with a person's cultural, economic, and environmental surroundings and conditions is important for professionals who interact with them in different roles. Business associates presumably work more effectively together if they understand each other's goals and preferences. Teachers in multicultural classrooms and training programs are likely to be more effective if they understand their students' values and social proclivities. Clinicians who deal with clients from different cultural backgrounds need to be sensitive to differences in assumptions, goals, and approved patterns of behavior.

Attachment researchers have generally accepted Bowlby's (1982) idea that continuity of attachment patterns across development is attributable in large part to what he called internal working models of self and others (in relationships). We know something about these models, which have been described using concepts such as "schemas" and "scripts" (e.g., Bretherton & Munholland, 2008; Waters & Waters, 2006). To date, such scripts have been studied mostly within the United States and other Western societies (e.g., Coppola, Vaughn, Cassibba, & Costantini, 2006). It will be interesting and enlightening to see whether self models and relational scripts vary systematically as a function of culture—a very likely possibility, in our opinion. The models and scripts are, in theory, a product of actual social experiences. So, to the extent that such experiences differ across cultures, the models and scripts should differ accordingly.

Conducting such cross-cultural research will be both theoretically and practically challenging for several reasons. When cross-cultural research requires the translation and adaptation of measures used in a different culture, as it usually does, it will be important to consider the ITC Guidelines for Test Adaptation and to deal with problems related to lack of conceptual, content, and semantic equivalence, as described in this chapter. It seems likely that there will be many small, and perhaps some substantial, differences across cultures in the best way to identify adults' primary attachment figures and capture individual differences in the ways in which adults relate to and mentally represent these figures. This is a challenging, but also a fascinating, prospect for future research.

REFERENCES

Ainsworth, M. D. S. (1967). *Infancy in Uganda: Infant care and the growth of love.* Baltimore, MD: Johns Hopkins University Press.

Ainsworth, M. D. S. (1973). The development of infant-mother attachment. In B. M. Caldwell & H. N. Ricciuti (Eds.), *Review of child development research* (Vol. 3, pp. 1–94). Chicago: University of Chicago Press.

Ainsworth, M. D. S. (1991). Attachment and other affectional bonds across the life cycle. In C. M. Parkes, J. Stevenson-Hinde, & P. Marris (Eds.), *Attachment across the life cycle* (pp. 33–51). New York: Routledge.

Ainsworth, M. D. S., Blehar, M. C., Waters, E., & Wall, S. (1978). *Patterns of attachment: Assessed in the strange situation and at home.* Hillsdale, NJ: Lawrence Erlbaum Associates.

Alonso-Arbiol, I., Balluerka, N., & Shaver, P. R. (2007). A Spanish version of the Experiences in Close Relationships (ECR) adult attachment questionnaire. *Personal Relationships, 14,* 45–63.

Alonso-Arbiol, I., Balluerka, N., Shaver, P. R., & Gillath, O. (2008). Psychometric properties of Spanish and American versions of the ECR adult attachment questionnaire: A comparative study. *European Journal of Psychological Assessment, 24,* 9–13.

Alonso-Arbiol, I., Shaver, P. R., & Yárnoz, S. (2002). Insecure attachment, gender roles, and interpersonal dependency in the Basque Country. *Personal Relationships, 9*, 479–490.

Baldwin, M. W., Fehr, B., Keedian, E., Seidel, M., & Thompson, D. W. (1993). An exploration of the relational schemata underlying attachment styles: Self-report and lexical decision approaches. *Personality and Social Psychology Bulletin, 19*, 746–754.

Balluerka, N., Gorostiaga, A., Alonso-Arbiol, I., & Haranburu, M. (2007). La adaptación de instrumentos de medidas de unas culturas a otras: Una perspectiva práctica. *Psicothema, 19*, 124–133.

Bartholomew, K., & Horowitz, L. M. (1991). Attachment styles among young adults: A test of a four-category model. *Journal of Personality and Social Psychology, 61*, 226–244.

Bowlby, J. (1973). *Attachment and loss: Vol. 2. Separation: Anxiety and anger.* New York: Basic Books.

Bowlby, J. (1980). *Attachment and loss: Vol. 3. Sadness and depression.* New York: Basic Books.

Bowlby, J. (1982). *Attachment and loss: Vol. 1. Attachment* (2nd ed.). New York: Basic Books.

Bowlby, J. (1988). *A secure base: Clinical applications of attachment theory.* London: Routledge.

Brassard, A., Shaver, P. R., & Lussier, Y. (2007). Attachment, sexual experience, and sexual pressure in romantic relationships: A dyadic approach. *Personal Relationships, 14*, 475–493.

Brennan, K. A., Clark, C. L., & Shaver, P. R. (1998). Self-report measurement of adult romantic attachment: An integrative overview. In J. A. Simpson & W. S. Rholes (Eds.), *Attachment theory and close relationships* (pp. 46–76). New York: Guilford Press.

Bretherton, I., & Munholland, K. A. (2008). Internal working models in attachment relationships: Elaborating a central construct in attachment theory. In J. Cassidy & P. R. Shaver (Eds.), *Handbook of attachment: Theory, research, and clinical applications* (2nd ed., pp. 102–127). New York: Guilford Press.

Cassidy, J., & Berlin, L. J. (1994). The insecure/ambivalent pattern of attachment: Theory and research. *Child Development, 65*, 971–981.

Cassidy, J., & Kobak, R. R. (1988). Avoidance and its relationship with other defensive processes. In J. Belsky & T. Nezworski (Eds.), *Clinical implications of attachment* (pp. 300–323). Hillsdale, NJ: Lawrence Erlbaum Associates.

Coan, J. A. (2008). Toward a neuroscience of attachment. In J. Cassidy & P. R. Shaver (Eds.), *Handbook of attachment: Theory, research, and clinical applications* (2nd ed., pp. 241–265). New York: Guilford Press.

Conradi, H. J., Gerlsma, C., van Duijn, M., & de Jonge, P. (2006). Internal and external validity of the Experiences in Close Relationships questionnaire in an American and two Dutch samples. *European Journal of Psychiatry, 20*, 258–269.

Coppola, G., Vaughn, B. E., Cassibba, R., & Costantini, A. (2006). The attachment script representation procedure in an Italian sample: Associations with Adult Attachment Interview scales and with maternal sensitivity. *Attachment and Human Development, 8*, 209–219.

Crawford, T. N., Livesley, W. J., Jang, K. L., Shaver, P. R., Cohen, P., & Ganiban, J. (2007). Insecure attachment and personality disorder: A twin study of adults. *European Journal of Personality, 21*, 191–208.

D'Cruz, P., & Bharat, S. (2001). Beyond joint and nuclear: The Indian family revisited. *Journal of Comparative Family Studies, 32*, 167–194.

Donnellan, M. B., Burt, S. A., Levendosky, A. A., & Klump, K. L. (2008). Genes, personality, and attachment in adults: A multivariate behavioral genetic analysis. *Personality and Social Psychology Bulletin, 34*, 3–16.

Feeney, J. A., & Noller, P. (1990). Attachment style as a predictor of adult romantic relationships. *Journal of Personality and Social Psychology, 58*, 281–291.

Feeney, J. A., Noller, P., & Hanrahan, M. (1994). Assessing adult attachment. In M. B. Sperling & W. H. Berman (Eds.), *Attachment in adults: Clinical and developmental perspectives* (pp. 128–152). New York: Guilford Press.

Fraley, R. C., & Shaver, P. R. (1998). Airport separations: A naturalistic study of adult attachment dynamics in separating couples. *Journal of Personality and Social Psychology, 75,* 1198–1212.

Fraley, R. C., & Shaver, P. R. (2000). Adult romantic attachment: Theoretical developments, emerging controversies, and unanswered questions. *Review of General Psychology, 4,* 132–154.

Fredrickson, B. L. (2001). The role of positive emotions in positive psychology: The broaden-and-build theory of positive emotions. *American Psychologist, 56,* 218–226.

Gillath, O., Mikulincer, M., Fitzsimons, G. M., Shaver, P. R., Schachner, D. A., & Bargh, J. A. (2006). Automatic activation of attachment-related goals. *Personality and Social Psychology Bulletin, 32,* 1375–1388.

Gillath, O., Shaver, P. R., Baek, J.-M., & Chun, D. S. (2008). Genetic correlates of adult attachment style. *Personality and Social Psychology Bulletin, 34,* 1396–1405.

Gillath, O., Shaver, P. R., Mikulincer, M., Nitzberg, R. A., Erez, A., & van IJzendoorn, M. H. (2005). Attachment, caregiving, and volunteering: Placing volunteerism in an attachment-theoretical framework. *Personal Relationships, 12,* 425–446.

Gore, M. S. (1965). The traditional Indian family. In M. F. Nimkoff (Ed.), *Comparative family systems* (pp. 209–231). Boston: Houghton Mifflin.

Grossmann, K. E., Grossmann, K., Huber, F., & Wartner, U. (1981). German children's behavior towards their mothers at 12 months and their fathers at 18 months in Ainsworth's Strange Situation. *International Journal of Behavioral Development, 4,* 157–181.

Gupta, G. R. (1992). Love, arranged marriage, and the Indian social structure. In J. J. Macionis & N. V. Benodraitis (Eds.), *Seeing ourselves: Classic, contemporary, and cross-cultural readings in sociology* (pp. 262–270). Upper Saddle River, NJ: Prentice Hall.

Hambleton, R. K. (1993). Translating achievement tests for use in cross-national studies. *European Journal of Psychological Assessment, 9,* 54–65.

Hambleton, R. K. (1994). Guidelines for adapting educational and psychological tests: Progress report. *European Journal of Psychological Assessment, 10,* 229–244.

Hambleton, R. K. (2005). Issues, designs, and technical guidelines for adapting tests into multiple languages and cultures. In R. K. Hambleton, P. F. Merenda, & C. D. Spielberger (Eds.), *Adapting educational and psychological tests for cross-cultural assessment* (pp. 3–38). Mahwah, NJ: Lawrence Erlbaum Associates.

Hazan, C., & Shaver, P. R. (1987). Romantic love conceptualized as an attachment process. *Journal of Personality and Social Psychology, 52,* 511–524.

Hazan, C., & Shaver, P. R. (1994). Attachment as an organizational framework for research on close relationships. *Psychological Inquiry, 5,* 1–22.

Hazan, C., & Zeifman, D. (1994). Sex and the psychological tether. In K. Bartholomew & D. Perlman (Eds.), *Advances in personal relationships: Attachment processes in adulthood* (Vol. 5, pp. 151–177). London: Jessica Kingsley.

Heinicke, C., & Westheimer, I. (1966). *Brief separations.* New York: International Universities Press.

Hesse, E. (2008). The Adult Attachment Interview: Protocol, method of analysis, and empirical studies. In J. Cassidy & P. R. Shaver (Eds.), *Handbook of attachment: Theory, research, and clinical applications* (2nd ed., pp. 552–598). New York: Guilford Press.

Hofstede, G. (2001). *Cultural consequences: Comparing values, behaviors, institutions, and organizations across the nations.* Thousand Oaks, CA: Sage.

Hui, C. H., & Triandis, H. C. (1985). Measurement in cross cultural psychology. *Journal of Cross-Cultural Psychology, 16,* 131–152.

Levine, R., Sato, S., Hashimoto, T., & Verma, J. (1995). Love and marriage in eleven cultures. *Journal of Cross-Cultural Psychology, 26*, 554–571.

Mace, D., & Mace, V. (1960). *Marriage: East and West*. New York: Doubleday.

Main, M., Kaplan, N., & Cassidy, J. (1985). Security in infancy, childhood, and adulthood: A move to the level of representation. *Monographs of the Society for Research in Child Development, 50*, 66–104.

Main, M., & Solomon, J. (1990). Procedures for identifying infants as disorganized/disoriented during the Ainsworth strange situation. In M. T. Greenberg, D. Cicchetti, & M. Cummings (Eds.), *Attachment in the preschool years: Theory, research, and intervention* (pp. 121–160). Chicago: University of Chicago Press.

Mallinckrodt, B., & Wang, C. C. (2004). Quantitative methods for verifying semantic equivalence of translated research instruments: A Chinese version of the Experiences in Close Relationship Scale. *Journal of Consulting Psychology, 51*, 368–379.

Medway, F. J., Davis, K. E., Cafferty, T. P., Chappell, K. D., & O'Hearn, R. E. (1995). Family disruption and adult attachment correlates of spouse and child reactions to separation and reunion due to Operation Desert Storm. *Journal of Social and Clinical Psychology, 14*, 97–118.

Mickelson, K. D., Kessler, R. C., & Shaver, P. R. (1997). Adult attachment in a nationally representative sample. *Journal of Personality and Social Psychology, 73*, 1092–1106.

Mikulincer, M., Birnbaum, G., Woddis, D., & Nachmias, O. (2000). Stress and accessibility of proximity-related thoughts: Exploring the normative and intraindividual components of attachment theory. *Journal of Personality and Social Psychology, 78*, 509–523.

Mikulincer, M., & Florian, V. (1998). The relationship between adult attachment styles and emotional and cognitive reactions to stressful events. In J. A. Simpson & W. S. Rholes (Eds.), *Attachment theory and close relationships* (pp. 143–165). New York: Guilford Press.

Mikulincer, M., & Florian, V. (2000). Exploring individual differences in reactions to mortality salience: Does attachment style regulate terror management mechanisms? *Journal of Personality and Social Psychology, 79*, 260–273.

Mikulincer, M., Florian, V., & Tolmacz, R. (1990). Attachment styles and fear of personal death: A case study of affect regulation. *Journal of Personality and Social Psychology, 58*, 273–280.

Mikulincer, M., Gillath, O., & Shaver, P. R. (2002). Activation of the attachment system in adulthood: Threat-related primes increase the accessibility of mental representations of attachment figures. *Journal of Personality and Social Psychology, 83*, 881–895.

Mikulincer, M., & Shaver, P. R. (2001). Attachment theory and intergroup bias: Evidence that priming the secure base schema attenuates negative reactions to out-groups. *Journal of Personality and Social Psychology, 81*, 97–115.

Mikulincer, M., & Shaver, P. R. (2007). *Attachment in adulthood: Structure, dynamics, and change*. New York: Guilford Press.

Mikulincer, M., Shaver, P. R., Cassidy, J., & Berant, E. (2009). Attachment-related defensive processes. In J. H. Obegi & E. Berant (Eds.), *Attachment theory and research in clinical work with adults* (pp. 17–45). New York: Guilford Press.

Moreira, J. M., Lind, W., Santos, M. J., Moreira, A. R., Gomes, M. J., Justo, J., … Faustino, M. (2006). Experiências em Relações Próximas, um questionário de avaliação das dimensões básicas dos estilos de vinculação nos adultos: Tradução e validação para a população Portuguesa. *Laboratório de Pscologia, 4*, 3–27.

Muñiz, J. (2000). Adaptación de los tests de unas culturas a otras. *Metodología de las Ciencias del Comportamiento, 2*, 129–149.

Muñiz, J., & Hambleton, R. K. (1996). Directrices para la traducción y adaptación de los tests. *Papeles del Psicólogo, 66*, 63–70.

Rothbaum, F., Weisz, J., Pott, M., Miyake, K., & Morelli, G. (2000). Attachment and culture: Security in the United States and Japan. *American Psychologist, 55,* 1093–1104.

Schmitt, D. E., Alcalay, L., Allensworth, M., Allik, J., Ault, L., Austers, I., … Zupanèiè, A. (2003). Are men universally more dismissing than women? Gender differences in romantic attachment across 62 cultural regions. *Personal Relationships, 10,* 307–331.

Schmitt, D. E., Alcalay, L., Allensworth, M., Allik, J., Ault, L., Austers, I., … Zupanèiè, A. (2004). Patterns and universals of adult romantic attachment across 62 cultural regions: Are models of self and of other pancultural constructs? *Journal of Cross-Cultural Psychology, 35,* 367–402.

Schwartz, S. (2009). Basic values: Motivating and inhibiting prosocial behavior. In M. Mikulincer & P. R. Shaver (Eds.), *Prosocial motives, emotions, and behavior* (pp. 221–241). Washington, DC: American Psychological Association.

Shaver, P. R., & Clark, C. L. (1994). The psychodynamics of adult romantic attachment. In J. M. Masling & R. F. Bornstein (Eds.), *Empirical perspectives on object relations theories* (pp. 105–156). Washington, DC: American Psychological Association.

Shaver, P. R., & Hazan, C. (1993). Adult romantic attachment: Theory and evidence. In D. Perlman & W. Jones (Eds.), *Advances in personal relationships* (Vol. 4, pp. 29–70). London: Jessica Kingsley.

Shaver, P. R., & Mikulincer, M. (2002). Attachment-related psychodynamics. *Attachment and Human Development, 4,* 133–161.

Shnabel, N., & Nadler, A. (2010). Perpetrators need acceptance and victims need power in order to reconcile: A needs-based model of reconciliation. In M. Mikulincer & P. R. Shaver (Eds.), *Prosocial motives, emotions, and behavior* (pp. 409–429). Washington, DC: American Psychological Association.

Simpson, J. A., & Belsky, J. (2008). Attachment theory within a modern evolutionary framework. In J. Cassidy & P. R. Shaver (Eds.), *Handbook of attachment: Theory, research, and clinical applications* (2nd ed., pp. 131–157). New York: Guilford Press.

Sireci, S. G., Patsula, L., & Hambleton, R. K. (2005). Statistical methods for identifying flaws in the test adaptation process. In R. K. Hambleton, P. F. Merenda, & S. D. Spielberger (Eds.), *Adapting educational and psychological tests for cross-cultural assessment* (pp. 93–115). Mahwah, NJ: Lawrence Erlbaum Associates.

Stern, J. (2003). *Terror in the name of God: Why religious militants kill.* New York: HarperCollins.

Tsagarakis, M., Kafetsios, K., & Stalikas, A. (2007). Reliability and validity of the Greek version of the Revised Experiences in Close Relationships measure of adult attachment. *European Journal of Psychological Assessment, 23,* 47–55.

van de Vijver, F. J. R., & Hambleton, R. K. (1996). Translating tests: Some practical guidelines. *European Psychologist, 1,* 89–99.

van de Vijver, F. J. R., & Poortinga, Y. H. (2005). Conceptual and methodological issues in adapting tests. In R. K. Hambleton, P. F. Merenda, & S. D. Spielberger (Eds.), *Adapting educational and psychological tests for cross-cultural assessment* (pp. 39–63). Mahwah, NJ: Lawrence Erlbaum Associates.

van IJzendoorn, M. H., Goosens, F. A., Kroonenberg, P. M., & Tavecchio, L. W. (1985). Dependent attachment: B-4 children in the Strange Situation. *Psychological Reports, 57,* 439–451.

van IJzendoorn, M. H., & Kroonenberg, P. M. (1988). Cross-cultural patterns of attachment: A meta-analysis of the strange situation. *Child Development, 59,* 147–156.

van IJzendoorn, M. H., & Sagi-Schwartz, A. (2008). Cross-cultural patterns of attachment: Universal and contextual dimensions. In J. Cassidy & P. R. Shaver (Eds.), *Handbook of attachment: Theory, research, and clinical applications* (2nd ed., pp. 880–905). New York: Guilford Press.

Vormbrock, J. K. (1993). Attachment theory as applied to wartime and job-related marital separation. *Psychological Bulletin, 114*, 122–144.

Waters, H. S., & Waters, E. (2006). The attachment working models concept: Among other things, we build script-like representations of secure base experiences. *Attachment and Human Development, 8*, 185–197.

Wei, M., Russell, D. W., Mallinckrodt, B., & Vogel, D. L. (2007). The Experiences in Close Relationships Scale (ECR)–Short Form: Reliability, validity, and factor structure. *Journal of Personality Assessment, 88*, 187–204.

Wei, M., Russell, D. W., Mallinckrodt, B., & Zakalik, R. A. (2004). Cultural equivalence of adult attachment across four ethnic groups: Factor structure, structured means, and associations with negative mood. *Journal of Counseling Psychology, 51*, 408–417.

Zhang, F., & Labouvie-Vief, G. (2004). Stability and fluctuation in adult attachment style over a 6-year period. *Attachment and Human Development, 6*, 419–437.

7

Cross-Cultural Adult Attachment Research
A Review of Methods and Measures

GÜNNUR KARAKURT, NİLÜFER KAFESCİOĞLU,
and MARGARET KEILEY*

CONTENTS

A substantial amount of cross-cultural research has been conducted on attachment over the last four decades. In this chapter, we will review the self-report measures of adult attachment, the Adult Attachment Interview, the Adult Attachment Q-sort, and narrative representations. Then, we will focus on some of the remaining methodological issues concerning cross-cultural studies on adult attachment.

---

* Karakurt and Kafescioğlu contributed equally to the chapter as first authors.

ATTACHMENT THEORY

Bowlby (1988) utilized an evolutionary perspective to account for the affectional ties between children and their primary caregivers. The evolutionary aspect of attachment theory implies that the sensory-behavioral attachment to a caregiver is universal in infants, regardless of the cultural context (van IJzendoorn & Sagi, 1999). Bowlby also suggested that the internal working models (IWMs) based on early secure-base behaviors with caregivers continue to influence subsequent relationships, including the emotional bonds between adult romantic partners (Hazan & Shaver, 1987).

Ainsworth's (1967) book on infant–mother attachment in Uganda was the first study of individual differences in attachment. Ainsworth observed the interactions of 28 infant–mother dyads and proposed different attachment patterns that might be present. With later observations in Baltimore, Ainsworth and Wittig (1969) created the Strange Situation Procedure based on Bowlby's work, showing that the presence of danger in the absence of an attachment figure elicited fear in infants. Ainsworth and Witting used separation from the caregiver to induce infants' anxiety in the Strange Situation. The procedures and measures developed after the Strange Situation assessment were mainly based on the results, comparisons, or improvements of the categories that were observed by Ainsworth.

Early studies on infants' attachment behaviors across different cultures revealed different distributions of attachment classifications in other countries when compared to the proportions in the United States. For example, a higher percentage of avoidant attachment was found in North Germany compared to the Baltimore sample (Grossmann, Grossmann, Spangler, Suess, & Unzner, 1985). In Israel (Sagi et al., 1985) and Japan (Miyake, Chen, & Campos, 1985) a larger number of infants were classified as insecure-anxious/ambivalent. Over time, three lines of research have emerged: one concentrating on the validity of the Strange Situation in different cultures, a second focusing more on the cultural differences in attachment behaviors across cultures, and a third focusing on expanding Bowlby's model of infant attachment to other developmental periods, including adulthood.

METHODOLOGIES IN CROSS-CULTURAL ADULT ATTACHMENT RESEARCH

Self-Report Measures

Hazan and Shaver's Adult Attachment Prototypes
Hazan and Shaver (1987) were first to expand attachment theory to adult romantic relationships. Adult attachment bonds were assumed to have the same functions as infant–caregiver bonds, which include proximity maintenance, separation protest, and a secure base (Weiss, 1991). They proposed that a peer, usually a sexual partner, is the primary attachment figure for adults (Hazan & Shaver, 1994). Prototypical adult attachment relationships involve the integration of three behavioral systems: attachment, caregiving, and sexual mating. Anxiety and distress at all ages cause proximity seeking, however, adult proximity seeking is also stimulated by protecting or offering comfort to the partner and engaging in sexual activity (Hazan & Shaver, 1994).

Hazan and Shaver (1987) developed three paragraphs describing individuals' general experiences in romantic relationships. They then asked participants which of these three descriptions (secure, avoidant, and anxious/ambivalent) best illustrated their experiences and behaviors in romantic relationships. These paragraphs characterize attachment prototypes as follows: (a) secure individuals find it relatively easy to get close to others and feel comfortable depending on others and others depending on them, (b) avoidant individuals are uncomfortable being close to others and find it difficult to trust others, and (c) anxious-ambivalent individuals have high fear of betrayal and worry about their partner abandoning them.

Their results and other studies using the same three-category measure indicated that individuals with different types of attachment styles were likely to report different experiences of romantic relationships. Securely attached individuals held positive mental representations of themselves and attachment figures. For example, they experienced happiness, friendship, and trust in their adult relationships, whereas avoidantly attached individuals experienced fear of closeness. Anxiously attached individuals, on the other hand, experienced a strong desire to be in almost constant contact with their adult romantic partner (Hazan & Shaver, 1987).

Hazan and Shaver's (1987) initial study was followed by a number of cross-cultural studies reporting replications and extensions of their findings. Most participants in the cultures that have been studied have been coded as securely attached. These cultures include United States (Hazan & Shaver, 1987), Australia (Feeney & Noller, 1990), Israel (Mikulincer, Florian, & Tolmacz, 1990), Canada (Baldwin & Fehr, 1995; Lapointe, Lussier, Sabourin, & Wright, 1994), and Portugal (Moreira et al., 1998). Two bilingual psychologists translated the scale into Hebrew. Factor structure of the Hebrew version yielded similar indices of factorial validity as did the English version (Mikulincer et al., 1990). In Canada, findings indicated that a substantial proportion of participants modified their classification over a relatively short period of time (ranging from one week to several months). Baldwin and Fehr (1995) were concerned that this lack of stability might be due to unreliable measurement. Another study in Canada, on the other hand, provided evidence for the convergent validity of the scale (Lapointe et al., 1994). With a Portuguese sample, Moreira et al. (1998) found similar results to those found in the United States, Canada, Australia, Israel, and Portugal. Moreira et al. highlighted a semantic equivalence instance in the translation of this scale to Portuguese; namely, the Portuguese word used for *depending* was also equivalent to *trusting*.

Researchers using this measure often called it a "conscious" measure of IWM (Mikulincer & Shaver, 2007). Due to its high face validity, brevity, and ease of administration, many social and personality researchers used this measure. However, shortly after the initial studies were conducted, limitations of this measure were noted: the measure asks only about the respondent's model of self and does not explicitly assess their model of the world (Collins & Read, 1990; Simpson, 1990).

Adult Attachment Questionnaire (AAQ)

Hazan and Shaver's (1987) adult attachment prototypes assume that individuals who fall into the same category are not different from each other. Early researchers converted these prototypes into more useful scales to overcome these limitations. By using the statements in Hazan and Shaver's paragraphs, Simpson (1990) created the 13 separate Likert-type items in the Adult Attachment Questionnaire (AAQ). The AAQ is different from Hazan and Shaver's prototypes in that it uses a two-dimensional representation for adult attachment, rather than a categorical representation. Simpson reported that these two dimensions represent two independent factors, attachment anxiety and avoidance, and both factors had adequate internal consistency ($\alpha > .70$).

A study conducted in France with the AAQ indicated similar indices of factorial validity, internal consistency, and stability as did the English version (Bouthillier, Tremblay, Hamelin, Julien, & Scherzer, 1996). Evaluation of the Chinese version concluded that AAQ is acceptably reliable and valid for assessing the attachment of Chinese adults (Li & Fu, 2001). Li and Fu (2001) found high internal consistency for the Chinese AAQ in a diverse sample of adolescents, parents, and clinical patients. However, the internal consistency they found was lower than the internal consistency in Western studies. Li and Fu also reported high discriminative power for the Chinese AAQ with clinical versus nonclinical participants as well as adults versus adolescents and significant correlations of attachment models between spouses.

Attachment Style Questionnaire (ASQ)

The ASQ is another self-report questionnaire developed by Feeney, Noller, and Hanrahan (1994) on a large sample of Australians to measure attachment with multiple items. The ASQ was constructed through factor-analytic procedures based on Bartholomew and Horowitz's (1991) four-category model of attachment. It has 40 items and five scales based on five factors that are related to attachment anxiety or attachment avoidance. The five factors of the ASQ include lack of confidence, discomfort with closeness, need for approval and confirmation, preoccupation with relationships, and viewing relationships as secondary. Respondents are asked to rate their feelings and behaviors in close relationships using a 6-point scale ranging from 1 (totally disagree) to 6 (totally agree).

Studies of the Italian (Fossati et al., 2003) and German versions (Hexel, 2004) of the ASQ have supported the five factors loading on attachment anxiety and avoidance. In the Italian study, the ASQ was used with a sample of clinical (psychiatric) and nonclinical participants. Inclusion of a clinical sample was a strength of this study since the ASQ had not been tested with such a sample before. Their nonclinical sample was also relatively diverse as it was not limited to college students (55%) but included workers (45%). Although the authors did not list cultural validation of the ASQ as one of their main goals, they explained how they ensured the Italian version was not different from the English version (e.g., back-translation, use of a professional translator). In the German study, the ASQ was again examined with both clinical and nonclinical participants. Factor analysis of the German version of the ASQ showed that it was congruent with its English version. Hexel suggested that the German version would be helpful in identifying attachment behaviors in German samples.

On the other hand, in a study with 356 French participants (Paquette, Bigras, & Parent, 2001) and in another with 69 Malaysian participants (Ng, Trusty, & Crawford, 2005) less supportive results for the cross-cultural validation of the ASQ were found. Paquette et al. (2001) found little validity for the five factors originally described by

Feeney et al. (1994). In this French study, two factors (avoidance of social relations and preoccupation with being loved) were found. In the Malaysian pilot study, Ng et al. (2005) studied the conceptual and linguistic equivalence of the ASQ and their findings did not support the use of the scale in this culture. Although the five scales of ASQ showed acceptable levels of reliability, there were problems with the reliability and validity of several items that influenced the overall validity of the measure. In terms of overall construct validity of ASQ, Ng et al. found some differences in interscale correlations when compared to Feeney et al.'s findings. A few participants also reported linguistic problems that might be due to differences in the cultural meanings of some words. These researchers suggested that the ASQ needs to be further studied with a larger and more representative Malaysian sample.

Adult Attachment Scale (AAS)   Collins and Read (1990) also independently converted Hazan and Shaver's (1987) adult attachment prototypes into an 18-item Likert scale, the Adult Attachment Scale (AAS). They extended it by including beliefs about the availability and responsiveness of attachment figures in times of need, and reactions to separation. Factor analysis of the AAS indicated a three-factor structure tapping into discomfort with closeness, discomfort with depending on others, and anxiety about being abandoned or not being lovable. Although several possible methods exist (e.g., cluster analyses) to reconstruct the attachment styles from these three dimensions, Collins and Read (1990) recommended using a dimensional rather than categorical method for examining attachment styles, thus not restricting method or theoretical variance.

Reliability, validity, and the factor structure of the AAS were found to be satisfactory and similar to previous findings when it was used with European American, Mexican American, and Asian Indian American samples (Rastogi & Wamples, 1999). When Rastogi and Wamples (1999) used this measure to investigate the dynamics of the mother–daughter relationship, they were challenged by the AAS's lack of sensitivity to the way that other cultures recognize closeness and dependency. However, the AAS was designed to measure discomfort with closeness, discomfort with depending on others, and anxiety about being abandoned or not being lovable in romantic relationships, rather than mother–daughter relationships, which might have contributed to this difficulty. The Dutch version of the AAS was found to have satisfactory internal consistency, convergent construct validity, and divergent validity by Heene, Buysse, and Van Oost (2000).

Four-Category Model: Relationship Questionnaire (RQ)   Bartholomew and Horowitz (1991) systematized Bowlby's conceptions of IWMs to explain adult attachment by combining model of self and model of the world. Both models were dichotomized as positive and negative. Model of self describes whether the self is seen as worthy or unworthy of love and support, and model of the world describes whether others are seen as trustworthy and available, or unreliable, cold, and rejecting.

Bartholomew and Horowitz's (1991) four-category model differs from Hazan and Shaver's (1987) typology in the categorization of avoidant attachment. In the four-category model, the avoidant category is split into two patterns: fearful avoidance and dismissing avoidance. Fearful avoidant attachment is characterized by a negative view of self and also a negative view of others. These individuals do not trust others and have difficulties in becoming close to them and relying on them. Dismissing avoidant attachment is characterized by a positive view of self but a negative view of others. These individuals minimize the importance of others but think highly of themselves. Preoccupied attachment, similar to the infant category of anxious ambivalent, is characterized by a negative view of self as unworthy and unlovable, but a positive view of others leading the preoccupied individuals to readily rely on others. Finally, secure attachment was characterized by a positive image of the self as loveable and worthy and a positive view of others as accepting and responsive.

The Relationship Questionnaire (RQ) involves four short paragraphs, each describing Bartholomew's four attachment prototypes (secure, preoccupied, fearful, and dismissing). Participants rate how much these paragraphs are like them on a 7-point Likert scale and also select the one paragraph that describes them best. Four continuous attachment ratings are used to compute scores for the mental models of self and the world (Griffin & Bartholomew, 1994b). The validity of the RQ was empirically supported by Griffin and Bartholomew (1994b).

The cross-cultural validity and the reliability of Bartholomew's four-category model, single (the RQ) and multi-item measures of attachment styles (the Relationship Scales Questionnaire [RSQ]) were examined by Sümer and Güngör (1999) in Turkey. Findings indicated that both measures had satisfactory levels of reliability, stability, and validity. The underlying dimensions of attachment were found to be associated with attachment-related outcome variables, such as trait anxiety and self-esteem. Results from a study comparing Turkish samples to U.S. samples revealed that the RQ and the RSQ were psychometrically compatible in these two cultures. Similar findings were observed in studies with Spanish samples (Alonso-Arbiol, Balluerka, & Shaver, 2007). The RQ and the RSQ were also examined in a Finnish sample with results supporting the four categories (Mannikko, 1999).

In another study, Schmitt and colleagues (2004) examined the cross-cultural validity of the RQ in 62 cultural regions including countries from North and South America; Western, Eastern, and Southern Europe; Middle East; Africa; Oceania; and South and East Asian regions in 30 different languages. Factor analytic findings demonstrated that the model of self and model of the world were supported as constructs of romantic attachment in almost all participating regions. This study also provided substantial cross-cultural evidence for the discriminant and convergent validity of the model of self (except for Brazil, Ethiopia, Bangladesh, Indonesia) and model of the world (except for Canada–French, Peru, Bolivia, Brazil, UK–England, France, Latvia, Lithuania, Jordan, Ethiopia, Tanzania, Zimbabwe, Fiji–Pacific Island, Bangladesh, Indonesia) showing that they were psychometrically valid within most cultures. However, these dimensions of the RQ did not factor the same way across all cultures to form the four categories of attachment outlined by Bartholomew and Horowitz (1991). Further analyses by Schmitt et al. also suggested that secure attachment was normative in 79% of cultures, whereas preoccupied attachment was more prevalent in East Asian cultures. Although the study included a broad range of cultural diversity among the countries, most of the samples were convenience samples of college students. This narrow sampling frame might make it difficult to draw conclusions about the use of the RQ in different cultures. Another limitation also identified by the authors was that all the translators in the study were not profession-als. That might have had an impact on the translation quality. Schmitt and colleagues (2004) suggested that their findings should be regarded as tentative until there are more cross-cultural studies with multi-item instruments of attachment.

Relationship Scales Questionnaire (RSQ)   Griffin and Bartholomew (1994a) developed the Relationship Scales Questionnaire (RSQ) by taking 30 items from Hazan and Shaver's (1987) adult attachment prototypes, Bartholomew and Horowitz's (1991) Relationship Questionnaire, and Collins and Read's (1990) Adult Attachment Scale. Participants are asked to rate these items on a 5-point scale to the extent each statement described their close relationships. The RSQ defines adult attachment patterns by the use of two underlying dimensions: the positivity of self (self worth) and the positivity of others (interpersonal trust). Griffin and Bartholomew (1994a) demonstrated the convergent and discrimi-nant validity of these two dimensions. Moderate to high test–retest reliability was also supported over an 8-month period ranging from .72 to .85 (Scharfe & Bartholomew, 1994). The RSQ indirectly measures the four attachment pat-terns: secure, fearful-avoidant, preoccupied, and dismissive avoidant.

In a Finnish sample results on the RSQ supported the four categories (Mannikko, 1999). Similarly, the RSQ was used successfully in German culture to understand the association between attachment and social relationships (Laireiter, Resch, & Sauer, 2007). It was also used to examine the effects of attachment patterns on the accul-turation process among Asian Indian mothers and their adult daughters (Singhal, 2005) as well as among Chinese Indonesians in the United States (Handojo, 2000). The Hungarian version of the RSQ was examined to determine the adaptability of the scale. However, the factor structure of the Hungarian and English versions of the RSQ were found not to be equivalent. These somewhat inconsistent results indicate that the RSQ is not always suitable in all cultures for measuring the four attachment categories (Csoka, Szabo, Safrany, Rochlitz, & Bodizs, 2007).

Experiences in Close Relationships (ECR)   In recent studies, underly-ing dimensions of attachment were reconceptualized. Brennan, Clark, and Shaver (1998) factor analyzed 14 attachment scales (60 subscales and 323 items) to obtain a two-factor solution containing 36 items, which they developed into a self-report measure of romantic attachment. They labeled these two factors as the anxiety and avoidance dimensions of attachment. These two major dimensions were then used to form the usual four attachment categories. Results indicated four distinct groups that were similar to Bartholomew and Horowitz's (1991) description of the secure, fearful, preoccupied, and dismissing categories.

Validation studies have shown that the factor structure of the Experiences in Close Relationships (ECR) survey was invariant across African, Asian, Hispanic, and White Americans (Wei, Russell, Mallinckrodt, & Zakalik, 2004). Studies have also further validated the translated versions of the ECR; for example, the Turkish ver-sion (Sümer, 2006; Sümer & Güngör, 1999), the Dutch version (Conradi, Gerlsma, van Duijn, & de Jonge, 2006), and the Chinese version (Wang & Mallinckrodt, 2006). A recent study using the ECR, the RQ, and the RSQ in Turkish culture indicated that attachment groups formed using the ECR anxiety and avoidance dimensions were more congruent as compared to attachment groups formed using the subscales of the RQ and the RSQ (Sümer, 2006).

To understand the semantic equivalence of the Chinese version of the ECR, Mallinckrodt and Wang (2004) used the dual-language, split-half (DLSH) method. They particularly searched for four kinds of quantitative evidence: (a) DLSH reliability, (b) internal reliability, (c) retest reliability, and (d) construct validity. Results indicated convincing evidence for the semantic equivalence of Chinese and English versions of the measure. However, the researchers also noted that construct equivalence of the anxiety subscale did not provide strong support. They also found that the standard for ideal attachment in Taiwan for both men and women involved significantly more anxiety and avoidance, as compared to Western beliefs about ideal attachment (Mallinckrodt & Wang, 2004; Wang & Mallinckrodt, 2006).

Fraley, Waller, and Brennan (2000) revised some of the items in the ECR to develop the ECR-Revised. Recent research indicated that the ECR-R Spanish version was useful for Spanish-speaking individuals and couples. However, this study also concluded that the translation of some items in the scale still needs improvement for better comprehensibility in Spanish (Alonso-Arbiol et al., 2007). Chinese, Greek, and German versions of the ECR-R have all demonstrated acceptable reliability and validity in assessing attachment (Jin & Tang, 2007; Neumann, Rohmann, & Bierhoff, 2007; Tsagarakis, Kafetsios, & Stalikas, 2007).

Adult Attachment Interview

The Adult Attachment Interview (AAI; George, Kaplan, & Main, 1985) is one of the first narrative measures used for assessing adult attachment representations. Before the development of the AAI, data for attachment research were primarily based on nonverbal behaviors observed in Ainsworth's Strange Situation Procedure (Hesse, 1999). Narrative measures enable researchers to assess behavioral and representational processes as they are reflected in language (Crowell, Fraley, & Shaver, 1999). The AAI is an hourlong, semistructured interview consisting of 18 questions regarding the person's life history. During the interview, the participants have ample time and opportunity to contradict themselves or support their descriptions of the experiences they have already mentioned (Main, 1996). More specifically, the participants are asked to describe their relationship with their parents in childhood; memories of their parents; parents' responses to the times when the person was upset, hurt, or ill; experiences with separation, rejection, discipline, and abuse; and the effects of these experiences on the person's development and personality. The interview is transcribed verbatim and coded and scored using a system that has been described in several publications (see Hesse, 1999). To learn about scoring, it is necessary to receive special training (Mikulincer & Shaver, 2007).

Main and Goldwyn (1985–1994) identified four adult attachment classifications through the use of AAI: (a) secure-autonomous, (b) dismissing, (c) preoccupied, and (d) unresolved-disorganized. Secure attachment is reflected in the coherent and collaborative nature of the person's narrative with sufficient elaboration regardless of the experiences described. In addition, the secure participants appear to value attachment relationships. Individuals with dismissing attachment tend to describe their parents in normalizing or positive terms, but are unable to support these descriptions with the memories they provide. In addition, they minimize the effect of negative experiences and tend to give short responses or lack memory of certain experiences. Preoccupied participants tend to give an angry account of their early experiences; they may also appear confused, passive, fearful, or overwhelmed. In addition, these individuals usually provide long and irrelevant responses and may use vague phrases. The interviews are classified as unresolved-disorganized when discussions of traumatic events such as loss or abuse show lapses in the monitoring of reasoning or discourse (Main, 1996).

Because the data collection and analyses of the AAI rely on verbal discourse, it poses a challenge for use in different cultures (Sagi et al., 1994). Bakermans-Kranenburg and van IJzendoorn (1993) demonstrated high reliability of the AAI classifications among 83 Dutch mothers over 2 months and across different interviewers. In another study Sagi et al. (1994) examined the stability and discriminant validity of the AAI in Hebrew with 59 Israeli students and found high interrater and test–retest reliability for the measure.

The AAI was recently used to examine Japanese mothers' attachment status in a study investigating the attachment distributions of mothers and their 6-year-old children (Behrens, Hesse, & Main, 2007). The interview was translated into Japanese by a professional translator and then back translated to check for its accuracy. The researchers reported some difficulties in coding the Japanese AAI due to differences between English and Japanese. For example, referring to a deceased person in the present tense has implications for the AAI coding, however it is perceived as an act of respect in the Japanese culture. Thus, the researchers studied Japanese tests to differentiate between normative or culturally sanctioned and nonnormative (i.e., lapses in speech) forms of this expression. Social desirability of vagueness and passivity in speech in Japanese culture (i.e., open-ended or incomplete sentences) also posed a difficulty in the AAI coding since vagueness and passivity of discourse is part of a scale in the AAI. However, the study coder was able to distinguish between normative incomplete sentences and nonnormative ones. The findings of this study suggested that Japanese mothers' AAI distribution yielded a higher proportion of secure and lower proportion of preoccupied classifications than the global norms. Similar to the findings of other studies the attachment security of Japanese mothers also appeared to transmit to their offspring.

In a study examining the predictive validity of different adult attachment measures with French-Canadian couples, the AAI classifications were predictive of proactive emotion regulation behaviors (Bouthillier, Julien, Dube, Belanger, & Hamelin, 2002). Study findings were consistent with other studies using the AAI: spouses with secure IWM endorsed higher levels of support-validation behaviors when compared to spouses with insecure IWM. In addition, men with secure IWM showed higher levels of communication expressiveness and lower levels of withdrawal compared to men with insecure IWM. Also couples with secure IWM showed higher levels of interactional synchrony and lower levels of dominance when compared to insecure ones.

Adult Attachment Q-Sort

The Adult Attachment Q-sort is an alternative scoring method for the AAI with an emphasis on the role of affect regulation in attachment representations (Kobak, 1993). With the Q-sort method, the interview transcript is scored according to a forced distribution of descriptors. Scoring results in two dimensions of emotional strategies along the continuum of security versus anxiety and deactivation versus hyperactivation. Deactivation refers to dismissing strategies and hyperactivation refers to preoccupied strategies (Crowell & Treboux, 1995). Sorting takes place among 100 Q-sort items between the individual's sort and a prototypic expert-based sort (Crowell et al., 1999). As in the original scoring of the AAI, security pertains to the coherence and collaboration within the interview and memories of attachment figures. The individual's sort is classified as secure on the basis of correlations with the secure prototype.

The Japanese adaptation of Kobak's (1993) attachment Q-sort method was used in a study with Japanese couples to examine the cultural variations in attachment (Onishi & Gjerde, 2002). In this study, the AAI was first modified in a pilot study to fit the Japanese culture and then administered to 39 Japanese couples. Onishi and Gjerde (2002) reported linguistic challenges for coding and scoring the AAI in Japanese similar to the ones mentioned by Behrens et al. (2007). For example, conversational cooperation, a determinant of attachment security in the AAI, appeared to be different in Japanese and English. Differences in expressions and use of long silences in Japanese, as well as exclusion of word spaces in written Japanese presented challenges with the AAI. Researchers used the Q-sort method adapted for use in Japan to overcome these challenges. They reported that using the Q-sort method provided the coders with the advantage of using their own cultural and linguistic understanding of the items. The researchers included two new items characteristic of Japanese families, rephrased some items to make them culturally more appropriate, and used back-translations to ensure cultural validation of the Japanese Q-sort method. Furthermore, a native Japanese speaker and a person who lived in Japan for an extended period of time defined the prototypical attachment patterns with high agreement, and Japanese psychology students blind to the purpose of the study and other measures evaluated the interviews. It is difficult to make generalizations of the use of the Japanese Q-sort method with this single study because the sample included only 39 young, middle-class, urban couples.

Narrative Representations

To assess secure-base representational knowledge, Waters, Rodrigues, and Ridgeway (1998) developed a scriptlike approach to study the mental representations of attachment. According to script theory, mental representations of events are generated in a temporal-causal manner with repeated experiences. Early researchers defined the script concept as a structure that describes appropriate series of events in a specific situation. Scripts also define actors, actions, and props needed to reach a goal, such as going to bed or going out for dinner (Nelson, 1986).

They can also be viewed as cognitive representations of routines or ways in which people usually approach errands and problems. Moreover, they provide cognitive tools to individuals to help them navigate their complex world (Nelson, 1986). The secure-base script provides a framework for understanding what has happened, the process for resolving difficulties, recovering, and returning back to normal. Scripted information about secure-base relationships better informs about key cognitive features underlying attachment representations and reflects typical experience in the domain of attachment relationships (Waters et al., 1998).

In the narrative representation procedure, word prompts are presented to the participants who have the chance to review the words then tell a story using those words. The generated stories are recorded. Scoring procedures include both content elaboration and prototypic scriptedness of the story completions (Waters et al., 1998). The generated stories are scored based on their content scriptedness, ranging from 1 (no secure-base script) to 7 (secure-base script). Validity of the script-base approach is being studied by various researchers (e.g., Guttmann-Steinmetz, Elliott, Steiner, & Waters, 2003).

Because the attachment script representation is one of the newest approaches to measuring attachment, only a handful of studies have used this protocol in non-English speaking cultures. Rodrigues-Doolabh, Zevallos, Turan, and Green (2003) examined the psychometric properties of the story score composites in diverse ethnic and cultural groups. These groups included samples from Peru, Switzerland, Turkey, United Arab Emirates, Zimbabwe, and the United States. Findings indicated that when presented with the word prompt list used with the initial American samples, mothers from these diverse groups created detailed and clear secure-base narratives. Results supported high internal consistency values across four secure-base stories in these samples. However, some of the word-prompt lists were modified to conform to cultural practices. This solution was successfully applied to the sample from the United Arab Emirates. Another study conducted by Vaughn et al. (2007) also indicated within-theme reliability (e.g., reliability within mother–child stories or adult–adult stories) in Colombia, Portugal, and the American cultures. However, the camping trip story theme did not apply in the Colombian sample; therefore, it was necessary to design a word-prompt list that was relevant to the Colombian cultural context. Furthermore, a more detailed study (Coppola, Vaughn, Cassibba, & Costantini, 2006) of the validation of attachment representations in an Italian sample provided findings similar to those that were reported by Rodrigues-Doolabh et al. (2003). Researchers can adapt narrative representation assessment with different sociocultural and linguistic groups as long as coders of the stories are adequately trained and narratives are accurately translated (Coppola et. al., 2006).

Measures Developed in Other Cultures

Influence of culture on adult attachment methodology can be observed in various ways. So far in our chapter, we have examined the localization and application of attachment measures that were mainly developed in North America. To understand the applicability of these measures in other cultures, researchers translated (and back-translated) these measures to languages other than English and examined their factor structures and psychometric properties with samples from different cultures. Furthermore, researchers around the world used these adapted measures to examine the attachment concepts in a number of individual and relationship processes. However, some researchers have developed instruments that were compatible with local culture. For example, Yoo (2004) formulated a mother–adult daughter attachment scale based on attachment concepts, such as emotional dependence, specificity, security, trust, proximity, and reciprocity as seen in Korean culture. This scale consists of 23 items that were developed by taking into account three existing attachment scales and in part by a review of Asian literature. Respondents are asked to rate the items using a 5-point scale ranging from strongly disagree to strongly agree. The mother–adult daughter attachment scale demonstrated satisfactory reliability and validity as an attachment instrument (Yoo, 2004).

To explore *emic* aspects of attachment, it is crucial to have indigenous measures/methodologies. These measures provide valuable information about attachment that is free from influence from Western cultures. Unfortunately, it is challenging to find additional studies focusing on attachment measures developed in other cultures because many of these studies are published in the native language of the particular culture. More connected international research communities might help to resolve this issue.

Clinical Implications

This chapter would be helpful to clinicians working with clients from different cultures especially in the assessment process of psychotherapy. Assessment is a vital part of therapy in identifying the client's problem; patterns of thinking, behaving, and feeling; clinical progress; and treatment outcomes. Clinicians can use an attachment theory framework and various methodologies described in this chapter to measure attachment security to objectify and organize their treatment efforts. Assessing clients' attachment security allows clinicians to better understand their experiences and presenting issues. Therapists could also use attachment information to conceptualize families' and couples' relationship problems within the attachment framework. With the use of instruments that have been validated culturally, clinicians could gain a culturally informed understanding of clients' attachment security/insecurity, which plays a significant role in their cognition, affect regulation, and interaction in close relationships. Because extant studies have revealed that some of the existing attachment measures lack cross-cultural validity, clinicians as well as researchers should only utilize measures that have demonstrated cross-cultural validity and reliability.

Case Example   A couple in their early 40s, married for more than 12 years and with two children, sought couples therapy. They both expressed unhappiness with their relationship for different reasons. The wife reported that she felt lonely in the relationship and described her husband as a workaholic. The husband agreed that he spent more time at his work than with his family but his main concern was jealousy. He had a hard time trusting his wife and especially feared that she might have had an affair with another man in the past. Even though the wife denied any affair, the husband did not believe her. The therapist suspected that attachment insecurity could play a significant role in the progress of therapy with this couple considering the husband's lack of trust and the wife's loneliness in the relationship. After searching for the right adult attachment measure to use in the cultural context with this couple, the therapist decided to administer the ECR-R as an assessment tool. The ECR-R has items such as "I often worry that my partner will not want to stay with me," "When my partner is out of sight, I worry that he or she might be interested in someone else," and "I find it difficult to allow myself to depend on my partner" (Fraley et al., 2000). After the administration of the measure, the therapist had a better understanding of the attachment positions of each partner and their affect regulation tendencies and experiences in the context of close intimate relationships. This understanding allowed the therapist to employ appropriate treatment strategies (e.g., emotionally focused couple therapy; Johnson, 2004) to help the couple to establish a more secure bond with each other.

CONCLUSION

Many measures have been developed to assess adult attachment. In this chapter, we reviewed interview, Q-sort, self-report, and projective narrative methods of assessing attachment in different cultures. Our review of these adult attachment measures and their use in different cultures revealed that some measures may be more appropriate or convenient to adapt to different cultures than others. Moreover, studies in different cultures with the same measure may show inconsistent findings in terms of cross-cultural psychometric invariance. This may be due to the differences between cultures or to different methodological strengths of the cross-cultural validation studies. Some of these measures may lack psychometric soundness. Cross-cultural validation of assessment tools pose certain challenges to researchers such as need for proper translation, and assessment of the equivalence or comparability of the test scores across cultures (see Ægisdottir, Gerstein, & Canel-Çinarbas, 2008, for a detailed description of the sources of bias in cross-cultural research including construct, method, and item bias). However, culturally valid instruments are needed to investigate adult attachment relationships beyond Western cultures and the responsible use of these measures in various cultures (Ng et al., 2005).

The interview techniques such as the AAI may pose certain difficulties for transcription, coding, and scoring in different languages. Meanings ascribed to expressions and verbal behaviors may change from culture to culture, which makes it difficult to adapt this method. It might be easier to adapt self-report measures, as has been done in many studies conducted with these measures in different cultures. A review of the self-report measures also showed that while most of them consistently revealed reliable and valid results in different cultures, some revealed different results across various cultures. For example, studies with the Italian and German versions of the ASQ revealed supportive results for the use of the measure in these cultures, whereas the studies with French and Malaysian versions showed less supportive findings. The use of narrative representations appeared promising in different cultures, but because this is a relatively new method, more research is needed to assess its validity and reliability in different cultures.

More studies and improvements are needed to develop better measures that are cross-culturally valid as well as indigenous measures that will account for culture-specific aspects of attachment. However, given the research findings and increasing cross-cultural collaborations among researchers, we have made a good start.

REFERENCES

Ægisdottir, S., Gerstein, L., & Canel-Çinarbas, D. (2008). Methodological issues in cross-cultural counseling research: Equivalence, bias and translations. *The Counseling Psychologist, 36,* 188–219.

Ainsworth, M. (1967). *Infancy in Uganda: Infant care and growth of love.* Baltimore: Johns Hopkins University Press.

Ainsworth, M., & Wittig, B. (1969). Attachment and the exploratory behavior of one year-olds in a strange situation. In B.M. Foss (Ed.), *Determinants of infant behavior* (Vol. 4, pp. 113–136). London: Methuen.

Alonso-Arbiol, I., Balleurka, N., & Shaver, P. (2007). A Spanish version of the Experiences in Close Relationships adult attachment questionnaire. *Personal Relationships, 14,* 45–63.

Bakermans-Kranenburg, M., & van IJzendoorn, M. (1993). A psychometric study of the adult attachment interview: Reliability and discriminant validity. *Developmental Psychology, 29,* 870–879.

Baldwin, M., & Fehr, B. (1995). On the instability of attachment style ratings. *Personal Relationships, 2,* 247–261.

Bartholomew, K., & Horowitz, L. (1991). Attachment styles among young adults: A test of a four-category model. *Journal of Personality and Social Psychology, 61,* 226–244.

Behrens, K., Hesse, E., & Main, M. (2007). Mothers' attachment status as determined by the adult attachment interview predicts their 6-year-olds' reunion responses: A study conducted in Japan. *Developmental Psychology, 43,* 1553–1567.

Bouthillier, D., Julien, D., Dube, M., Belanger, I., & Hamelin, M. (2002). Predictive validity of adult attachment measures in relation to emotion regulation behaviors in marital interactions. *Journal of Adult Development, 9,* 291–305.

Bouthillier, D., Tremblay, N., Hamelin, F., Julien, D., & Scherzer, P. (1996). French-Canadian translation of a questionnaire evaluating adult attachment styles. *Canadian Journal of Behavioural Science, 28,* 74–77.

Bowlby, J. (1988). *A secure base: Parent-child attachment and healthy human development.* New York: Basic Books.

Brennan, K., Clark, C., & Shaver, P. (1998). Self-report measurement of adult romantic attachment: An integrative overview. In J. Simpson & W. Rholes (Eds.), *Attachment theory and close relationships* (pp. 46–76). New York: Guilford Press.

Collins, N., & Read, S. (1990). Adult attachment, working models, and relationship quality in dating couples. *Journal of Personality and Social Psychology, 58,* 644–663.

Conradi, H., Gerlsma, C., van Duijn, M., & de Jonge, P. (2006). Internal and external validity of the Experiences in Close Relationships questionnaire in an American and two Dutch samples. *European Journal of Psychiatry, 20,* 258–269.

Coppola, G., Vaughn, B., Cassibba, R., & Costantini, A. (2006). The attachment script representation procedure in an Italian sample: Associations with AAI scales and with maternal sensitivity. *Attachment & Human Development, 8,* 209–219.

Crowell, J., Fraley, R., & Shaver, P. (1999). Measurement of individual differences in adolescent and adult attachment. In J. Cassidy & P. R. Shaver (Eds.), *Handbook of attachment: Theory, research, and clinical applications* (pp. 434–465). New York: Guilford Press.

Crowell, J., & Treboux, D. (1995). A review of adult attachment measures: Implications for theory and research. *Social Development, 4*, 294–327.

Csoka, S., Szabo, G., Safrany, E., Rochlitz, R., & Bodizs, R. (2007). An attempt to measure adult attachment: The Hungarian version of the relationship scale questionnaire. *Pszichologia: Az MTA Pszichologiai Intezetenek folyoirata, 27*, 333–355.

Feeney, J., & Noller. P. (1990). Attachment style as a predictor of adult romantic relationships. *Journal of Personality and Social Psychology, 58*, 281–291.

Feeney, J., Noller, P., & Hanrahan, M. (1994). Assessing adult attachment. In M. Sperling & W. Berman (Eds.), *Attachment in adults: Clinical and developmental perspectives* (pp. 128–152). New York: Guilford Press.

Fossati, A., Feeney, J., Donati, D., Donini, M., Novella, L., Bagnato M., ... Maffei, C. (2003). On the dimensionality of the Attachment Style Questionnaire in Italian clinical and nonclinical participants. *Journal of Social and Personal Relationships, 20*, 55–79.

Fraley, R., Waller, N., & Brennan, K. (2000). An item response theory analysis of self-report measures of adult attachment. *Journal of Personality & Social Psychology, 78*, 350–365.

George, C., Kaplan, N., & Main, M. (1985). *The Adult Attachment Interview*. Unpublished protocol, Department of Psychology, University of California, Berkeley.

Griffin, D., & Bartholomew, K. (1994a). The metaphysics of measurement: The case of adult attachment. In K. Bartholomew & D. Perlman (Eds.), *Advances in personal relationships: Attachment processes in adulthood* (pp. 17–52). London: Jessica Kingsley.

Griffin, D., & Bartholomew, K. (1994b). Models of the self and other: Fundamental dimensions underlying measures of adult attachment. *Journal of Personality and Social Psychology, 67*, 430–445.

Grossmann, K., Grossmann, K., Spangler, G., Suess, G., & Unzner, L. (1985). Maternal sensitivity and newborns' orientation responses as related to quality of attachment in Northern Germany. *Monographs of the Society for Research in Child Development, 50*, 233–256.

Guttmann-Steinmetz, S., Elliott, M., Steiner, M., & Waters, H. (2003). *Co-constructing script-like representations of early secure base experience*. Poster symposium presented at the biennial meeting of the Society for Research in Child Development, Tampa, Florida.

Handojo, V. (2000). Attachment styles, acculturation attitudes/behaviors, and stress among Chinese Indonesian immigrants in the United States. *Dissertation Abstracts International: Section A. Humanities and Social Sciences, 61*(4-B), 2271.

Hazan, C., & Shaver, P. (1987). Romantic love conceptualized as an attachment process. *Journal of Personality and Social Psychology, 52*, 511–524.

Hazan, C., & Shaver, P. (1994). Attachment as an organizational framework for research on close relationships. *Psychological Inquiry, 5*, 1–22.

Heene, E., Buysse, A., & Van Oost, P. (2000). Assessment of marital distress: Dutch adaptation and psychometric analysis of marital self report questionnaires. *Nederlands Tijdschrift voor de Psychologie en haar Grensgebieden, 55*, 203–216.

Hesse, E. (1999). The adult attachment interview: Historical and current perspectives. In J. Cassidy & P. R. Shaver (Eds.), *Handbook of attachment: Theory, research, and clinical applications* (pp. 395–433). New York: Guilford Press.

Hexel, M. (2004). Validation of the German version of the Attachment Style Questionnaire (ASQ) in participants with and without psychiatric diagnosis. *Zeitschrift fur Klinische Psychologie und Psychotherapie: Forschung und Praxis, 33*, 79–90.

Jin, Y., & Tang, R. (2007). A preliminary study on ECR-R for Chinese college students. *Chinese Journal of Clinical Psychology, 15*, 242–243.

Johnson, S. M. (2004). *The practice of emotionally focused couples therapy* (2nd ed.). New York: Brunner-Routledge.

Kobak, R. (1993). *The Attachment Interview Q-Set*. Unpublished manuscript, University of Delaware.

Laireiter, A., Resch, A., & Sauer, J. (2007). Attachment, social network, and social support in adolescents. *Zeitschrift fur Gesundheitspsychologie, 15*, 187–192.

Lapointe, G., Lussier, Y., Sabourin, S., & Wright, J. (1994). The nature and correlates of attachment in couple relationships. *Canadian Journal of Behavioural Science, 26*, 551–565.

Li, F., & Fu, G. (2001). A preliminary study on the Adult Attachment Questionnaire. *Chinese Journal of Clinical Psychology, 9*, 190–192.

Main, M. (1996). Introduction to the special section on attachment and psychopathology: 2. Overview of the field of attachment. *Journal of Consulting and Clinical Psychology, 64*, 237–243.

Main, M., & Goldwyn, R. (1985–1994). *Adult attachment scoring and classification system*. Unpublished manuscript, Department of Psychology, University of California, Berkeley.

Mallinckrodt, B., & Wang, C. (2004). Quantitative methods for verifying semantic equivalence of translated research instruments: A Chinese version of the experiences in close relationship scale. *Journal of Counseling Psychology, 51*, 368–379.

Mannikko, K. (1999). How to assess adult attachment. *Psykologia, 34*, 199–209.

Mikulincer, M., Florian, V., & Tolmacz, R. (1990). Attachment styles and fear of personal death: A case study of affect regulation. *Journal of Personality and Social Psychology, 58*, 273–280.

Mikulincer, M., & Shaver, P. (2007). *Attachment in adulthood: Structure, dynamics, and change*. New York: Guilford Press.

Miyake, K., Chen, S., & Campos, J. (1985). Infant temperament, mother's mode of interaction, and attachment in Japan. An interim report. *Monographs of the Society for Research in Child Development, 50*(1–2), 276–297.

Moreira, J., Bernardes, S., Andrez, M., Aguiar, P., Moleiro, C., & de Fatima, S. (1998). Social competence, personality and adult attachment style in a Portuguese sample. *Personality and Individual Differences, 24*, 565–570.

Nelson, K. (1986). *Event knowledge: Structure and function in development*. Hillsdale, NJ: Lawrence Erlbaum Associates.

Neumann, E., Rohmann, E., & Bierhoff, H. (2007). Development and validation of scales for measuring avoidance and anxiety in romantic relationships: The Bochurn Adult Attachment Questionnaire. *Diagnostica, 53*, 33–47.

Ng, K., Trusty, J., & Crawford, R. (2005). A cross-cultural validation of the Attachment Style Questionnaire: A Malaysian pilot study. *The Family Journal, 13*, 416–426.

Onishi, M., & Gjerde, P. (2002). Attachment strategies in Japanese urban middle-class couples: A cultural theme analysis of asymmetry in marital relationships. *Personal Relationships, 9*, 435–455.

Paquette, D., Bigras, M., & Parent, S. (2001). La validation du QSA et la prevalence des styles d'attachement adulte dans un echantillon francophone de Montreal. *Canadian Journal of Behavioural Science, 33*, 88–96.

Rastogi, M., & Wamples, K. (1999). Adult daughters' perceptions of the mother-daughter relationship: A cross-cultural comparison. *Family Relations, 48*, 327–336.

Rodrigues-Doolabh, L., Zevallos, A., Turan, B., & Green, K. (2003, April). *Attachment scripts across cultures: Further evidence for a universal secure-base script*. Poster symposium presented at the biennial meetings of the Society for Research in Child Development, Tampa, Florida.

Sagi, A., Lamb, M., Lewkowicz, K., Shoham, R., Dvir, R., & Estes, D. (1985). Security of infant-mother, father, and metapelet attachments among kibbutz-reared Israeli children. *Monographs of the Society for Research in Child Development, 50,* 257–275.

Sagi, A., van IJzendoorn, M., Scharf, M., Koren-Karie, N., Joels, T., & Mayseless, O. (1994). Stability and discriminant validity of the adult attachment interview: A psychometric study in young Israeli adults. *Developmental Psychology, 30,* 771–777.

Scharfe, E., & Bartholomew, K. (1994). Reliability and stability of adult attachment patterns. *Personal Relationships, 1,* 23–43.

Schmitt, D., Alcalay, L., Allensworth, M., Allik, J., Ault, L., Austers, I., … Zupanèiè, A. (2004). Patterns and universals of adult romantic attachment across 62 cultural regions: Are models of self and of other pancultural constructs? *Journal of Cross-Cultural Psychology, 35,* 367–402.

Simpson, J. A. (1990). Influence of attachment styles on romantic relationships. *Journal of Personality and Social Psychology, 59,* 971–980.

Singhal, S. (2005). Effects of attachment patterns on levels of acculturation and mother-daughter relationship among Asian Indian immigrant mothers and their adult daughters. *Dissertation Abstracts International: Section A. Humanities and Social Sciences, 66,* 1788.

Sümer, N. (2006). Categorical and dimensional comparison of the adult attachment measures. *Turk Psikoloji Dergisi, 21,* 1–22.

Sümer, N., & Güngör, D. (1999). Yetişkin bağlanma stilleri ölçeklerinin Türk örneklemi üzerinde değerlendirmesi ve kültürlerarası bir karşılaştırma. *Türk Psikoloji Dergisi, 14,* 71–106.

Tsagarakis, M., Kafetsios, K., & Stalikas, A. (2007). Reliability and validity of the Greek version of the Revised Experiences in Close Relationships measure of adult attachment. *European Journal of Psychological Assessment, 23,* 47–55.

van IJzendoorn, M. H., & Sagi, A. (1999). Cross-cultural patterns of attachment: Universal and contextual dimensions. In J. Cassidy & P. Shaver (Eds.), *Handbook of attachment: Theory, research, and clinical applications* (pp. 713–734). New York: Guilford Press.

Vaughn, B., Coppola, G., Verissimo, M., Monteiro L., Santos, A. J., Posada, G., … Korth, B. (2007). The quality of maternal secure-base scripts predicts children's secure-base behavior at home in three sociocultural groups. *International Journal of Behavioral Development, 31,* 65–76.

Wang, C., & Mallinckrodt, B. S. (2006). Differences between Taiwanese and U.S. cultural beliefs about ideal adult attachment. *Journal of Counseling Psychology, 53,* 192–204.

Waters, H. S., Rodrigues, L. M., & Ridgeway, D. (1998). Cognitive underpinnings of narrative attachment assessment. *Journal of Experimental Child Psychology, 71,* 211–234.

Wei, M., Russell, D. W., Mallinckrodt, B., & Zakalik, R. A. (2004). Cultural equivalence of adult attachment across four ethnic groups: Factor structure, structure means, and associations with negative mood. *Journal of Counseling Psychology, 51,* 408–417.

Weiss, R. (1991). The attachment bond in childhood and adulthood. In C. Parkes (Ed.), *Attachment across the life cycle* (pp. 66–76). London: Tavistock/Routledge.

Yoo, G. (2004). Attachment relationships between Korean young adult daughters and their mothers. *Journal of Comparative Studies, 35,* 21–32.

8

The Utility of the Adult Attachment Interview in the United States
Effects of Ethnicity and Age Group

AMY MORGENSTERN and CAROL M. MAGAI

CONTENTS

*T*he Adult Attachment Interview (AAI; Main & Goldwyn, 1984) has added considerably to the adult attachment literature, particularly in regard to longitudinal and intergenerational patterns of attachment. Although the validity of the interview in various cultures and non-English languages has been explored (Bakermans-Kranenburg & van IJzendoorn, 1993; Sagi et. al., 1994; van IJzendoorn et al., 1997; see also Karakurt, Kafescioğlu, & Keiley, Chapter 7, this volume), its utility with nonnormative samples continues to raise some concerns. In this chapter, we review a brief history of the interview itself. We then explore lessons learned from our own research (Morgenstern, 2008), in which we administered AAIs to approximately 150 elderly participants from three urban-dwelling ethnic groups in the United States: Caucasian, African American, and African Caribbean.

We review concerns about the applicability of some of the interview questions and the validity of individual rating scales with these participants. We then examine the differential impact of ethnicity on attachment classification in our research as compared to previous findings using self-report measures of adult attachment. Clinical implications and possibilities for future research are considered.

THE ADULT ATTACHMENT INTERVIEW

The past three decades have reflected an influx of interest in patterns of attachment among adults, resulting in the development of a variety of methods of assessing and conceptualizing the phenomenon. Consequently, many attachment researchers have developed self-report measures based on adult attachment and its influence on romantic and interpersonal behaviors (Bartholomew & Horowitz, 1991; Brennan, Clark, & Shaver, 1998; Crowell, Fraley, & Shaver, 1999; Hazan & Shaver, 1987). Although the adult attachment literature has supported the empirical value of these measures, their scope is limited in that they measure social behaviors in relationships rather than assessing unconscious processes or states of mind with respect to attachment (Bernier & Dozier, 2002; DeHaas, Bakermans-Kranenburg, & van IJzendoorn, 2001; Jacobvitz, Curran, & Moller, 2002; Robson & Savage, 2001). Many critics of the self-report measures have supported the use of the AAI (Main & Goldwyn, 1984), a semistructured 18-item interview that reflects an attempt to move away from simple behavioral reports and toward the level of representation (Main, Kaplan, & Cassidy, 1985).

The methodical coding system that accompanies the AAI balances two separate variables: the speaker's reported attachment experiences, which are primarily content based, and the manner in which he or she describes these experiences within the context of the interview. These are scored with a series of discriminatory scales, the *experience* scales and the *state of mind* scales, respectively. Individual scale scores are derived in a bottom-up manner based on a very close reading of transcribed adult attachment interviews. Subsequent to the scoring of each scale, the interview is analyzed again, and a top-down analysis is conducted to assign the interview to a specific attachment category.

The experience scales of the AAI coding system reflect the degree to which early attachment relationships with caregivers may be characterized by a variety of early attachment experiences, including but not limited to caregivers' love, rejection, role reversal, and neglect. To some extent, each of these is correlated with different attachment patterns in adulthood. For example, high loving scores for early attachment relationships are usually associated with secure states of mind with respect to attachment in adulthood, whereas high rejecting scores tend to be correlated with dismissing states of mind and high role reversal scores are generally linked with preoccupied states of mind.

Although early attachment experiences exert undeniable influence on later attachment patterns, one of the basic tenets of the AAI is that adult attachment patterns cannot be assessed based on this information alone (Hesse, 1999; Main & Goldwyn, 1984). Rather, these experiences must be understood within the context of the state of mind of the individual reporting them. It is this notion that resulted in the development of the second set of AAI scales—those measuring state of mind with respect to attachment (Hesse, 1999; Main & Goldwyn, 1984). These scales examine the participant's language and ability to provide a coherent, consistent, and integrated account of early experiences, particularly when the attachment system is activated. Unlike the experience scales, which are content based, the state of mind scales are believed to reflect participants' internal working models, indicating both conscious and unconscious rules for organizing and utilizing attachment information (Main et al., 1985). Like the experience scales, each state of mind scale is associated with a different style of attachment.

As a general rule, secure, or autonomous, state of mind is associated with early experiences of loving and valuing relationships with caregivers (Main & Goldwyn, 1984). The interviews of securely attached individuals tend to be objective and consistent in the recounting of past attachment experiences (Hesse, 1999). Although the content of the attachment histories are not necessarily positive in nature, secure participants are able to reflect upon them in a thoughtful and coherent manner.

The interviews of people with dismissing attachment generally contain reports of early experiences of harsh and rejecting attachment figures, and are typically associated with a tendency to idealize caregivers without providing much concrete support, and to minimize, dismiss, or underreport early attachment experiences (Hesse, 1999).

Preoccupied, or entangled, interviews usually contain themes of caregivers who were overly involved or intrusive in the participants' lives, thereby making themselves the object of the majority of participants' early attention and care (Main & Goldwyn, 1984). In adulthood, these participants continue to be preoccupied with early attachment experiences, so much so that it is reflected in their capacity for coherent conversation (Hesse, 1999).

Another category is the unresolved or disorganized group. These interviews are linked with experiences of loss or abuse about which participants continue to demonstrate significant lapses in awareness or reasoning. Protocols with high scores in this area are often marked by long silences or illogical thinking specifically in response to participants' recollection of early traumatic experiences (Hesse, 1999).

The AAI has proven to be a valuable addition to attachment theory and research. Perhaps most significantly, it has been demonstrated that states of mind with respect to attachment, as measured by the interview, are consistently correlated with secure-base behavior of interviewees (Hesse, 1999; Waters, Crowell, Elliott, Corcoran, & Trebeaux, 2002) as well as of the Strange Situation behaviors of interviewees' children (Hesse, 1999). Thus, research in this domain has added considerably to the overall adult attachment literature, particularly that related to developmental patterns of attachment and the intergenerational effects of attachment patterns.

CROSS-CULTURAL RESEARCH USING THE ADULT ATTACHMENT INTERVIEW

The AAI was initially developed with a nonclinical sample of middle-class parents to examine potential correlations between their attachment patterns and the Strange Situation behaviors of their young children (Hesse, 1999). Although the utility of the interview as a research tool with psychiatric (Fonagy, Steele, Steele, Moran, & Higgitt, 1991; Hesse, 1999; Lee, Polan, & Ward, 1998) and forensic populations (van IJzendoorn et al., 1997) has had a growing place in the research, there is still relatively little information regarding its applicability to culturally diverse samples. In fact, while cross-cultural research has examined the impact of race, ethnicity, and culture on self-reported adult attachment patterns (Mickelson, Kessler, & Shaver, 1997, and the validity of the measure in various non–English speaking countries has been established [see Karakurt et al., Chapter 7, this volume, for a review]), an extensive review of the literature has yielded virtually no empirical exploration of the impact of ethnicity on AAI outcomes per se. Research exploring the impact of age on the AAI is similarly sparse.

In our own research examining adult attachment patterns among elderly adults ranging in age from 72 to 99 years (Morgenstern, 2008), we conducted AAIs with three ethnic groups: African Americans, Caucasians, and Afro-Caribbeans, all of whom were dwelling in Brooklyn, New York. Our research yielded two distinct but overlapping issues that deserve further attention: those related to the applicability of the interview questions to various demographic groups and those having to do with inherent differences in adult attachment patterns among these groups. The following is an analysis of each of these matters in turn. The first section is a review of the outstanding concerns regarding the validity of the AAI with an ethnically diverse population, focusing particularly on the individual experience and state of mind scales. This is followed by an examination of the inherent differences in adult attachment patterns among the various ethnic groups, focusing on global attachment categories as determined by the AAI.

ADULT ATTACHMENT INTERVIEW SCALES: CONCERNS WITH VALIDITY

As mentioned, the AAI coding system evaluates individual scales of experience and state of mind with respect to attachment, as well as overall categorical state of mind classification (Main et al., 1985). The scales are coded in a bottom-up manner that adheres closely to the content and style of the narrative of the interview, whereas the categories are determined in a more top-down or gestalt manner, which is therefore less vulnerable to individual anomalies of content or narrative style. Although the distribution of attachment categories among the participants in our research (Morgenstern, 2008) paralleled categorical distributions reflected in past studies with younger and less ethnically diverse participants (Roisman, Fraley, & Belsky, 2007; van IJzendoorn & Bakermans-Kranenburg, 1996), the individual experience and state of mind scales were not quite as impervious to the impact of participants' demographic differences relative to the initial norming sample. These results suggested that a number of methodological concerns must be considered during the coding of these scales with ethnically diverse samples (Morgenstern, 2008). Though the following discussion has been divided into two sections, ethnicity and birth cohort, there is a great deal of overlap among these concepts and each is best understood within the context of the other.

Ethnicity

Our research (Morgenstern, 2008) highlighted a number of distinct methodological concerns with the applicability of the AAI to a Caribbean sample. The first of these is related to the relative difficulty that many of the Caribbean participants had answering the interview question, "Who would you say raised you?" and their subsequent struggle to identify one or two primary caregivers to discuss during the interview. Many of the Caribbean-born participants in our research were raised in large households by extended family, including aunts, uncles, and grandparents, and they frequently moved from home to home during childhood. Their parents were sometimes members of these households and sometimes not. For example, when asked who she considered to be her primary caretaker in childhood, one Caribbean woman responded, "Really hard to say. All these women. My aunt's husband died when I was 13. So it was only women in the family and they raised me. My grandmother, my grandaunt, and my two aunts."

Whereas many of the fathers of our Caribbean participants were active members of their households, others had fathers who lived nearby but were minimally involved in their lives (Morgenstern, 2008). Caribbean participants' relationships with their mothers were frequently more complicated; some of their mothers lived in the community and even in the participants' own homes, but were still not considered by participants to be primary caregivers. For example, one participant who identified her grandmother as her primary caregiver failed to disclose that her mother lived "400 yards away" until she was probed for this information. Other participants had mothers who lived and worked in neighboring towns or villages during the week and who returned home only on weekends, but whom they did consider to be their primary caregivers. One such participant stated, "My mother was a person that worked with some White people in another district. So when she goes she never come home until, like, every other weekend. So, that's where I grew up with my grandmother, and my aunt and my uncle."

Relative to other ethnic groups, Caribbean participants in our study were more likely to move from one household to another during childhood (Morgenstern, 2008). Often, they were sent to live with wealthier family members, such as one participant who reported that "in those days, Trinidad was much more advanced than St. Vincent so [my parents] left us to grow there … and we get our education in Trinidad." This participant saw his parents on vacations, but considered his aunt and uncle to be his primary caregivers. Another was sent to live with "rich White people" because her mother could not afford to raise her.

Early cross-cultural research with children from multiple caregiver homes has suggested that there is no correlation between number of caregivers and security of attachment (van IJzendoorn & Sagi, 1999). In fact, research examining child rearing practices in Uganda (Ainsworth, 1967), Kenya (Kermoian & Leiderman, 1986), and kibbutz practice in Israel (Rabin & Beit-Hallahmi, 1982) has demonstrated that a child's attachment security is based more on continuity and quality of caretaker–child interaction than upon number of caregivers per se (van IJzendoorn & Sagi, 1999). Nonetheless, key attachment figures must be identified during the

AAI to ascertain that that the interview taps into early attachment experiences (Turton, McGauley, Marin-Avellan, & Hughes, 2001). Unfortunately, our own research (Morgenstern, 2008) indicated that even the best-trained interviewers were not able to isolate key attachment figures with a Caribbean population. In fact, many of the participants in this study had difficulty understanding the very notion of having only one or two primary caregivers. Unfortunately, repeating the same interview questions too many times can weaken the overall impact of the interviewer's ability to surprise the unconscious, thereby limiting the number of caregivers an interviewer can ask about in each AAI (Turton et al., 2001). Therefore, we suggest training interviewers to do their best to select two to three primary caregivers about whom to query and to query about important attachment figures as they come up.

Cohort Effects

In her research examining life-span changes in adult attachment patterns, Magai (2001, 2008; Magai et al., 2001) demonstrated the impact of birth cohort effects on the distribution of self-reported patterns of attachment behaviors among older participants. She highlighted the way in which the distribution of attachment style within a generation is directly impacted by the specific historical challenges and rules of child rearing to which that generation was exposed. Thus we can expect systematic differences in attachment patterns between participants from earlier birth cohorts and those from later ones. Later research has suggested the presence of a birth cohort effect on AAI outcomes as well (Morgenstern, 2008). This effect is important in that it speaks to the applicability of the AAI questions and coding system to older and ethnically diverse participants.

Among the U.S.-born participants in our research (Morgenstern, 2008), the potential for birth cohort effects was due in part to their having been raised during the period of the Great Depression. Participants who were fortunate enough to have caregivers who were employed often described rarely seeing them as a result of their working 15-hour days. Many recalled seeing their fathers for a few hours only when they brought their suppers to them at work or on weekends. One such participant stated that her "relationship [with my father] was just on Sunday, that's the only time I saw him. To me it wasn't strange because I thought that's how other relationships were." Others' parents were physically present, often as a result of being out of work, but deeply depressed and thus emotionally unavailable. One participant, in describing her mother's transition from a wealthy family in Poland to a life of relative poverty in the United States stated that her mother "would go into depression … she was very unhappy. She had a very unhappy life." Another explained her mother's tendency to scold her by stating, "She was depressed about a lot of things, it was hard times and sometimes she would just, you know, not meaning to but would let it out to me … she was always worried where the next dollar was coming from, so she would skimp and save."

Similar factors seemed to come into play for the Caribbean participants, who also suffered from severe poverty and deprivation during their childhoods. As one Trinidadian man described, "Christmas time, I can remember, things was bad with us. It was war days. Germany was fighting England, and things wasn't coming from England to Trinidad, cause we were owned by the British government. So … y'know the family had to go to the place to get rice and stuff. Everything was rationed in them there. But my mother, she'd grow her food, and she'd dig it up and she'd cook for us." As mentioned, many of the Caribbean participants' parents were forced to leave their communities to find work elsewhere, and the study participants were often sent away to live with wealthier friends or family members.

Participants in our study (Morgenstern, 2008) were also reared during the rise of the influence of Watsonian behaviorism, which emphasized the value of withholding affection from children (Magai, 2008). Interestingly, about a third of the participants across ethnic groups answered no in response to the query regarding whether their caregivers held them when they were upset, hurt, or ill. This statistic is quite remarkable even among individuals raised within the Watsonian era. As one participant stated, "Well they would talk to you, but nobody was coming to hold you or mother you like they do with these kids now."

Similar to the high proportion of emotionally withholding caregivers among our participants is that of corporal punishment at the hands of early caregivers (Morgenstern, 2008). Although physical punishments were described by all three ethnic groups, the Caribbean participants were particularly likely to tell stories of whoopings and licks in childhood. Although the standards dictated by the AAI coding system would likely identify these transcripts as including situations of trauma and abuse (and thereby require that they be coded for degree of resolution of such experiences), this style of parenting was apparently culturally normative during the period in which our participants were raised, thereby making it difficult to score according to the dictums of the AAI coding system. For example, one participant stated, "My relationship with my mother was very good. She loved me a lot. (Mhmm.) She cared for me, cause she send me to school in the daytime … to come back from school was a problem. I come home late I get licks. That's just how it went."

Parental preoccupation with financial concerns, their relative inability to provide gifts or other material things to their children, and their tendency to be emotionally withholding and to participate in corporal punishment, certainly sets the early experiences of these participants apart from those of the younger, presumably more affluent, norming sample on which the AAI was initially developed. For this reason, the applicability of the AAI coding system to an older, ethnically diverse group is called into question. A strict reading of the AAI coding manual dictates that the experiences associated with security of attachment are related to the consistent availability and attention of caregivers. Such child-centered parenting was simply not as possible for the caregivers of participants growing up during the period in which our participants were raised. Adherence to the manual would therefore result in lower loving scores and higher scores of neglect and rejection relative to a younger and presumably more affluent sample. Furthermore, high idealizing scores might also be assigned to interviews in which caregivers were remembered kindly in spite of their apparent abuse or neglect. Such designations all contribute to insecure attachment categorization and are likely to result in high loadings on the preoccupied and dismissing categories.

It is recommended, then, that the AAIs of nonnormative samples be examined within the context of the environment in which the participant's early attachment experiences occurred. This may require educating oneself about the history and the norms of the time to determine which types of rearing techniques were typical and which were not. Nonetheless, it is difficult, if not impossible, to maintain validity in working with populations to whom the coding system does not directly apply, and this is certainly a matter for future investigation.

ADULT ATTACHMENT INTERVIEW SCALES: DISCUSSION

As mentioned, the AAI coding system was developed and normed with a culturally circumscribed sample, and although subsequent studies have explored its applicability to various other demographic groups (Bakermans-Kranenburg & van IJzendoorn, 1993; Sagi et al., 1994; van IJzendoorn et al., 1997), this research is far from inclusive. Our own research (Morgenstern, 2008) indicated a number of important factors for which the individual scales could not sufficiently account, including the failure of older participants to recall specific accounts of childhood, the impact of extreme poverty and deprivation on early childhood experiences, and the effect of distinct but culturally normative environmental factors, such as general parenting style, on current state of mind. It is likely that future work with different populations will result in the identification of other complications regarding the applicability of the scales to diverse groups.

Perhaps most relevant to this discussion, we contend that the structure of the interview generally fails to detect many nonnormative early attachment experiences, particularly those distinctly related to ethnicity and culture. Specifically, the AAI does not universally pick up on subtle but nevertheless essential differences in early caregiving experiences, above and beyond one's relationships with one or two primary caregivers. For example, the interview does not necessarily elicit an exploration of one's relationships with other potential members of his or her caregiving community, including extended family members, teachers, religious leaders, or neighbors. While proponents of the interview would certainly point out that the interview leaves room for discussion of such caregivers (i.e., "Were there any other adults with whom you were close, like parents, as a child?"), our research suggests that it is just as likely that such relationships might be overlooked completely (Morgenstern, 2008).

Similarly, the coding system draws a rather direct line between certain caregiver behaviors and the degree to which the caregiver is assessed as loving, and we contend that this association may be much more complex within certain cultures. For example, the narratives of our Caribbean participants imply that a loving parent may actually utilize more corporal punishment, not less. Similarly, among our participants whose parents worked through the Great Depression, the loving ones might indeed have been those who worked 70-hour weeks, not necessarily those who were home in time for dinner.

It is arguable that to criticize the AAI in this manner is perhaps to miss the point of the interview's main purpose. The AAI is not a comprehensive assessment of all early interpersonal experiences, but rather an attempt at activating one's attachment system to analyze the current state of mind within that context (Main et al., 1985). From this perspective, one might contend that to make the interview any longer or more inclusive would only take away its power to surprise the unconscious, thereby diminishing its overall effectiveness. However, we assert that the alternative is to overlook the many unconventional attachment experiences that are specific to cultures other than that of the initial norming sample, a notion that is certainly supported by our own research (Morgenstern, 2008). There is clearly no simple solution to this matter but it is an issue that requires further attention if we are to continue to administer the AAI to ethnically diverse groups.

ADULT ATTACHMENT INTERVIEW CATEGORICAL ANALYSIS: DIFFERENTIAL DISTRIBUTION AMONG ETHNIC GROUPS

While the potential impact of age, ethnic group, and birth cohort on individual state of mind scales is related to issues of methodological validity, the statistical relation between ethnic group and attachment category reflects an inherent differential distribution of attachment representations among ethnic groups. This is supported by the literature, which indicates that the distribution of self-reported attachment behavior varies by culture (Magai, 2008; van IJzendoorn & Kroonenberg, 1988) and by local values and norms (Magai, 2008; Weisner, 2005), and that the environments and cultures in which these participants' early attachment experiences occurred undoubtedly impact their current attachment patterns.

In our own research with older adults (Morgenstern, 2008), ethnicity and attachment category were found to be directly related in some rather surprising ways. First, African American participants were significantly more likely to be in the unresolved category than would otherwise be expected. Importantly, an anecdotal review of the content of the interviews of these participants did not reflect any more loss or trauma among this group compared to Caucasian or Caribbean participants, nor were there any significant differences between any of the three groups' experience scales. Therefore, this overrepresentation of unresolved attachment among the African Americans seems to speak to differential degrees of resilience to loss among ethnic groups.

Whereas some past researchers have failed to find a correlation between ethnic group and resilience to loss (Bonanno, Moskowitz, Papa, & Folkman, 2005; Carr, 2004), others have found that compared to Caucasians, African Americans maintain a stronger continuing bond with the deceased other, more pronounced grief in response to the loss of kin beyond the immediate family, and higher levels of complicated grief symptoms overall, particularly when they do not seek outside support (Laurie & Neimeyer, 2008). These latter results are consistent with the outcome of our research and suggest that African Americans may simply be more vulnerable to prolonged mourning than other ethnic groups.

There are various reasons for such differences in resilience. Bowlby (1980) suggested that chronic mourning is related to a lack of responsiveness on the part of early caregivers, which ultimately heightens individuals' sensitivity regarding loss and abandonment. This is supported by past research which has suggested that mothers' security can serve as a protective factor against passing their own unresolved attachment patterns along to their children (Schuengel, Bakermans-Kranenburg, & van IJzendoorn, 1997; van IJzendoorn & Bakermans-Kranenburg, 2008). Although the content of the interviews in the study gave no indication that the African American participants' caregivers were any less responsive than those of other ethnic groups, an analysis of the content of the interviews suggests that African Americans were more likely to be raised in single-parent households relative to the other two ethnic groups. Therefore, it is possible that there are subtle experiences associated with being raised by a single parent that add a new and as yet undiscovered dimension to the AAI coding system. Future research must further explore this association.

Our research (Morgenstern, 2008) also indicated that Caucasian participants represented a higher proportion of dismissing attachment than would be expected. This outcome is in direct opposition to much of the adult attachment research using self-report methods, which suggests that respondents classified as secure are more likely to be Caucasian, whereas those classified as avoidant are more likely to be Black or Other, and those classified as anxious are more likely to be Black or Hispanic (Mickelson et al., 1997). As described earlier, the content of the interviews in our study did reflect a great deal of experience with harsh and withholding caregivers. An anecdotal analysis of the interviews in our study gave no indication that such early experiences were more prevalent among the Caucasian participants than the members of the other two ethnic groups, nor were there any differences in experience scales among ethnic groups. However, it is imperative to keep in mind that one of the primary characteristics of a dismissing narrative is that negative caregiving experiences are minimized or thoroughly disregarded. Therefore, it is quite possible that the Caucasian participants in the study did in fact have more such experiences and simply failed to report them due specifically to their dismissing style.

If the overrepresentation of dismissing attachment among our Caucasian participants cannot be explained by differential early experiences, it is reasonable to consider that the Caucasian group was somehow more vulnerable to the impact of such experiences (Morgenstern, 2008). Our research indicates that one potential reason for this is that relative to the other ethnic groups, Caucasian participants may have had fewer people available to serve as surrogate attachment figures when their caregivers were not emotionally or physically available. An anecdotal review of the interviews in our study suggests that the Caribbean and African American participants had more siblings and larger extended families than the Caucasian participants did. Therefore, these two groups were likely to seek and develop secure relationships with surrogate attachment figures within their extended family network, thus resulting in the development of secure attachment patterns. Caucasian participants, on the other hand, seemed not to have had such opportunities.

ADULT ATTACHMENT INTERVIEW CATEGORICAL ANALYSIS: DISCUSSION

In many ways, our analysis of the impact of ethnicity on attachment category leaves us with more questions than answers. While our own research indicated a distinct effect of ethnic group on attachment category (Morgenstern, 2008), the absence of prior research examining the relation between ethnicity and AAI categories prohibits a thorough understanding of the degree to which this effect is limited to this study or if it is universal, as well as of the degree to which birth cohort plays a role in this association.

Our findings that African American participants were more likely than expected to be unresolved with respect to attachment, while the Caucasian participants were more likely than expected to be dismissive, were not only inconsistent with research using self-report measures of attachment but were also virtually impossible to explain with simple content analysis of the interviews. While future analysis necessitates a detailed exploration of differential childhood experiences and current characteristics that moderate the relationship between ethnicity and attachment category, we also believe that a more culturally conscious version of the interview would inherently answer some of the questions raised in our research.

SUMMARY

Taken as a whole, there are a number of methodological concerns regarding the applicability of the AAI coding system in its current form to demographically diverse populations. Although the results of our research (Morgenstern, 2008) examining the relation between ethnic group and attachment category led to more questions than answers, it certainly paved the way for future research in this domain. An increased understanding of the vulnerability of different ethnic groups to various early attachment experiences would certainly shed light on culturally appropriate research in this domain as well as more sensitive and suitable clinical interventions.

The effects of age, ethnicity, and birth cohort on the coding of the individual scales of the AAI reflect the importance of taking cultural context into account when analyzing the transcripts of nonnormative samples. However, it bears repetition that our concerns about the validity of the measure are related primarily to the individual experience scales and state of mind scales of the interview and that our research (Morgenstern, 2008) indicated no reason to question the validity of the overall categorical classification of attachment style. In fact, we suspect that the reason that most research using the AAI relies primarily on categorical analysis and not on an examination of individual scales is that the former tends to be much more impervious to individual anomalies, thereby retaining its validity across nonnormative samples.

Although the applicability of the AAI scales to nonnormative samples is primarily a matter of methodological concern, it brings to light some of the theoretical questions underlying the development of the coding system itself. For example, do individuals with atypical early attachment experiences follow similar developmental trajectories to those with one or two primary caregivers and minimal early trauma? Are those who minimize early attachment experiences in old age necessarily as dismissing as those who do so when they are younger? Must adult attachment theorists develop an entirely new set of AAI coding rules for these populations, or can the current system be adapted to suit the variety of early experiences reflected in their interviews? Future research must certainly continue to parse out methodological concerns from theoretical ones before tackling these and similar questions. Until then, it is imperative that future AAI coders be trained to deal with issues related to demographic and cultural differences to ensure that the system is being properly utilized and to maintain reliability across AAI studies.

Until recently, the Adult Attachment Interview has served primarily as a research measure; however, its utility as a clinical tool has recently been explored. Steele and Steele (2008) explore 10 distinct ways to use the AAI clinically, including facilitating the therapeutic alliance, uncovering trauma that may otherwise have remained hidden, and assessing level of reflective function. While we believe that the AAI has such use in all clinical settings, our research indicates that clinicians working with nonnormative samples should proceed with caution. The inherent assumptions with which AAI operates as a research tool would certainly impact its utility in a clinical setting as well. Such assumptions would certainly harm the therapeutic relationship rather than cultivate it. Therefore, we encourage the use of the AAI as a clinical tool with the same cultural awareness that we hope all clinicians bring to the treatment room in any context.

Whatever one's actual early attachment experiences, results of the AAI shed light on his current frame of mind regarding these experiences. Therefore, results of AAI research such as ours has notable use in a clinical setting, in that they permit a window into the individual's autobiographical memory and for the opportunity to help him to develop and modify this personal story through therapeutic intervention (van IJzendoorn & Bakermans-Kranenburg, 2008). Therefore, our results regarding ethnic distinctions in attachment patterns have clinical implications that exist on a global level, even when individual administrations of the AAI are not feasible.

It is our sincere hope that future work with the AAI will aim at incorporating a more thorough analysis of the impact of various and nonnormative early attachment experiences on later attachment patterns to expand our understanding of the differential impact of culture in this regard. In this way, its utility as a research tool and a method of clinical assessment will be increasingly sensitive and valid across demographic groups.

REFERENCES

Ainsworth, M. S. (1967). *Infancy in Uganda: Infant care and the growth of love.* Baltimore: Johns Hopkins University Press.
Bakermans-Kranenburg, M. J., & van IJzendoorn, M. H. (1993). A psychometric study of the adult attachment interview: Reliability and discriminant validity. *Developmental Psychology, 29,* 870–879.
Bartholomew, K., & Horowitz, L. (1991). Attachment styles among young adults: A test of a four-category model. *Journal of Personality and Social Psychology, 61,* 226–244.
Bernier, A., & Dozier, M. (2002). Assessing adult attachment: Empirical sophistication and conceptual bases. *Attachment and Human Development, 4,* 171–179.
Bonanno, G. A., Moskowitz, J. T., Papa, A., & Folkman, S. (2005). Resilience to loss in bereaved spouses, bereaved parents, and bereaved gay men. *Journal of Personality and Social Psychology, 88,* 827–843.
Bowlby, J. (1980). *Attachment and loss: Volume 3. Loss: Sadness and depression.* New York: Basic Books.

Brennan, K. A., Clark, C. L., & Shaver, P. R. (1998). Self-report measurement of adult attachment: An integrative overview. In J. A. Simpson & W. S. Rholes (Eds.), *Attachment theory and close relationships* (pp. 46–76). New York: Guilford Press.

Carr, D. (2004). Black/white differences in psychological adjustment to spousal loss among older adults. *Research on Aging, 26,* 591–622.

Crowell, J. A., Fraley, R. C., & Shaver, P. R. (1999). Measurement of individual differences in adolescent and adult attachment. In J. Cassidy & P. R. Shaver (Eds.), *Handbook of Attachment: Theory, research, and clinical applications* (pp. 434–465). New York: Guilford Press.

DeHaas, M. A., Bakermans-Kranenburg, M. J., & van IJzendoorn, M. H. (2001). The adult attachment interview and questionnaires for attachment style, temperament, and memories of parental behavior. *The Journal of Genetic Psychology, 155,* 471–486.

Fonagy, P., Steele, M., Steele, H., Moran, G., & Higgitt, A. C. (1991). The capacity for understanding mental states: The reflective self in parent and child and its significance for security of attachment. *Infant Mental Health Journal, 12,* 201–218.

Fonagy, P., & Target, M. (1997). Attachment and reflective function: Their role in self-organization. *Development and Psychopathology, 9,* 679–700.

Hazan, C., & Shaver, P. (1987). Romantic love conceptualized as an attachment process. *Journal of Personality and Social Psychology, 52,* 511–524.

Hesse, E. (1999). The adult attachment interview: Historical and current perspectives. In J. Cassidy & P. R. Shaver (Eds.), *Handbook of attachment: Theory, research, and clinical applications* (pp. 295–433). New York: Guilford Press.

Jacobovitz, D., Curran, M., & Moller, N. (2002). Measurement of adult attachment: The place of self-report and interview methodologies. *Attachment and Human Development, 4,* 207–215.

Kermoian, R., & Leiderman, P. H. (1986). Infant attachment to mother and child caretaker in an East African community. *International Journal of Behavioral Development, 9,* 455–469.

Laurie, A., & Neimeyer, R. A. (2008). African Americans in bereavement: Grief as a function of ethnicity. *Omega: Journal of Death and Dying, 57,* 173–193.

Lee, S. S., Polan, H. J., & Ward, M. J. (1998). *Internal working models of attachment and psychopathology in a non-clinical sample of adult women.* Manuscript submitted for publication.

Magai, C. (2001). Emotions over the lifespan. In J. E. Birren & K. W. Schaie (Eds.), *Handbook of the psychology of aging* (5th ed., pp. 310–344). San Diego, CA: Academic Press.

Magai, C. (2008). *Attachment in middle and later life.* In J. Cassidy & P. R. Shaver (Eds.), *Handbook of attachment: Theory, research, and clinical applications* (2nd ed., pp. 532–551). New York: Guildford Press.

Magai, C., Cohen, C., Milburn, N., Thorpe, B., McPherson, R., & Peralta, D. (2001). Attachment styles in older European American and African American adults. *The Journals of Gerontology Series B: Psychological Sciences and Social Sciences 56,* S28–S35.

Main, M., & Goldwyn, R. (1984). *Adult attachment scoring and classification system.* Unpublished manuscript, University of California at Berkeley.

Main, M., Kaplan, N., & Cassidy, J. (1985). Security in infancy, childhood and adulthood: A move to the level of representation. In I. Bretherton & E. Waters (Eds.), Growing points in attachment theory and research. *Monographs of the Society for Research in Child Development, 50*(Serial No. 209), 66–104.

Mickelson, K. D., Kessler, R. C., & Shaver, P. R. (1997). Adult attachment in a nationally representative sample. *Journal of Personality and Social Psychology, 73,* 1092–1106.

Morgenstern, A. (2008). *Saving grace: The role of attachment to God in the relation between adult attachment patterns and bereavement among the elderly* (Doctoral dissertation). Long Island University, Brooklyn, New York.

Rabin, A. I., & Beit-Hallahmi, B. (1982). *Twenty years later*. New York: Springer.

Robson, K., & Savage, A. (2001). Assessing adult attachment: Interview course with Patricia Crittenden, November 2000–April 2001. *Child Abuse Review, 10*, 440–447.

Roisman, G. I., Fraley, R. C., & Belsky, J. (2007). A taxometric study of the Adult Attachment Interview. *Developmental Psychology, 43*, 675–686.

Sagi, A., van IJzendoorn, M. H., Scharf, M., Koren-Karie, N., Joels, T., & Mayseless, O. (1994). Stability and discriminant validity of the adult attachment interview: A psychometric study in young Israeli adults. *Developmental Psychology, 30*, 771–777.

Schuengel, C., Bakermans-Kranenburg, M. J., & van IJzendoorn, M. H. (1997). Frightening maternal behavior linking unresolved loss and disorganized infant attachment. *Journal of Consulting and Clinical Psychology, 67*, 54–63.

Steele, H., & Steele, M. (2008). Ten clinical uses of the Adult Attachment Interview. In H. Steele & M Steele (Eds.), *Clinical applications of the Adult Attachment Interview.* (pp. 3–30). New York: Guildford Press.

Turton, P., McGauley, G., Marin-Avellan, L., & Hughes, P. (2001). The Adult Attachment Interview: Rating and classification problems posed by non-normative samples. *Attachment and Human Development, 3*, 284–303.

van IJzendoorn, M. H., & Bakermans-Kranenburg, M. J. (1996). Attachment representations in mothers, fathers, adolescents, and clinical groups: A meta-analytic search for normative data. *Journal of Consulting and Clinical Psychology, 64*, 8–21.

van IJzendoorn, M. H., & Bakermans-Kranenburg, M. J. (2008). The distribution of adult attachment representations in clinical groups: A meta-analytic search for patterns of attachment in 105 AAI studies. In H. Steele & M. Steele (Eds.), *Clinical applications of the Adult Attachment Interview* (pp. 69–96). New York: Guildford Press.

van IJzendoorn, M. H., Feldbrugge, J. T., Derks, F. C., De Ruiter, C., Verhagen, M. F., Philipse, M. S., … Riksen-Walraven, J. M. A. (1997). Attachment representations of personality disordered criminal offenders. *American Journal for Orthopsychiatry, 67*, 449–459.

van IJzendoorn, M. H., & Kroonenberg, P. M. (1988). Cross-cultural patterns of attachment: A meta-analysis of the Strange Situation. *Child Development, 5*, 147–156.

van IJzendoorn, M. H., & Sagi, A. (1999). Cross-cultural patterns of attachment: Universal and contextual dimensions. In J. Cassidy & P. R. Shaver (Eds.), *Handbook of attachment: Theory, research, and clinical applications* (pp. 713–734). New York: Guilford Press.

Waters, E., Crowell, J., Elliott, M., Corcoran, D., & Trebeaux, D. (2002). Bowlby's secure base theory and the social/personality psychology of attachment styles: Work(s) in progress. *Attachment and Human Development, 4*, 230–242.

Weisner, T. S. (2005). Attachment as a cultural and ecological problem with pluralistic solutions. *Human Development, 48*, 89–94.

Section *III*

Child–Caregiver Attachment

9

A Cross-Cultural Study of Attachment in Korea and the United States
Infant and Maternal Behavior During the Strange Situation

MI KYOUNG JIN, DEBORAH JACOBVITZ, and NANCY HAZEN*

CONTENTS

---

* This chapter is based on the first author's dissertation (Jin, 2005), "A Cross-Cultural Study of Infant Attachment Patterns in Korea and the U.S.: Associations Among Infant Temperament, Maternal Personality, Separation Anxiety, and Depression."

A ccording to attachment theory, infant–mother attachment is a universal evolutionary adaptation that helps ensure the survival of the helpless infant (Bowlby, 1982). All human infants are presumed to have evolved attachment behaviors that serve to elicit the mother's care and keep her in proximity. The mother thus serves as a secure base from which the infant, feeling protected and secure, may explore. Studies of infant attachment have been conducted worldwide to examine the extent to which patterns of mother–infant attachment behaviors are universal across cultures and to provide evidence for the cross-cultural validity of the Strange Situation as a measure of mother–infant attachment security. Most of these studies have replicated Ainsworth's (Ainsworth, Blehar, Waters, & Wall, 1978) pioneering research using the Strange Situation Procedure in finding similar distributions of secure, insecure-avoidant, and insecure-resistant attachment patterns across cultures (van IJzendoorn & Sagi-Schwartz, 2008). However, attachment researchers using the Strange Situation in two East Asian cultures, Japan and Indonesia, have found an overrepresentation of resistant attachment and little or no avoidant attachment (Takahashi, 1986; Zevalkink, Riksen-Walraven, & Van Lieshout, 1999). Some researchers have argued that these findings cast doubt on the cross-cultural validity of the Strange Situation and even on the basic universal premises of attachment theory. Further studies on East Asian cultures that have similar patterns of infant caregiving as Japan and Indonesia are needed to clarify the extent to which cultural differences in infant caregiving might affect patterns of infant–mother attachment. Thus, the goal of the present study is to extend cross-cultural research on attachment by examining attachment patterns in Korea, another East Asian culture that has infant caregiving customs similar to Japan and Indonesia.

ATTACHMENT AND CAREGIVING PATTERNS IN JAPAN AND INDONESIA

One of the earliest cross-cultural studies on attachment was conducted on 60 mother–infant dyads in Sapporo, Japan (Miyake, Chen, & Campos, 1985; Nakagawa, Lamb, & Miyaki, 1992; Takahashi, 1986). In this sample, 68% of the infants were classified as securely attached, 32% as resistant, and 0% as avoidant. A meta-analysis of 2,000 infant–parent dyads assessed in the Strange Situation, including several studies done in non-Western cultures, found a global distribution of 65% secure infants, 14% resistant, and 21% avoidant (van IJzendoorn & Kroonenberg, 1988). Even though a normative proportion of secure infants were found in Sapporo, the striking divergence in the distribution of avoidant versus resistant attachment has led to considerable controversy concerning the cross-cultural validity of the Strange Situation and the universality of some core assumptions of attachment theory. Takahashi (1986, 1990) suggested that the Strange Situation Procedure probably underestimated the number of secure and avoidant children in Sapporo, and overestimated the number of resistant children, and was therefore invalid in Japanese culture. She argued that this was because Japanese customs surrounding infant care are very different from Western infant caregiving practices. In traditional Japanese culture, children under 7 are regarded as personifications of God and are treated very indulgently. A deep emotional bond between mother and infant is culturally valued, and infants are almost constantly within mother's reach. Cosleeping and cobathing of mother and infant is common, and mothers rarely leave their infants, even with the father or grandparent. Infants unaccustomed to separations from their mothers are thus likely to become more distressed by the separations in the Strange Situations. Thus, Takahashi (1990) argued that the Strange Situation Procedure is inherently invalid in Japan because it is too stressful for Japanese infants. However, the separations in the Sapporo study were at least two minutes long, following Ainsworth's original instructions (Ainsworth et al., 1978). Since infants experiencing extreme distress for that long may be very difficult to comfort even if secure, Main (1990) later changed the maximum suggested separation time for infants showing distress to 10 to 30 seconds, with Ainsworth's agreement.

Even more challenging to attachment theory, the Sapporo studies of infant–mother attachment have been cited as evidence that key assumptions of attachment theory are not universal, and that attachment researchers have been culturally biased in applying Western ideas about optimal patterns of infant care and infant security to other cultures. Specifically, Rothbaum and his colleagues argue that mother–infant relationships in Japan may be more accurately characterized by the concept of *amae* than by secure-base attachment (Rothbaum, Weisz, Pott, Miyake, & Morelli, 2000). According to Doi (1992), a Japanese psychiatrist, *amae* means, "to depend and presume upon another's love or bask in another's indulgence" (p. 8). Thus, Rothbaum et al. (2000) assert that in Japan, the attachment system promotes dependence rather than exploration, and that "attachment theorists would be hard pressed to explain the many similarities between descriptions of insecure-ambivalent behaviors and behaviors widely regarded as adaptive in Japan (i.e., characteristic of *amae*)" (p. 1100), including infant passivity and extreme expressions of dependency such as clinging.

On the other side of the controversy, Behrens (2004) argued that in Japanese society, *amae* is actually a multifaceted concept with both positive and negative dimensions. She further argues that insecure-resistant infant behaviors, including those expressing a high degree of dependency or passivity, are viewed as similar only to those particular types of *amae* behavior that are viewed by Japanese mothers as negative. In support of her arguments, Behrens cites research by Vereijken, Riksen-Walraven, and Van Lieshout (1997) in which Japanese mothers performed a criterion sort of their view of the ideal child using a Japanese version of the Attachment Q-sort. These sorts revealed that behaviors that Japanese mothers rated as *amae* were related to dependency rather than secure attachment, and behaviors they rated as consistent with secure attachment as more characteristic of the ideal infant secure-base behaviors than dependent behaviors.

Further support for Behrens's view that attachment patterns in Japan share the universal characteristic of secure-base dynamics was obtained in a recent replication and extension of the Sapporo study by Behrens, Main, and Hesse (2007). In this study, 43 mother–child dyads from Sapporo were observed in Main and Cassidy's (1988) reunion procedure for assessing security of attachment in 6-year-olds.

The distribution of three-way attachment classifications (with disorganized attachment forced into its best-fitting alternative) was 70% secure, 23% avoidant, and 7% ambivalent; very similar to the global distribution found by van IJzendoorn and Kroonenberg (1988). Behrens et al. (2007) cautioned that although Strange Situation classifications found in infancy have been found to predict those at age 6, it is nonetheless possible that mother–infant attachment classifications in infancy might have been more similar to those found in the earlier Sapporo study in which no avoidant infants and an overrepresentation of resistant infants were found.

The only other study examining the Strange Situation in an East Asian culture in which mother–infant closeness is highly valued and separations are rare was done in West Java, Indonesia (Zevalkink et al., 1999). In this culture, infants are almost never separated from the mother; they are carried next to the mother's body on a *sledang* (carrying cloth) for the first year, are breast fed on demand until age 2 or 3 years, and cosleep with the mother for the first 4 years. Also, as in Japan, mothers in West Java anticipate their infants' needs and respond quickly to any signs of distress. In this small sample of 46 mother–child pairs, the distribution of attachment classifications was similar to that in the original Sapporo study: 57% secure, 33% resistant, and only 7% avoidant. In this study, unlike the Sapporo study, separations in the Strange Situations were curtailed quickly when infants became distressed, so it is less likely that the relatively high proportions of resistant attachment were due to children who were really secure or avoidant becoming so distressed that they could not be comforted. In addition, secure infant attachment was predicted by higher levels of maternal support, suggesting that secure attachment was assessed accurately even though proportions of avoidant and resistant insecurity differed from global distributions. Clearly, further studies of mother–infant attachment patterns in East Asian cultures are needed to clarify the reasons for these discrepant findings.

INFANT CAREGIVING CUSTOMS AND ATTACHMENT IN KOREA

Korea is another East Asian culture in which a very close relationship between mother and infant is culturally valued and infants are rarely separated from the mother. Korean society emphasizes interpersonal harmony in child rearing and values the interrelatedness of mother and child (Triandis, 2001). Kim and Choi (1994) suggested that two key concepts are critical to understanding maternal behavior in Korea: *T'aekyo* and *maternal dew*. *T'aekyo* is a set of guidelines for pregnant women about what they should do and should not do during pregnancy based on the long-standing Korean belief that a mother's experiences during pregnancy have a direct effect on the baby (Yu, 1984). For example, *t'aekyo* guidelines recommend that mothers should eat only good-looking fruits, see pretty babies, and have positive thoughts if they want to produce a pretty baby. Maternal dew refers to an intrinsic bond between mothers and their children that is perceived to have special healing powers promoting psychological well-being and ameliorating physical ailments (Kim & Choi, 1994). For example, Korean mothers believe that if they touch their baby's stomach when it is upset, their baby will feel better. Both concepts illustrate how the baby is thought to be one with the mother. Although Korean mothers have increasingly come to consider concepts such as *t'aekyo* and maternal dew as unscientific, they are nonetheless reluctant to break old customs.

Concepts of oneness and relatedness between mother and child explain the generosity and devotion that Korean mothers give to their children (Kim & Choi, 1994). Korean mothers are very flexible and not discipline-oriented with infants. For example, they do not emphasize weaning or toilet training, but instead emphasize more empathic understanding of children's desires. As such, Korean mothers regard their children as an extension of themselves and give continuous support for children throughout their lives. Thus, we expect insecure patterns of attachment in Korea to be more resistant than avoidant, because Korean mothers are culturally more likely to show enmeshed overinvolvement or interference toward their infants rather than rejection.

However, we also expect secure infant attachment to be the norm in Korea, and we expect that attachment serves the same universal secure base function in Korea that it does in Western cultures. Attachment theorists have argued that although the secure base function of attachment is universal, cultural variations in the behaviors that infants and their caregivers may use to meet this function should vary in accordance with cultural values and practices surrounding infant caregiving (van IJzendoorn & Sagi-Schwartz, 2008). For example, to the extent that very close infant–mother relationships are culturally valued and mother–infant separations are rare, infants might learn to count on their mothers to maintain proximity. Thus, they may show greater distress due to separation than infants who are more accustomed to separations from the mother, but they may also have learned to count on the mother to be the one to maintain proximity.

GOALS AND PREDICTIONS OF THE PRESENT STUDY

The present study has two primary goals. The first goal is to examine whether the distribution of Strange Situation classifications in Taegu, Korea, replicates those reported in Japan and Indonesia. Based upon the cultural similarities in caregiving in these three cultures, we predict that insecure mother–infant dyads in Taegu, like those in Japan and Indonesia, will be less likely than insecure mother–infant dyads in a U.S. sample (obtained in Austin, Texas) and in the global distribution to be classified as anxious-avoidant and more likely to be classified as anxious-resistant. Nonetheless, we also expected the proportion of secure infants in Korea to be similar to the proportion of secure infants in Austin and in the global distribution. In addition to examining the distribution of three-way classifications (secure, resistant, and disorganized), we also examined four-way classifications to explore whether the percentage of infants classified as disorganized in Taegu would be similar to that found in the United States (approximately 15%; True, Pisani, & Oumar, 2001).

The second goal of the present study was to explore whether mother–infant caregiving behavior in the Strange Situations differs in predictable ways for the

Taegu and Austin samples. We expected to find culturally based differences in infant attachment behaviors and maternal caregiving styles between the two cultures, despite equal proportions of securely attached dyads. For example, we expected that within each attachment classification, Taegu mothers would stay closer to their infants than would Austin mothers. Taegu mothers were expected to maintain proximity to their infants even when the infants are not distressed, whereas Austin mothers were expected to be more likely to move away from their infants once they are settled so as to encourage their exploration and autonomy. We also expected that within each attachment classification, Taegu infants would become more distressed by separations. Thus, secure Taegu mothers should be more likely to stay close to their infants than secure Austin mothers, and secure Taegu babies should become more distressed than secure Austin babies, but nonetheless, the secure Taegu babies were expected to be equally successful as Austin babies in gaining access to the mother and in being comforted as a result.

METHOD

Participants

Taegu Sample   Mothers and their 12- to 15-month-olds ($N = 87$) residing in Taegu, one of the five largest cities in South Korea, were recruited with flyers while visiting their pediatricians at Kyungpook National University Hospital for their babies' 1-year immunizations. Mothers whose infants were already immunized were contacted by telephone. Mothers ranged in age from 26 to 37 years ($M = 29$; $SD = 3.22$) and most reported education levels beyond high school with 81% having earned a bachelor's or graduate degree. The median family income was between US$24,000 and US$30,000.

Austin Sample   The comparison sample of mothers was drawn from a larger longitudinal study investigating the transition to first-time parenthood (Jacobvitz, Hazen, Curran, & Hitchens, 2004). In the larger study, 125 women in their third trimester of a first-time pregnancy were recruited through birthing classes, public service announcements, and flyers. Mothers ranged in age from 16 to 41 ($M = 29.48$, $SD = 4.73$). Sixty percent had a bachelor's or graduate degree and another 30% had some college or trade/business school coursework. Most of the mothers were Caucasian (85%), but 8% were Hispanic, 3% African American, and 4% endorsed Other and/or biracial heritage. The median family income was $30,000 to $45,000. To match the Taegu and Austin sample on income level, nine families in the larger sample whose income was below poverty level were not included; thus, 104 mothers and infants were included in the present study.

Procedures and Measures

Infant Attachment Security (12–18 Months)   The Strange Situation was used to assess mother–infant attachment security following the standard procedures specified by Ainsworth (Ainsworth et al., 1978). Separation episodes were curtailed if infants were highly distressed and did not settle after 30 seconds. In Taegu, mothers and infants visited a laboratory at Kyungpook National University Hospital to participate in the Strange Situation Procedure. In Austin, mothers and infants visited a University of Texas laboratory. A standardized set of instructions from the workshop training manual was given to mothers in both samples prior to the Strange Situation Procedure.

For the Austin sample, one trained primary coder coded all of the Strange Situations for both the three-way classification (A, B, and C) and for D versus not D. Two other trained coders also coded 82 videotapes (65%) to obtain inter-rater reliability for the three-way classification (A, B, and C); $k = .79, p < .001$. Two additional trained coders coded 45 (40%) of the videotapes for D versus not D; $k = .95, p < .001$. For the Taegu sample, interrater agreement was obtained for four-way classifications, A, B, C, and D; $k = .93, p < .001$. All coders had been previously trained to achieve high reliability $(r > .90)$ on 30 test cases, and were blind to scores on the maternal and infant behavior scales developed for this study.

Infant Distress   Infant distress was coded separately for each of the three separation episodes. Infants who cried were placed in the *distressed* group, and those who appeared to be immediately comforted by the stranger were placed in the *nondistressed* group. Two coders, one from Korea and the other from the United States, independently coded all of the Taegu and Austin videotapes. Interrater agreement was high $(k = .89, p = .00)$.

Physical Proximity   Whether mothers stayed on the floor next to their babies during the entire reunion episode or sat in their chair for some or the entire the episode, and whether the babies approached their mother during the reunion were assessed. Maternal and infant behavior was coded separately. The interrater reliability obtained on 25 cases from each sample was high for ratings of mothers' behavior $(k = .90, p = .00)$ and babies' behavior $(k = .86, p = .00)$.

RESULTS

Distribution of Attachment Classifications

The distribution of attachment classifications in Taegu was 66 secure (78%), one avoidant (1%), and 18 resistant (21%), whereas the distribution in Austin was 58 secure (60%), 16 avoidant (17%), and 22 resistant (23%). The proportions of secure versus insecure infants in both samples are similar to the global distribution of 70% secure based on results from a meta-analysis including nearly 2,000 Strange Situations across 18 samples from eight countries (van IJzendoorn & Kroonenberg, 1988). However, with respect to the three-way attachment classifications (secure, avoidant, and resistant), fewer Taegu babies were classified as avoidant (only 1%), compared with the Austin sample (17%) and the global distribution (23%). The proportions of resistant infants in Taegu (21%) and Austin (23%) were similar, and both were somewhat higher than the cross-national distribution (14%). With respect to the disorganized category, only 9% of Taegu infants were classified as disorganized, which is somewhat lower than the average of about 15% percent in North America and Europe (Lyons-Ruth & Jacobvitz, 1999).

Infant Distress Displayed in Separation Episodes

Previous studies have shown that infant distress during separation more often occurred among babies classified as anxious resistant than those classified as secure (Sagi & Lewkowicz, 1987). To control for differences in the incidence of babies classified as resistant in Taegu and Austin, the frequency of crying was compared for infants assigned the same attachment classification in Taegu and Austin using chi-square analyses. Specifically, secure Taegu babies were compared with secure Austin babies, and resistant Taegu babies were compared with resistant Austin babies. No analyses were conducted to compare avoidant infants in Austin and Taegu because only one baby in Taegu was classified as avoidant.

Regarding the secure infants, during the first separation, significantly fewer Taegu infants cried compared with the Austin infants (11% vs. 28%, χ^2 (1, $N = 119$) = 7.11, $p < .05$). In contrast, during the second separation, Taegu infants cried more than the Austin infants, both when they were left alone (85% vs. 70%, χ^2 (1, $N = 119$) = 3.89, $p < .05$) and when alone with the stranger (40% vs. 19%, χ^2 (1, $N = 119$) = 7.21, $p < .01$). Among babies in the resistant group, Taegu infants cried more than Austin infants during the first separation (56% vs. 37%), but the difference was not statistically significant. During the second separation, Taegu and Austin infants were equally highly distressed when left alone (100% and 97% cried, respectively), but significantly more Taegu infants than Austin infants cried when left with the stranger during the second separation (94% vs. 66%, χ^2 (1, $N = 50$) = 5.25, $p < .05$).

Mothers' Physical Proximity to Their Infants Following Separations

Finally, we compared the likelihood that Taegu versus Austin mothers would stay with their infants versus sit in their chairs throughout the reunion episode, versus stay by the baby, regardless of whether the infants expressed distress. In the secure group, Taegu mothers were much less likely than Austin mothers to sit in their chairs during both the first reunion (53% vs. 96%, (1, $N = 119$) = 27.37, $p < .001$) and during the second reunion (24% vs. 94%, (1, $N = 119$) = 58.47, $p < .001$). Similarly, in the resistant group, Taegu mothers were much less likely than Austin mothers to sit in their chairs during both the first reunion (28% vs. 97%, χ^2 (1, $N = 50$) = 27.28, $p < .001$) and second reunion (75% vs. 6%, χ^2 (1, $N = 50$) = 22.22, $p < .001$). Moreover, in both countries mothers more often sat in their chairs during the first reunion as compared to the second reunion.

It is possible that Taegu infants were less likely to approach their mothers because, unlike the Austin mothers, Taegu mothers more often went immediately to their infant rather than waiting by the door for their infants to approach them. That is, Taegu infants may have learned that their mothers will come to them when they are distressed. To investigate this possibility, we examined whether Taegu infants were less likely to approach their mothers the moment they were reunited with their mother following the brief separation. In the Austin sample, no differences between secure and resistant infants were uncovered in terms of the infants' approach following separation. A comparison of infant behavior in Taegu and Austin revealed that secure Taegu infants were significantly less likely than secure Austin infants to approach their mother following both the first reunion (26% vs. 60% approached, χ^2 (1, N = 119) = 14.55, p < .001); and second reunion (58% vs. 77%, χ^2 (1, N = 119) = 5.16, p < .05). However, more Taegu infants approached their mothers during the second reunion as compared with the first reunion. In the resistant group, there were no differences between the two samples; all resistant infants were likely to approach the mother following both first separation (67% in Taegu and 78% in Austin) and the second separation (94% in Taegu and 87% in Austin).

DISCUSSION

Results of the present study support the idea that cultural differences in caregiving are related to patterns of infant–mother attachment. Compared with mothers in the United States, Taegu mothers tended to stay closer to their babies even when their babies were not distressed, initiated contact more quickly, and more often picked up their babies following a brief separation. Consequently, only one Taegu infant (1%) was classified as avoidant compared with 23% in the global distribution and 17% in Austin. These findings replicated the distribution of classifications found in Japan (Takahashi, 1986) and Indonesia (Zevalkink et al., 1999). Taken together, these findings suggest that in cultures that value very close mother–infant relationships and a lack of separation between mother and infant, avoidant patterns of attachment may be very rare, since cold or rejecting behavior toward infants is viewed very negatively by the culture. Insecure attachment is more likely to be resistant because mothers are more likely to err on the side of being too intrusive, overinvolved, overprotective, or inconsistent.

As expected, however, most of the infants in the Taegu sample were securely attached. In fact, the proportion of secure versus insecure infants in Taegu (78% secure) was quite high; somewhat higher than the proportion of secure infants in the Austin sample (60%) and in the global distribution (65%). The fact that the Strange Situation may be more stressful for babies in Korea who have rarely been left alone or with a stranger might raise questions about the validity of using the Strange Situation Procedure in Korea. Even though all separations were terminated after only 20 to 30 seconds if the infants continued to cry, Taegu infants classified as secure were significantly more likely than the secure U.S infants to cry during the second separation, both when alone and when they were with the stranger, and the resistant Taegu infants were more likely than resistant Austin infants to cry during the second reunion when they were with the stranger. Yet, despite the fact that the Taegu infants appeared more distressed when separated from the mother and left alone with the stranger, a very high proportion of them (78%) did settle when their mother returned and were classified as secure. Thus, we argue that the Strange Situation is a valid assessment of secure versus insecure mother–infant attachment even if Korean infants perceive it as more stressful than babies in some other cultures. Future research should further investigate the validity of the Strange Situation classifications in Korea by examining whether secure attachment is predicted by sensitive maternal caregiving and whether it predicts later social competence.

It is possible that some of the infants in the original Sapporo study who were actually securely attached were misclassified as resistant because separations were not quickly curtailed even when the infants were very distressed (Takahashi, 1986). However, results from the present study as well as the study of attachment in Indonesia (Zevalkink et al., 1999) suggest that the Strange Situation is likely to be a valid measure of attachment even in cultures in which mother–infant separation is rare, as long as separations are limited to 20 to 30 seconds when infants become distressed. In the Indonesian study, the validity of the Strange Situation is supported by the finding that secure attachment was predicted by higher support from the mother, as predicted by attachment theory. And in the present study, given that such a large percentage of infants showed secure attachment, it is very unlikely that misclassification was a problem. Thus, we argue that the existing evidence suggests that the core secure-base model of infant–mother attachment is universal across cultures. That is, in every culture sampled to date, when infants are distressed, they utilize attachment behaviors such as crying or seeking proximity to get the caregiver's attention, and the caregiver usually responds by trying to comfort and soothe the infant. Also, the majority of infants in every culture are able to get the comfort they need; that is, most are secure, indicating that the attachment system functions effectively across cultures.

Nonetheless, although we believe that the core function of the attachment system is universal, the data suggest that there are cultural variations in the specific behaviors that mothers and infants use to meet this function. These cultural variations are clearly reflected in the differences in maternal and infant behaviors in the Strange Situation between the Taegu sample and the Austin sample. First, secure Taegu babies were less likely to seek proximity to their mothers, compared to secure babies in the Austin sample. One explanation may be that Korean mothers view their infants as passive dependent creatures whose needs are to be met without delay (Kim & Choi, 1994). In the present study, 44 of the 87 Taegu mothers did not pause when entering the room following the separations even though they were instructed to do so. In contrast, Austin mothers given the same instructions were more likely to pause for a moment, giving their infants a chance to approach them. In addition to initiating contact quickly during the reunion, Taegu mothers were more likely to sit on the floor with their babies during the entire reunion episode, even though they were instructed to take their seat when they thought their baby had settled. The 44 mothers who did not follow the directions to wait by the door and take their seat if their baby had settled were asked individually why they behaved as they did. Forty-two of the 44 (95%) mothers told the researcher that their baby had never been alone with a stranger and they were very worried about their baby. Of the 19 mothers who worked full time, only 1 mother reported putting her infant in a childcare setting. The rest reported that they left their babies with a close relative. In contrast to the Taegu mothers, nearly all of the Austin mothers waited for their infants to approach them during the reunions, and then returned to their chairs as soon as their infants were settled. In fact, some of the mothers of the resistant babies in Austin returned to their chairs before the infants were settled. Thus, secure Taegu infants may come to expect their caregivers to come to them quickly, thus, they were less likely than the secure Austin infants to approach their mothers upon reunion.

Recent trends toward Western industrialization in Korea have led many young Korean women to put a greater emphasis on academic achievement, social assertiveness, and attaining professional status than they did in the past (Park & Cheah, 2005). Nonetheless, findings of this study indicate that Korean mothers have retained traditional child rearing values inherited from their Confucian beliefs such that priority is given to emotional relationships in the family and constant attention to infants. Rarely would these mothers withdraw and ignore their infants' signals, which may be why only 1.2% of the Taegu infants in this study were classified as avoidant, compared with 17% in Austin and 21% in the global distribution (van IJzendoorn & Kroonenberg, 1988).

In addition, the Korean mother–infant dyads showed a different pattern of secure base behavior than the Austin mother–infant dyads. Taegu mothers were more likely than Austin mothers to take the lead in seeking proximity to their infants, rather than waiting for their infants to come to them, and the Taegu infants, especially those who were securely attached, seemed to expect this. Thus, when distressed, they would cry but would not actively seek proximity, instead waiting for their mother to come to them. Rothbaum et al. (2000) reported similar patterns of infant care in Japanese mothers, noting that they try to anticipate their infants' needs and take steps to minimize infants' distress before it happens. Rothbaum et al. argued that these differences in maternal caregiving patterns are designed to foster dependence and *amae* rather than to foster exploration and autonomy, thus supporting their view that secure-base behavior is not universal across cultures. We argue, however, that the secure-base function of attachment theory is universal, but may be achieved by different means in different cultures. The universal core of attachment theory is that infants use their caregiver as a secure haven when they are distressed and the caregiver, then, provides comfort to the infant. This function can be met by the infant approaching the caregiver when distressed, or by the caregiver staying nearby and anticipating the infant's distress. In either case, once comforted, the infant can choose to explore away from the mother or to play with her.

Finally, the percentage of disorganized babies in Taegu was similar but somewhat lower than that found in the global distribution (15%). It is possible that Korean mothers are less likely to behave in ways that frighten their babies, which has been associated with attachment disorganization in previous studies (Jacobvitz, Leon, & Hazen, 2006; Schuengel, van IJzendoorn, Bakermans-Kranenberg, & Blom, 1998). However, this study is one of the first to examine infant disorganization in an Eastern culture. In the Indonesian sample, nine infants (19.6%) were disorganized, which is close to the global distribution. Also, a high percentage of 6-year-olds (46%) were classified as disorganized in the attachment study in Sapporo done by Behrens et al. (2007). Clearly, much further research on the disorganized classification across cultures and its relation to variations in caregiving practices and child outcomes is needed.

This study is one of the first to compare the ways that cultural differences in infant–caregiver interactions in the Strange Situation relate to infant's security of attachment. The fact that mothers in both samples were from middle socioeconomic backgrounds and resided in an urban city limits the generalizability of the findings. Future studies should include more heterogeneous samples and examine the potential influence of education and rural–urban differences in parenting.

CLINICAL IMPLICATIONS

The clinical implications of mother–infant attachment in Korea should also be examined. Longitudinal studies in the United States have documented that attachment security during infancy has important clinical implication in that secure attachment facilitates children's later social–emotional adjustment, and insecure attachment predicts later emotional and behavior problems. For example, secure attachment in infancy predicts enhanced exploration during toddlerhood (Matas, Arend, & Sroufe, 1978) and the ability to form friendships during the preschool years (Sroufe, 1983). In contrast, avoidant infant attachment has been associated with higher levels of aggression and resistant infant attachment has forecast shyness as rated by preschool teachers (Renken, Egeland, Marvinney, Mangelsdorf, & Sroufe, 1989) and anxiety at age 7 as rated by the children themselves (Kaufman et al., 2005). Attachment disorganization during infancy forecasts internalizing and externalizing behavior during middle childhood and symptoms of dissociation at ages 17 and 19½ (Fury, Carlson, & Sroufe, 1997). Although the overall prevalence of particular disorders in Korean children has not been identified, children in Korea appear to have similar kinds of emotional and behavior problems as those found in the United States, including anxiety, depression, attention deficit and hyperactivity disorders, and conduct disorders (Yun & Kim, 1996). Studies following Korean children over time are needed to uncover whether forming a resistant or disorganized attachment with the caregiver during infancy predicts later psychopathology.

Finally, the findings of the present study suggest that it may be possible to incorporate caregiving behavior shown by Korean mothers into intervention programs in the United States designed to reduce the likelihood that infants will form an avoidant attachment. In the United States, interventions that reduce the incidence of an avoidant attachment help the mother to perceive and empathize with her infant's distress and respond with sensitivity (van den Boom, 1997). Feeling loved and cared for, these infants will be able to more fully explore their environment and develop a sense of mastery and autonomy. In addition, therapists in Korea could draw upon caregiving behaviors shown by mothers in the United States to develop interventions aimed at reducing the incidence of a resistant attachment. For example, it might be important for Korean mothers to give their infants more time to regulate their emotions and organize a response following stressful experiences.

REFERENCES

Ainsworth, M. D. S., Blehar, M. C., Waters, E., & Wall, S. (1978). *Patterns of attachment.* Hillsdale, NJ: Erlbaum.

Behrens, K. (2004). A multifaceted view of the concept of *amae*: Reconsidering the indigenous Japanese concept of relatedness. *Human Development, 47*, 1–27.

Behrens, K., Main, M., & Hesse, E. (2007). Mothers' attachment status as determined by the Adult Attachment Interview predicts their 6-year-olds' reunion responses: A study conducted in Japan. *Developmental Psychology, 43*, 1553–1567.

Bowlby, J. (1982). *Attachment and loss: Vol. I* (2nd ed.). New York: Basic Books.

Doi, T. (1992). On the concept of *amae*. *Infant Mental Health Journal, 13*, 7–11.

Fury, G., Carlson, E. A., & Sroufe, A. (1997). Children's representations of attachment relationships in family drawings. *Child Development, 68(6)*, 1154–1164.

Jacobvitz, D., Hazen, N., Curran, M., & Hitchens, K. (2004). Observations of early triadic family interactions: Boundary disturbances in the family predict depressive, anxious, and ADHD symptoms in middle childhood. *Development and Psychopathology, 16*, 577–592.

Jacobvitz, D., Leon, K., & Hazen, N. (2006). Does expectant mothers' unresolved/disorganized trauma predict frightened/frightening (FR) maternal behavior? Risk and protective factors. *Development and Psychopathology, 18*, 363–379.

Jin, M. K. (2005). A cross-cultural study of infant attachment patterns in Korea and the U.S.: Associations among infant temperament, maternal personality, separation anxiety, and depression. Unpublished doctoral dissertation, The University of Texas at Austin.

Kaufman, N. K., Rohde, P., Seeley, J. R., Clarke, G. N., & Stice, E. (2005). Potential mediators of cognitive-behavioral therapy for adolescents with comorbid major depression and conduct disorder. *Journal of Consulting and Clinical Psychology, 73*, 38–46.

Kim, U., & Choi, S. H. (1994). Individualism, collectivism, and child development: A Korean perspective. In P. M. Greenfield & R. R. Cocking (Eds.), *Cross-cultural roots of minority child development* (pp. 227–257). Hillsdale, NJ: Erlbaum.

Lyons-Ruth, K., & Jacobvitz, D. (1999). Attachment disorganization: Unresolved loss, relational violence, and lapses in behavioral and attentional strategies. In J. Cassidy & P.R. Shaver (Eds.), *Handbook of attachment: Theory, research, and clinical applications* (pp. 520–554). New York: Guilford Press.

Main, M. (1990). Cross-cultural studies of attachment organization: Recent studies, changing methodologies, and the concept of conditional strategies. *Human Development, 33*, 48–61.

Main, M., & Cassidy, J. (1988). Categories of response to reunion with the parent at age 6: Predictable from infant attachment classifications and stable over a 1-month period. *Developmental Psychology, 24*, 415–426.

Matas, L., Arend, R. A., & Sroufe, L. A. (1978). Continuity of adaptation in the second year: The relationship between quality of attachment and later competence. *Child Development, 49*, 547–556.

Miyake, K., Chen, S. J., & Campos, J. J. (1985). Infant temperament, mother's mode of interaction, and attachment in Japan: An interim report. In I. Bretherton & E. Waters (Eds.), Growing points of attachment theory and research. *Monographs of the Society for Research in Child Development, 50*, 276–297.

Nakagawa, M., Lamb, M., & Miyaki, K. (1992). Antecedents and correlates of the strange situation behavior of Japanese infants. *Journal of Cross-Cultural Psychology, 23*, 300-310.

Park, S. Y., & Cheah, C. S. (2005). Korean mothers' proactive socialisation beliefs regarding preschoolers' social skills. *International Journal of Behavioral Development, 29*, 24–34.

Renken, B., Egeland, B., Marvinney, D., Mangelsdorf, S., & Sroufe, L. A. (1989). Early childhood antecedents of aggression and passive-withdrawal in early elementary school. *Journal of Personality, 57*, 257–281.

Rothbaum, F., Weisz, J., Pott, M., Miyake, K., & Morelli, G. (2000). Attachment and culture: Security in the United States and Japan. *American Psychologist, 55*, 1093–1104.

Sagi, A., & Lewkowicz, K. S. (1987). A cross-cultural evaluation of attachment research. In L. W. C. Tavecchio & M. H. van IJzendoorn (Eds.), *Attachment in social networks* (pp. 427–459). Amsterdam, NL: Elsevier Science.

Schuengel, C., van IJzendoorn, M., Bakermans-Kranenberg, M., & Blom, M. (1998). Frightening, frightened and/or dissociated behavior, unresolved loss, and infant disorganization. *Journal of Reproductive and Infant Psychology, 16*, 277–283.

Sroufe, L. A. (1983). Infant-caregiver attachment and patterns of adaptation in pre-school. The roots of maladaptation and competence. In M. Perlmutter (Ed.), *Minnesota Symposium on Child Psychology* (Vol. 16, pp. 41–81). Hillsdale, NJ: Erlbaum.

Takahashi, K. (1986). Examining the strange-situation procedure with Japanese mothers and 12-month-old infants. *Development Psychology, 22*, 265–270.

Takahashi, K. (1990). Are the key assumptions of the strange situation procedure universal? A view from Japanese research. *Human Development, 33*, 23–30.

Triandis, H. C. (2001). Individualism-collectivism and personality. *Journal of Personality, 69*, 907–924.

True, M. M., Pisani, L., & Oumar, F. (2001). Infant-mother attachment among the Dogon of Mali. *Child Development, 72*, 1451–1466.

van den Boom, D. C. (1997). Sensitivity and attachment: Next steps for developmentalists. *Child Development, 68*, 592–594.

van IJzendoorn, M. H., & Kroonenberg, P. M. (1988). Cross-cultural patterns of attachment: A meta-analysis of the strange situation. *Child Development, 59*, 147–156.

van IJzendoorn, M. H., & Sagi-Schwartz, A. (2008). Cross-cultural patterns of attachment: Universal and contextual dimensions. In J. Cassidy & P. R. Shaver (Eds.), *Handbook of attachment: Theory, research, and clinical applications* (2nd ed., pp. 880–905). New York: Guilford Press.

Vereijken, C. J. J. L., Riksen-Walraven, J. M., & Van Lieshout, C. F. M. (1997). Mother-infant relationships in Japan: Attachment, dependency, and amae. *Journal of Cross-Cultural Psychology, 28*, 442–462.

Yu, A. C. (1984). *The child rearing practices in the traditional Korean society*. Seoul: Jungminsa.

Yun, K. W., & Kim, G. H. (1996). A study on the behavior, adaptability and intelligence of child and adolescents at the children's medical examination center in a general hospital. *Ewha Medical Journal, 19*, 165–171.

Zevalkink, J., Riksen-Walraven, J. M., & Van Lieshout, C. F. M. (1999). Attachment in the Indonesian caregiving context. *Social Development, 8*, 21–40.

10

Culturally Relevant Parenting Predictors of Attachment Security
Perspectives From Turkey

NEBI SÜMER and ÇIĞDEM KAĞITÇIBAŞI

CONTENTS

*T*he ways parents socialize their children show cultural variation. Recent conceptualizations on both parenting (e.g., Kağıtçıbaşı, 2005, 2007) and attachment security (e.g., Rothbaum, Weisz, Pott, Miyake, & Morelli, 2000; van IJzendoorn & Sagi, 1999) have specifically emphasized the central role of culture and have called for testing the validity of "individualistic" assumptions in cross-cultural settings. Although attachment theory has been extensively studied in the last four decades, two main issues still call for further exploration and clarification. The first one is whether and to what extent the findings of attachment relationships in early years can be generalized to later developmental phases (e.g., Thompson, 1999). The second is how cultural differences in parenting and, thus, attachment behaviors can be explained by or integrated into the core assumptions of attachment theory (Rothbaum et al., 2000; van IJzendoorn & Sagi, 1999).

In this study, we examined the impact of parenting behaviors in both general (i.e., emotional warmth and rejection) and more "culturally relevant" domains (i.e., overprotection, comparing and contrasting the child with similar others, love withdrawal, intrusion, and guilt induction) in predicting attachment security in a relatively less studied developmental stage, namely, middle childhood (Mayseless, 2005; Sümer & Anafarta, 2009) among Turkish school children. Based on Kağıtçıbaşı (1990, 2005, 2007) theoretical perspectives on *family change* and the *autonomous-related self*, we tested two specific assumptions. First, we assumed that (over)protection and intrusion/guilt induction, both of which are generally assumed to have negative implications in individualistic cultures, would not have necessarily negative effects on attachment security in the Turkish cultural context. Second, considering the cultural adaptiveness of "anxious parenting" and critical implications of avoidance in collectivistic "cultures of relatedness," we expected that attachment avoidance of parents, especially mothers, rather than attachment anxiety, would primarily predict attachment security of children.

CULTURE AND ATTACHMENT

From the first studies of Ainsworth (1967), the role of cultural context in the formation, maintenance, and intergenerational transmission of attachment behavior has received attention from attachment researchers (e.g., Main, 1990; van IJzendoorn & Kroonenberg, 1988). However, early attachment studies focused mainly on the proximal familial context rather than larger societal and cultural context (see Ainsworth & Bowlby, 1991; Bretherton, 1992). Although the first study was run in a non-Western culture, almost all of the later work was conducted in Western cultures, and in Bretherton's words, "systematic work on the more fascinating topic of how different cultures—especially non-Western cultures—fit attachment behaviors and relationships into their overall social organization has barely begun … in the 1990s" (1992, p. 770).

Theoretical attempts aiming to explain cultural differences in caregiver or parental behaviors associated with attachment security have been rarely offered with a few exceptions (e.g., Voelker, Keller, Lohaus, Cappenberg, & Chasiotis, 1999). Van IJzendoorn and Sagi (1999) documented cross-cultural differences in attachment behavior while supporting the overarching universal validity of attachment theory. Based on a meta-analysis, they organized the findings from numerous studies within the four assumptions of attachment theory: *universality* (i.e., infants develop attachment to caregivers in all cultures), *normativity* (i.e., secure attachment is the ideal style in all cultures), *sensitivity* (i.e., sensitive parenting leads to secure attachment), and *competence* (i.e., secure attachment enhances social and cognitive competence of children). Although infants' specific attachment behaviors varied across cultures, they all showed behavioral patterns indicative of attachment to caregivers, supporting the universality hypothesis. The normativity hypothesis also received wide support, though with a fewer number of studies.

Evidence supporting the cross-cultural validity of the sensitivity and the competence hypotheses, however, was relatively weak, suggesting that cultural variation increases when attachment behaviors are associated with specific parenting behaviors. Van IJzendoorn and Sagi (1999) also noted that only a small number of studies from the non-Western cultures were included in the meta-analyses and that "data on attachment in India and the Islamic world are still completely lacking" (p. 731).

A radical challenge to the fundamental assumptions of attachment theory was posited by Rothbaum, Pott, Azuma, Miyake, and Weisz (2000), contrasting the differences between Western and Japanese parenting patterns. These authors asserted that observed extensive cross-cultural differences regarding the sensitivity and competence hypotheses, indeed, reflect a qualitative difference in parents' socialization goals between *interdependent* Japanese and *independent* North American cultures. For example, they claimed that sensitive parenting in Japan involves responding to situational cues reflecting a child's needs rather than to direct signals or demands from the child. By contrast, sensitive parenting in North America involves responding to direct signals from the child. These behaviors are seen as adaptive and culture-specific paths in close relationships.

There may be some alternative explanations as to why maternal sensitivity may not be linked with attachment security in many cultures. For example, Voelker et al. (1999) asserted that maternal sensitivity in early years predicts different aspects of attachment security. Specifically, they expected that, whereas maternal behavioral contingency toward the infant's signals is related to later security of attachment, maternal warmth is related to later emotional closeness. They tested their assumptions on German infants and found evidence demonstrating that emotional closeness and behavioral contingency had different adaptive values for attachment security. Given that maternal warmth and emotional closeness, as opposed to behavioral contingency, are common in many collectivist contexts including Turkey (Kağıtçıbaşı, 2005, 2007), these may be related to attachment security more in collectivist cultures than in individualistic ones.

Attachment styles and the underlying internal working models of the self and the other influence all sorts of close relationships including parent–child relations (George & Solomon, 1999). In recent conceptualization, insecure attachment behaviors are best systematized into two general dimensions: *attachment anxiety* (i.e., a strong desire for closeness and intense worry about others' availability, and one's own value in partner's eyes) and *avoidance* (i.e., discomfort with closeness and dependence to others, and a preference for emotional distance and self-reliance). Whereas attachment anxiety taps the dynamics of the mental (working) model of self and is related with compulsively using *hyperactivating* strategies in family and close relationships, attachment avoidance taps the mental model of others and is related to using *deactivating* strategies in relationships (see Brennan, Clark, & Shaver, 1998; Mikulincer & Shaver, 2007). Four attachment styles are produced at the interaction of the anxiety and avoidance dimensions: secure (both low anxiety and avoidance), fearful avoidant (both high anxiety and avoidance), dismissing avoidant (low anxiety but high avoidance), and preoccupied or anxious-ambivalent (high anxiety but low avoidance).

It may be suggested that attachment anxiety is more prevalent in collectivist cultures and attachment avoidance in individualistic cultures. For example, using samples from 64 cultures, Schmitt et al. (2004) found that positivity of the self model is lower than the model of others and that preoccupied romantic attachment, which is marked with high attachment anxiety and low avoidance, is particularly prevalent in East Asian cultures. This pattern was reversed in Western cultures. Rothbaum, Rosen, Ujiie, and Uchida (2002) assert that extreme dependency is functional, and thus, preoccupied (or anxious ambivalent) attachment and high attachment anxiety should not be seen as abnormal or maladaptive in cultures with extremely close and interdependent mother–child interactions. However, as attachment avoidance may imply complete rejection, exclusion can be maladaptive in such cultures. In other words, since anxious behaviors of mothers serve the purpose of optimal safety for children, such behaviors can be seen as adaptive in this specific context (Crittenden, 2000). Therefore, it can be expected that on the dimensional level, parental, especially maternal, attachment avoidance, and on the categorical level, dismissing-avoidant attachment patterns are more maladaptive, and thus, would be predictive of children's attachment (in)security in cultures valuing closely knit relatedness. Furthermore, given the gender-specific parental role divisions, characterized by the nurturing and "warm" mother and the disciplining, distant father, paternal anxiety rather than avoidance can be a maladaptive paternal behavior.

ATTACHMENT AND PARENTING

Attachment theory was built on the hypothesis that sensitive caregiving is the primary antecedent of attachment security (Bowlby, 1982). Following Ainsworth, Blehar, Waters, and Wall's (1978) robust finding pointing to a strong link between maternal sensitivity and infant attachment, maternal sensitivity has been used almost exclusively as the predictor of security. Sensitive caregiving was defined as "a parent being readily available, sensitive to her child's signals, and lovingly responsive when s/he seeks protection and/or comfort and/or assistance" (Bowlby, 1988, p. 4). This definition also refers to the *acceptance* dimension of parenting (Baumrind, 1991; Darling & Steinberg, 1993). As indicated by Bretherton, Golby, and Cho (1997), although maternal sensitivity in attachment theory and *authoritative parenting* (defined as warm involvement, psychological autonomy granting, and behavioral control or monitoring) refer to similar characteristics (e.g., Baumrind, 1991), attachment and parenting (child socialization) literatures have followed separate lines for decades, using different labels for similar constructs.

Research on parenting styles commonly uses the degree of *acceptance/involvement* and *control/discipline* parents show as the two fundamental dimensions of child socialization attitudes. Crossing these two dimensions has produced four parenting styles. Whereas high levels of acceptance and control correspond to *authoritative* parenting, low levels in both dimensions correspond to *neglectful* parenting. Whereas low levels of acceptance combined with high levels of control typify *authoritarian* parenting, the opposite pattern typifies *permissive* or *indulgent* parenting (Darling & Steinberg, 1993; Kağıtçıbaşı, 1996, 2007; Lamborn,

Mounts, Steinberg, & Dornbusch, 1991). Parallel to insensitive caregiving leading to insecure attachment, authoritarian and neglectful parenting are associated with negative child outcomes (e.g., Lamborn et al., 1991). Recent studies have revealed that parental warmth (acceptance) and authoritative parenting are the significant predictors of attachment security (e.g., Karavasilis, Doyle, & Markiewicz, 2003; Sümer & Engin, 2004).

There are at least three concerns to be addressed in predicting attachment security from maternal sensitivity and parenting styles. The first is whether maternal sensitivity and parenting styles predict a unique and independent variance in attachment security. That is, what is the contribution of parenting styles on attachment security above and beyond the effects of maternal sensitivity? Second, considering that parenting behaviors, especially parental control (Barber, 1996; Barber & Harmon, 2002), are more sensitive to cultural variations (e.g., Carlson & Harwood, 2003; Kağıtçıbaşı, 2005), what is the predictive power of culturally relevant parenting behaviors over and above the more universal parenting behaviors, such as warmth and rejecting parenting? Third, given that in the majority of cultures mothers still serve as the *nurturing* agent and fathers as the *controlling* agent, do maternal and paternal parenting behaviors differ in predicting attachment security?

Regarding the first and second concerns, past studies have shown that different aspects of maternal sensitivity, such as expression of positive affect and emotional availability, are consistently associated with attachment security. In their extensive meta-analysis, De Wolff and van IJzendoorn (1997) examined the impact of a number of parental behaviors, including maternal sensitivity, and found a moderate effect size ($r = .22$) between maternal sensitivity and attachment security. They also showed that maternal sensitivity was not the unique predictor of security. Parental behaviors, such as *synchrony* and *mutuality* had relatively higher effect sizes than sensitivity (.26 and .32, respectively). De Wolff and van IJzendoorn concluded that "sensitivity has lost its privileged position as the only important causal factor" (p. 585) and those different aspects of parenting play a role similar to sensitivity in predicting attachment. As indicated by these authors, however, parental behaviors were limited to the general domains of warmth and acceptance, and aspects that are related to parental control were left unexamined in the reviewed studies. Therefore, it is important to examine whether culturally defined aspects of parental control have unique power in predicting attachment security.

Within the framework of attachment theory, maternal control, as a form of intrusive behavior, is associated with insecure attachment (Ainsworth et al., 1978). However, in cultures where parents are expected to structure and guide the child's environment in the absence of an explicit demand from the child, parental control is used for *order setting* and the maintenance of *connectedness* within the family (Kağıtçıbaşı, 2005, 2007; Lau, Lew, Hau, Cheung, & Berndt, 1990). In these cultures, maternal sensitivity may involve different types of control (e.g., Carlson & Harwood, 2003; Kağıtçıbaşı, 2005; Rothbaum et al., 2000).

Psychological parental control is a multidimensional concept that includes different aspects of parenting entailing strict control, guilt induction, intrusion, love, and withdrawal to overprotection. Past research in Western cultural contexts has demonstrated that high levels of psychological control predict a number of adjustment problems (Barber, 1996). However, depending on their cultural relevance and adaptive value, different aspects of psychological control may function differently in different settings. In general, as indicated by Kağıtçıbaşı (2007), "higher levels of parental control are seen in sociocultural contexts where independence of the child is not a goal of parenting" (p. 175).

FAMILY CHANGE THEORY

Kağıtçıbaşı's (1990, 1996, 2005, 2007) theory of family change has the potential to explain why certain aspects of parental control may be adaptive in the collectivist cultures of relatedness, whereas they may be maladaptive or dysfunctional in the individualistic Western middle-class contexts. Three family models are distinguished that have distinct familial and societal antecedents, and implications for parental goals and behaviors as well as for the development of the self.

The *model of independence* is prototypical of the individualistic Western, especially American, family culture involving self-reliance and autonomy in child rearing toward the goal of the development of an autonomous and separate self. In the contrasting family model, that of *interdependence*, which is prototypical of the traditional agrarian society, children provide for their parents material and economic benefits especially when they grow up. Thus, intergenerational interdependence is adaptive for family well-being. To ensure this, obedience- and (inter)dependence-oriented parenting is adaptive toward the development of a related self.

It is commonly assumed that through global socioeconomic development and urbanization there is a shift from the family model of interdependence to that of independence (i.e., modernization toward the Western model). However, a growing amount of both historical and contemporary empirical evidence shows this not to be the case (for extensive reviews, see Kağıtçıbaşı, 1990, 2007). Although there is a decline in material interdependencies between generations (i.e., decreased dependence on the adult offspring for material old-age security and family livelihood), psychological interdependencies continue to exist in collectivist cultures of relatedness where closely knit interpersonal ties are cherished. Instead, a third family model emerges, that of the *psychological/emotional interdependence*, which is indeed a dialectical synthesis of the models of independence and interdependence though considerably different from them. Most important, with increased affluence, urbanization, and socioeconomic development, parents' material dependency on their offspring diminishes. However, interdependence in the psychological realm continues, since this is not incompatible with changing life styles.

The family model of psychological/emotional interdependence has important implications for parental goals involving the continued adaptiveness of parental control. That is, when material interdependencies diminish (i.e., the material contribution of the offspring is no longer required for family well-being), there is more room for autonomy in child rearing, and children's autonomy is not seen as a threat to family integrity. Nevertheless, because emotional interdependence and connectedness continue to be treasured, given the collectivistic culture of relatedness, the psychological closeness of the growing child is aspired. Thus, although complete obedience and loyalty of the child are no longer needed, there is still a need for firm parental control because independence of the child leading to separation is not wanted. Parents are therefore motivated to have control and child management strategies, such as (over)protection and guilt induction to ensure the emotional relatedness and psychological interdependence of the child.

The theory also has implications for the development of the self. In the model of emotional interdependence there is a child-rearing orientation that integrates autonomy with control and relatedness leading to the development of the *autonomous-related self*. This self-construal is different from the autonomous-separate self and the heteronomous (dependent)-related self, which characterize the family models of independence and interdependence, respectively. This model of self-development and family functioning is relevant especially in urbanized and socioeconomically more developed contexts in collectivistic cultures of relatedness where autonomy becomes functional for higher education status and more specialized urban life styles. Given the strong global urbanization trends in the Majority World (see Kağıtçıbaşı, 2007, p. 45), this self-construal is prevalent. Furthermore, Kağıtçıbaşı asserts that it is also of universal relevance as a healthy self model, since it involves and satisfies both of the basic human needs for autonomy and relatedness (for further discussion and empirical evidence supporting the theory, see Kağıtçıbaşı, 2005, 2007).

Thus, in the Turkish urban, middle-class contexts, which suit the family model of psychological/emotional interdependence, parents use specific types of psychological control behaviors to create the contingencies for related (emotionally interdependent) but autonomous children. In this cultural context, children perceive these parental control behaviors as normal, not a reflection of rejection, exclusion, or intrusion. Therefore, we maintain that parental control behaviors, such as guilt induction, love withdrawal, and (over)protection, are culturally adaptive and do not necessarily have a negative effect on child's attachment security. This is also consistent with past and recent research from diverse cultural contexts showing that, where normative, strong parental control can be perceived as a sign of warmth and involvement, and is not detrimental to healthy development (e.g., Deater-Deckard, & Dodge, 1997; Dekovic, Pels, & Model, 2006; Lansford, Deater-Deckard, Dodge, Bates, & Pettit, 2003; Rohner & Pettengill, 1985; Rudy & Grusec, 2001).

THE PRESENT STUDY AND HYPOTHESES

In this study, we aimed to test two hypotheses to clarify two major pathways through which cultural parental patterning affects attachment security during middle childhood. First, considering the fundamental assumptions of attachment theory and the cultural adaptiveness assumption, we hypothesize that parents' attachment avoidance, especially maternal avoidance, rather than attachment anxiety predicts children's attachment security to their parents in the Turkish cultural context. Accordingly, we also expect that dismissing maternal attachment, which can be depicted with a specific interaction between (low) attachment anxiety and (high) avoidance, would predict insecure attachment to parents. Therefore, we aim to test both main effects and the interactions between parents' attachment anxiety and avoidance in predicting attachment to parents. Second, based on Kağıtçıbaşı's (2005, 2007) model of psychological/emotional interdependence, we hypothesize that although the universal dimensions of parenting, such as parental warmth and rejection, are linked to attachment security consistent with the predictions of attachment theory, culturally endorsed parenting control behaviors, namely, guilt induction, overprotection, and making comparisons with other children, do not have negative effects on children's attachment security in the Turkish cultural context.

METHOD

Participants

This study is part of a larger project on parenting behaviors and attachment during middle childhood conducted by the first author. Fourth- and fifth-grade students ($N = 797$, females = 52%) from two major cities in Turkey participated in this study. Four elementary schools were randomly selected from each city and all of the students attending the fourth and fifth grades were targeted as the sample. Only those children whose parents agreed and signed the parental approval and informed consent form were asked to fill out the questionnaires. About 85% of the parents allowed their children to participate in the study. After children completed the questionnaires they were given two sealed envelopes containing the questionnaires for their mothers and fathers. Children brought back the questionnaires completed by their parents using the sealed envelopes. The return rate for the mothers and fathers were 73% ($n = 582$) and 64%, ($n = 508$), respectively. We had data from both parents of 502 participating students. Thus in the analyses that included parents and children together, the sample size was reduced to 502. However, the sample size was 797 for the analyses on the data reported by children.

Of the students, 45% were in the fourth grade and 55% were in the fifth grade. All the children were from two-parent families and the mean age for the sample was 10.74 years ($SD = 1.09$). Mean age for mothers was 36.93 years ($SD = 4.94$) and for fathers was 41.55 years ($SD = 5.40$). Sample groups were mostly from middle and lower middle-class families. Of the mothers 28.4% were elementary school graduates, 45.4% were middle and high school graduates, and 26% were two- or four-year college graduates. Of the fathers 15.6% were elementary school graduates, 46.4% were middle and high school graduates, and 38.0% were two- or four-year college graduates.

Measures

Some of the scales and items used in the present study were adopted into Turkish following translation and back-translation procedures (e.g., Sümer, 2006; Sümer & Anafarta, 2009). Parents and children completed a number of questionnaires, and demographic information was obtained. In this section, the measures used in the study are presented.

Experiences in Close Relationships-Revised (ECR-R)

The 36-item Experiences in Close Relationships-Revised (ECR-R) developed by Fraley, Waller, and Brennan (2000), was used to measure parents' attachment. Both parents separately filled out the reworded version of the ECR for married couples so that the term "my partner" was replaced with "my spouse." The ECR-R was shown to have good psychometric properties for Turkish samples (Selcuk, Gunaydın, Sümer, & Uysal, 2005; Sümer, 2006). The ECR-R has two 18-item subscales assessing attachment avoidance (i.e., discomfort with interpersonal closeness, dependence, and self-disclosure) and attachment anxiety (i.e., fear of abandonment but desire for intimacy). The ECR-R has good internal consistency coefficients for its two subscales for both parents in this study (see Table 10.1 later).

Kerns Security Scale (KSS)

Children completed the Kerns Security Scale (KSS) developed by Kerns, Klepac, and Cole (1996) for childhood from ages 8 to 12. The 15-item KKS measures the degree to which children evaluate their parents as responsive, reliable, and available. Children completed the KSS for each parent separately. Items were rated using Harter's "Some kids ... Other kids ..." format. Children were asked to indicate which statement was more characteristic of them and then to indicate whether this statement was really true for them or sort of true for them. Each item was scored on a scale from 1 to 4, with higher scores indicating a more secure parent–child attachment. The KSS was shown to have good psychometric qualities for Turkish school children (Sümer & Anafarta, 2009). In the current study, alphas for mother and father subscales were satisfactory (.79 and .82, respectively).

Measure for Parenting Behaviors

To assess both general and specific parental behaviors that we believe to be common among Turkish families, we used a set of items derived from different parenting measures. We also added items to tap culturally relevant parenting behaviors. We used the EMBU-C (a Swedish acronym for My Memories of Upbringing for Children; Markus, Lindhout, Boer, Hoogendijk, & Arrindell, 2003). The EMBU-C has been developed to assess children's perception of parental rearing practices. The EMBU-C consists of four subscales: emotional warmth, rejection, overprotection, and favoring. We used the emotional warmth and rejection subscales to measure general parenting behaviors. Emotional warmth refers to acceptance and involvement, giving special attention, praising for approved behavior, unconditional love, and affection. Rejection refers to hostility, punishment, harsh discipline, and blaming of the child. We omitted the favoring subscale and used some items from the overprotection subscale. The emotional warmth subscale includes eight items, and the rejection subscale includes 10 items.

We selected items from different parenting scales including Barber's (1996) psychological control scales to measure a number of specific parenting behaviors. We aimed to assess different aspects of parental psychological control, including overprotection, comparison (i.e., comparing children with others), guilt induction/love withdrawal, and intrusive parenting. A total of 34 items were used for the culture-relevant parenting measures.

We used principal factor analyses with Promax rotation on the 34 items and found four specific factors: *comparison, overprotection, guilt induction,* and *intrusion/love withdrawal.* Those representing comparison had six items (e.g., "Does your mom/dad compare you with your friends about your courses and grades?"); overprotection had four items (e.g., "Does your mom/dad check you to see if you are sweating or not?"); guilt induction had eight items (e.g., "Does your mom/dad tell you how much she/he has worked all for you?"); and intrusion/love withdrawal (labeled as "intrusion" for the sake of brevity) had 13 items (e.g., "Does your mom/ dad complete your sentences as you are talking?" for intrusion and "Does your mom/dad behave less sympathetic towards you when you disagree with her/him?" for love withdrawal). Children completed the scales for mothers and fathers separately using 4-point scales (1 = no, 2 = sometimes, 3 = most of the time, and 4 = always).

All of the parenting subscales had acceptable to good degree of internal consistencies with the exception of the overprotection (.52) and guilt induction (.53) subscales since they included few items (Table 10.2). (Complete set of items and results of the factor analyses may be obtained from the first author.)

RESULTS

We tested our hypotheses via regression analyses following preliminary analyses of the major variables. The first analysis examined if attachment anxiety and avoidance reported by parents predicted children's reported attachment security to parents. Table 10.1 presents descriptive statistics and pairwise correlations between parents and children attachment variables. Attachment to mothers and attachment to fathers were strongly correlated ($r = .62, p < .001$) as expected. Whereas mother attachment anxiety was not significantly correlated with attachment to parents, mother attachment avoidance was significantly correlated with both attachment to mothers ($r = -.14, p < .01$) and attachment to fathers ($r = -.11, p < .05$). Father anxiety, however, was significantly correlated with both attachment to mothers

TABLE 10.1   Descriptive Statistics and Correlations Among Parental and Children Attachment Variables ($N = 502$)

	1	2	3	4	5	6
1. Attachment to mother	(.79)					
2. Attachment to father	.62°°	(.82)				
3. Mother attachment anxiety	−.06	−.04	(.79)			
4. Mother attachment avoidance	−.14°°	−.11°	.41°°	(.88)		
5. Father attachment anxiety	−.11°	−.15°°	.21°°	.24°°	(.71)	
6. Father attachment avoidance	−.04	−.08	.22°°	.31°°	.38°°	(.84)
Mean	3.33	3.23	2.28	1.74	2.11	1.73
SD	.47	.49	.64	.67	.57	.63

Note: Cronbach's alpha values were given at diagonals.
°$p < .05$. °°$p < .001$.

$(r = -.11, p < .05)$ and attachment to fathers $(r = -.15, p < .01)$. Father avoidance was not significantly correlated with attachment to parents.

Hierarchical regressions were used separately to predict attachment to fathers and mothers reported by children. Sex and age of the children, and mothers' and fathers' level of education were entered as covariates on the first step to control for their effects, followed by both parents' attachment anxiety and avoidance reported by parents on the second step. The six interactions between father and mother attachment anxiety and avoidance were entered on the third step. As seen in Table 10.2, in predicting attachment to mothers, mothers' level of education was significant on the first step $(\beta = .10, p < .05)$ suggesting that as mothers' education increases children report more secure attachment to their mothers. As expected, only mother attachment avoidance significantly and negatively predicted secure attachment to mothers $(\beta = -.14, p < .01)$ in the second step. The interaction between mother attachment anxiety and avoidance also significantly predicted attachment to mothers $(\beta = .19, p < .001)$ in the third step. In predicting attachment to fathers, first, children's age was significant $(\beta = -.10, p < .05)$, suggesting that as they get older to preadolescent ages, their attachment to fathers was slightly decreasing. In the second step, father attachment anxiety was significant $(\beta = .13,$

TABLE 10.2   Predicting Child-Reported Attachment to Parents From Parent-Reported Attachment Anxiety and Avoidance $(N = 471)$

Analysis	Attachment to Mother		Attachment to Father	
	β	ΔR²	β	ΔR²
Step 1: Demographics		.03°		.02
Gender	−.06		−.01	
Age	−.08		−.10°	
Mother education	.10°		.05	
Step 2: Main effects		.02°		.03°
Mother attachment anxiety	.01		.01	
Mother attachment avoidance	−.14°		−.10	
Father attachment anxiety	−.10		−.13°	
Father attachment avoidance	−.02		−.02	
Step 3: Interaction terms		.04°		.03°
MANX × MAVO	.19°°		.13°	
FANX × FAVO	.05		.10°	
MANX × FANX	−.06		−.04	
MANX × FAVO	−.05		−.05	
MAVO × FANX	.01		.00	
MAVO × FAVO	.04		.05	
	R^2 total = .09		R^2 total = .08	

Notes: MANX = mother attachment anxiety; MAVO = mother attachment avoidance; FANX = father attachment anxiety; FAVO = father attachment avoidance. β values were obtained from the last step.
$°p < .05. °°p < .001.$

$p < .01$). In the last step, the interactions between mother anxiety and avoidance, and between father anxiety and avoidance, signifying specific attachment styles, were also significant in predicting attachment to fathers ($\beta = .13$, $p < .01$; $\beta = .10$, $p < .05$, respectively) above and beyond the main effects of the four parent attachment variables.

These interactions were plotted following the procedures proposed by Aiken and West (1991). As seen in Figure 10.1, when mother attachment anxiety was used as a moderating variable, the regression coefficient for high attachment anxiety was not significant. However, the coefficient for the low attachment anxiety was significant ($\beta = -.30$, $p < .001$). As predicted, those mothers with low anxiety and high avoidance, corresponding to dismissing attachment style, had children with lowest attachment to their mothers. However, when mothers have both low levels of attachment avoidance and anxiety, corresponding to secure attachment style, children had the highest attachment security to mothers. The same pattern was observed in predicting attachment to fathers (the beta for low mother attachment anxiety was significant only; $\beta = -.31$, $p < .001$), suggesting that when their mothers were *dismissing*, children also reported the lowest level of attachment to their fathers, and when their mothers were *secure*, they reported the highest level of attachment to their fathers (see Figure 10.2). The plotting of the interaction between father anxiety and avoidance also depicted the same pattern that was observed for

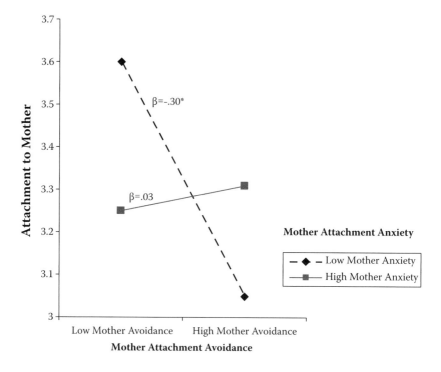

Figure 10.1   Plotting of the interaction between mother attachment avoidance and anxiety predicting child attachment to mother.

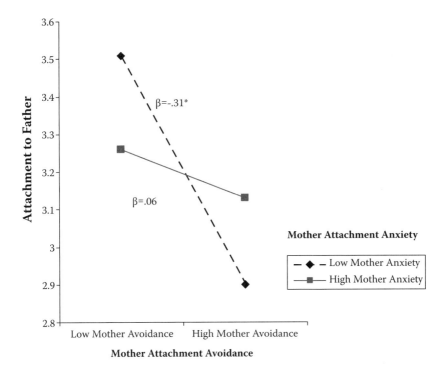

Figure 10.2   Plotting of the interaction between mother attachment avoidance and anxiety in predicting child attachment to father.

mothers. As seen in Figure 10.3, when the fathers had a dismissing pattern (i.e., the combination of low anxiety and high avoidance, $\beta = -.25$, $p < .001$), children reported the lowest attachment to their father. This pattern, however, was reversed for secure fathers (i.e., the combination of both low anxiety and avoidance).

In testing the second hypothesis we used the child-reported data only. The correlations between attachment to parents and parenting behaviors are presented in Table 10.3. As seen in Table 10.3, children's reports of maternal and paternal parenting behaviors were strongly correlated (.52 between mother and father rejection and .65 between mother and father overprotection). As expected, attachment to parents were strongly and positively correlated with emotional warmth and negatively correlated with rejection for both mother and father parenting, confirming their universal significance in forming attachment security. However, the pattern of correlations varied when we examined the correlations with the parental control variables. Whereas attachment to both parents was negatively and relatively strongly correlated with intrusion, correlations for other parenting variables differed. Attachment to parents was relatively weakly, but negatively, correlated with comparison and guilt induction. They were, however, positively correlated with overprotection. When the correlations among the parenting variables were examined, although the pattern of the correlations were in the expected direction, both

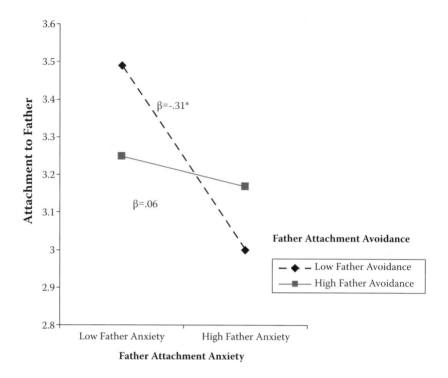

Figure 10.3   Plotting of the interaction between father attachment avoidance and anxiety in predicting child attachment to father.

mother and father emotional warmth were significantly and positively correlated with overprotection and guilt induction.

To specifically examine the hypothesis that culturally relevant parenting predicts attachment to parents in culturally adaptive ways, we ran two hierarchical regression analyses for mother and father variables separately. In these analyses, considering that the child's reports of mother and father parenting behaviors were strongly correlated, we predicted attachment to mothers and fathers separately by using mother variables for predicting attachment to mothers and father variables for predicting attachment to fathers. In both analyses we entered demographic variables (sex, age, mothers' or fathers' level of education) to control for their effects in the first step, and then, six parenting variables for each parent were entered on the second step. As depicted in Table 10.4, among the demographic variables in the first step, only age weakly but significantly and negatively predicted attachment to mothers ($\beta = -.06$, $p < .05$). In the second step, mother emotional warmth ($\beta = .41$, $p < .001$), intrusion ($\beta = -.19$, $p < .01$) and comparison ($\beta = -.08$, $p < .05$) significantly predicted attachment to mothers. Maternal rejection, overprotection, and guilt induction did not have significant effects. All predictors accounted for 31% of the variance in attachment to mothers.

Results indicated that only age significantly and negatively predicted attachment to fathers in the first step ($\beta = -.09$, $p < .01$). In the second step, similar to

TABLE 10.3   Descriptive Statistics and Correlations Among the Major Variables Reported by Children ($N = 797$)

	1	2	3	4	5	6	7	8	9	10	11	12	13	14
1. Att to Mother	(.79)													
2. Att to Father	.55**	(.82)												
3. Mother RJC	−.42**	−.33**	(.83)											
4. Mother WR	.48**	.31**	−.47**	(.77)										
5. Mother CM	−.27**	−.25**	.46**	−.14**	(.78)									
6. Mother OP	.08	.07	.01	.41**	.17**	(.51)								
7. Mother GI	−.10**	−.15**	.31**	.15**	.32**	.34**	(.49)							
8. Mother INT	−.38**	−.34**	.63**	−.21**	.56**	.20**	.42**	(.72)						
9. Father RJC	−.27**	−.43**	.52**	−.27**	.26**	.00	.23**	.47**	(.88)					
10. Father WR	.36**	.54**	−.34**	.62**	−.11**	.33**	.04	−.20**	−.42**	(.76)				
11. Father CM	−.13**	−.26**	.28**	−.07	.59**	.14**	.32**	.43**	.48**	−.09*	(.78)			
12. Father OP	.07	.20**	−.06	.34**	.05	.65**	.20**	.08**	−.01	.49**	.11**	(.52)		
13. Father GI	−.10*	−.07	.29**	.10**	.32**	.29**	.62**	.37**	.36**	.16**	.47**	.33**	(.53)	
14. Father INT	−.23**	−.34**	.38**	−.08	.36**	.19**	.35**	.63**	.67**	−.19**	.57**	.18**	.46**	(.74)
Mean	3.35	3.23	1.22	3.43	1.77	2.68	2.01	1.53	1.22	3.32	1.62	2.40	1.97	1.43
SD	.47	.51	.34	.54	.64	.64	.46	.39	.37	.60	.60	.66	.47	.38

Notes: Att = attachment; RJC = rejection; WR = warmth; CM = comparison; OP = overprotection; GI = guilt induction; INT = intrusion. Cronbach's alphas for the measures were given at diagonals.

*p < .05. **p < .001.

TABLE 10.4   Predicting Attachment to Mothers and Fathers Using Parental Variables ($N = 767$)

Analysis	Attachment to Mother		Attachment to Father	
	β	ΔR²	β	ΔR²
Step 1: Demographic		.02°		.02°
Gender	.01		.05	
Age	−.06°		−.09°	
Mother/father education	.03		.01	
Step 2: Parenting variables		.29°°°		.34°°°
Mother/father warmth	.41°°°		.45°°°	
Mother/father rejection	−.04		−.09°	
Mother/father comparison	−.08°		−.10°°	
Mother/father overprotection	.03		.02	
Mother/father guilt induction	−.04		−.01	
Mother/father intrusion	−.19°°°		−.14°°°	
		R^2 total = .31		R^2 total = .36

°$p < .05$. °°$p < .01$. °°°$p < .001$.

maternal variables, paternal emotional warmth ($\beta = .45, p < .001$), intrusion ($\beta = -.14, p < .001$) and comparison ($\beta = -.10, p < .01$) significantly predicted attachment to fathers. Father rejection also significantly predicted attachment to fathers ($\beta = -.09, p < .01$). All predictors accounted for 36% of the variance on attachment to fathers. In sum, emotional warmth was the strongest predictor of attachment security; intrusion and comparison also negatively and significantly predicted attachment to parents, although of relatively weak magnitude. Overprotection and guilt induction, however, did not predict attachment to parents.

DISCUSSION

The present study examined the interplay between child-reported parenting behaviors, and both child- and parent-reported attachment security during middle childhood in a Turkish cultural context. We expected that culturally adaptive attachment dimensions (i.e., maternal attachment anxiety and paternal avoidance) and parental control behaviors (i.e., (over)protection, comparison, and guilt induction) would not have a negative impact on attachment to parents in Turkish cultural context.

Although the strength of the association is relatively weak, as expected, mothers' attachment avoidance significantly and negatively predicted attachment to mothers, whereas father attachment anxiety significantly and negatively predicted attachment to fathers. Furthermore, as expected, significant interactions between attachment anxiety and avoidance yielded clear patterns in explaining cultural relevance of these variables. The three significant interactions between attachment anxiety and avoidance revealed almost an identical pattern demonstrating that when mothers or fathers had the combination of high attachment avoidance and low anxiety, which typifies dismissing attachment style, their children had the lowest (insecure) attachment to their parents. This pattern seems to be stronger for maternal avoidance. Given that child-reported attachment security to parents was predicted by parent-reported attachment dimensions, completely eliminating common method variance, these findings signify that maternal avoidance rather than anxiety is a risk factor for secure attachment to parents in the Turkish cultural context. This is in line with Kağıtçıbaşı's family change theory, since in the family contexts of total interdependence and psychological/emotional interdependence close-knit family ties are valued and nurtured.

Predictive power of attachment anxiety, however, differed depending on parents' gender. As expected, whereas maternal attachment anxiety was not predictive of child attachment, paternal attachment anxiety significantly predicted attachment to fathers. Consistent with traditional, culturally defined gender-based expectations that, as compared to mothers, fathers should be relatively distant and even avoid showing emotional closeness to children, paternal avoidance was not a critical risk factor. Rothbaum et al. (2002) claim that extremely high levels of mother–child closeness and avoidance of father are typical normative patterns in Japan. There appears to be a similar pattern in traditional sex-typed collectivistic societies where gender roles are divergent, such as among low- and middle-class Turkish contexts from which the sample of this study was drawn.

These findings suggest that mothers' attachment anxiety, or preoccupied attachment, that is seen as an *overinvolved* or *enmeshed* mother–child interaction pattern in Western conceptualization (Rothbaum et al., 2002), may not be maladaptive (may even be normative) in cultures valuing psychological interdependence (Kağıtçıbaşı, 2007). In contrast, preoccupied or anxious-ambivalent attachment has been shown to have more negative effects on child's attachment security and psychological well-being in Western cultures (Rothbaum et al., 2002; van IJzendoorn & Sagi, 1999). These results show that although attachment security has much commonality across cultures, insecure attachment, especially the distinction between dismissing and preoccupied patterns, should be interpreted considering the cultural relevance of associated behaviors. Indeed, some inconsistencies observed regarding the predictive power of attachment anxiety or the working model of self (e.g., Pietromonaco & Barrett, 2000) might be related to cultural variations in the conceptualization of anxious attachment behaviors. Supporting this, Schmitt and his colleagues (2004) showed that the preoccupied attachment pattern was correlated with collectivism and was more common among East Asian cultures.

Our results further show that beyond parental attachment anxiety and avoidance, the impact of parenting behaviors on attachment security should also be evaluated considering cultural relevance of these behaviors. As expected, the effect of parental control variables on attachment to parents differed depending on the specific behaviors. Overall, we found that when the effect of parenting behaviors on attachment were evaluated on the basis of higher order categories of parenting dimensions, such as emotional warmth and rejection, there should be no major cultural differences. However, when parenting behaviors are examined in middle or lower order categories, such as the dimension of parental control, the effects vary depending on the normative and adaptive nature of the specific behaviors. Although overprotection and guilt induction are assumed to be insensitive and intrusive behaviors that result in insecure attachment in Western cultures (Ainsworth et al., 1978; Rothbaum et al., 2000), these behaviors did not have negative effects on attachment to parents in the current study. Indeed, according to family change theory (Kağitçibaşi, 1990, 2005, 2007) parental control is an important aspect of parenting in both the family model of interdependence and of psychological/emotional interdependence.

Thus a cross-cultural perspective can detect some individualistic or cultural biases in psychological theorizing that claim universality. The very term *overprotection* appears to be culturally bound. It appears to be a detrimental parental behavior in the family model of independence, where the child's autonomy and separation are nurtured. In contrast, in the psychologically/emotionally interdependent family, which nurtures closely knit relatedness, protection is an inherent aspect of positive parenting and can coexist with autonomy. It is not seen as overprotection, therefore, it turns out not to be detrimental.

Similarly, considering that guilt induction was found to be positively correlated with perceived emotional warmth from both mothers and fathers, it appears that guilt induction is interpreted as a sign of involvement and attention from the parents. Again an assumedly detrimental parenting behavior takes on a different meaning in a different family culture. This is another manifestation of the closely knit relatedness in the family model of psychological/emotional interdependence.

Results demonstrated that intrusion/love withdrawal and comparison are consistently different from the other parenting control variables. Intrusion negatively and significantly predicted attachment security to parents and had negative correlations with parental warmth for both parents. Although its effect was relatively weaker than intrusion, comparison also negatively predicted attachment security to both parents. Although some kinds of intrusive controlling seem relatively common in collectivist contexts, strict intrusion, especially when accompanied with love withdrawal, is perceived as an intrusion to personal autonomy.

Autonomy is the key concept in identity formation and parenting because of its universal value for healthy personal growth. Autonomy as a basic need cannot be equated with independence or individualism (Chirkov, Ryan, Kim, & Kaplan, 2003; Kağitçibaşi, 2005; Ryan & Deci 2003), and regardless of the context, autonomy represents the means for effective transmission and internalization of prevalent cultural values. Comparing children with similar others (i.e., comparison) can also be evaluated as an intrusive behavior limiting personal autonomy and uniqueness. Therefore, given that autonomy is a basic need in actualizing the self in all cultures, whether they value psychological interdependence or independence, excessive intrusion is likely to be perceived as a violation of autonomy and as a sign of rejection. Future studies should further explore both universal and culturally relevant dimensions of parental control using culturally informed approaches that see autonomy and relatedness in a balanced functional system (e.g., Imamoğlu, 2003; Kağitçibaşi, 2005).

These findings point to the need to consider what is a normative form of maternal (or parental) sensitivity in a cultural context. Past studies showed that whereas the mother's behavior contingency is a sign of maternal sensitivity in Western cultures, emotional warmth and support are the predictors of sensitivity in collectivist cultures (De Wolff & van IJzendoorn, 1997; Voelker et al., 1999). The present study corroborates those findings. It is also in line with other research showing that strong parental control, even physical punishment (not abuse), while detrimental in the individualistic Western middle-class contexts is not so among, for example, Afro-American (Deater-Deckart & Dodge, 1997; Lansford et al., 2003) and ethnic minority families in Europe and the United States (Dekovic et al., 2006; Harwood, Handwerker, Schoelmerich, & Leyendecker, 2001). Clearly, cultural norms regarding parenting play a role in the definitions and perceptions of what is "normal" and therefore acceptable. It is not only children's perceptions that count but going beyond that, the same behavior can take on different meanings for everyone concerned. Thus in individualistic contexts where intrusive behavior and strong discipline are not normative and are not endorsed, such parenting can indeed indicate pathology.

IMPLICATIONS FOR APPLICATIONS

The implications for applications are considerable. Cultural variations are seen even in parenting of infants where commonalities are the greatest (Carlson & Harwood, 2003; Keller, 2003; Voelker et al., 1999). With increasing age, from middle childhood toward adolescence, cultural diversity increases, which calls for culturally sensitive analyses. The issue is particularly notable in culture contact situations involving immigration and ethnic relations. For example, Gonzales, Cauce, and Mason (1996) noted that ethnic minority parents are often labeled authoritarian because they appear to be too controlling. Yet, as we have seen in this study, acceptable, nondomineering parental control is not detrimental to attachment; neither does it mean lack of love (Dekovic et al., 2006; Kağıtçıbaşı, 2007).

Attachment researchers have found that attachment anxiety and related hyperactivating strategies, rather than attachment avoidance, are more detrimental for interpersonal conflict, relationship quality, and attachment security in Western cultures (e.g., Campbell, Simpson, Boldry, & Kashy, 2005; Mikulincer & Shaver, 2007). Our findings, however, imply that attachment avoidance may be more predictive of attachment insecurity and potential relationship conflict in Turkish cultural contexts. Consistent with the culturally adaptive value of attachment anxiety and avoidance, their predictive power differs across cultures. These differences have critical implications for therapeutic interventions.

First, therapists working with clients with emotionally interdependent self-construals should acknowledge that attachment avoidance rather than anxiety may create a critical barrier for building therapeutic alliance, healthy transference, and effective intervention. Indeed, past studies show that although people with different insecure patterns benefit almost equally from therapeutic intervention, those with high avoidance (i.e., dismissing people) are less likely to seek treatment and also they are less emotionally committed to treatment (Daniel, 2006). These findings suggest that although avoidant people from collectivist or emotionally interdependent cultures feel more distress when they have relationship conflicts than avoidant people from individualist cultures, the former are less likely to seek help and treatment. Therapists should consider these culture-specific effects of attachment patterns and their possibly divergent effects on the interpersonal problems to employ effective treatment strategies.

Second, comparing Western and Japanese ways of relationship styles and parenting practices, Rothbaum and his colleagues (2002) argued that behaviors associated with high anxiety and high avoidance patterns have different implications for family dynamics and child functioning in individualist and collectivist cultures. Furthermore, given that Kağıtçıbaşı's (2007) model of emotional interdependence proposes that these two opposite patterns can be functionally integrated, basic attachment dimensions can be manifested in family dynamics differently in cultures that do not typically belong to these two extremes. Therefore, therapists should consider the cultural relevance and adaptive value of attachment style differences in intervention. For instance, those with emotionally interdependent family relationships may not tolerate much interpersonal distance, which is relatively common in Western cultures. These individuals may perceive formal and distant relationships that are open to confrontation as more threatening and stressful than those with emotionally independent family relationships. In sum, considering that cultural differences are reflected in the attachment relationships, therapists should acknowledge and hence should be able to tailor their intervention strategies accordingly.

Third, since very close and overprotective mother–child relationships are culturally adaptive in non-Western cultures, therapists should not immediately see these "enmeshed" patterns of parenting as dysfunctional or problematic. Also, as suggested by Rothbaum et al. (2002), therapists should pay more attention to nonverbal cues especially if the clients are from non-Western cultures. Finally, past studies have shown that the interaction between therapist and client attachment patterns has an effect on the effectiveness of treatment (Daniel, 2006). For instance, if a therapist with high attachment anxiety is working with a client with high attachment avoidance (especially if the client is from a collectivist culture) this may result in the least effective treatment outcome.

These issues appear critical especially if the therapist and the client are from different cultural contexts. If health workers, social workers, therapists, and other service professionals do not understand these culturally sensitive issues, they may misjudge and mislead families. Thus, comparative cross-cultural theory and research are promising in informing both science and practice.

ACKNOWLEDGMENT

This research was supported by the Scientific and Technological Research Council of Turkey (TUBITAK), grant No. 105K102. We thank Mehmet Harma for his help and useful comments.

REFERENCES

Aiken, L. S., & West, S. G. (1991). *Multiple regression: Testing and interpreting interactions*. Newbury Park, CA: Sage.

Ainsworth, M. D. S. (1967). *Infancy in Uganda: Infant care and the growth of love*. Baltimore: Johns Hopkins University Press.

Ainsworth, M. D. S., Blehar, M., Waters, E., & Wall, S. (1978). *Patterns of attachment: A psychological study of the strange situation*. Hillsdale, NJ: Lawrence Erlbaum Associates.

Ainsworth, M. D. S., & Bowlby, J. (1991). An ethological approach to personality development. *American Psychologist, 46*, 331–341.

Barber, B. K. (1996). Parental psychological control: Revisiting a neglected construct. *Child Development, 67*, 3296–3319.

Barber, B. K., & Harmon, E. L. (2002). Violating the self: Parental psychological control of children and adolescents. In B. K. Barber (Ed.), *Intrusive parenting: How psychological control affects children and adolescents* (pp. 15–52). Washington, DC: American Psychological Association.

Baumrind, D. (1991). Effective parenting during the early adolescent transition. In P. Cowan & E. M. Hetherington (Eds.), *Family transitions: Advances in family research series* (pp. 111–163). Hillsdale, NJ: Lawrence Erlbaum Associates.

Bowlby, J. (1982). *Attachment and loss: Vol. 1. Attachment* (2nd ed.). New York: Basic Books.

Bowlby, J. (1988). Developmental psychiatry comes of age. *American Journal of Psychiatry, 145*, 1–10.

Brennan, K. A., Clark, C. L., & Shaver, P. R. (1998). Self-report measurement of adult attachment: An integrative overview. In J. A. Simpson & W. S. Rholes (Eds.), *Attachment theory and close relationships* (pp. 46–76). New York: Guilford Press.

Bretherton, I. (1992). The origins of attachment theory: John Bowlby and Mary Ainsworth. *Developmental Psychology, 28*, 759–775.

Bretherton, I., Golby, B., & Cho, E. (1997). Attachment and the transmission of values. In J. Grusec & L. Kucszynski (Eds.). *Parenting and children's s internalization of values* (pp. 103–134). New York: Wiley.

Campbell, L., Simpson, J. A., Boldry, J. G., & Kashy, D. (2005). Perceptions of conflict and support in romantic relationships: The role of attachment anxiety. *Journal of Personality and Social Psychology, 88*, 510–531.

Carlson, V. J., & Harwood, R. L. (2003). Attachment, culture, and the caregiving system: The cultural patterning of everyday experiences among Anglo and Puerto Rican mother-infant pairs. *Infant Mental Health Journal, 24*, 53–73.

Chirkov, V., Ryan, R. M., Kim, Y., & Kaplan, U. (2003). Differentiating autonomy from individualism and independence: A self-determination theory perspective on internalization of cultural orientation, gender and well-being. *Journal of Personality and Social Psychology, 84*, 97–110.

Crittenden, P. M. (2000). A dynamic-maturational exploration of the meaning of security and adaptation: Empirical, cultural, and theoretical considerations. In P. M. Crittenden and A. H. Claussen (Eds). *The organization of attachment relationships: Maturation, culture, and context* (pp. 358–384). New York: Cambridge University Press.

Daniel, S. I. F. (2006). Adult attachment patterns and individual psychotherapy: A review. *Clinical Psychology Review, 26*, 968–984.

Darling, N., & Steinberg, L. (1993). Parenting style as context: An integrative model. *Psychological Bulletin, 113*, 487–496.

Deater-Deckard, K., & Dodge, K. A. (1997). Externalizing behavior problems and discipline revisited: Nonlinear effects and variation by culture, context, and gender. *Psychological Inquiry, 8*, 161–175.

Dekovic, M., Pels, T., & Model, S. (Eds.). (2006). *Unity and diversity in child rearing: Family life in a multicultural society.* Lewiston, NY: Edwin Mellen Press.

De Wolff, M. S., & van IJzendoorn, M. H. (1997). Sensitivity and attachment: A meta-analysis on parental antecedents of infant attachment. *Child Development, 68,* 571–591.

Fraley, R. C., Waller, N. G., & Brennan, K. A. (2000). An item response theory analysis of self-report measures of adult attachment. *Journal of Personality and Social Psychology, 78,* 350–365.

George, C., & Solomon, J. (1999). Attachment and caregiving: The caregiving behavioral system. In J. Cassidy & P. R. Shaver (Eds.), *Handbook of attachment* (pp. 649–670). New York: Guilford Press.

Gonzales, N. A., Cauce, A. M., & Mason, C. A. (1996). Interobserver agreement in the assessment of parental behavior and parent-adolescent conflict: African American mothers, daughters, and independent observers. *Child Development, 67,* 1483–1498.

Harwood, R. L., Handwerker, W. P., Schoelmerich, A., & Leyendecker, B. (2001). Ethnic category labels, parental beliefs, and the contextualized individual: An exploration of the individualism-sociocentrism debate. *Parenting: Science and Practice, 1,* 217–236.

Imamoğlu, E. O. (2003). Individuation and relatedness: Not opposing but distinct and complementary. *Genetic, Social and General Psychology Monographs, 129,* 367–402.

Kağıtçıbaşı, C. (1990). Family and socialization in cross-cultural perspective: A model of change. In J. Berman (Ed.), *Cross-cultural perspectives: Nebraska symposium on motivation, 1989* (pp. 135–200). Lincoln: University of Nebraska Press.

Kağıtçıbaşı, C. (1996). The autonomous-relational self: A new synthesis. *European Psychologist, 1*(3), 180–186.

Kağıtçıbaşı, C. (2005). Autonomy and relatedness in cultural context: Implications for self and family. *Journal of Cross-Cultural Psychology, 36,* 403–422.

Kağıtçıbaşı, C. (2007). *Family, self and human development across cultures: Theory and applications* (Rev. 2nd ed.). Hillsdale, NJ: Lawrence Erlbaum Associates.

Karavasilis, L., Doyle, A. B., & Markiewicz, D. (2003). Associations between parenting style and attachment orientation in middle childhood and early adolescence. *International Journal of Behavioural Development, 27,* 153–164.

Keller, H., Papaligoura, Z., Kunsemuller, P., Voelker, S., Papaeliou, C., Lohaus, A., … Mousouli, V. (2003). Concepts of mother- infant interaction in Greece and Germany. *Journal of Cross Cultural Psychology, 34,* 677–689.

Kerns, K. A., Klepac, L., & Cole, A. (1996). Peer relationships and preadolescents' perceptions of security in the child-mother relationship. *Developmental Psychology, 32,* 457–466.

Lamborn, S. D., Mounts, N. S., Steinberg, L., & Dornbusch, S. M. (1991). Patterns of competence and adjustment among adolescents from authoritative, authoritarian, indulgent, and neglectful families. *Child Development, 62,*1049–1065.

Lansford, J. E., Deater-Deckard, K., Dodge, K. A., Bates, J. E., & Pettit, G. S. (2003). Ethnic differences in the link between physical discipline and later adolescent externalizing behaviors. *Journal of Child Psychology and Psychiatry, 44,* 1–13.

Lau, S., Lew, W. J. F., Hau, K. T., Cheung, P. C., & Berndt, T. J. (1990). Relations among perceived parental control, warmth, indulgence, and family harmony of Chinese in Mainland China. *Developmental Psychology, 26,* 674–677.

Main, M. (1990), Cross-cultural studies of attachment organization: Recent studies, changing methodologies, and the conditional strategies. *Human Development, 33,* 48–61.

Markus, M. T., Lindhout, I. E., Boer, F., Hoogendijk, T. H. G., & Arrindell, W. A. (2003). Factors of perceived parental rearing styles: The EMBU-C examined in a sample of Dutch primary school children. *Personality and Individual Differences, 34,* 503–519.

Mayseless, O. (2005). Ontogeny of attachment in middle childhood: Conceptualization of normative changes. In K. A. Kerns & R. A. Richardson (Eds.), *Attachment in middle childhood* (pp. 1–23). New York: Guilford Press.

Mikulincer, M., & Shaver, P. R. (2007). *Attachment in adulthood: Structure, dynamics, and change*. New York: Guilford Press.

Pietromonaco, P. R., & Barrett, L. F. (2000). The internal working models concept: What do we really know about the self in relation to other? *Review of General Psychology, 2*, 155–175.

Rohner, R. P., & Pettengill, S. M. (1985). Perceived parental acceptance-rejection and parental control among Korean adolescents. *Child Development, 56*, 524–528.

Rothbaum, F., Pott, M., Azuma, H., Miyake, K., & Weisz, J. (2000). The development of close relationships in Japan and the United States: Paths of symbiotic harmony and generative tension. *Child Development, 71*(5), 1121–1142.

Rothbaum, F., Rosen, K., Ujiie, T., & Uchida, N. (2002). Family systems theory, attachment theory, and culture. *Family Process, 41*, 328–350.

Rothbaum, F., Weisz, J., Pott, M., Miyake, K., & Morelli, G. (2000). Attachment and culture. *American Psychologist, 55*, 1093–1104.

Rudy, D., & Grusec, J. E. (2001). Correlates of authoritarian parenting in individualist and collectivist cultures and implications for understanding the transmission of values. *Journal of Cross-Cultural Psychology, 32*, 202–212.

Ryan, R. M., & Deci, E. L. (2003). On assimilating identities to the self: A self-determination theory perspective on internalization and integrity within cultures. In M. R. Leary & J. P. Tangney (Eds.), *Handbook of self and identity* (pp. 253–272). New York: Guilford Press.

Schmitt, D. P., Alcalay, L., Allensworth, M., Allik, J., Ault, L., Austers, I., … Zupanèiè, A. (2004). Patterns and universals of adult romantic attachment across 62 cultural regions: Are models of self and other pancultural constructs? *Journal of Cross-Cultural Psychology, 35*, 367–402.

Selçuk, E., Günaydın, G., Sümer, N., & Uysal A. (2005). Yetişkin baglanma boyutları için yeni bir ölçüm: Yakın Ilişkilerde Yaşantılar Envanteri-II'nin Türk örnekleminde psikometrik açıdan degerlendirilmesi [A new measure for adult attachment styles: The psychometric evaluation of Experiences in Close Relationships-Revised (ECR-R) on a Turkish sample]. *Türk Psikoloji Yazıları, 8*, 1–11.

Sümer, N. (2006). Yetişkin bağlanma ölçeklerinin kategoriler ve boyutlar düzeyinde karşılaştırılması [Categorical and dimensional comparison of the adult attachment measures]. *Türk Psikoloji Dergisi, 21*, 1–22.

Sümer, N., & Anafarta-Şendağ, M. (2009). Orta Çocukluk Döneminde Ebeveynler Bağlanma, Benlik Algısı ve Kaygı [Attachment to parents during middle childhood, self perceptions, and anxiety]. *Türk Psikoloji Dergisi, 24*, 86–101.

Sümer, N., & Engin, E. (2004, July). Role of parenting styles in predicting attachment anxiety and avoidance. Paper presented at the International Association for Relationship Research Conference, Madison, WI.

Thompson, R. A. (1999). Early attachment and later development. In J. Cassidy & P. R. Shaver. (Eds.), *Handbook of attachment: Theory, research, and clinical applications* (pp. 265–286). New York: Guilford Press.

van IJzendoorn, M. H., & Kroonenberg, P. (1988). Cross-cultural patterns of attachment: A meta-analysis of the strange situation. *Child Development, 59*, 147–156.

van IJzendoorn, M. H., & Sagi, A. (1999). Cross-cultural patterns of attachment: Universal and contextual dimensions. In J. Cassidy, & P. R. Shaver (Eds.), *Handbook of attachment: Theory, research, and clinical applications* (pp. 713–734). New York: Guilford Press

Voelker, S., Keller, H., Lohaus, A., Cappenberg, M., & Chasiotis, A. (1999). Maternal interactive behaviour in early infancy and later attachment. *International Journal of Behavioral Development, 23*, 921–936.

11

Attachment Theory, Culture, and Africa
Past, Present, and Future

MARK TOMLINSON, LYNNE MURRAY, and PETER COOPER

CONTENTS

Although Bowlby is undoubtedly the architect of attachment theory, the role of Mary Ainsworth cannot be underestimated. For the purposes of this chapter, two of her seminal contributions to attachment theory will serve as the starting point. The first is her ethological study of the Ganda in Uganda (Ainsworth, 1977), the first study of attachment and culture, a study which in fact presages by a number of years Bowlby's (1969) three central attachment texts. The second was her development of the Strange Situation Procedure (SSP; Ainsworth, Blehar, Waters, & Wall, 1978), which enabled the empirical testing of Bowlby's ideas, including the role of maternal sensitivity to infant signals in the development of attachment. In this chapter we will focus on attachment studies in Africa, highlighting the paucity of research conducted there and suggesting how this can be rectified. To the best of our knowledge there are no empirical data on adult attachment in Africa and therefore we focus on parent–child attachment in this chapter. We argue that the range of circumstances in which children in Africa are reared, particularly insofar as they contrast with conditions in the developed world, provides evidence of considerable value in evaluating the general usefulness of attachment theory, as well as in refining our understanding of the nature of attachment. Although not a central plank of attachment theory itself, a major concern of research in the developed world has been to identify the conditions under which sensitive parenting, and thus secure infant attachment, occurs. In general, poorer parental sensitivity has been found to arise in the context of socioeconomic adversity and the presence of mental health problems (Valenzuela, 1990). Nevertheless, developed world populations are often relatively homogeneous, and the fact that developing world populations are likely to include a far wider range of rearing conditions means that results from their study stand to make an important contribution to this aspect of the understanding of attachment and its workings. Finally, we discuss the future for attachment theory in the African research agenda.

ATTACHMENT THEORY AND CULTURE

Bowlby's (1969) depiction of early human life on the savanna grasslands of Africa as instrumental in the development of infant distress signals and secure base behavior, together with Ainsworth's (1977) Ganda studies, firmly positioned Africa in the inception of attachment theory. However, the principal measure used in research on attachment, the SSP (Ainsworth et al., 1978), was developed as an assessment of infant attachment quality in a middle-class White population in the United States of America, and the precursors and sequelae of such attachment have also been principally investigated in this context. Although the use of the SSP is being increasingly extended to other developed world cultures (e.g., Japan, Germany, Israel), the relevance to developing world contexts of conclusions deriving from this method is in need of investigation.

Criteria for the Cross-Cultural Applicability of Attachment Theory

Bowlby (1969) saw attachment theory as being a universal evolutionary one, applicable (albeit with particular caretaking variations between cultures) to all cultures. Van IJzendoorn and Sagi (1999) have outlined four hypotheses that they argue need to be confirmed or discounted in attempting to answer the question about the cross-cultural applicability of attachment theory and the SSP. In this section we will outline the four hypotheses and then go on to show how studies of childrearing practices and attachment in six African populations provide considerable support for the cross-cultural applicability of attachment theory, and at the same time extend and enrich attachment theory.

The Four Hypotheses

The idea that all infants become attached to one or more caregivers (parental or nonparental), except in cases such as those of extreme mental retardation (van IJzendoorn & Sagi, 1999) or the profound neglect characteristic of some Romanian orphanages (Chisholm, Carter, Ames, & Morrison, 1995), is termed the *universality hypothesis*. Although this hypothesis has been confirmed in several Western samples (van IJzendoorn & Sagi, 1999), part of the cross-cultural question requires its confirmation/disconfirmation among other cultures and countries.

The *normativity hypothesis* concerns the idea that security of attachment is the norm. The majority of infants in Western societies assessed using the SSP have, indeed, been found to be securely attached (van IJzendoorn & Kroonenberg, 1988; van IJzendoorn, Sagi, & Lambermon, 1992), but it needs to be demonstrated that this holds in other cultures.

The *sensitivity hypothesis*, perhaps the central tenet of attachment theory, holds that it is the ability of the caregiver to respond sensitively and promptly to the infant's signals that will ensure the development of a secure attachment (Ainsworth et al., 1978; De Wolff & van IJzendoorn, 1997). The importance of such antecedent features of early parenting in the development of attachment security has been confirmed in many studies in Western countries; and cross-cultural applicability requires that this is also true elsewhere.

Attachment theory's predictions concerning the sequelae of different attachment patterns are characterized by van IJzendoorn and Sagi (1999) as the *competency hypothesis*. Thus, securely attached infants in Western studies have been found to be more autonomous; less likely to have behavior problems; and more likely to form close, stable peer relationships than insecure children. This needs to be confirmed in studies of non-Western children.

ATTACHMENT STUDIES IN AFRICA

Considering that Ainsworth's theory and subsequent development of the SSP originated in her study of the Ganda (Ainsworth, 1977), the paucity of research on attachment patterns and processes in Africa is striking. Few studies have been published on attachment in Africa (van IJzendoorn & Sagi, 1999) and of these few have employed the SSP. In the following, we consider each of the African studies concerned with attachment relationships, focusing specifically on the question of the relevance of their findings to the core attachment theory hypotheses.

The Gusii Study

Kermoian and Leiderman (1986), in the context of multiple caregiving among the Gusii of Kenya, tested whether different attachment relationships developed between infants and their mothers compared to those between infants and other caregivers. A modified SSP was implemented with two separation–reunion episodes each for the mother, caregiver, and stranger. In terms of daily caregiving, caretakers other than the mother (usually older siblings) care for Gusii infants for most of the day. Nevertheless, the role of these caregivers is strictly limited to social and playful interactions, while the biological mother is responsible for most of the physical care and health of the child. This study therefore addresses a number of questions: first, whether the secure pattern of attachment manifest in the SSP occurs in a very different context; second, whether it occurs with similar frequency; and third, whether it depends on care that includes meeting primary infant biological needs (as provided by the mother), or whether it also emerges in the context of other kinds of relationship (as with the other caregivers).

Kermoian and Leiderman (1986) also investigated the question of whether security showed the same relationship to other aspects of child functioning as in developed world samples, in this case cognitive development; and they also investigated background predictors of attachment security. With regard to the first two questions, results showed similar patterns of secure attachment, and similar rates of security in relation to the mother (61%), as those found in developed world samples. However, although the insecure behavior patterns were not described in detail, it was noted that, during the procedure, insecure children were prone to explore the environment visually rather than manipulatively (Kermoian & Leiderman, 1986). With regard to the third and fourth questions, it was notable that similar rates of security applied to relationships with nonmaternal caregivers (54%). Furthermore, and in contrast to findings from developed world samples, no relationship was found between attachment security to the mother and infant cognitive development, whereas secure attachment to their nonmaternal caregiver was associated with better infant cognitive functioning. These findings suggest, therefore, a specificity of effect not always evident in developed world samples. In this context it is possible that improved cognitive functioning derives from relationships that have more potential for cognitive stimulation, like the stimulating play that occurred in nonmaternal care, whereas more basic caretaking aspects of attachment may not confer cognitive benefit. Although this study concerned a small sample and validated measures of caregiving were not used, the findings are important in that they both lend support for the cross-cultural validity of the hypotheses concerning applicability of attachment theory, as set out by van IJzendoorn and Sagi (1999), and they also help to refine and develop attachment theory accounts of the role of relationships in child development. One of the most important contributions of the Kermoian and Leiderman (1986) study was the inclusion of relationships to nonmaternal caregivers. As van IJzendoorn and Sagi point out, most attachment research has focused on the dyadic interactions between mother and child, and it is cross-cultural studies of attachment that have sensitized the field to the importance of the infant's wider social network.

The Hausa Study

Marvin, VanDevender, Iwanaga, LeVine, and LeVine (1977) observed 18 infants between the ages of 6 months and 14 months among the Hausa of Nigeria. The economy is largely agricultural and the religion Islamic, with men able to take as many as four wives. While men work in the fields, wives tend gardens in their living compounds. The Hausa live and work in a context of high social density; typically, two or three co-wives are in the compound at all times and are thus in close physical proximity to one another throughout the day, and the care of infants is one of their shared household responsibilities. Nevertheless, this sharing does not imply that there is no role differentiation, as the biological mother takes almost complete responsibility for feeding, bathing, and other routine physical activities (Marvin et al., 1977). Other caregiving activities, such as comforting the infant and playing with or vocalizing to the infant, are shared by the familiar adults and in some cases by older children.

With regard to caregiver responsiveness to the infant's signals, Marvin et al. (1977) posit that an indulgent, as well as restrictive, caregiving stance operates. While awake, Hausa infants are almost always in close physical proximity to one or more adult caregivers. As a result, infant signals, such as crying, are responded to promptly by adults or older children—an indulgent response (Marvin et al., 1977). On the other hand, because of the dangers involved in the infants' exploring the wider environment, they are not allowed to explore alone—a restrictive response. Marvin et al. argue that this restriction of exploratory locomotion results in the infants utilizing their caregiver as a secure base in a different way from the one usually understood. Marvin et al. describe the Hausa infants as exploring the environment in a visual and manipulatory fashion, providing that they are in close physical proximity to their caregiver. As soon as the caregiver leaves the room or compound, however, infants cease this form of exploration, thereby supporting the hypothesis concerning the link between the presence of the secure base of the attachment figure and exploration of the environment.

Although the Hausa infants appear to be attached to three or four different figures (including fathers), most are primarily attached to one. Importantly, the principal figure is not necessarily the mother, who is solely responsible for feeding, but rather the person who holds and otherwise interacts with the infant the most. As in the study of Kermoian and Leiderman (1986), this finding helps refine the understanding of the caretaking conditions under which secure attachments are likely to develop, underlining the importance of social, rather than purely biological, care functions. Van IJzendoorn and Sagi (1999) note that while this study documents the existence of multiple attachments, it also shows infant preference for one attachment figure, and in this respect it provides support for the universality hypothesis. In addition, it refines the understanding of attachment by illustrating that the form of attachment-seeking behaviors is variable and depends on the particular living conditions.

The !Kung Study

The !Kung (or Bushmen) of Botswana way of life is prototypical of forager populations (Tronick, Morelli, & Ivey, 1992). !Kung infants are fed on demand, leading to brief but frequent feedings, even during the night, with infants feeding while their mother sleeps (Konner, 1977). Physical contact is high, with infants carried around in slings on their mother's body as well as sleeping in close proximity to their mother. In fact, !Kung infants are in physical contact with their mothers 70% to 80% of the time in the first year of life, thereby experiencing a far more exclusive relationship than that of either the Gusii or the Hausa. During the second year of life, the social network expands, and these children spend much of their time in multiage peer groups in which they are able to form new bonds. Interactions with these peers occur most often in the context of play. Konner (1977) argues that the high social density of the child-rearing environment allows mothers to be very indulgent and highly sensitive to the signals of their infant. Van IJzendoorn and Sagi (1999) argue that the !Kung example provides support for both the universality hypothesis (it is the mother–infant bond that fulfills the function of protection and stimulation), and the sensitivity hypothesis, with the early intimate and sensitive relationship evolving into more independent affiliations with peers.

The Efe Study

The Efe are a group of foragers living in Zaire. Groups usually comprise about 20 individuals, several extended families and a few visitors (Tronick et al., 1992). The Efe subsist through hunting small game and by gathering food such as nuts and fruit from the forest. Food resources are unpredictable, with the result that the economic activities of the men and the women are diverse (Tronick et al., 1992). Men may accompany the women as they forage, and women may assist on a hunt, flushing out the animals.

As is the case with the Hausa and the Gusii, but unlike the !Kung, the Efe employ a system of multiple caregivers, and because their day-to-day activities are relatively uncoordinated, there is an almost continuous presence of people in the camp (Morelli & Tronick, 1991; Tronick et al., 1992). This allows mothers the opportunity to leave their children in the camp while they forage. Efe infants and toddlers therefore spend about half of their time in social contact with people who are not their mothers. Unlike the Hausa, Gusii, and !Kung, the physical care of the Efe infants is not the sole responsibility of the mother, and Efe infants are allowed to nurse with other adult women, even in the presence of the mother herself (Morelli & Tronick, 1991). The network of alternative caregivers is also larger than for the Hausa and Gusii (Tronick, Morelli, & Winn, 1987). As is the case with the !Kung, infant distress is responded to promptly—mostly as a consequence of the high social network density (Morelli & Tronick, 1991).

In spite of their experience of multiple carers, even in intimate situations such as feeding, during the second half of the first year Efe infants begin showing a preference for the care of their mother. Morelli and Tronick (1991) believe that one of the reasons for this is the care that occurs at night, care that in this case is the sole responsibility of the mother. Morelli and Tronick describe playful interactions between mother and child interrupting sleep throughout the night. Van IJzendoorn and Sagi (1999) postulate that, from the point of view of attachment theory, night is a particularly stressful time where protection from a caregiver is most important, but it is also notable that mothers seek opportunities for other kinds of contact with their infants at this time, and these occasions may also be important in forging special bonds.

Tronick et al. (1992) argue that the focus of attachment theory on the quality of the relationship between infant and mother (as the prototypical form) is of limited relevance to the Efe. They argue that Efe infants and toddlers experience a changing pattern of multiple and simultaneous relationships and may represent their social world as a landscape populated with several secure bases (Tronick et al., 1992). Indeed, Tronick et al. question what they describe as the hierarchical epigenetic view of social development in which the infant progresses from a primary relationship with one individual (invariably the mother) to relationships with others (usually peers). In their view, the Efe pattern of care supports a socioecological model of caretaking, where multiple simultaneous relationships may each have independent developmental effects and consequences for later development and relationships (Tronick et al., 1992). While the multiplicity of Efe relationships is undoubtedly of central importance to the development of children in this culture, it is nevertheless notable that a preferential attachment to the mother does generally develop.

The Dogon Study

True, Pisani, and Oumar (2001) investigated attachment relationships among the Dogon ethnic group of Mali in West Africa. This was the first published African study to use the traditional SSP assessment. The sample consisted of 42 mother–infant pairs, divided into two subsamples: a village sample of 15 mother–infant pairs and a town sample of 27 mother–infant pairs. The Dogon economy is based on the subsistence farming of millet. Variable food supplies, diseases, and impure drinking water result in health problems for all residents, but mostly the children, with malnutrition being a particular problem (True et al., 2001). The majority of residents are Muslim, with most households comprising a father, his wife and co-wives, and their children (True et al., 2001). All the mothers and infants live in compounds that consist of an open courtyard where most daily activities take place. True et al. state that there is no "typical" childcare arrangement, with some infants cared for by their mother, others by a grandmother, and others by both the mother and another family member. Biological mothers nurse infants in the first year, and infants are breastfed frequently and on demand. Infant mortality rates are high with as many as 25% of children dying before their fifth birthday. Van IJzendoorn and Sagi (1999) speculate that this threatening ecology is one of the reasons for demand breastfeeding and the fact that the infants are kept in close physical proximity almost all of the time.

Mother–infant dyads were filmed in the traditional SSP, as well as being observed twice in the stressful setting of a weigh-in that formed part of a standardized well-baby examination. Results indicated high levels of both secure attachment (69%) and disorganized attachment (23%). A few resistant mother–infant dyads were also found (8%), but the avoidant classification was entirely absent (True et al., 2001). When infants classified as disorganized were "forced" into the best fitting attachment classification of the tripartite system (Lyons-Ruth & Jacobvitz, 1999), 88% were classified as secure and 12% as resistant.

With regard to the formulation that infant disorganization reflects the infant's experience of their parent as frightened/frightening, True et al. (2001) found a link between "dysfluent" mother–infant communication and infant disorganization. In addition, the mothers of disorganized infants were rated significantly higher than other mothers for frightened or frightening behaviors (True et al., 2001). True et al. note that the indices of frightened/frightening used were mild to moderate and that there was no sign of physical abuse. Van IJzendoorn and Sagi (1999) suggest that the True et al. study provides evidence for the universality hypothesis (i.e., the ABCD coding system can be applied in an African culture) as well as for the normativity hypothesis (most infants were classified as securely attached); and the study also provides evidence of consistent associations between the quality of care and attachment type (supporting the sensitivity hypothesis).

The Khayelitsha, South Africa, Study

South Africa is a developing country characterized by high levels of poverty and inequality. As a result of its apartheid past, conditions of adversity disproportionately affect the Black South African population. The effects of poverty and the inequalities in South Africa are evident across all aspects of child development, and are apparent in the high infant mortality rate, stunted growth, high rates of early drop out from school and general low levels of educational attainment, high rates of homelessness, and criminality. The occurrence of such hardship is associated with high rates of child psychological disturbance. Indeed, a study of children living in Khayelitsha, a periurban settlement of the outskirts of Cape Town, found that as many as 40% of the children exposed to community violence (a common occurrence in this area) were found to have one or more psychiatric disorders (Lockhat & Van Niekerk, 2000).

An important question in seeking to understand the development of children growing up in settlements like Khayelitsha concerns the nature of the parenting that is possible under the conditions of pervasive adversity. Preoccupation with external problems (e.g., poverty, lack of partner support), as well as more immediate difficulties (e.g., trauma and losses), may directly affect the parent's capacity to be responsive to his or her child. This difficulty may be further compounded by maternal mental health problems, in particular, by the occurrence of depression. Indeed, an epidemiological study found the point prevalence of maternal depression in Khayelitsha at 2 months postpartum to be 34.7% (Cooper et al. 1999), a prevalence almost 3 times that of Western samples (O'Hara, 1997). With regard to the mother–infant relationship, Cooper et al.'s study also showed that depressed mothers in Khayelitsha were significantly less sensitive to their infants in early face-to-face interactions than were nondepressed mothers; and, the infants of depressed mothers were less positively engaged with their mothers.

Further assessment of infant attachment was conducted in this sample using the SSP (Tomlinson, Cooper, & Murray, 2005). Given the high levels of postpartum depression and associated disturbances in the mother–infant relationship, as well as the high levels of socioeconomic adversity in Khayelitsha, rates of insecure infant attachment were expected to be high, and to be predicted by dimensions of risk and maternal depression, and associated interaction difficulties. As hypothesized, maternal interaction difficulties (intrusive-coercion and remote disengagement at 2 months, and insensitivity at 18 months) were associated with insecure attachments. Furthermore, when account was taken of these patterns of maternal interaction, the mother's depression and lack of partner support were no longer significant predictors. In spite of these systematic associations, contrary to expectations, 61.9% of the sample was securely attached, in line with proportions in many cross-cultural studies of infant attachment where rates of 67% (using the original Ainsworth ABC classifications; van IJzendoorn & Kroonenburg, 1988) and 55% (van IJzendoorn, Goldberg, Kroonenberg, & Frenkel, 1992) have been found in meta-analytic studies (van IJzendoorn & Sagi, 1999). This high rate of security in the context of Khayelitsha was particularly unexpected given the extreme levels of social adversity. Nevertheless, results of other studies of developing world populations are consistent with this figure. Thus, Zevalkink, Riksen-Walraven, and van Lieshout (1999) found similar rates of secure attachment in a high-risk Indonesian sample and argue that, despite adverse living conditions, mothers of secure children were able to create a sufficiently good personal environment for the healthy emotional development of their children. Similarly, True et al. (2001) found high levels of secure attachment in Mali, in a community characterized by extremely high levels of adversity.

Discussion of Findings

Together these studies suggest that the mechanisms operating in the developing world may be different from those in high-risk samples in the developed world, where rates of insecure attachment are typically high (Cichetti & Barnett, 1991). Belsky (1999), commenting on the fact that rates of secure attachment seldom fall below 50%, argues that a basic level of security is a prerequisite for a community to be able to survive. While this might well be the case, in each instance an account is required of how this level is achieved. One possible explanation for the unexpectedly high rate of secure attachments in Khayelitsha is the protective contribution of Xhosa social and cultural organization (even in the midst of extreme poverty). Thus, despite the extreme levels of adversity and the legacy of the apartheid system that systematically attempted to destroy family structures and community cohesion, there still exists a humanity and compassion in Khayelitsha for neighbors and the wider community. In African parlance this notion of community spirit and compassion for others is known as *Ubuntu*. Infants and young children are seen as belonging, to some extent, to the community; and responsibility for their safety and well-being is seen as a collective concern. In addition, the combination of extremely close dwellings and small houses facilitates a great deal of social interaction in the narrow portions of space in front of houses or in the street. This high-density living, and the communal nature of much of Xhosa culture (Chalmers, 1990), combined with the survival imperatives of living in extreme poverty (many mothers depend at times on the assistance of friends and neighbors to, quite literally, feed their children) may mean that some of the more negative social consequences of poverty that are often present in more developed societies do not arise. An understanding of the distinctive patterns of social arrangement regarding infant care in different cultures is of critical importance in evaluating the cross-cultural applicability of attachment theory.

The investigation of subtypes of attachment quality is similarly informative with regard to the understanding of how particular cultural practices may influence attachment quality. In Khayelitsha, a quarter of the attachments were found to be disorganized (Tomlinson et al., 2005), compared to 15% in the meta-analysis of van IJzendoorn, Goldberg, et al. (1992). While these rates of disorganized attachment are high, they are consistent with rates of disorganized infants in other low-income samples such as those in the Mali study (van IJzendoorn, Schuengel, & Bakermans-Kranenburg, 1999). In both Mali and in Khayelitsha, mothers of disorganized infants had significantly higher levels of frightened or frightening behaviors than other mothers. In light of this, it is worth noting the possible preoccupations that many of the women in Khayelitsha experience and how these might contribute to a frightening interaction style. Lyons-Ruth and Block (1993) noted that disorganized infant attachment behaviors occur predominantly in the context of maternal childhood experiences of family abuse or violence, and that the severity of this violence was related to hostile and intrusive maternal behavior. Levels of family violence, rape, and sexual and physical abuse are extremely high in South Africa (Dawes, 2002). In addition, the impact of HIV/AIDS as a factor in the preoccupations of women is crucial. HIV/AIDS prevalence rates are high in South Africa (with a prevalence of almost 30% among women attending antenatal clinics) and are a common source of concern in communities like Khayelitsha. Given the similar distributions of disorganized attachment found in Mali and in Khayelitsha, it is possible that it is the high level of psychosocial stress obtained in both samples that, by virtue of its impact on maternal preoccupations, accounts for the predominance of disorganization in these samples.

In contrast to the level of disorganized attachment in Khayelitsha, only 4.1% of the infants were classified as avoidant (compared to 22% in the van IJzendoorn, Goldberg, et al., 1992, study), and both the True et al. (2001) and the Zevalkink et al. (1999) studies found similar low levels of the avoidant pattern in Mali and Indonesia, respectively. True and colleagues argue that the caregiving practices associated with infant avoidance, such as rejection of attachment bids and the lack of close physical contact or tender holding, are simply not found among the Dogon. Zevalkink and colleagues (1999) make a similar argument in accounting for the low rate of infant avoidance in their sample. The Indonesian norm of responding to crying, they argue, makes a rejecting or neglecting attitude of the mother more difficult to develop. Many of the homes in Khayelitsha consist of only one room, resulting in all the mother's daily activities occurring in the presence of the infant. Together with demand feeding and close sleeping arrangements (in this sample 96% of the infants were still sharing a bed with their mother at 18 months), this contributes to high levels of maternal physical availability. This close proximity makes maternal rejection of infant attachment bids during distress less likely.

Furthermore, just as in Mali and Indonesia, the norm in Khayelitsha is to respond to the crying of the infant with feeding. Much like Ainsworth's (1977) description of the Ganda infants, infants in Khayelitsha are breastfed on demand, making the attachment figure and the source of nourishment the same. In addition, weaning usually takes place between a year and two years, once an attachment has already been established. True et al. (2001) argue that in a context where mothers "often enough" respond to hunger and distress signals with breastfeeding, nursing operates as an intermittent reinforcer of the infant's attachment bids. In line with this idea, Kermoian and Leiderman (1986) found in their work with the Gusii, that the only infants in their sample who were classified as avoidant were those who were not breastfed by their mothers.

An additional factor that may contribute to the low level of avoidant attachment in Khayelitsha is the practice of infant carrying. Infants are frequently carried on their mothers' backs. Notably, Anisfield, Casper, Nozyce, and Cunningham (1990) found that increased physical contact between mother and infant (by way of a baby carrier) promoted secure attachment among infants of low-income, inner-city mothers in the United States; and that the rate of avoidant infant attachment was significantly lower among those who used the baby carriers.

CONCLUSIONS

Although small in number, studies of child-rearing practices and attachment in six African populations provide considerable support for the cross-cultural applicability of attachment theory, and at the same time they both extend and enrich it. First, all studies confirm the universality hypothesis that infants will tend to form particular attachment relationships, even in the context of multiple caregivers. This is most strikingly illustrated in relation to the Efe, where multiple caretakers are the norm during daytime. Second, and perhaps most notable, is the finding that, in spite of very adverse living conditions, secure patterns of attachment are common, thus supporting the normative hypothesis. The high rates of security in adverse conditions in some of the African populations are particularly striking in comparison to rates in high-risk populations in developed countries, where insecure attachments are far more prevalent (Cichetti & Barnett, 1991). Consideration of the differences between these African cultures and high-risk populations in the developed world are, therefore, instructive: in these African cultures, despite considerable hardship, social relationships are often close knit, and there is a high degree of interdependency lacking in developed world high-risk samples, and it is the general concern for infant well-being that appears to promote infant security. This aspect of the African situation helps, therefore, extend the understanding of the conditions promoting satisfactory childcare arrangements, and the nature of sensitivity underpinning secure attachments.

More limited evidence is available concerning the competency hypothesis, and long-term follow-up studies of African populations are required. Nevertheless, the finding from the Gusii study regarding infant cognitive development is notable, and helps refine our understanding of the specific features of caregiving associated with different child outcomes.

FUTURE DIRECTIONS FOR ATTACHMENT RESEARCH IN AFRICA

This chapter has served to provide a summary of attachment research in Africa. The current cross-cultural attachment database is small (van IJzendoorn & Sagi, 1999), and the African database is just a subset of this. Further, several of the studies conducted to date in Africa have not used standardized, validated assessments of caretaking quality, or indeed of attachment itself, as assessed in the SSP. In spite of this, the question arises whether, in the context of the resource-constrained settings that characterize most of Africa, the focus of future attachment-based research should be on producing more controlled, representative demographic data. Conducting such attachment research is time consuming and costly. In our view, although more generally descriptive than the standard attachment research base, the findings that have emerged from the diverse African communities described in this chapter already lend consistent support for the cross-cultural applicability of attachment theory, and the additional contribution to the validation of attachment theory's core principles that may be yielded by further epidemiological studies is likely to be of limited value. Given this, we consider that two further directions for attachment work may be more promising.

First, there is a need, as indicated earlier, to know more about the sequelae of early attachments in African societies. This is a particular challenge in contexts such as Khayelitsha, where infant attachments are in general secure, yet high rates of behavior disturbance exist among children of school age. How early attachment patterns either become modified, or else translate into subsequent maladaptive patterns of functioning, is in urgent need of investigation. Second, what attachment theory has to contribute to intervention development is an important area for further research. Compelling evidence of the effectiveness of early interventions in improving a variety of maternal and child health outcomes has accumulated in relation to high-risk populations in the developed world (e.g., Olds, Kitzman, Cole, & Robinson, 1997). Notably, the content and methods of some of the most effective interventions have the principles of attachment theory at their core (Olds et al., 1997). Attachment is fundamentally about relationships, and we would argue that the provision of supportive relationships to parents, and the promotion of good parent–child relationships, should be at the core of all early intervention models.

Africa is facing a huge human resource crisis, with the result that health interventions are increasingly being implemented using community health workers or paraprofessionals. As interventions are scaled up across the continent, the training and supervision of increasing numbers of such community health workers is assuming critical importance. A challenge for attachment theory for the future in Africa is, therefore, to establish itself as a core component in the design of such intervention programs. This is self-evidently sound in early interventions for child psychosocial functioning, but we would also argue that it is as sound and evidence-based for early interventions that attempt to improve core child health outcomes, such as rates of exclusive breastfeeding as a means by which to prevent the transmission of HIV from mother to child or those designed to improve child survival in the developing world (Ranson & Urichuk, 2008).

REFERENCES

Ainsworth, M. D. S. (1977). *Infancy in Uganda*. Baltimore: Johns Hopkins.

Ainsworth, M. D. S., Blehar, M., Waters, E., & Wall, S. (1978). *Patterns of attachment: A psychological study of the Strange Situation*. Hillsdale, NJ: Lawrence Erlbaum Associates.

Anisfield, E., Casper, V., Nozyce, M., & Cunningham, N. (1990). Does infant carrying promote attachment? An experimental study of the effects of increased physical contact on the development of attachment. *Child Development, 61*, 1617–1627.

Belsky, J. (1999). *Interactional and contextual determinants of attachment security*. In J. Cassidy & P. R. Shaver (Eds.), *Handbook of attachment: Theory, research, and clinical applications* (pp. 249–264). New York: Guilford Press.

Bowlby, J. (1969). *Attachment*. Harmondsworth, UK: Penguin.

Chalmers, B. (1990). *African birth: Childbirth in cultural transition*. Johannesburg: Berev Publications.

Chisholm, K., Carter, M. C., Ames, E. W., & Morrison, S. J. (1995). Attachment security and indiscriminately friendly behaviour in children adopted from Romanian orphanages. *Development and Psychopathology, 7*, 283–297.

Cichetti, D., & Barnett, D. (1991). Attachment organization in maltreated preschoolers. Special issue: Attachment and developmental psychopathology. *Development and Psychopathology, 3*, 397–411.

Cooper, P. J., Tomlinson, M., Swartz, L., Woolgar, M., Murray, L., & Molteno, C. (1999). Postpartum depression and the mother-infant relationship in a South African peri-urban settlement. *British Journal of Psychiatry, 175*, 554–558.

Dawes, A. (2002). *Sexual offences against children in South Africa: Considerations for primary prevention* [Submission to parliament, Cape Town, South Africa]. Cape Town: Human Sciences Research Council.

De Wolff, M. S., & van IJzendoorn, M. H. (1997). Sensitivity and attachment: A meta-analysis on parental antecedents of infant attachment. *Child Development, 68*, 571–591.

Kermoian, R., & Leiderman, P. (1986). Infant attachment to mother and child caretaker in an East African community. *International Journal of Behavioral Development, 9*, 455–469.

Konner, M. (1977). Infancy among the Kalahari Desert San. In P. H. Leiderman, S. R. Tulkin, & A. Rosenfeld (Eds.), *Culture and infancy: Variations in human experience* (pp. 287–328). New York: Academic Press.

Lockhat, R., & Van Niekerk, A. (2000). South African children: A history of adversity, violence and trauma. *Ethnicity and Health, 5*, 291–302.

Lyons-Ruth, K., & Block, D. (1993). The disturbed caregiving system: Conceptualizing the impact of childhood trauma on maternal caregiving behavior during infancy. In J. Solomon (Chair), *Defining the caregiving system*. Symposium conducted at the biennial meeting of the Society for Research in Child Development, New Orleans, LA.

Lyons-Ruth, K., & Jacobvitz, D. (1999). Attachment disorganization: Unresolved loss, relational violence, and lapses in behavioral and attentional strategies. In J. Cassidy & P. R. Shaver (Eds.), *Handbook of attachment* (pp. 520–554). New York: Guilford Press.

Marvin, R. S., VanDevender, T. L., Iwanaga, M. I., LeVine, S., & LeVine, R. A. (1977). Infant-caregiver attachment among the Hausa of Nigeria. In H. McGurk (Ed.), *Ecological factors in human development* (pp. 247–260). New York: North Holland.

Morelli, G., & Tronick, E. (1991). Efe multiple caretaking and attachment. In J. Gewirtz & W. Kurtines (Eds.), *Intersections with attachment* (pp. 41–51). Hillsdale, NJ: Lawrence Erlbaum.

O'Hara, M. W. (1997). The nature of postpartum depressive disorders. In L. Murray & P. J. Cooper (Eds.), *Postpartum depression and child development* (pp. 3–31). New York: Guilford Press.

Olds, D., Kitzman, H., Cole, R., & Robinson, J. (1997). Theoretical foundations of a program of home visitation for pregnant women and parents of young children. *Journal of Community Psychology, 25,* 9–25.

Ranson, K. E., & Urichuk, L. J. (2008). The effect of parent-child attachment relationships on child biopsychosocial outcomes: A review. *Early Child Development and Care, 178,* 129–152.

Tomlinson, M., Cooper, P., & Murray, L. (2005). The mother-infant relationship and infant attachment in a South African peri-urban settlement. *Child Development, 76,* 1044–1054.

Tronick, E. Z., Morelli, G. A., & Ivey, P. K. (1992). The Efe forager infant and toddler's pattern of social relationships: Multiple and simultaneous. *Developmental Psychology, 28,* 568–577.

Tronick, E. Z., Morelli, G. A., & Winn, S. (1987). Multiple caretaking of Efe (Pygmy) infants. *American Anthropologist, 89,* 96–106.

True, M. M., Pisani, L., & Oumar, F. (2001). Infant-mother attachment among the Dogon of Mali. *Child Development, 72,* 1451–1466.

Valenzuela, M. (1990). Attachment in chronically underweight young children. *Child Development, 61,* 1984–1996.

van IJzendoorn, M. H., Goldberg, S., Kroonenberg, P. M., & Frenkel, O. J. (1992). The relative effects of maternal and child problems on the quality of attachment: A meta-analysis of attachment in clinical samples. *Child Development, 63,* 840–858.

van IJzendoorn, M. H., & Kroonenberg, P. M. (1988). Cross-cultural patterns of attachment: A meta-analysis of the Strange Situation. *Child Development, 59,* 147–156.

van IJzendoorn, M. H., & Sagi, A. (1999). Cross-cultural patterns of attachment: Universal and contextual dimensions. In J. Cassidy & P. R. Shaver (Eds.), *Handbook of attachment: Theory, research and clinical applications* (pp. 713–734). New York: Guilford Press.

van IJzendoorn, M. H., Sagi, A., & Lambermon, M. W. E. (1992). The multiple caretaker paradox: Data from Holland and Israel. *New Directions for Child Development, 57,* 5–24. San Francisco: Jossey-Bass.

van IJzendoorn, M., Schuengel, C., & Bakermans-Kranenburg, M. J. (1999). Disorganized attachment in early childhood: Meta-analysis of precursors, concomitants, and sequelae. *Development and Psychopathology, 11,* 225–249.

Zevalkink, J., Riksen-Walraven, J. M., & van Lieshout, C. F. M. (1999). Attachment in the Indonesian caregiving context. *Social Development, 8,* 21–40.

Section IV

Adult Attachment

12

Adult Attachment in Cross-Cultural and International Research
Universality Issues

ALEV YALÇINKAYA, KIMBERLY RAPOZA, and KATHLEEN MALLEY-MORRISON

CONTENTS

*I*n this chapter we consider the debate over the universality of attachment theory and the cross-cultural generalizability of research findings associated with theories of infant and adult attachment. We first provide a brief overview of representative attachment theories and controversies concerning their cross-cultural generalizability, and then review empirical evidence shedding light on the universality of attachment theory constructs and assumptions. Although we briefly discuss the controversy over universality in regard to infant attachment, our primary focus is on issues related to adult attachment and its correlates, and the potential universal applicability of attachment theory and assessment tools.

ATTACHMENT THEORY

Attachment theory has been investigated widely ever since John Bowlby (1969, 1982) identified a human need—attachment—for developing individuals to have a special bond with a primary caregiver. According to Bowlby, if caregivers are generally available and responsive, infants feel secure and rely on caregivers to be available when needed. However, in the absence of sensitive and consistent caregiving, infants form an insecure attachment to caregivers that can generalize to other relationships. During the early years, the quality of attachment experiences shapes the child's internal working models of the self and representations of the availability and responsiveness of others. These working models influence relationships throughout the life span.

Informed by Bowlby's original attachment theory, Ainsworth, Blehar, Waters, and Wall (1978) observed infants and mothers in laboratory settings (the Strange Situation test) and identified three attachment styles. When briefly separated from their primary caregivers, *securely attached* children initially displayed mild distress but showed an ability to calm down when the caregiver returned. *Anxious/ ambivalent* children showed intense distress following caregiver departure and had difficulty calming down at her return. *Anxious/avoidant* children showed little distress and seemed rather apathetic both when caregivers left and when they returned.

These three infant attachment styles were formulated into a model of adult attachment by Hazan and Shaver (1987), who organized individual cognitive, affective, and behavioral differences around three prototypical attachment types: (a) secure attachment, characterized by finding it easy to get close to others, being comfortable depending on others, and having few fears about close intimacy with a partner; (b) anxious/ambivalent attachment, characterized by excessive worrying that one is not loved by one's partner and that the partner will leave; and (c) avoidant attachment, characterized by discomfort with closeness, and difficulty allowing oneself to be dependent on and trusting of others.

Bartholomew and Horowitz (1991) extended the conceptualization and investigation of adult attachment by developing a four-category model of adult attachment with distinctions between attachment styles centering on positive or negative views of the self and others. In this model, the secure attachment style is characterized by a positive view of a self seen as worthy of love, and a positive expectation that others will be accepting and reliable in their responsiveness. The dismissive attachment style is characterized by a positive view of the self as worthy of love, but a negative view of others, leading to a predisposition toward independence and maintaining interpersonal distance. The preoccupied style is characterized by a negative view of a self seen as unworthy of love and a positive view of others, leading to a preoccupation with maintaining the affections of others and using clinging behavior aimed at eliciting acceptance and preventing abandonment. The fearful attachment style involves negative views of self and of others, who are seen as rejecting and unresponsive to one's intimacy needs, thereby creating an approach-avoidance conflict in regard to intimate relationships. Moreover, among individuals with serious psychological problems, those with a negative model of others have been shown to be less likely to seek counseling for their problems than those with a positive model of others (Lopez, Melendez, Sauer, Berger, & Wyssmann, 1998).

Some researchers have argued that assessing infant and adult attachment patterns with typological models is a weak approach that has not yet been validated. They recommend focusing instead on the dimensions underlying the proposed attachment types. Underlying the four attachment types posited by Bartholomew and Horowitz (1991) is a dimensional model of the self that can range from a strong sense of self-worth to anxiety related to a belief in one's unworthiness and a dimensional model of the other ranging from substantial trust in and comfort with intimate others to considerable mistrust and a desire to avoid close relationships. Much of the attachment research has focused on these underlying dimensions rather than the attachment types representing four points of integration of the self and other orientations. For instance, in a study of attachment patterns in 1,139 15-month-old children, Fraley and Spieker (2003) found support for a dimensional interpretation of attachment; specifically, a two-dimensional model, with one dimension representing proximity-seeking versus avoidant strategies (the degree to which the child engages in the goal of proximity seeking), and the other dimension involving angry and resistant strategies (level of conflict and anger toward the caregiver). One of the more widely used adult attachment dimensional measures is the Experiences in Close Relationships (ECR) survey—created by Brennan, Clark, and Shaver (1998)—based on a factor analysis of 320 items derived from available attachment measures and yielding two independent dimensions related to classic attachment theory: avoidance and anxiety.

THE UNIVERSALITY DEBATE

Bowlby (1969) and Ainsworth et al. (1978) both assumed that attachment behaviors and the development of the attachment system had an evolutionary basis. Both also assumed that the development of the attachment system during infancy and childhood was influenced by the responsiveness of primary caregivers to the needs of the dependent child, and that based on these influences, fairly stable patterns of security, anxiety, or avoidance in close relationships develop within individuals as part of their internalization of models of self and other. Both assumed that an attachment orientation characterized by a high level of felt security in relationships was more adaptive for the individual in regard to adult family relationships (as partners and parents) and other aspects of adult functioning, and both were concerned that disruptions in early attachment relations and interference in the development of secure attachment could lead to adult pathology. Bowlby (1988) put particular emphasis on the role of attachment theory in psychotherapy.

Attachment theory has stimulated much debate concerning the extent to which it and its principal constructs (e.g., the attachment types or dimensions) have applicability independent of culture (Wang & Mallinckrodt, 2006; Wei, Russell, Mallinckrodt, & Zakalik, 2004). Infant attachment theory, as articulated by Bowlby (1969) and Ainsworth et al. (1978) and investigated by dozens of researchers, has been labeled ethnocentric and biased toward Western values, and even as reflective of a "history of colonialism, which is also the history of psychology" (Burman, 2007, p. 194). Rothbaum, Weisz, Pott, Miyake, and Morelli (2000) describe and then challenge what they see as the three "core hypotheses" of attachment theory:

(a) the sensitivity hypothesis postulating that the mother's ability to respond sensitively is the most important predictor of the extent to which infants become securely or insecurely attached; (b) the competence hypothesis, postulating that securely attached children become more competent, both socially and emotionally, than insecurely attached children; and (c) the secure base hypothesis, which predicts that securely attached infants are more comfortable exploring their environments within the protective context of their mother's presence than insecurely attached infants. Rothbaum et al. (2000) argue that these hypotheses "are embedded in Western historical, social, political, economic, demographic, and geographic realities" (p. 1095) and urge "greater context specificity in theorizing about attachment relationships" (p. 1102).

The universality debate has several different levels. On one level, the debate is not just theoretical but ideological. Identifying the theory as part of "broader military-political agendas that have called forth and continue to structure (Western and non-Western) psychology" (Burman, 2007, p. 194) appears itself to be an expression of a political agenda and difficult to challenge empirically. At the theoretical level, the debate also focuses on the issue of whether, because of its origins, the theory puts too much emphasis on Western constructs of individuation and separation and not enough emphasis on Eastern constructs of connectedness and dependence (Burman, 2007). This debate, too, is in part ideological.

On another level, the debate is empirical. In this chapter, we examine international and cross-cultural empirical findings as we address the following questions concerning the extent to which classic attachment theory deals with a universal process: (a) To what extent can the secure and insecure adult attachment types, as identified in the Western theories, be identified across different cultures with the Western attachment type measures that have been developed? This is the universality of types question. (b) Does adult attachment have an underlying structure that tends to generalize across cultures? This is the universality of structure question. (c) To what extent do patterns of parental responsiveness predict later attachment across cultures? This is the universality of predictors question. (d) Is there cross-cultural support for the assumption that secure attachment is associated with more positive outcomes than insecure attachment? This is the universality of outcomes question. All of the research discussed here is subject to classic problems related to sampling and measurement; consequently, failure to find construct validity for any attachment construct is not the same as showing that the construct has no validity, and a failure to find cross-cultural support for any hypothesis derived from attachment theory does not necessarily invalidate the theory or close the question of universality.

The Universality of Types Issue

Studies examining the relative distribution of adult participants into the adult attachment style types have used a number of different attachment measures and have found somewhat different patterns using these measures. For example, using the structured, semiclinical Adult Attachment Interview (AAI; George, Kaplan, & Main, 1996) with a sample of Japanese mothers, Behrens, Hesse, and Main (2007) found that their attachment type distributions differed only very slightly (but statistically significantly) from global norms, with larger proportions being classified as secure and smaller proportions as preoccupied. In studies using Bartholomew and Horowitz's (1991) four-category Relationships Questionnaire (RQ), Schmitt et al. (2004) found that preoccupied attachment was particularly prevalent in East Asian cultures. You and Malley-Morrison (2000) found that Korean students scored higher on preoccupied attachment than European American students, and both Yalçınkaya (1997) and Sümer and Güngör (1999) found that Turkish participants scored higher in preoccupied attachment than U.S. participants. On the other hand, although Yalçınkaya found a lower percentage of Turkish women (32.4%) than American women (47%) in the secure category, Sümer and Güngör found no differences between a Turkish and a U.S. sample in secure attachment. Based on this sample of studies, we conclude that it is clearly possible to identify patterns of adult attachment security and insecurity across cultures, although the relative frequency of membership in different categories seems to vary somewhat not just by culture but also by type of attachment measure. Certainly different relative frequencies do not invalidate the generalizability of the theoretical constructs or the tools used to assess them.

The Universality of Structure Issue

The major approach to assessing the extent to which the underlying structure of the attachment system is universal involves factor analyses and other intercorrelational analyses of various attachment measures in different cultures. Factor-analytic studies have been done with attachment measures composed of multi-item scales for each of the purported attachment styles or dimensions. For example, using Sümer and Güngör's (2000) Turkish translation of Brennan et al.'s (1998) ECR measure with a student sample, Selçuk, Günaydın, Sümer, and Uysal (2005) found support for the original two-factor solution representing attachment-related avoidance and attachment-related anxiety, as well as other support for the validity, internal consistency, and test–retest reliability of the ECR in the Turkish culture. Exploratory and confirmatory factor analytic results of a Greek version of the ECR also showed a two-factor structure consistent with the original findings (Tsagarakis, Kafetsios, & Stalikas, 2007). Using a Spanish version of the ECR, Alonso-Arbiol, Balluerka, Shaver, and Gillath (2008) found similar factor structures across Spanish and English versions.

In a related study, Rapoza and Yalçınkaya (1998) used exploratory factor analysis to investigate adult attachment style structure in 133 Turkish women who completed Mikulincer, Florian, and Tolmacz's (1990) Attachment Questionnaire (AQ). A statistical test of model fit, specifically for smaller sample sizes, indicated a good model fit for the Turkish data, although they did not coincide with secure and insecure dimensions. This model identified four factors, which Rapoza and Yalçınkaya described as representing fear of closeness in relationships, dependency, fear of abandonment, and fear of union with another; two of these factors (fear of closeness and fear of union) appear consistent with the avoidance dimension identified by Brennan et al. (1998), and the other two (dependency and fear of abandonment) reflect the anxiety dimension. Thus, this study provides additional support for the generalizability of a dimensional model of adult attachment.

Because Bartholomew and Horowitz's (1991) RQ consists of single-item scales for the four attachment styles, factor analysis is not appropriate. However, several studies have examined correlations among items in the scale to explore the attachment structure and test hypotheses derived from self-model/other model attachment theory. The most broad-based study of adult attachment (Schmitt et al., 2004) involved more than 100 researchers who administered the Bartholomew and Horowitz RQ to 17,804 participants from 62 cultural regions (including five different cultural areas within the United States). This research team was particularly interested in the generalizability of the model of self and model of other constructs and scales from the Bartholomew and Horowitz four-category model of attachment. Although the results of the analyses confirmed the psychometric validity of the model of self and model of other scales cross-culturally, the analyses also revealed that the two models operated somewhat differently across cultures. For example, one prediction from a universal two-dimensional structure of the self and other model would be that scores on the secure scale (positive other) should be negatively correlated with scores on the fearful scale (negative other) and that scores on the dismissive scale (positive self) should be negatively correlated with scores on the preoccupied scale (negative self). However, in the Schmitt et al. (2004) analyses, the predicted negative correlations occurred primarily only in Western cultures.

These studies provide mixed evidence concerning the extent to which the attachment system has an underlying structure that generalizes across cultures. The strongest evidence for a universal structure comes from the studies using a dimensional attachment measure (the ECR) assessing the underlying dimensions of attachment and avoidance. Cross-cultural support for the generalizability of a four-prototype system based on a positive and negative self and a positive and negative other comes primarily from Western cultures, and may not be generalizable to Eastern cultures, although Fraley and Shaver (2000) consider the positive and negative self models to be largely equivalent to their two-dimensional avoidance and anxiety model.

The Universality of Predictors Issue

One of the strongest predictions generated by Bowlby's and Ainsworth's attachment theories is that parental responsiveness is the major predictor of infant attachment and the internalized models of self and other that are carried into adulthood. Studies in Western cultures have found support for theoretically based links between parents' behavior and attachment styles. For example, Bartholomew (1993) found that securely attached people described their childhood relationships with parents more positively than did insecure individuals. Bringle and Bagby (1992) reported that in both males and females, warm mothering and warm fathering were positively related to secure attachment, a lack of warm mothering was related to avoidant attachment, and cold fathering was associated negatively with secure style. Carnelley, Pitromonaco, and Jaffe (1994) found that women reporting less positive childhood experiences with their mothers and fathers had higher scores on the avoidant and preoccupied attachment styles, and women with more controlling fathers scored higher on avoidant attachment. McCormick and Kennedy (1994) found that students who classified themselves as securely attached rated their parents as high in encouraging independence and in acceptance.

Although attachment theorists and researchers from the West have emphasized the importance of parental warmth in contributing to the development of a secure base, parental control—which could be viewed as representing another form of parental responsiveness, but not necessarily a positive one—may also contribute to the development of the attachment system. Kağıtçıbaşı (1996, 2007) suggested that normative context has an influence on the nature of control and its meanings for the parent, which in turn affects the child's early development. This context may be one in which parental control is common, accepted, and perceived as normal by the child (e.g., in Taiwan, Hong Kong, Japan, Korea, Turkey) or one in which control is perceived as parental hostility or rejection (e.g., in North America and Germany; Kağıtçıbaşı, 1996). Depending on the context, it is possible that parental control could contribute to either secure or insecure attachment.

Cross-cultural findings concerning the relationship between parental control and child attachment outcomes do vary in relation to the sociocultural context. Focusing on parental predictors of adult attachment styles as assessed with Mikulincer et al.'s (1990) 15-item, three-prototype attachment measure, Yalçınkaya (1997), in her study of 158 Turkish women, explored the relationship between recollections of mothers' and fathers' acceptance and control, and daughters' attachment styles and relationship beliefs. The findings revealed that parental acceptance and control during childhood, as reported by the young adult women, were associated with their adult attachment styles. For example, not only was level of parental acceptance positively associated with secure adult attachment, it was also negatively correlated with avoidant attachment—the higher the acceptance, the lower the avoidance. Mothers' level of acceptance was also negatively related to anxious avoidance in their daughters—the higher the maternal acceptance, the lower the anxious attachment. These findings are quite consistent with what would be expected from classic attachment theory. Yalçınkaya also found that maternal control was negatively related to adult attachment security but not related to any of the insecure attachment styles, suggesting that in Turkish culture maternal control does not play the same positive role in the development of secure attachment that maternal acceptance plays.

Building on the Yalçınkaya (1997) study, Yalçınkaya, Rapoza, and Malley-Morrison (1998) examined the relationship between parental acceptance and control and adult attachment styles in a U.S. sample ($n = 47$) as well as in a roughly matched Turkish sample ($n = 74$). A series of one-way analyses of variance (ANOVAs) showed that U.S. participants scored higher on anxious-ambivalent and avoidant attachment (as measured by Mikulincer et al.'s, 1990, Attachment Questionnaire), and described their mothers and fathers as more controlling and accepting than Turkish participants did. In regard to parental acceptance as recalled from childhood, within both the Turkish and the U.S. samples, reported acceptance by the father was significantly positively associated with secure attachment scores and significantly negatively correlated with avoidant attachment scores. Although maternal acceptance was positively associated with secure attachment within both samples, it was negatively associated with avoidant attachment in the U.S. sample but with none of the insecure attachment scores in the Turkish sample. In regard to parental control, mother's level of controlling behavior was negatively associated with secure attachment in the Turkish sample and positively correlated with anxious-ambivalent attachment in the U.S. sample. These findings support the cross-cultural generalizability of at least some of the basic assumptions associated with classic attachment theory as developed in an individualistic culture—specifically, that parental acceptance contributes to the development of secure attachment and parental control contributes to the development of insecure attachment.

Not all cross-cultural findings are consistent with this pattern. For example, Carlson and Harwood (2003) found that middle-class Puerto Rican mothers used more physical control in their interactions with their infants during the first year of life than Anglo mothers did, and that high physical control in Puerto Rican mothers was associated with secure attachment. On the other hand, Carlson and Harwood also found that high use of maternal physical control in Anglo mother–infant pairs was associated with insecure avoidant attachment. Such findings further confirm a link between maternal responsiveness and the development of attachment, but also indicate that maternal responsiveness may be more complex than originally assumed and that various forms of maternal responsiveness may contribute to different attachment outcomes, depending on the sociocultural context of the interactions.

The Universality of Outcomes Issue

Several investigators have challenged the universality of a connection between secure attachment in adulthood and indices of adaptiveness. For example, You and Malley-Morrison (2000) suggested that in a collectivistic culture, which can be both authoritarian and socially hierarchical, it is possible that social inhibition, shyness, and anxiety (characteristics of various forms of insecure attachment) are not necessarily associated with negative outcomes, because they may be encouraged within the culture as desirable signs of maturity and self-control. Kondo-Ikemura (2001) also suggested that the attachment styles labeled as insecure in classic attachment theory might be more adaptive in some cultures than in others. For example, based on her review of findings from attachment studies in Japan, Kondo-Ikemura concluded that some behaviors characteristic of ambivalent attachment might be adaptive in Japan.

Despite these possibilities, the majority of findings of relevant cross-cultural studies are generally consistent with classic attachment theory, thereby supporting the universality of the secure attachment–positive outcome relationship and insecure attachment–negative outcome relationship. For example, in a Turkish study of insulin-dependent diabetes mellitus patients, dismissing attachment was predictive of poor adjustment to diabetes (Turan, Osar, Turan, Ilkova, & Damcı, 2003). In a much broader study across 47 nations, Schmitt (2005) found the following relationships across cultures: (a) secure attachment was associated with high self-esteem, high extroversion, and high levels of agreeableness (low neuroticism); (b) dismissive attachment was linked to low agreeableness; and (c) preoccupied and fearful attachment were associated with low self-esteem and low emotional stability.

On the other hand, several researchers (e.g., Minuchin, 2002; Rothbaum, Rosen, Ujiie, & Uchida, 2002) have warned against the tendency of some clinicians to interpret psychiatric symptoms from an attachment theory perspective, particularly within non-Western cultures. Rubin (2003) described Delfina Ortega, a 23-year-old college student who, after a severe panic attack requiring hospitalization was brought into the clinic in which Rubin practices. At a case conference, one of Rubin's colleagues described Ortega as "stubbornly resistant and decidedly paranoid," (p. 132) demonstrating a lack of trust indicative of insecure attachment, consistent with her reports on her mother's ambivalent parenting. Rubin challenged the attachment theory interpretation of the case, noting, "No one, neither [the therapist] nor anyone else in the room, seemed to see significance in the fact that Ms. O had grown up in a Latino working-class family. Instead, the conversation was totally focused on her internal dynamics: on her relationships in the family, on the primitive nature of her anxiety, on the possibility that her panic was a response to some repressed experience" (p. 133).

THE UNIVERSALITY ISSUE REVISITED

Dilemmas characteristic of all cross-cultural research include difficulty in finding adequate equivalents of constructs across cultures, different meanings constructs can have within different contexts, and difficulties in determining the extent to which the researcher's background and worldviews affect research conduct and outcomes. Based on Bronfenbrenner's (1979) ecological model, Kağıtçıbaşı (2007) recommended one possible resolution to the conflict over the universality of attachment versus contextual variation in regard to both the antecedents and consequences of attachment. Specifically, Kağıtçıbaşı suggested an integrative synthesis "combining the concept of adaptive or optimal attachment as a person–environment interaction variable in the early microsystem that would feed into later development but that could also be affected by the ever-changing context" (p. 172). Kağıtçıbaşı's approach parallels that of Harwood, Miller, and Irizzary (1995), who emphasized the "importance of contextual meanings in shaping the universality of social, emotional, and linguistic expressiveness into culturally specific elaborations, attenuations, and conceptualizations" (p. 141). In a model of the person–environment interaction, Harwood and colleagues (1995) asked Anglo and Puerto Rican mothers to describe their child's desirable and undesirable behavior in culturally sensitive Strange Situation scenarios. They found that Anglo mothers preferred that toddlers balance autonomy and relatedness and disliked clinginess; whereas Puerto Rican mothers preferred that toddlers display respectfulness and disliked highly active or avoidant behaviors.

Space limitations have prevented us from reviewing all the relevant attachment research related to the universality issue. However, we believe that the sources we have selected provide a good window into the potential universality of various constructs and hypotheses derived from classic attachment theory. Based on this review, we have several observations and recommendations. First, we believe Bowlby was correct in identifying a universal human need for connectedness with others, present at birth and modifiable in various ways depending on experience. Bowlby (1969), Ainsworth et al. (1978), and others were also correct in assuming that the constructs of secure and insecure had universal applicability; however, the relative benefits of, for example, two-prototype, three-prototype, or four-prototype systems has not been definitively established. We also believe that the Bartholomew and Horowitz (1991) RQ provides meaningful data across cultures (particularly with the continuous scores for each attachment style), and the positive/negative self/other framework is valuable.

On the other hand, in explorations of the universality of classic attachment theory constructs and hypotheses, attachment dimensions (for example, views on the self and views on the other that range from positive to negative, or levels of anxiety and avoidance) are probably more promising for statistical as well as other reasons than are typologies. Moreover, the insecure attachment labels may have negative connotations that may be inappropriate cross-culturally. Characteristics appearing to be maladaptive in Western majority cultures may be viewed differently and have different predictors and outcomes that are not necessarily negative in other societies. For example, after describing several Western clinical cases portraying a preoccupied mother overinvested in her son and thwarting his autonomy needs, Rothbaum et al. (2000) pointed out that in Japan, sensitive caregiving is characterized by a nearly symbiotic relationship between mother and child and that the kind of interdependence, rather than being pathological, contributes to the social harmony that is so prized in Japan. Moreover, there may be many contexts where the most adaptive attachment pattern is moderate security combined with moderate anxiety or avoidance. Particularly in patriarchal societies or cultural contexts tolerant of female abuse, a strongly secure attachment orientation combined with low levels of anxiety and avoidance could put women at risk in intimate relationships.

Despite promising evidence in support of many aspects of classic attachment theory, we recommend greater attention to the demands of particular cultural contexts for the development of individuals within those contexts. For example, in Turkey, child socialization occurs in a context of gender and generational hierarchy (Fişek, 1991) that allows a balance among high levels of proximity, less articulated personal boundaries between family members (Levi, 1994), and differentiation of self and other (Sunar & Fişek, 2005). Not only is respect desirable in children even among immigrant Turks (Harwood, Yalçınkaya, Çıtlak, & Leyendecker, 2006), but disrespect is considered abusive (Yalçınkaya, 2004; Yalçınkaya, Mandıracıoğlu, & Turan, 2006). Accepting parental authority, subordinating personal interests and ambitions, and cultivating a sensitivity to the need of other family members is expected of children in both rural and urban settings (Sunar & Fişek, 2005), although the importance of the child's individual achievement increases in educated, urban, middle-class families (Kağıtçıbaşı, 1996). In this context, preoccupied attachment, defined as a negative view of the self and a positive view of others (Bartholomew & Horowitz, 1991), might not only be socially appropriate and functional but might also develop independently of orientations toward the sense of feeling secure.

Finally, we believe it is important to examine further the correlates (both predictors and outcomes) of the different attachment styles in different cultural contexts and in relation to other characteristics, such as gender, if a culturally sensitive understanding of the concept of attachment is to be achieved.

REFERENCES

Ainsworth, M. D., Blehar, M., Waters, E., & Wall, S. (1978). *Patterns of attachment.* Hillsdale, NJ: Lawrence Erlbaum Associates.

Alonso-Arbiol, I., Balluerka, N., Shaver, P. R., & Gillath, O. (2008). Psychometric properties of the Spanish and American versions of the ECR Adult Attachment Questionnaire: A comparative study. *European Journal of Psychological Assessment, 24*(1), 9–13.

Bartholomew, K. (1993). From childhood to adult relationships: Attachment theory and research. In S. Duck (Ed.), *Learning about relationships* (pp. 30–62). Newbury Park, CA: Sage.

Bartholomew, K., & Horowitz, L. M. (1991). Attachment styles among young adults: A test of a four-category model. *Journal of Personality and Social Psychology, 61*, 226–244.

Behrens, K. Y., Hesse, E., & Main, M. (2007). Mothers' attachment status as determined by the Adult Attachment Interview predicts their 6-year-olds' reunion responses: A study conducted in Japan. *Developmental Psychology, 43*(6), 1553–1567.

Bowlby, J. (1969). *Attachment and loss: Vol. 1. Attachment.* New York: Basic Books.

Bowlby, J. (1982). *Attachment and loss: Vol. 1. Attachment* (2nd ed.). New York: Basic Books.

Bowlby, J. (1988). *A secure base: Parent-child attachment and healthy human development.* New York: Basic Books.

Brennan, K. A., Clark, C. L., & Shaver, P. R. (1998). Self-report measurement of adult attachment: An integrative overview. In J. A. Simpson & W. S. Rholes (Eds.), *Attachment theory and close relationships* (pp. 46–76). New York: Guilford Press.

Bringle, R. G., & Bagby, G. J. (1992). Self-esteem and perceived quality of romantic and family relationships in young adults. *Journal of Research in Personality, 26*, 340–356.

Bronfenbrenner, U. (1979). *The ecology of human development: Experiments by nature and design.* Cambridge, MA: Harvard University Press.

Burman, E. (2007). Between orientalism and normalization: Cross-cultural lessons from Japan for a critical history of psychology. *History of Psychology, 10*, 179–198.

Carlson, V. J., & Harwood, R. L. (2003). Attachment, culture, and the care giving system: The cultural patterning of everyday experiences among Anglo and Puerto Rican mother-infant pairs. *Infant Mental Health Journal, 24*, 53–73.

Carnelley, K. B., Pitromonaco, P. R., & Jaffe, K. (1994). Depression, working models of others, and relationship functioning. *Journal of Personality and Social Psychology, 66*, 127–140.

Fişek, G. O. (1991). A cross-cultural examination of proximity and hierarchy as dimensions of family structure. *Family Process, 30*, 121–133.

Fraley, R. C., & Shaver, P. R. (2000). Adult romantic attachment: Theoretical developments, emerging controversies, and unanswered questions. *Review of General Psychology, 4*, 132–154.

Fraley, R. C., & Spieker, S. J. (2003). Are infant attachment patterns continuously or categorically distributed? A taxometric analysis of strange situation behavior. *Developmental Psychology, 39*, 387–404.

George, C., Kaplan, N., & Main, M. (1996). *Adult Attachment Interview* (3rd ed.). Unpublished manuscript, Department of Psychology, University of California, Berkeley. (Original work published 1985)

Harwood, R. L., Miller, J. G., & Irizzary, N. L. (1995). *Culture and attachment: Perceptions of the child in context.* New York: Guilford.

Harwood, R. L., Yalçınkaya, A., Çıtlak, B., & Leyendecker, B. (2006). Exploring the concept of respect among Turkish and Puerto Rican migrant mothers. *New Directions in Child and Adolescent Development, 114*, 9–24. San Francisco: Jossey-Bass.

Hazan, C., & Shaver, P. R. (1987). Conceptualizing romantic love as an attachment process. *Journal of Personality and Social Psychology, 52*, 511–524.

Kağıtçıbaşı, Ç. (1996). *Family and human development across cultures.* Mahwah, NJ: Lawrence Erlbaum Associates.

Kağıtçıbaşı, Ç. (2007). *Family, self and human development across cultures: Theory and applications* (2nd ed.). Mahwah, NJ: Lawrence Erlbaum Associates.

Kondo-Ikemura, K. (2001). Insufficient evidence. *American Psychologist, 56*, 825–826.

Levi, H. R. (1994). The relationship between self and self-objects: A demonstration of Kohut's self psychology outside the clinical setting. *Dissertation Abstracts International, 58*(10), 5649B. (UMI No. 9811588)

Lopez, F. G., Melendez, M. C., Sauer, E. M., Berger, E., & Wyssmann, J. (1998). Internal working models, self-reported problems, and help-seeking attitudes among college students. *Journal of Counseling Psychology, 45*, 79–83.

McCormick, C. B., & Kennedy, J. H. (1994). Parent-child attachment working models and self esteem in adolescence. *Journal of Youth and Adolescence, 23*, 1–18.

Mikulincer, M., Florian, V., & Tolmacz, R. (1990). Attachment styles and fear of personal death: A case study of affect regulation. *Journal of Personality and Social Psychology, 58*, 273–280.

Minuchin, P. (2002). Cross-cultural perspectives: Implications for attachment theory and family therapy. *Family Process, 41*, 546–550.

Rapoza, K., & Yalçınkaya, A. (1998). *Turkish and U.S. adult attachment styles: A cross-cultural examination.* Paper presented at the meeting of the American Psychological Association, San Francisco, CA.

Rothbaum, F., Rosen, K., Ujiie, T., & Uchida, N. (2002). Family systems theory, attachment theory, and culture. *Family Process, 41*, 3, 328–350.

Rothbaum, F., Weisz, J., Pott, M., Miyake, K., & Morelli, G. (2000). Attachment and culture: Security in the United States and Japan. *American Psychologist, 55*, 1093-1104.

Rubin, L. B. (2003). *The man with the beautiful voice.* Boston: Beacon Press.

Schmitt, D. P. (2005). Is short-term mating the maladaptive result of insecure attachment? A test of competing evolutionary perspectives. *Personality and Social Psychology Bulletin, 31*, 747–768.

Schmitt, D. P., Alcalay, L., Allensworth, M., Allik, J., Ault, L., Austers, I., … Zupanèiè, A. (2004). Patterns and universals of adult romantic attachment across 62 cultural regions: Are models of self and of other pancultural constructs? *Journal of Cross-cultural Psychology, 35*, 367–402.

Selçuk, E., Günaydın, G., Sümer, N., & Uysal, A. (2005). Yetişkin bağlanma boyutları için yeni bir ölçüm: Yakın İlişkilerde Yaşantılar Envanteri-II'nin Türk örnekleminde psikometrik açıdan değerlendirilmesi [A new measure for adult attachment styles: The psychometric evaluation of Experiences in Close Relationships– Revised (ECR-R) on a Turkish sample]. *Türk Psikoloji Yazıları, 8*, 1–11.

Sümer, N., & Güngör, D. (1999). Yetişkin bağlanma stilleri ölçeklerinin Türk örneklemi üzerinde psikometrik değerlendirmesi ve kültürlerarası bir karşılaştırma. [Psychometric evaluation of adult attachment measures on Turkish samples and a cross-cultural comparison]. *Türk Psikoloji Dergisi, 14*, 71–106.

Sümer, N., & Güngör, D. (2000, June–July). *The relationships between anxiety and avoidance dimensions of adult attachment and affective aspects of the self.* International Conference on Personal Relationships, Brisbane, Australia.

Sunar, D., & Fişek, G. O. (2005). Contemporary Turkish families. In J. L. Roopnarine & U. P. Gielen (Eds.), *Families in global perspective.* Boston: Allyn & Bacon.

Tsagarakis, M., Kafetsios, K., & Stalikas, A. (2007). Reliability and validity of the Greek version of the Revised Experiences in Close Relationships measure of adult attachment. *European Journal of Psychological Assessment, 23,* 47–55.

Turan, B., Osar, Z., Turan, J. M., Ilkova, H., & Damcı, T. (2003). Dismissing attachment and outcome in diabetes: The mediating role of coping. *Journal of Social and Clinical Psychology, 22,* 607–626.

Wang, C. D. C., & Mallinckrodt, B. S. (2006). Differences between Taiwanese and U.S. cultural beliefs about ideal adult attachment. *Journal of Counseling Psychology, 53,* 192–204.

Wei, M., Russell, D. W., Mallinckrodt, B., & Zakalik, R. A. (2004). Cultural equivalence of adult attachment across four ethnic groups: Factor structure, structure means, and associations with negative mood. *Journal of Counseling Psychology, 51,* 408–417.

Yalçınkaya, A. (1997). Turkish daughters' attachment styles, romantic relationships and recollections of parental acceptance and control. *Dissertation Abstracts International, 58*(02), 1027B. (UMI No. 9723725)

Yalçınkaya, A. (2004). Turkey. In K. Malley-Morrison (Ed.), *International perspectives on family violence and abuse: A cognitive ecological approach* (pp. 151–163). Hillsdale, NJ: Lawrence Erlbaum Associates.

Yalçınkaya, A., Mandıracıoğlu, A., & Turan, F. (2006). Turkey: A pilot study of elder mistreatment in a convenience sample. *Journal of Elder Abuse and Neglect 18,* 105–121.

Yalçınkaya, A., Rapoza, K., & Malley-Morrison, K. (1998, February). *Parenting practices and attachment styles in the U.S. and Turkey.* In K. Malley-Morrison (Chair), *Family processes and interactions: A cross-cultural perspective.* Paper symposium conducted at the meeting of the Eastern Psychological Association, Boston, MA.

You, H. S., & Malley-Morrison, K. (2000). Young adult attachment styles and intimate relationships with close friends: A cross-cultural study of Koreans and Caucasian Americans. *Journal of Cross-Cultural Psychology, 31,* 528–534.

13

Romantic Attachment From Argentina to Zimbabwe
Patterns of Adaptive Variation Across Contexts, Cultures, and Local Ecologies

DAVID P. SCHMITT

CONTENTS

*I*n this chapter, I review evidence of romantic attachment variation across cultures focusing on findings from the International Sexuality Description Project (ISDP; see Schmitt et al., 2003, 2004) and the International Sexuality Description Project 2 (ISDP-2; see Schmitt et al., 2008). The ISDP and ISDP-2 involved the collaborative research efforts of more than 150 scientists from around the world. Among the primary aims of the ISDP and ISDP-2 was to uncover the ways in which gender, personality, and culture influence romantic attachment and basic human mating strategies.

The current findings pertain to four specific research questions on romantic attachment variability across cultures. First, do the theoretical internal working models of attachment—models of self and models of other—underlie romantic attachment styles in a similar way across cultures (Bartholomew, 1990)? Second, is the "secure" romantic attachment style normative (i.e., is it the most common) across cultures (see van IJzendoorn & Sagi, 1999)? Third, are East Asians particularly high in the preoccupied form of insecure romantic attachment (Soon & Malley-Morrison, 2000), and if so, why? Fourth, do cross-cultural patterns of attachment relate to local ecologies in predictable ways from an evolutionary perspective (Belsky, Steinberg, & Draper, 1991; Chisholm, 1999)? I begin with a review of attachment theory and its relevance to adult romantic relationships (see also Mikulincer & Goodman, 2006; Simpson & Rholes, 1998).

ATTACHMENT THEORY, PARENT–CHILD ATTACHMENT, AND ROMANTIC RELATIONSHIPS

According to Bowlby's (1969/1982, 1988) classic theory of attachment, humans possess a behavioral–motivational system that is shared with other primates (Fraley, Brumbaugh, & Marks, 2005) and that protects children as they pass through several developmental phases (Marvin & Britner, 1999). Childhood experiences that include responsive, supportive, and consistent caregiving are thought to adaptively leave children with an abiding sense of high self-worth and lasting feelings of comfort about depending on others. These thoughts and feelings can eventually crystallize into internal working models or basic cognitive–emotional attitudes that securely assert that the self is valuable and worthy of love (i.e., children develop a positive model of self) and that others are valuable and worthy of trust (i.e., children develop a positive model of other). Unresponsive, abusive, or inconsistent caregiving experiences, in contrast, are thought to leave children with negative or dysfunctional internal working models. Dysfunctional models may consist of a negative model of other (via distrust and low valuing of the parent), a negative model of self (via low self-esteem and sensitivity to rejection), or negative models of both the self and others (Bartholomew, 1990).

Evidence suggests internal working models of self and other persist over time, affecting our ability to relate to others in close personal relationships well into adulthood (Fraley, 2002; Waters, Merrick, Treboux, Crowell, & Alberstein, 2000), at least at a general level (Overall, Fletcher, & Friesen, 2003). In the mid-1980s, researchers began to investigate how attachment styles and orientations might apply to people's cognitive–emotional attitudes toward romantic love and sexual relationships (Hazan & Shaver, 1987). For example, variation in romantic attachment has been linked to individual differences in sexual motivations and behaviors (Cooper et al., 2006; Schachner & Shaver, 2004; Stephan & Bachman, 1999), sexual offending and coercion (Bogaert & Sadava, 2002; Campagna, 2007; Davis, 2006), intimate partner violence (Finkel, 2007), and stalking (Wilson, Ermshar, & Welsh, 2006). Parent–child and romantic attachment processes and outcomes do share several similarities, such as involving proximity maintenance and close physicality, safe haven functioning for emotional comfort, secure base functioning for confidence and exploration, and involving separation distress when the secure base (parent or romantic partner) is unavailable.

Indeed, over the last decade and a half a growing body of evidence has shown that attachment deeply influences the way people think and feel about their most important romantic relationships (Feeney & Noller, 1996; Klohnen & John, 1998). Variation in attachment has been linked to romantic relationship patterns of conflict, stress, and affect regulation (Feeney, 1994; Mikulincer, Shaver, & Pereg, 2003); romantic satisfaction, love, and harmony (Brennan & Shaver, 1995; Kirkpatrick & Davis, 1994); as well as the temporal duration of romantic relationships (Kirkpatrick, 1998; Schmitt, 2005a; Simpson, 1999).

Even though many attachment researchers regard the key developmental processes of attachment—the processes that give rise to internal working models of self and other—as a human universal (Main, 1990; van IJzendoorn & Sagi, 1999), some have argued that the core assumptions of attachment theory are biased toward Western ways of thinking. For example, Rothbaum and his colleagues question whether the secure base of attachment universally fosters adaptation through exploration and individuation (Rothbaum, Weisz, Pott, Miyake, & Morelli, 2000). Indeed, many cultural differences have previously been implicated as moderators of childhood attachment behaviors (Ainsworth & Marvin, 1995). Because the view of the two-dimension model of self and other of romantic attachment has not been widely examined in non-Western cultures (cf. Sümer & Güngör, 1999), it remains unclear whether this view of romantic attachment is a universal feature of human psychology or whether it differs in important ways across diverse human cultural forms (Morelli & Rothbaum, 2007).

MODELS OF SELF AND OTHER ACROSS CONTEXTS AND CULTURES

Given the prominent role that culture plays in child development and parenting (Cronk, 1999; Gardner & Kosmitzki, 2002; Rohner & Britner, 2002), in one's attitudes toward the self and others (Glick, 2006; Markus & Kitayama, 1991), and in romantic relationship desires and dynamics (Schmitt, 2006; Tolman & Diamond, 2001), it seems likely that internal working models of romantic attachment may be at least partly influenced or moderated by context and culture. The degree of this influence is to a large degree unknown, however, because very few studies have simultaneously looked at romantic attachment styles across more than two contexts or cultures (cf. Sprecher et al., 1994). Only one study has examined the two-factor view of romantic attachment, based on models of self and other from the Relationship Questionnaire (RQ; Bartholomew & Horowitz, 1991) across multiple non-Western cultures (Schmitt et al., 2004).

If internal working models of self represent feelings and attitudes toward the self across all cultures, including whether the self is lovable and worthy of attention (see Bowlby, 1988), then within each culture models of self as measured by the RQ should positively correlate with measures of self-worth (e.g., self-esteem as measured by the Rosenberg Self-Esteem Scale; Rosenberg, 1965). The tendency for models of self to positively correlate with self-esteem was documented in a large cross-cultural study of romantic attachment across 56 nations—the ISDP (see Schmitt, 2008; Schmitt et al., 2004). This provided some evidence for the universality of the model of self construct. Moreover, Model of Self scores from the RQ were largely unrelated to measures unassociated with self-worth, providing cross-cultural evidence of the discriminant validity of the model of self construct. Similarly, the model of other scale from the RQ—theoretically representing feelings and attitudes toward others (including whether others are valuable, dependable, and worthy of love)—was usually positively correlated with measures of prosociality, such as with agreeableness as measured by the Big Five Inventory (BFI; Benet-Martinez & John, 1998), and largely unrelated to measures unassociated with prosociality (see Schmitt et al., 2004).

Based on the series of statistical tests originally used by Bartholomew and Horowitz (1991), Schmitt and his colleagues (2004) found conflicting evidence concerning the cultural universality of the two-dimension/four-category structure of romantic attachment. Some evidence clearly showed that the four-category structure was not universal across all cultures. For example, the four attachment scales of the Relationship Questionnaire did not interrelate across cultures as predicted by the two-dimension/four-category model of Bartholomew and Horowitz (1991). Secure and fearful forms of romantic attachment were negatively correlated, as predicted, in 63% of cultures, but preoccupied and dismissing attachment were negatively correlated in only 25% of cultures. The latter percentage clearly falls short of a "cultural universality" threshold. Of particular importance is the fact that specific world regions, and not just those cultures with smaller sample sizes, tended to fail tests of universality. For example, none of the seven African cultures displayed a significant negative correlation between secure and fearful attachment. In South/Southeast Asia, the secure–fearful relationships were equally inconsistent, with a peculiar correlation in the opposite of the predicted direction in Malaysia. Moreover, factor analyses demonstrated that the four categories of romantic attachment do not align as predicted within two-dimensional space in the world regions of South America, Western Europe, Eastern Europe, the Middle East, Africa, and East Asia (see Schmitt et al., 2004).

On the other hand, a considerable amount of evidence supported the universality of the basic two-dimensional structure of romantic attachment. For example, factor analytic results suggested that two dimensions underlie romantic attachment across all world regions. In almost all individual cultures, models of self and other formed *independent* dimensions. In addition, there was evidence of convergent and discriminant validity for the model of self and model of other scales within most cultures, as noted earlier. Individuals with more positive models of self tended to have higher self-worth but did not tend to have higher levels of prosociality. Individuals with positive models of other tended to have higher prosociality but did not tend to have higher self-worth. Finally, models of self and other were relatively reliable over time, as noted by comparing their nation-level scores in the ISDP and the ISDP-2. For example, national levels of model of self, $r(43) = 0.58, p < .001$, and model of other, $r(43) = 0.62, p < .001$, were strongly positively correlated.

Although it is difficult to draw strong inferences given the measurement limitations of the RQ as a brief measure of attachment (Brennan, Clark, & Shaver, 1998; cf. Sibley, Fischer, & Liu, 2005) and the sampling limitations of the ISDP, such as almost all participants were college students (see Schmitt et al., 2004), it may be reasonable to tentatively conclude that in nearly all cultures people possess basic cognitive–emotional attitudes that constitute romantic attachment models of self and other. These internal working models likely exist as pancultural constructs, forming independent dimensions that underlie romantic attachment types across cultures. Nevertheless, the four categories or types of romantic attachment outlined by Bartholomew and Horowitz (1991)—secure, dismissing, preoccupied, and fearful—seem not to reside within this two-dimensional space in precisely the same way across all regions of the world. It is unclear why cultures would vary in romantic attachment structure, especially given the strong theoretical rationale for thinking that internal working models of self and other are elemental components of human psychology (Bowlby, 1988). Perhaps response biases or translation difficulties were a factor in the ISDP. What is clear is that more work is needed to reveal why certain cultures vary in the psychological structure of romantic attachment.

IS THE SECURE STYLE OF ROMANTIC ATTACHMENT UNIVERSALLY NORMATIVE?

Previous research has suggested that secure attachment is the most common type of parent–child attachment across cultures (van IJzendoorn & Sagi, 1999). The idea that most children develop (and should develop) secure attachment styles has been called the normativity hypothesis, and it is a core assumption of attachment theory (see Rothbaum et al., 2000). Empirically, it does appear that secure parent–child attachment is the most prevalent form in Westernized cultures (Ainsworth, 1991), and several studies have documented the preponderance of secure parent–child attachment in non-Western cultures, including in Uganda (57% of children studied were classified as secure), China (68%), and Japan (68%; see van IJzendoorn & Sagi, 1999). A logical implication of the normativity hypothesis, combined with the presumption that attachment styles are reasonably stable over time (Waters et al., 2000), is that secure attachment should be the most common form of *romantic* attachment across all cultures.

Given the large number of cultures in the ISDP (i.e., 56 nations across 10 major world regions) and the ISDP-2 (i.e., 58 nations across 11 major world regions), evidence of universality in the ISDP/ISDP-2 would provide compelling support for the normativity hypothesis. Descriptive information from this diverse collection of cultures also may help to reveal why some clusters of romantic attachment across cultures deviate from this normative trend. In the ISDP, secure attachment was the highest rated form of romantic attachment across 79% of ISDP cultures, qualifying this as a "near universal" of human psychology (Schmitt et al., 2004). However, secure romantic attachment was significantly lower than dismissing, preoccupied, or fearful romantic attachment in several cultures. In addition, the three forms of insecure attachment, in combination, were typically more prevalent

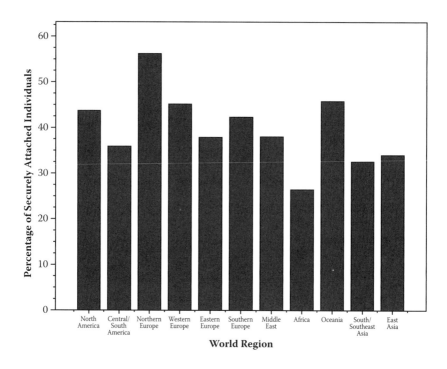

Figure 13.1   Percentage of "securely" attached individuals across world regions.

than secure attachment. Figure 13.1 displays the percentage of secure individuals across the 11 world regions of the ISDP-2. Only in Northern Europe was secure attachment prevalent in more than 50% of individuals. These findings provide only qualified support for the normativity hypothesis.

Looking across demographic contexts of the ISDP-2 (see Table 13.1), secure attachment was significantly associated with several different statuses. For example, secure attachment was significantly related to age, $\chi^2(7) = 104.14$, $p < .001$, with the percentage of secure attachment among 18-year-olds (38%) less than the percentage of securely attached individuals 41 and older (54%). Secure attachment was also associated with having less relationship experience (especially for virgins, among whom only 30% are securely attached), having a bisexual sexual orientation (only 30% are secure in romantic attachment), having a lower socioeconomic status (32% are secure), and residing in a rural community (39% are secure). The finding that in most demographic statuses fewer than 50% of individuals are secure in romantic attachment orientation provides further reason to question the normativity hypothesis.

Why is secure attachment not always the highest rated form of romantic attachment across contexts and cultures? One possibility is that the local ecologies of some cultures may naturally elicit more insecure forms of romantic attachment and sexual behavior (Belsky et al., 1991; Schmitt, 2005b). For example, in several African and South/Southeast Asian cultures—cultures that experience high

TABLE 13.1 Prevalence of Secure Romantic Attachment Across Demographic Contexts of the ISDP-2

Demographic Status	Percentage of Securely Attached Individuals
Gender ($\chi^2(1) = 0.25$)	
Men ($n = 10{,}011$)	41%
Women ($n = 14{,}588$)	41%
Age ($\chi^2(7) = 104.14$***)	
18 ($n = 3{,}023$)	39%
19 ($n = 3{,}978$)	38%
20 ($n = 3{,}954$)	39%
21–25 ($n = 9{,}505$)	42%
26–30 ($n = 1{,}975$)	44%
31–35 ($n = 676$)	46%
36–40 ($n = 390$)	52%
41 and older ($n = 634$)	54%
Current Relationship Status ($\chi^2(6) = 644.55$***)	
Married ($n = 1{,}542$)	50%
Engaged ($n = 1{,}507$)	47%
Cohabiting ($n = 1{,}647$)	56%
Dating one person ($n = 8{,}030$)	46%
Dating multiple people ($n = 1{,}308$)	37%
Not currently involved ($n = 6{,}111$)	34%
Never had sex ($n = 3{,}495$)	30%
Sexual Orientation ($\chi^2(2) = 38.72$***)	
Heterosexual ($n = 22{,}393$)	42%
Homosexual ($n = 620$)	38%
Bisexual ($n = 702$)	30%
Current Socioeconomic Status ($\chi^2(4) = 101.18$***)	
Upper ($n = 566$)	44%
Upper-middle ($n = 5{,}643$)	46%
Middle ($n = 13{,}635$)	40%
Lower-middle ($n = 3{,}110$)	37%
Lower ($n = 711$)	32%
Current Residence ($\chi^2(2) = 13.70$***)	
Rural ($n = 3{,}325$)	39%
Suburban ($n = 6{,}142$)	43%
Urban ($n = 13{,}760$)	41%

Note: ISDP-2 = International Sexuality Description Project 2.
***$p < .001$.

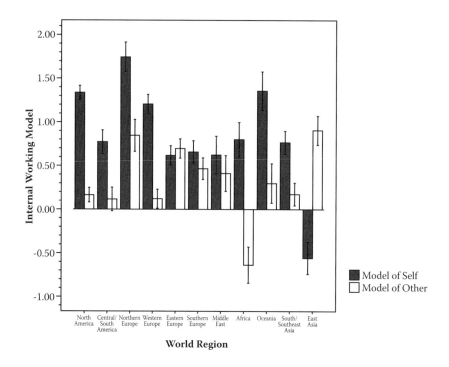

Figure 13.2   Internal working models of self and other across world regions.

levels of stress—insecure forms of romantic attachment tend to be quite high. In addition, the sociohistorical forces that presumably cause certain people to exhibit more interdependent or collectivist interpersonal orientations across cultures may similarly impact their basic romantic attachment orientations (Markus & Kitayama, 1991). In Japan and Taiwan, for example, levels of secure romantic attachment are lower than preoccupied romantic attachment levels (see Schmitt et al., 2004). Geographic variations in romantic attachment may be further caused by regionally shared religious, political, or socioeconomic factors.

To examine the geographic patterns of romantic attachment, Figure 13.2 displays the average model of self and model of other scores across the 11 major world regions of the ISDP-2. Models of self and other are generally positive, suggesting most regions are typically secure in orientation. However, in Africa the average model of other score drops below zero, suggesting people in these regions may typically develop dismissing romantic orientations. Similarly low model of other scores, compared to model of self scores, are seen in North America, Central/South America, Western Europe, Oceania, and South/Southeast Asia. In contrast, the region of East Asia possesses an average model of self score below the zero point, a score that is dwarfed by their high model of other scores. In Southern Europe, as well, models of other are, on average, higher than models of self. It seems likely that regionally shared religious, political, or economic factors play a role in these patterned deviations from normative secure attachment.

ARE EAST ASIANS PARTICULARLY PREOCCUPIED IN ROMANTIC ATTACHMENT?

Markus and Kitayama (1991) have suggested that Japanese individuals tend to evaluate the self primarily in terms of interdependent relationships (see also Singelis, 1994; Triandis, 1995). One's self-worth, it is argued, depends in large part on whether one's groups are collectively valued (see also Kitayama, Markus, Matsumoto, & Norasakkunkit, 1997). This has led to the hypothesis that East Asian individuals would be particularly prone to preoccupied romantic attachments, given that they may strive for self-acceptance by focusing on the approval of highly valued others (e.g., Soon & Malley-Morrison, 2000).

According to findings from the ISDP, East Asian cultures are particularly high on the preoccupied form of romantic attachment (Schmitt et al., 2004). This result may reflect the fact that in many East Asian cultures psychological validation (in this case romantic validation) is heavily dependent upon the opinion of others. Such a finding would be consistent with cultural variation in parent–child attachment (van IJzendoorn & Sagi, 1999). As expected, in the ISDP Schmitt and his colleagues (2004) found that national levels of preoccupied attachment correlated negatively with national rates of individualism (Hofstede, 2001), $r(47) = -0.45$, $p < .001$. This finding was replicated in the ISDP-2, $r(39) = -0.46$, $p < .001$ (see Figure 13.3). Thus, it appears that more collectivist nations such as those in East Asia tend to judge the

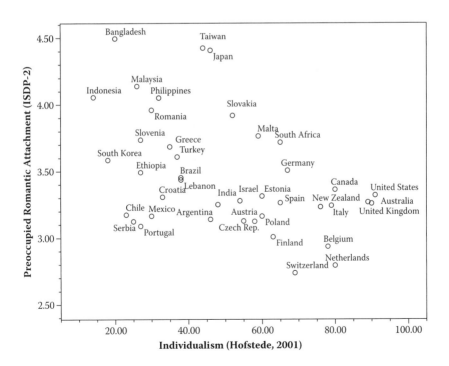

Figure 13.3   Individualism related to preoccupied romantic attachment across 41 nations.

romantic self primarily in terms of interconnectedness and the value provided to others (i.e., collective attachments; see also Oishi & Diener, 2001).

IS DISMISSING ROMANTIC ATTACHMENT ASSOCIATED WITH HIGH ECOLOGICAL STRESS?

According to the evolutionary theory of human sexuality proposed by Belsky et al. (1991), early social experiences adaptively channel children down one of two reproductive pathways. Those people who are socially exposed to high levels of stress—especially insensitive/inconsistent parenting, harsh physical environments, and economic hardship—tend to develop insecure attachment styles that are associated with short-term reproductive strategies (see also Schmitt, 2005a). Individuals from social contexts with lower stress, such as people from cultures with ample resources, should develop more secure attachment styles that are associated with long-term reproductive strategies (Belsky, 1997). Chisholm (1999) has argued further that in cultures with fewer resources, the optimal mating strategy is to reproduce early and often, a strategy rooted in high fertility rates, insecure romantic attachments, promiscuous sexual relationships, and an overall focus on short-term temporal horizons or future discounting (Wilson & Daly, 2006). In cultures that have abundant resources, the optimal strategy is to invest heavily in fewer numbers of offspring, a strategy associated with low fertility, secure romantic attachment, monogamous mating behavior, and long-term temporal horizons.

Findings from the ISDP and the ISDP-2 largely supported these evolutionary theories (see Schmitt et al., 2004). Those nations with lower human development indexes (including lower gross domestic product per capita; United Nations Development Programme, 2007/2008) had higher levels of dismissing attachment (data from the ISDP-2 are presented in Figure 13.4). Moreover, ISDP-2 results confirmed national levels of dismissing attachment are related to lower life expectancy, $r(54) = -0.40$, $p < .001$; lower adult literacy, $r(54) = -0.54$, $p < .001$; and lower political freedom, $r(55) = -0.50$, $p < .001$ (see Schmitt et al., 2008). Dismissing attachment was also linked to higher fertility, $r(54) = 0.52$, $p < .001$; higher rates of low birth weight newborns, $r(51) = 0.41$, $p < .001$; higher tuberculosis rates, $r(53) = 0.40$, $p < .001$; and higher average daily temperature, $r(28) = 0.41$, $p < .01$. Overall, it appears that there is a consistent relationship between indexes of cultural stress and dismissing attachment, a finding that supports Kirkpatrick's (1998) assertion that dismissing romantic attachment, among the various forms of insecure attachment, is most closely associated with short-term temporal horizons (Chisholm, 1999), including short-term mating strategies (Belsky et al., 1991; Schmitt, 2005a).

CLINICAL IMPLICATIONS

Each of the major questions addressed in this chapter may have implications for the clinical diagnosis and treatment of attachment-related phenomena. For example, if the underlying psychologies of the different forms of attachment are

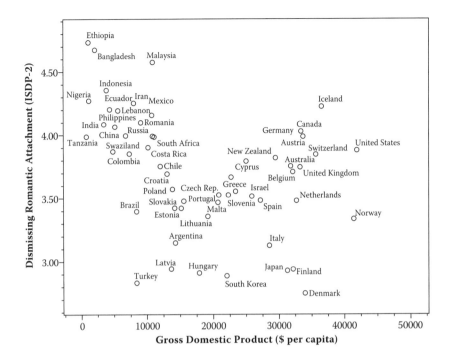

Figure 13.4   Gross domestic product related to dismissing romantic attachment across 55 nations.

found to fluctuate across cultures, this would inform our fundamental understanding of romantic relationship processes and outcomes (Schmitt, 2002, 2005a), as well as our use of treatments for attachment-related disorders in those cultures (Slade, 1999). If fearful attachment was found to be unassociated with models of other in a particular culture, the therapeutic emphasis in that culture for treating symptoms of fearful attachment should not focus on increasing the value that fearful patients place on others. Instead, clinical efforts may be more efficiently allocated toward increasing a fearful individual's positive attitudes toward the self (Blatt, 1995). Such caveats to clinical treatment would apply to variations in the underlying structures of dismissing, preoccupied, and even secure attachments, as well.

Several African and South/Southeast Asian cultures, in which individuals tend to experience high levels of stress, possessed especially high levels of dismissing forms of romantic attachment. This form of attachment insecurity may be beneficial to individuals who mature within cultures of high pathogens, high mortality, prolific reproduction, and short-term temporal orientations (Chisholm, 1999). The forces that presumably cause certain people to exhibit more collectivistic interpersonal orientations across cultures tended also to lead to preoccupied romantic attachments. If dismissing and preoccupied attachment styles are functional in these different ecological, political, and socioeconomic contexts, clinicians may wish to be cautious in trying to intervene to instill more secure attachments.

For example, therapeutic interventions involving individual, couple-based, or school-based programs that are designed to reduce dismissing attachment could, in fact, be harmful within a cultural context wherein trust in others and doubts about oneself are physically and emotionally hazardous. Instead, perhaps therapists should investigate an intervention target's context as an ecologically, politically, and socioeconomically distinct culture, within which treatments should need to be individually tailored. In some cases, dismissing attachment may be reduced in ways that lead to more secure interpersonal functioning. In other cases, dismissing attachment may be the most functional strategy and it is preoccupied individuals that need interventions to maximize mental health and interpersonal functioning. It is hoped that the clinical and research questions addressed in this chapter will stimulate future large-scale studies into the diversity of developmental causes and clinically relevant relationship consequences of adult romantic attachment variability.

CONCLUSION

This review addressed four specific issues concerning culture and romantic attachment. First, some evidence suggested that models of self and models of other serve as a fundamental two-dimensional structure of romantic attachment within most cultures, though these dimensions do not always underlie the categories of attachment in the same way across cultures. Second, in the ISDP, secure attachment among adults was normative across only 79% of cultures. Most often, the three forms of insecure attachment were more common than secure attachment. Third, East Asians, when insecurely attached, appear particularly prone to preoccupied attachment. Fourth, cross-cultural patterns of attachment are related to local ecologies in ways that support evolutionary theories of human sexuality (Belsky et al., 1991; Burton, 1990; Chisholm, 1999). It appears that high levels of ecological stress lead to insecurities that activate an adaptive developmental path that involves dismissing parent–child attachment, tendencies toward interpersonal distrust, and the pursuit of short-term reproductive strategies in adulthood (Ellis, McFadyen-Ketchum, Dodge, Pettit, & Bates, 1999; Schmitt, 2005a).

Beyond the four questions addressed here, the results from the ISDP and ISDP-2 may help to answer other questions (Schmitt et al., 2003, 2004). Previous cross-cultural reports of romantic attachment have been collected at varying points in time and different measures of adult romantic attachment have fallen in and out of favor over the years (Bartholomew & Shaver, 1998), rendering archival cross-cultural comparisons somewhat problematic. If meaningful patterns and universals of romantic attachment do exist across cultures, the best method for detecting and clarifying these patterns is to conduct large studies such as the ISDP and the ISDP-2 in which primary data are simultaneously collected from all cultures using identical romantic attachment measures. Reporting romantic attachment scores across the cultures of the ISDP and ISDP-2 (see Schmitt et al., 2004) may therefore provide a unique and needed quantitative benchmark for future investigators looking to relate romantic attachment patterns to other nation-level constructs of human sociality, psychology, and culture.

Still, there are some serious limitations to utilizing the ISDP and ISDP-2 results. For example, there are uncertainties as to whether the etically imposed measurement method used in these studies captured the full spectrum of romantic attachment psychology across cultures, whether self-report measures of adult romantic attachment assess the same constructs as other important assessment methods (Bartholomew & Shaver, 1998), and whether childhood attachment is truly a precursor of adult romantic attachment (though see Waters et al., 2000). As a result, researchers should not make overly broad or sweeping conclusions about the romantic attachment psychology of entire cultural regions or nations based solely on the limited self-report data derived from the ISDP and ISDP-2. Nevertheless, these results may serve as a useful heuristic for framing and stimulating important discussions about the precise nature and cultural contexts of romantic attachment psychology.

REFERENCES

Ainsworth, M. D. S. (1991). Attachments and other affectional bonds across the life cycle. In C. M. Parkes, J. Stevenson-Hinde, & P. Marris (Eds.), *Attachment across the life cycle* (pp. 33–51). London: Routledge.

Ainsworth, M. D. S., & Marvin, R. S. (1995). On the shaping of attachment theory and research: An interview with Mary D. S. Ainsworth (Fall 1994). *Monographs of the Society for Research in Child Development, 60,* 3–21.

Bartholomew, K. (1990). Avoidance of intimacy: An attachment perspective. *Journal of Social and Personal Relationships, 7,* 147–178.

Bartholomew, K., & Horowitz, L. M. (1991). Attachment styles in young adults: A test of a four-category model. *Journal of Personality and Social Psychology, 62,* 226–244.

Bartholomew, K., & Shaver, P. R. (1998). Methods of assessing adult attachment: Do they converge? In J. A. Simpson & W. S. Rholes (Eds.), *Attachment theory and close relationships* (pp. 25–45). New York: Guilford Press.

Belsky, J. (1997). Attachment, mating, and parenting: An evolutionary interpretation. *Human Nature, 8,* 361–381.

Belsky, J., Steinberg, L., & Draper, P. (1991). Childhood experience, interpersonal development, and reproductive strategy: An evolutionary theory of socialization. *Child Development, 62,* 647–670.

Benet-Martinez, V., & John, O. P. (1998). Los Cinco Grandes across cultures and ethnic groups: Multitrait-multimethod analyses of the Big Five in Spanish and English. *Journal of Personality and Social Psychology, 75,* 729–750.

Blatt, S. (1995). Representational structures in psychopathology. In D. Cicchetti & S. L. Toth (Eds.), *Rochester symposium on developmental psychology: Vol. 6. Emotion, cognition, and representation* (pp. 1–33). Rochester, NY: University of Rochester Press.

Bogaert, A. F., & Sadava, S. (2002). Adult attachment and sexual behavior. *Personal Relationships, 9,* 191–204.

Bowlby, J. (1982). *Attachment and loss: Vol. I. Attachment.* New York: Basic Books. (Original work published 1969)

Bowlby, J. (1988). *A secure base: Parent-child attachment and healthy human development.* New York: Basic Books.

Brennan, K. A., Clark, C. L., & Shaver, P. R. (1998). Self-report measurement of adult attachment: An integrative overview. In J. A. Simpson & W. S. Rholes (Eds.), *Attachment theory and close relationships* (pp. 46–76). New York: Guilford Press.

Brennan, K. A., & Shaver, P. R. (1995). Dimensions of adult attachment, affect regulation, and romantic relationship functioning. *Personality and Social Psychology Bulletin, 21*, 267–283.

Burton, L. M. (1990). Teenage childbearing as an alternative life-course strategy in multi-generational black families. *Human Nature, 1*, 123–144.

Campagna, A. F. (2007). Review of attachment and sexual offending: Understanding and applying attachment theory to the treatment of juvenile sex offenders. *Journal of the American Academy of Child & Adolescent Psychiatry, 46*, 892–893.

Chisholm, J. S. (1999). Steps to an evolutionary ecology of the mind. In A. L. Hinton (Ed.), *Biocultural approaches to the emotions* (pp. 117–149). Cambridge, UK: Cambridge University Press.

Cooper, M. L., Pioli, M., Levitt, A., Talley, A., Micheas, L., & Collins, N. (2006). Attachment styles, sex motives, and sexual behavior: Evidence for gender-specific expressions of attachment dynamics. In M. Mikulincer & G. S. Goodman (Eds.), *Dynamics of romantic love: Attachment, caregiving, and sex* (pp. 243–274). New York: Guilford Press.

Cronk, L. (1999). *That complex whole: Culture and the evolution of human behavior*. Boulder, CO: Westview Press.

Davis, D. (2006). Attachment-related pathways to sexual coercion. In M. Mikulincer & G. S. Goodman (Eds.), *Dynamics of romantic love: Attachment, caregiving, and sex* (pp. 293–336). New York: Guilford Press.

Ellis, B. J., McFadyen-Ketchum, S., Dodge, K. A., Pettit, G. S., & Bates, J. E. (1999). Quality of early family relationships and individual differences in the timing of pubertal maturation in girls: A longitudinal test of an evolutionary model. *Journal of Personality and Social Psychology, 77*, 387–401.

Feeney, J. A. (1994). Attachment style, communication patterns, and satisfaction across the life cycle of marriage. *Personal Relationships, 1*, 333–348.

Feeney, J. A., & Noller, P. (1996). *Adult attachment*. Thousand Oaks, CA: Sage.

Finkel, E. J. (2007). Impelling and inhibiting forces in the perpetration of intimate partner violence. *Review of General Psychology, 11*, 193–207.

Fraley, R. C. (2002). Attachment stability from infancy to adulthood: Meta-analysis and dynamic modeling of developmental mechanisms. *Personality and Social Psychology Review, 6*, 123–151.

Fraley, R. C., Brumbaugh, C. C., & Marks, M. J. (2005). The evolution and function of adult attachment: A comparative and phylogenetic analysis. *Journal of Personality and Social Psychology, 89*, 731–746.

Gardner, H. W., & Kosmitzki, C. (2002). *Lives across cultures: Cross-cultural human development* (2nd ed.). Boston: Allyn & Bacon.

Glick, P. (2006). Ambivalent sexism, power distance, and gender inequality across cultures. In S. Guimond (Ed.). *Social comparison and social psychology: Understanding cognition, intergroup relations, and culture* (pp. 283–302). New York: Cambridge University Press.

Hazan, C., & Shaver, P. R. (1987). Romantic love conceptualized as an attachment process. *Journal of Personality and Social Psychology, 52*, 511–524.

Hofstede, G. (2001). *Culture's consequences*. Thousand Oaks, CA: Sage.

Kirkpatrick, L. A. (1998). Evolution, pair-bonding, and reproductive strategies: A reconceptualization of adult attachment In J. A. Simpson & W. S. Rholes (Eds.), *Attachment theory and close relationships* (pp. 353–393). New York: Guilford Press.

Kirkpatrick, L. A., & Davis, K. E. (1994). Attachment style, gender, and relationship stability: A longitudinal analysis. *Journal of Personality and Social Psychology, 66*, 502–512.

Kitayama, S., Markus, H. R., Matsumoto, H., & Norasakkunkit, V. (1997). Individual and collective processes in the construction of the self: Self-enhancement in the United States and self-criticism in Japan. *Journal of Personality and Social Psychology, 72*, 1245–1267.

Klohnen, E. C., & John, O. P. (1998). Working models of attachment: A theory-based prototype approach. In J. A. Simpson & W. S. Rholes (Eds.), *Attachment theory and close relationships* (pp. 115–140). New York: Guilford Press.

Main, M. (1990). Cross-cultural strategies of attachment and attachment organization: Recent studies, changing methodologies, and the concept of conditional strategies. *Human Development, 33,* 48–61.

Markus, H. R., & Kitayama, S. (1991). Culture and the self: Implications for cognition, emotion, and motivation. *Psychological Review, 98,* 224–253.

Marvin, R. A., & Britner, P. A. (1999). Normative development: The ontogeny of attachment. In J. Cassidy & P. R. Shaver (Eds.), *Handbook of attachment* (pp. 44–67). New York: Guilford Press.

Mikulincer, M., & Goodman, G. S. (Eds.). (2006). *Dynamics of romantic love: Attachment, caregiving, and sex.* New York: Guilford.

Mikulincer, M., Shaver, P. R., & Pereg, D. (2003). Attachment theory and affect regulation: The dynamics, development, and cognitive consequences of attachment-related strategies. *Motivation and Emotion, 27,* 77–102.

Morelli, G. A., & Rothbaum, F. (2007). Situating the child in context: Attachment relationships and self-regulation in different cultures. In S. Kitayama & D. Cohen (Eds.), *Handbook of cultural psychology* (pp. 500–527). New York: Guilford Press.

Oishi, S., & Diener, E. (2001). Goals, culture, and subjective well-being. *Personality and Social Psychology Bulletin, 27,* 1674–1682.

Overall, N. C., Fletcher, G. J. O., & Friesen, M. D. (2003). Mapping the intimate relationship mind: Comparisons between three models of attachment representations. *Personality and Social Psychology Bulletin, 29,* 1479–1493.

Rohner, R. P., & Britner, P. A. (2002). Worldwide mental health correlates of parental acceptance-rejection: Review of cross-cultural and intracultural evidence. *Cross-Cultural Research, 36,* 16–47.

Rosenberg, M. (1965). *Society and the adolescent self-image.* Princeton, NJ: Princeton University Press.

Rothbaum, F., Weisz, J., Pott, M., Miyake, K., & Morelli, G. (2000). Attachment and culture: Security in the United States and Japan. *American Psychologist, 55,* 1093–1104.

Schachner, D. A., & Shaver, P. R. (2004). Attachment dimensions and sexual motives. *Personal Relationships, 11,* 179–195.

Schmitt, D. P. (2002). Personality, attachment, and sexuality related to dating relationship outcomes: Contrasting three perspectives on personal attribute interaction. *British Journal of Social Psychology, 41,* 589–610.

Schmitt, D. P. (2005a). Is short-term mating the maladaptive result of insecure attachment? A test of competing evolutionary perspectives. *Personality and Social Psychology Bulletin, 31,* 747–768.

Schmitt, D. P. (2005b). Sociosexuality from Argentina to Zimbabwe: A 48-nation study of sex, culture, and strategies of human mating. *Behavioral and Brain Sciences, 28,* 247–275.

Schmitt, D. P. (2006). Evolutionary and cross-cultural perspectives on love: The influence of gender, personality, and local ecology on emotional investment in romantic relationships. In R. J. Sternberg & K. Weis (Eds.), *The new psychology of love* (pp. 249–273). New Haven, CT: Yale University Press.

Schmitt, D. P. (2008). Attachment matters: Patterns of romantic attachment across gender, geography, and cultural forms. In J. Forgas & J. Fitness (Eds.), *Social relationships: Cognitive, affective, and motivational processes* (pp. 75–97). New York: Psychology Press.

Schmitt, D. P., Alcalay, L., Allensworth, M., Allik, J., Ault, L., Austers, I., … Zupanèiè, A. (2003). Are men universally more dismissing than women? Gender differences in romantic attachment across 62 cultural regions. *Personal Relationships, 10,* 307–331.

Schmitt, D. P., Alcalay, L., Allensworth, M., Allik, J., Ault, L., Austers, I., … Zupanèiè, A. (2004). Patterns and universals of adult romantic attachment across 62 cultural regions: Are models of self and of other pancultural constructs? *Journal of Cross-Cultural Psychology, 35,* 367–402.

Schmitt, D. P., Alcalay, L., Allik, J., Alves, I. C. B., Anderson, C. A., … Youn, G. (2008). *Evolutionary and cross-cultural perspectives on the "Dark Triad" of personality traits: Explaining patterns and universals of Machiavellianism, Narcissism, and psychopathy across 58 nations.* Manuscript in preparation.

Sibley, C. G., Fischer, R., & Liu, J. H. (2005). Reliability and validity of the revised experiences in close relationships (ECR-R) self-report measure of adult romantic attachment. *Personality and Social Psychology Bulletin, 31,* 1524–1536.

Simpson, J. A. (1999). Attachment theory in modern evolutionary perspective. In J. Cassidy & P. R. Shaver (Eds.), *Handbook of attachment* (pp. 115–140). New York: Guilford Press.

Simpson, J. A., & Rholes, W. S. (Eds.). (1998) *Attachment theory and close relationships.* New York: Guilford Press.

Singelis, T. (1994). The measurement of independent and interdependent self-construals. *Personality and Social Psychology Bulletin, 20,* 580–591.

Slade, A. (1999). Attachment theory and research: Implications for the theory and practice of individual psychotherapy with adults. In J. Cassidy & P. R. Shaver (Eds.), *Handbook of attachment* (pp. 575–594). New York: Guilford Press.

Soon, H., & Malley-Morrison, K. (2000). Young adult attachment styles and intimate relationships with close friends: A cross-cultural study of Koreans and Caucasian Americans. *Journal of Cross-Cultural Psychology, 31,* 528–534.

Sprecher, S., Aron, A., Hatfield, E., Cortese, A., Potapova, E., & Levitskaya, A. (1994). Love: American style, Russian style, and Japanese style. *Personal Relationships, 1,* 349–369.

Stephan, C. W., & Bachman, G. F. (1999). What's sex got to do with it? Attachment, love schemas, and sexuality. *Personal Relationships, 6,* 111–123.

Sümer, N., & Güngör, D. (1999). Psychometric evaluation of adult attachment measures in Turkish samples and a cross-cultural comparison. *Turkish Journal of Psychology, 14,* 71–109.

Tolman, D. L., & Diamond, L. M. (2001). Desegregating sexuality research: Cultural and biological perspectives on gender and desire. *Annual Review of Sex Research, 12,* 33–74.

Triandis, H. C. (1995). The self and social behavior in differing cultural contexts. In N. R. Goldberger & J. B. Veroff (Eds.), *The culture and psychology reader* (pp. 326–365). New York: New York University Press.

United Nations Development Programme. (2007/2008). *Human development report 2007.* New York: Oxford University Press.

van IJzendoorn, M. H., & Sagi, A. (1999). Cross-cultural patterns of attachment: Universal and contextual dimensions. In J. Cassidy & P. R. Shaver (Eds.), *Handbook of attachment* (pp. 713–734). New York: Guilford Press.

Waters, E., Merrick, S., Treboux, D., Crowell, J., & Alberstein, L. (2000). Attachment security in infancy and early adulthood: A twenty-year longitudinal study. *Child Development, 71,* 684–689.

Wilson, J. S., Ermshar, A. L., & Welsh, R. K. (2006). Stalking as paranoid attachment: A typological and dynamic model. *Attachment & Human Development, 8,* 139–157.

Wilson, M., & Daly, M. (2006). Are juvenile offenders extreme future discounters? *Psychological Science, 17,* 989–994.

14

Culture, Attachment Style, and Romantic Relationships

ELAINE HATFIELD and RICHARD L. RAPSON

CONTENTS

Researchers have proposed that culture and attachment style may have a profound impact on the way people think, feel, and behave in love and sexual relationships. Scholars interested in this topic have generally examined three factors: (a) cultural background (see Schmitt, 2008); (b) cultural values (whether participants are individualistic or collectivist in orientation; see Doherty, Hatfield, Thompson, & Choo, 1994); and (c) participants' love schemas, a measure designed to assess six popular attachment styles (see Hatfield & Rapson, 2005). Scholars have discovered that in a wide variety of cultures and ethnic groups, with people possessing diverse cultural values, people's attachment styles have a profound impact on their romantic preferences, their comfort when facing serious romantic commitments, the dynamics of romantic and marital relationships, and how people react when romantic and marital relationships fall apart.

HABITS OF THE HEART

In an influential theoretical paper, Hazan and Shaver (1987) proposed that childhood attachments may have a profound impact on men's and women's later romantic and sexual attachments. In the subsequent two decades, a number of scholars have amassed a plethora of evidence in support of Hazan and Shaver's contention that people possess a variety of cognitive schemas concerning the nature of love. Most theorists consider the three attachment styles, originally proposed by Ainsworth, Blehar, Waters, and Wall (1978) and later applied by Hazan and Shaver, to be of crucial importance, but some scholars have proposed that people possess four, five, or even six attachment styles (see Bartholomew & Horowitz, 1991; Hatfield & Rapson, 2005; and Hazan & Shaver, 1987, for a description of these various theoretical perspectives). In an attempt to integrate these perspectives and to allow scholars to talk about theorists' diverse research within a single framework, we proposed the following integrative model, referred to as the love schemas model (Hatfield & Rapson, 2005). We hope that scholars who prefer one or another theoretical perspective will have no trouble translating the findings we present into their own terminologies.

Love Schemas

Developmental theorists point out that, as important as infancy is, young people may learn even more about passionate love and intimacy in adolescence. Erikson (1982) observed that infants, children, adolescents, and adults face a continuing series of developmental tasks. Generally, attachment theorists have focused primarily on infants' first developmental task: attachment (in Hazan & Shaver's, 1987, terms) or learning to trust (in Erikson's, 1982, terminology). But there is more learning to come. In early, middle, and late childhood, children learn to know their own minds, to develop a sense of purpose, to take initiative, and to work hard. The next two stages are those in which we are primarily interested. In adolescence, teenagers must develop some sense of their own identity. Only when they have formed a relatively stable, independent identity are they able to tackle the next developmental task—to learn how to love someone and to become deeply intimate with them. Mature relationships, according to Erikson, involve an ability to balance intimacy and independence. In the love schemas model, we placed people into six possible categories, depending on how comfortable they are with independence and intimacy.

> Secure—The secure are comfortable with both emotional closeness and independence. They may be swept up in romantic love affairs, but they know that if things fall apart, they will survive. Some attachment theorists have labeled such people as securely attached.

Clingy—The clingy desire a great deal of closeness but feel uneasy when forced to be independent. Such people have been labeled the preoccupied, the socially absorbed, the anxious, or the fearful.

Skittish—The skittish desire a great deal of independence, but if forced to get too close, they may feel smothered and flee. Such people have been labeled as dismissing, socially individuated, and avoidant.

Fickle—The fickle are uneasy with closeness or independence. They yearn for what they do not have. They tend to fall in love with people who are not interested in them. If they finally succeed in capturing the other's interest, they soon get bored, irritated, anxious, and eventually bolt. Should the other begin to forget them or get involved with someone else, however, they often conclude they have made a terrible mistake and begin courting, sometimes desperately, the other again. And so it goes, on and on and on. Such people have been labeled as ambivalent.

Finally, there are two types of people who are simply not much interested in relationships.

Casual—The casual are only interested in relationships that are problem free.

Uninterested—The uninterested are simply not interested in relationships, romantic or otherwise, with anyone or at anytime. As some clinicians point out, "Emotional intimacy is not for everyone" (Marcus, 2006, p. D5). Such people have been labeled as dismissive-avoidant.

Hatfield and Rapson (2005) designed the Love Schema (LS) scale to measure these six attachment styles. For information on the reliability and validity of this measure see Bachman (1996a, 1996b); Choo, Levine, and Hatfield (1996); and Stephan, Singelis, Bachman, and Choo (1999).

SECURE ATTACHMENT: A CULTURAL UNIVERSAL?

In a landmark study, Schmitt (2008) interviewed 17,000 men and women from 56 nations. As predicted, he found that in most cultures, most people claim to possess a secure attachment style. The author argues that secure caretaker–child bonds (and later attachments) are near universal in human psychology. (For a discussion of the similarities and differences in cross-cultural patterns of attachment, see Imamoğlu & Imamoğlu, 2006; van IJzendoorn & Sagi, 1999; Wang & Mallinckrodt, 2006).

Sprecher et al. (1994) interviewed Americans, Russians, and Japanese. They found that in all three cultures, men and women generally identified themselves as secure in their love relationships. In all three, similar percentages of men and women identified with the various categories on the LS scale as well. For example, similar percentages considered themselves to be clingy, skittish, and so forth. Doherty and his colleagues (1994), who interviewed Americans of Chinese, European, Japanese, and Pacific Islander ancestry, secured similar results.

SECURE ATTACHMENT: CULTURAL VARIATIONS

Culture does, however, have some impact on how men and women classify themselves. Sprecher et al. (1994), for example, found that American men are more likely to possess a secure schema than are Russian or Japanese men. American and Japanese women are more likely to possess secure schemas than are Russian women. Soon and Malley-Morrison (2000) argue that, in general, East Asians' orientations are less individualistic and more collectivist than are their Western peers. They are more likely to strive for self-acceptance via the approval of highly valued others. Thus, we argue, East Asians should be particularly prone to preoccupied (i.e., clingy) romantic attachments. In his study of 56 nations, Schmitt (2008) found that this was so. In East Asian cultures, the preoccupied style was particularly prevalent. As Schmitt predicted, insecure romantic attachments were also most prevalent in high-stress social environments (i.e., societies where there was a great deal of political or religious turmoil, where life was harsh, disease prevalent, and life expectancy low).

Chisholm (1999), among others, attempted to provide an evolutionary explanation for societal differences in people's love schemas. He argued that in cultures with abundant resources, people can afford to possess long-term temporal horizons. In such societies, the optimal strategy is to invest in secure romantic attachments, monogamy, and a few high-quality offspring. By contrast, in cultures of poverty, people are forced to adopt short-term temporal horizons. In these societies, the optimal mating strategy is to engage in promiscuous sexual affairs, to reproduce often and early, and to invest minimally in any single relationship (see Brumbaugh & Fraley, 2006, for a further discussion of the evolution of attachment in adult love relationships).

Scholars have also predicted that culture and gender might interact in shaping men's and women's attachment styles. Useful insights as to the impact of culture on men's and women's attachment styles in various cultures may also be gleaned from historical research into private lives, which has expanded greatly in the past two decades (see Coontz, 2005; Hatfield & Rapson, 1993; and Stone, 1990, for an overview of this research). Historians contend that throughout most of time, gender inequality prevailed. Women were profoundly oppressed and often considered to be of less value than farm animals, especially horses. In such circumstances, women were almost always dependent upon fathers, husbands, and mates for survival. By necessity and circumstance, they clearly would have fallen into the clingy or dependent love category. Men, on the other hand, probably filled the ranks of the casual and uninterested. Historians also contend that the global movement toward gender equality will be a significant factor in encouraging men and women to think of themselves as secure and deserving the same benefits as their partners. In those parts of the world today where gender inequality still prevails, female dependency and male casualness and indifference in love may still prevail. However, times are changing in many places, though hardly everywhere. Thus, in time scholars might expect existing gender differences in attachment to decrease.

Culture, Love Schemas, and Romantic Behavior

Cultures differ greatly in values (Schwartz, 1992), self-schemas (Marcus & Kitayama, 1991), and cultural orientations (Triandis, 1992; Triandis, McCusker, &

Hui, 1990). Researchers have proposed that culture and people's love schemas may have a profound impact on their romantic attitudes and behavior. Specifically, cultural factors may shape romantic preferences, young people's comfort when faced with serious romantic commitments, the fate of romantic and marital relationships, and the ways people react to separation and the termination of romantic and marital relationships (Choo et al., 1996; Hatfield, Rapson, & Martel, 2007; Hatfield, Singelis, et al., 2007). We will discuss evidence in support of these contentions in the next few sections.

Culture, Love Schemas, and Romantic Preferences

Social psychologists have amassed considerable evidence that in a variety of cultures and ethnic groups, people's attachment styles may have a profound impact on their romantic preferences. In a study at the University of Hawaii, for example, Hatfield, Singelis, et al. (2007) invited 204 men and women to participate in a study of dating relationships. As is typical of Hawaii's multicultural population, the respondents came from a variety of cultural and ethnic backgrounds. They identified their ancestry as African, Chinese, European, Filipino, Hawaiian, Japanese, Korean, Samoan, Spanish/Mexican, and Vietnamese. The participants also identified with an array of religious groups and varied markedly in socioeconomic status and educational attainment.

In this study, Hatfield, Singelis, et al. (2007) told participants they were crafting a computer matching service similar to e-Harmony.com, PerfectMatch.com, or Chemistry.com. Participants were told they would be paired up with suitable partners, which would give scientists a chance to determine how well various types of matches worked out. To this end, participants were given a set of six personality profiles, which were designed to make it clear that potential dates differed in their love schemas. Respondents were asked to rank the profiles in order of preference and to indicate how appealing each of the potential dating partners was on a 10-point scale, ranging from 10 (extremely appealing) through 1 (not at all appealing), to 0 (would not consider this person).

As predicted, men and women generally preferred potential dates who possessed an "ideal" love schema. Specifically, they preferred potential dates and mates who possessed a secure love schema. Men's first choice was the secure woman (77% of the time); women's first choice was the secure man (91% of the time). Similar results were found by Latty-Mann and Davis (1996). In the event that an ideal partner was unavailable, men and women were most willing to settle for potential dates or mates whose love schemas matched their own. Cultural analyses made it clear that these preferences held true for people in all ethnic groups.

Culture, Love Schemas, and the Intensity of Passionate Love

In a variety of cultures and ethnic backgrounds, people's attachment styles have been found to influence how likely they are to fall in love and how passionately they love their romantic partners. Doherty et al. (1994), for example, interviewed 308 men and women from the University of Hawaii, who identified with four different ethnic backgrounds (Chinese, European, Japanese, or Pacific Island ancestry). First, participants were asked to complete the Individualism/Collectivism (I/C) scale developed by Triandis and his colleagues (Triandis, 1992; Triandis et al., 1990). The I/C scale is designed to assess individualism (idiocentrism) and collectivism (allocentrism). As predicted, Hawaii students of differing ancestry possessed very different orientations toward life. The European Americans were most individualistic, the Japanese Americans and Pacific Islanders were intermediate in I/C, and the Chinese Americans were the most collectivist in their orientations.

Respondents from the various ethnic groups also differed in how likely they were to be in love. When asked: "Are you in love with anyone right now?" Pacific Islanders were most likely to be currently in love, and the European Americans were least likely to be in love. Men and women from the various ethnic groups, or who were more or less individualistic or collectivist, did not differ in the intensity of their love, however. What turned out to be important in predicting men's and women's feelings were not culture, ethnicity, or I/C score, but their love schema profiles. Students who rated themselves as secure, clingy, or skittish were asked to fill out the Passionate Love Scale (PLS), which assesses how wildly in love people are, and the Companionate Love Scale (CLS), which measures how much people love and like their partners. As predicted, it was the clingy who loved most passionately. They were most likely to be in love at the present time and to score higher on the PLS than did any other group. As before, it was the skittish who were the least likely to have ever felt passionately about another. A look at men's and women's CLS scores adds a missing piece to the puzzle. Those who felt secure about love were most likely to love and like their partners. They were more committed to them, and their relationships were more intimate, than were those of their peers. Not surprisingly, it was the skittish who secured the lowest CLS scores.

Similar results were secured by Singelis, Choo, and Hatfield (1995), who interviewed 235 men and women from the University of Hawaii. As before, participants came from a variety of ethnic and socioeconomic groups. As in the previous study, the authors also asked men and women to complete the LS scale and assessed how much they loved and liked their partners. As predicted, they found that the more strongly people endorsed the clingy schema (and to some extent the secure schema), the more susceptible they were to love's ecstatic heights and agonizing abysses (i.e., the higher their scores on the PLS). The casual and uninterested were the most resistant to falling in love. Secure men and women received the highest scores on the CLS. Men and women who were skittish, fickle, casual, or uninterested in closeness, also shied away from close, intimate involvements. They received fairly low scores on the CLS. A number of studies have been conducted with samples from a variety of cultures (Cassidy & Shaver, 2008; Mikulincer & Shaver, 2007). Briefly what researchers find is that regardless of culture or ethnicity, certain patterns of relationships between love schemas and romantic behaviors tend to hold. These conclusions could change, of course, once research is conducted in a wider array of cultures. Let us now review some of these results.

The secure—The secure are susceptible to the charms of passionate love. Yet, a steady personality does not guarantee smooth sailing in romantic waters. Love is difficult for everyone and the vast majority of love affairs fail (Hatfield, Pillemer, O'Brien, & Le, 2008). Nonetheless, the secure do seem to do better than most at negotiating stable, companionate, intimate love relationships (see Doherty et al., 1994, and Hazan & Shaver, 1987, for evidence in support of these contentions).

The clingy—Researchers generally find that those who are clingy are most vulnerable to neurotic love. The clingy have low self-esteem, but idealize their romantic partners and obsess about the other's feelings. They often criticize their partners for their failure to make a commitment and to take care of them in the way they yearn to be cared for. Because they are so focused on what they want from an affair, they are oblivious to the fact that others might have different feelings and needs. They are addicted to relationships and are dependent on them, and they are often viewed as on an emotional roller coaster: elated one minute then anxious, frightened, and lonely the next. They have trouble finding a stable, committed, companionate relationship, and their insatiable demands tend to drive others away. For evidence in support of these propositions, see Bartholomew and Horowitz (1991), Collins and Read (1990), Feeney and Noller (1996), Hazan and Shaver (1987), Shaver and Hazan (1993), and Singelis et al. (1995).

The skittish—The skittish seem to fear romantic intimacy. They are pessimistic about love and avoid intimate social contact, especially emotional confrontations. Instead, they focus their attention on their work or on nonsocial activities. If their partners disclose too much, they become uncomfortable. They prefer uncommitted sexual relationships, and their love relationships rarely go well. However, breakups are usually not terribly upsetting to them. The work of a variety of researchers leads us to these conclusions (Bartholomew & Horowitz, 1991; Collins & Read, 1990; Feeney & Noller, 1990; Hazan & Shaver, 1987; Shaver & Hazan, 1993; Singelis et al., 1995).

The fickle—The fickle suffer terribly in their fleeting love relationships. They experience little joy and a great deal of anxiety, sadness, and anger in their passionate encounters (Singelis et al., 1995).

The casual and uninterested—The casual and the uninterested find the bittersweet emotion of passionate love to be a matter of some indifference. Caught up in a passionate affair, these two groups rarely feel joy. Instead, if anything, they are more likely to feel sadness and anger. Perhaps it is not surprising that these types tend to shy away from romantic encounters (Singelis et al., 1995).

Culture, Love Schemas, and Sexual Fantasies, Desires, and Behavior

Research suggests that people with different love schemas differ markedly in their sexual fantasies, desires, and behavior (see Davis et al., 2006; Feeney, 1999; Stephan

& Bachman, 1999). Stephan and Bachman (1999), for example, interviewed men and women from New Mexico State University. The students came from a variety of ethnic backgrounds: American Indian/Alaskan native, Asian/Pacific Islander, African American, European American, and Hispanic. Respondents were asked to complete the following assessments: a Partner Characteristics scale, which assesses what young people desire in a sexual partner; the Sociosexual Orientation Inventory, which assesses the extent to which they feel comfortable with unrestricted/restricted sexual activity; a Love Obsession scale, which measures people's desire for love and tendency to jealousy; the Emotionless Sex scale, which measures participants' interest in romantic love versus casual sex; a Low Commit/ High Fantasy scale, which assesses people's sexual fantasies for "forbidden" sexual partners; a Bad Lover scale, which measures the extent to which people are willing to risk engaging in sexual behavior destructive to a relationship; and a Sexual Exploration measure, which assesses people's sexual experience and willingness to take sexual risks. As predicted, the authors found clear evidence that men's and women's love schemas (i.e., their six LS scores) had a considerable impact on sexual fantasies, desires, and behaviors as measured by the preceding scales. For a review of work linking attachment style and sexual jealousy, see Levy, Kelly, and Jack (1996). Once again, cultural analyses revealed that in all ethnic groups, the same relationships between love schemas and sexual fantasies, desires, and behaviors were found.

In a Web-based study, Davis and her colleagues (2006) attempted to determine the impact of secure/insecure attachment style on sexual communication and sexual satisfaction. They interviewed 1,999 men and women from a variety of cultural and ethnic backgrounds. As predicted, the secure experienced the most emotional and physical satisfaction in their relationships. The clingy suffered from sexual anxiety, deferred too much to their partners needs, and sacrificed their own wishes. The skittish were poor communicators. As a consequence, both the clingy and the skittish found their sexual relationships to be unsatisfying. A number of other scholars have explored the link between culture, attachment style, and sexuality. For a comprehensive review of this research, see Cooper et al. (2006) and Feeney (1999).

Culture, Love Schemas, and Commitment

Let us now move to the second stage in the mate selection process—the point at which young men and women find themselves on the brink of making a serious commitment to another. There is considerable evidence that in a variety of cultures, participants' love schemas affect their cognitions, feelings, and behaviors when considering a serious romantic commitment. This appears to be true whether couples are heterosexual, gay, lesbian, or bisexual, although there is not so much evidence as scholars might wish concerning the dynamics of these latter groups in love relationships. See Diamond (1996) and Mohr (1999) for a review of existing research.

Hatfield, Singelis, et al. (2007) interviewed 242 men and women from the University of Hawaii. As is typical of Hawaii's multicultural population, respondents came from diverse ethnic and religious backgrounds. Participants were asked whether they had ever been "right on the brink of making a serious commitment to someone they loved (thinking about, say, going steady, living together, becoming engaged, or married)" (p. 14). The vast majority of people described a heterosexual commitment. Only a few described a homosexual attachment. The authors then asked respondents about their reaction at this juncture via the Reactions to Commitment scale. The authors proposed that regardless of cultural background, participants' love schemas would shape how calm and confident (as opposed to anxious, insecure, fearful, and trapped) young people felt when faced with a serious romantic commitment. As predicted, the scholars found that whatever their cultural background, the more secure men and women were (as assessed by the LS scale), the more calm and confident they felt when facing a commitment. Endorsement of any of the other schemas (clingy, skittish, fickle, casual, or uninterested) was negatively correlated with feelings of calm and confidence, and positively associated with feeling fearful and trapped when finding themselves on the brink of commitment. The clingy, for example, tended to experience considerable anxiety when faced with the possibility of a serious commitment. They reported: "I tried desperately to win his/her approval"; "I felt compelled to have sexual relations with my partner in order to keep him/her satisfied"; "I became extremely anxious whenever _____ failed to pay enough attention to me"; "I was constantly jealous" (p. 15).

The skittish admitted they went to great lengths to avoid commitment. When faced with the necessity of making a serious commitment, they admitted to two serious concerns: "I often worried that I was making a big mistake by getting so involved so soon" and "I often felt trapped; I needed a lot more time to be alone" (Hatfield, Singelis, et al., 2007, p. 15). Not surprisingly, the fickle, casual, and uninterested expressed such concerns as well. One finding is of special interest. The fickle appeared to be plagued with the problems that both the clingy and the skittish faced (i.e., they desired what they did not have, but fled from what lay within their grasp). When commitment loomed, they felt both anxious and wary of commitment. They felt trapped and worried that it was too much, too soon.

As was observed earlier, when reviewing this research, a cultural researcher cannot help but wish that more cross-cultural research linking culture, attachment style, and reactions to commitment existed. In societies with arranged marriages, for example, when there is no possibility except submitting to one's fate, are people relatively calm when commitments loom or are people in such situations as concerned as anyone else? Does attachment style affect one's reactions? As yet scholars do not know.

Culture, Attachment Styles, and the Nature of Intimate Relationships

Only a few cultural or cross-cultural theorists have investigated the impact of couple's love schemas on long-term intimate relationships, in spite of the fact that many sociologists and social psychologists have studied this topic. Theorists have, however, conducted a great deal of research in the West, with a wide variety of ethnic groups, that suggests that people's schemas may well have a profound impact on how they think, feel, and behave in their most important romantic relationships (see Charania & Ickes, 2007; Collins & Read, 1990; Cooper et al., 2006; Davis, Shaver, & Vernon, 2004; Schachner & Shaver, 2004; Schmitt, 2008). Scholars have found, for example, that in a variety of Western ethnic groups (including American Indian/Alaskan native, Asian/Pacific Islander, African American, European American, and Hispanic) the following relationships hold true.

The secure and perhaps the clingy are far better communicators than their peers. They are more likely to engage in open communication and sharing (Bachman, 1996a, 1996b; Feeney, 1999; Mohr, 1999). Their messages are more supportive and, in turn, they are more likely to receive support from lovers, friends, and family (Bachman, 1996a, 1996b). Bachman (1996a, 1996b), for example, found that in a variety of ethnic groups, the secure score higher on self-disclosure to their intimate partners than do their skittish, fickle, or casual peers. They are more able to talk about their hopes, dreams, and fears than are their peers.

The secure tend to be trusting and caring (Bachman, 1996a, 1996b), and more emotionally supportive, less emotionally abusive, and more responsive to their partners' needs than their peers (Collins, Guichard, Ford, & Feeney, 2006; O'Hearn & Davis, 1997). They also perceive others as more emotionally supportive than do their peers (Bachman, 1996a, 1996b). A number of scholars have also conducted studies linking attachment styles to emotional and physical violence (Mikulincer, Shaver, & Pereg, 2003; Rholes, Simpson, & Stevens, 1998). Bachman (1996b), in a study at New Mexico State University with participants from a variety of ethnic groups, asked students to complete a Social Support Appraisal Scale. He found that the secure felt more cared for—more liked, loved, and valued by their partners and more convinced that their needs were likely to be met—than were most of their peers.

The secure tend to be more satisfied in their relationships than their peers (Feeney, 1998; Kirkpatrick & Hazan, 1994; Mohr, 1999). Additionally, the secure's intimate relationships are more stable and longer lasting than are those of their peers (Belsky, 1999; Kirkpatrick, 1997; Kirkpatrick & Hazan, 1994; O'Hearn & Davis, 1997).

Culture, Attachment Styles, and Relationship Endings

People differ in how they react to the breakup of love relationships. Some mend quickly when a love affair falls apart. Others never fully recover. As one might expect, in a variety of cultural and ethnic groups, men's and women's attachment styles have been found to have a profound impact on how upsetting a breakup is, and in the strategies men and women employ to cope with loss.

Choo et al. (1996) interviewed 250 men and women from the University of Hawaii, who came from diverse ethnic backgrounds (African, Chinese, European, Filipino, Hawaiian, Japanese, Korean, and mixed ethnic backgrounds). Respondents were asked if they ever had the experience of being passionately in love, dating for a while, and then breaking up, and if so, how had they reacted emotionally to the breakup. They were also asked what strategies they had employed to cope with their tumultuous feelings and with the practical problems they faced in the week or two after the breakup. Men and women were found to differ somewhat in their reactions to breakups. Men were less likely to report experiencing joy or relief immediately after a breakup than were women. Men and women also relied on somewhat different coping strategies for dealing with a breakup. Although men and women were equally critical of their own roles in breakups, women were more likely to blame their partners than were men. Men were more likely to bury themselves in work or sports. No ethnic group differences were found in the strategies men and women used, however.

Love schemas were also correlated with reactions to breakups. Once again, regardless of respondents' ethnicity, the same patterns tended to hold true. These patterns are described next.

The secure—The more secure people found it easier to cope and were less likely than their peers to blame themselves or their partners for their predicament. They were also less likely to cope with the end of an affair by drinking or taking drugs than were others.

The clingy—Not surprisingly, it was the clingy who suffered the most after a breakup. After a love affair ended, they felt less joy and relief, and more sadness, fear, and anger than did their peers. They tended to blame themselves for breakups and were more likely than their peers to describe the following behaviors: "I spent a great deal of time trying to figure out what I might have done wrong"; "I spent a great deal of time trying to figure out what I could do to save our relationship"; "I spent a great deal of time talking to my friends, trying to figure out what I had done wrong"; and "I spent a great deal of time talking to my friends, trying to figure out if there was anything we could do to save the relationship" (Choo et al., 1996, p. 149).

The skittish—The skittish were most likely to feel good after a breakup, experiencing both joy and relief. They were unlikely to blame either themselves or their partners for the breakup. Typical comments included the following: "I spent a great deal of time thinking about how badly my partner had treated me" and "I spent a great deal of time talking to my friends—almost all of them agreed that my partner was really the one who had problems" and "I told myself 'I'm lucky to have gotten out of that relationship'" (Choo et al., 1996, p. 149). The skittish (and the fickle) tended to drink or take drugs. It is probably not too encouraging for those men and women, who go to a singles' bar in the hope of finding someone to casually date or spend a relaxing night with, to discover that they may well bump into the skittish and the fickle recovering from their last blighted love affair.

Other researchers have also found attachment styles to be important in shaping reactions to separation and breakup, regardless of participants' ethnicity (Bachman, 1996a, 1996b; Birnbaum, Orr, Mikulincer, & Florian, 1997). It seems logical to argue that culture and gender ought to interact in shaping men's and women's reaction to a breakup. In some cultures divorce is impossible; or men may divorce their wives but not vice versa. In some societies, where women are confined to family and home, divorce may be virtually a death sentence for women. In such circumstances, culture and attachment style may have profoundly different dynamics on reactions to a breakup. Scholars can only hope that such cultural research will be conducted in the near future.

CONCLUSIONS AND CLINICAL IMPLICATIONS

Unfortunately, the scholarly research exploring the impact of culture, gender, and attachment style on romantic relations remains sparse. Ideally, we would know a great deal about people's visions of love in profoundly religious communities (such as Iran) and secular ones (such as Norway, Sweden, and Denmark); in communist and socialist countries (such as Cuba, North Korea, and Laos) as well as fiercely capitalist ones (such as Singapore and Taiwan); in peaceful communities and in warlike ones; in urban and rural communities; and in affluent and poor countries. Given the tremendous popularity of attachment style research, however, the current neglect of culture is bound to change and the change will be for the good. Cross-cultural attachment research could contribute significantly to our understanding of the attachment process.

Currently, a few scholars argue that attachment style is a cultural universal. As we have seen, there is considerable evidence for their contention. Researchers and clinicians generally find that in a wide variety of cultures, the attachment paradigm is a surprisingly good predictor of how men and women will think, feel, and behave in their love relationships. In this chapter, for example, we have seen that in an array of cultural and ethnic groups, people's love schemas do appear to influence their romantic attitudes and behavior. Specifically, in all of the cultures studied, men and women's love schemas were found to shape romantic preferences, the comfort of young people when faced with serious romantic commitments, the fate of romantic and marital relationships, and the way people react to separation and loss. Such consistency provides clinicians with an increased confidence in the validity of the basic attachment paradigm. However, as we study a wider range of cultural groups, if we find impressive cultural differences in the way love schemas shape romantic attitudes, preferences, and behaviors, that confidence would be shaken. Consequently, as clinicians encounter cultural groups that do not adhere to the norms of attachment theory, they must be sensitive to such differences.

In truth, it would not come as a surprise to discover that in different societies, people's attachment prototypes differ as a consequence of their different childhood experiences. As historians point out, culture and time often have a dramatic impact on the way children are raised, and clinicians need to be particularly responsive to these impacts when working with their clients. In some tribal societies, for example, it does take a village to raise a child. In the West, before the 15th century, children were generally considered miniature adults. There is only scant evidence to suggest that childhood was even considered a separate stage in the life cycle. Children were often raised by wet nurses, strangers, or left to fend for themselves, and almost as soon as they could walk, they were sent out to work alongside adults. Even as recently as the early 1900s, psychologists such as J. B. Watson were advising mothers that infants should never be coddled or touched, and that such coddling would make them clingy and dependent, and expose them to killer infections. A few years decades later, pediatricians like Dr. Benjamin Spock were counseling mothers that it was impossible to spoil infants, and the more love and attention children received, the better (Blum, 2002).

The cultural and historical work of the future should provide some ideas of the importance of culture versus the biological "wiring" of humankind in shaping behavior. If scholars secure large cultural differences, that would suggest that humans are indeed protean and flexible, even in these most fundamental areas of human behavior. If we find that in most cultures caretaker–child relationships follow much the same patterns, that will say a great deal about the architecture of the mind laid down during humankind's long evolution. At the moment, most historians emphasize change through time and differences between cultures. However, they are not of one mind with those conclusions, and many see the emergence of a common global culture (Rapson, 2007; Stone, 1977).

Currently, we can only wish that cultural researchers and clinicians will devote more time and energy to this topic and attempt to fill the gaps in the literature. In this chapter, we were often forced to speculate about cultural differences based on studies conducted in the West with various ethnic groups. We need hardly say that while this is a beginning, it is not good enough—not by a long shot. We can only hope that this paucity of evidence is remedied in the future. We suspect it will be, given the importance of this fascinating topic, including insights that open a window on how culture and biology interact in shaping humanity's deepest of relationships.

REFERENCES

Ainsworth, M. D. S., Blehar, M. C., Waters, E., & Wall, S. (1978). *Patterns of attachment: A psychological study of the strange situation.* Hillsdale, NJ: Lawrence Erlbaum Associates.

Bachman, G. F. (1996a). *"Do you come here too?" "Gee, Did I forget to say goodbye?" Attachment styles and strategies in initiating and terminating romantic relationships* (Unpublished master's thesis). New Mexico State University, Las Cruces, NM.

Bachman, G. F. (1996b). *Love schemas, perceived social support, and self-disclosure in romantic relationships.* Paper presented at the 4th annual Arizona State University Communication Studies Student Conference, Tempe, AZ.

Bartholomew, K., & Horowitz, L. M. (1991). Attachment styles among young adults: A test of a four-category model. *Journal of Personality and Social Psychology, 61,* 226–244.

Belsky, J. (1999). Modern evolutionary theory and patterns of attachment. In J. Cassidy & P. R. Shaver (Eds.), *Handbook of attachment: Theory, research, and clinical applications* (pp. 141–161). New York: Guilford Press.

Birnbaum, G. E., Orr, I., Mikulincer, M., & Florian, V. (1997). When marriage breaks up: Does attachment style contribute to coping and mental health? *Journal of Social and Personal Relationships, 14,* 643–654.

Blum, D. (2002). *Love at Goon Park: Harry Harlow and the science of affection.* New York: John Wiley & Sons.

Brumbaugh, C. C., & Fraley, C. (2006). The evolution of attachment in romantic relationships. In M. Mikulincer & G. S. Goodwin (Eds.), *Dynamics of romantic love: Attachment, caregiving, and sex* (pp. 71–101). New York: Guilford Press.

Cassidy, J., & Shaver, P. R. (2008). *Handbook of attachment: Theory, research, and clinical applications* (2nd ed.). New York: Guilford Press.

Charania, M. R., & Ickes, W. (2007). Predicting marital satisfaction: Social absorption and individuation versus attachment anxiety and avoidance. *Personal Relationships, 14,* 187–208.

Chisholm, J. S. (1999). Steps to an evolutionary ecology of the mind. In A. L. Hinton (Ed.), *Biocultural approaches to the emotions* (pp. 117–149). Cambridge, UK: Cambridge University Press.

Choo, P., Levine, T., & Hatfield, E. (1996). Gender, love schemas, and reactions to a romantic breakup. *Journal of Social Behavior and Personality, 11,* 143–160.

Collins, N. L., Guichard, M. C., Ford, M. B., & Feeney, B. C. (2006). In M. Mikulincer & G. S. Goodwin (Eds.), *Dynamics of romantic love* (pp. 149–190). New York: Guilford Press.

Collins, N. L., & Read, S. J. (1990). Adult attachment, working models, and relationship quality in dating couples. *Journal of Personality and Social Psychology, 58,* 644–663.

Coontz, S. (2005). *Marriage: A history.* New York: Viking.

Cooper, M. L., Pioli, M., Levitt, A., Talley, A. E., Micheas, L., & Collins, N. (2006). Attachment styles, sex motives and sexual behavior: Evidence for gender-specific expressions of attachment dynamics. In M. Mikulincer & G. S. Goodman (Eds.), *Dynamics of romantic love: Attachment, caregiving, and sex* (pp. 243–274). New York: Guilford Press.

Davis, D., Shaver, P. R., & Vernon, M. L. (2004). Attachment style and subjective motivations for sex. *Personality and Social Psychology Bulletin, 30,* 1076–1090.

Davis, D., Shaver, P. R., Widaman, K. F., Vernon, M. L., Follette, W. C., & Beitz, K. (2006). "I can't get no satisfaction": Insecure attachment, inhibited sexual communication, and sexual dissatisfaction. *Personal Relationship 13,* 465–483.

Diamond, L. M. (1996). How do I love thee?": Implications of attachment theory for understanding same-sex love and desire. In M. Mikulincer & G. S. Goodwin (Eds.), *Dynamics of romantic love* (pp. 275–292). New York: Guilford Press.

Doherty, R. W., Hatfield, E., Thompson, K., & Choo, P. (1994). Cultural and ethnic influences on love and attachment. *Personal Relationships, 1,* 391–398.

Erikson, E. (1982). *The life cycle completed: A review.* New York: Norton.

Feeney, J. A. (1998). Adult attachment and relationship-centered anxiety: Responses to physical and emotional distancing. In J. A. Simpson & W. S. Rholes (Eds.), *Attachment theory and close relationships* (pp. 189–218). New York: Guilford Press.

Feeney, J. A. (1999). Adult romantic attachment and couple relationships. J. Cassidy & P. R. Shaver (Eds.), *Handbook of attachment: Theory, research, and clinical applications* (pp. 355–377). New York: Guilford Press.

Feeney, J. A., & Noller, P. (1990). Attachment style as a predictor of adult romantic relationships. *Journal of Personality and Social Psychology, 58,* 281–291.

Feeney, J. A., & Noller, P. (1996). *Adult attachment.* Thousand Oaks, CA: Sage Publications.

Hatfield, E., Pillemer, J. T., O'Brien, M. U., & Le, Y. L. (2008). The endurance of love: Passionate and companionate love in newlywed and long-term marriages. *Interpersona: An International Journal of Personal Relationships, 2,* 35–64. Retrieved January 1, 2009, from http://www.interpersona.org/issues.php?section=viewfulltext&issue=3&area=14&id=int485ee26d5859b&fulltextid=14&idiom=1

Hatfield, E., & Rapson, R. L. (1993). *Love, sex, and intimacy: Their psychology, biology, and history.* New York: Harper/Collins.

Hatfield, E., & Rapson, R. (2005). *Love and sex: Cross-cultural perspectives.* Lanham, MD: University Press of America.

Hatfield, E., Rapson, R. L., & Martel, L. D. (2007). Passionate love and sexual desire. In S. Kitayama & D. Cohen (Eds.), *Handbook of cultural psychology* (pp. 760–779). New York: Guilford Press.

Hatfield, E., Singelis, T., Levine, T., Bachman, G., Muto, K., & Choo, P. (2007). Love schemas, preferences in romantic partners, and reactions to commitment. *Interpersona: An Interdisciplinary Journal on Personal Relationships, 1,* 1–24. Retrieved January 1, 2009, from http://www.interpersona.org/issues.php?section=view&issue=1&area=6&id=int466c8cee6e240

Hazan, C., & Shaver, P. (1987). Romantic love conceptualized as an attachment process. *Journal of Personality and Social Psychology, 52,* 511–524.

Imamoğlu, S., & Imamoğlu, E. O. (2006). Relationship between general and context-specific attachment orientations in a Turkish sample. *The Journal of Social Psychology, 146,* 261–274.

Kirkpatrick, L. A. (1997). Evolution, pair-bonding, and reproductive strategies: A reconceptualization of adult attachment. In J. A. Simpson & W. S. Rholes (Eds.), *Attachment theory and close relationships* (pp. 353–393). New York: Guilford Press.

Kirkpatrick, L. A., & Hazan, C. (1994). Attachment styles and close relationships: A four-year prospective study. *Personal Relationships, 1,* 123–142.

Latty-Mann, H., & Davis, K. E. (1996). Attachment theory and partner choice: Preference and actuality. *Journal of Personal and Social Relationships, 13,* 5–23.

Levy, K. N., Kelly, K. M., & Jack, E. L. (1996). Sex differences in jealousy: A matter of evolution or attachment history? In M. Mikulincer & G. S. Goodwin (Eds.), *Dynamics of romantic love* (pp. 128–148). New York: Guilford Press.

Marcus, E. N. (2006, November 21). Cases: Like a fish needs a bicycle: For some people intimacy is toxic. *New York Times,* p. D5.

Markus, H. R., & Kitayama, S. (1991). Culture and self: Implications for cognition, emotion, and motivation. *Psychological Review, 98,* 224–253.

Mikulincer, M., & Shaver, P. R. (2007). *Attachment in adulthood: Structure, dynamics, and change.* New York: Guilford Press.

Mikulincer, M., Shaver, P. R., & Pereg, D. (2003). Attachment theory and affect regulation: The dynamics, development, and cognitive consequences of attachment-related strategies. *Motivation and Emotion, 27,* 77–102.

Mohr, J. J. (1999). Same-sex romantic attachment. In J. Cassidy, & P. R. Shaver (Eds.), *Handbook of attachment: Theory, research, and clinical applications* (pp. 378-394). New York: Guilford Press.

O'Hearn, R. E., & Davis, K. E., (1997). Women's experience of giving and receiving emotional abuse. *Journal of Interpersonal Violence, 12,* 375–391.

Rapson, R. L. (2007). *Magical thinking and the decline of America.* Philadelphia: Xlibris.

Rholes, W. S., Simpson, J. A., & Stevens, J. G. (1998). Attachment orientations, social support, and conflict resolution in close relationships. In J. A. Simpson & W. S. Rholes (Eds.), *Attachment theory and close relationships* (pp. 166–188). New York: Guilford Press.

Schachner, D. A., & Shaver, P. R. (2004). Attachment dimensions and sexual motives. *Personal Relationships, 11,* 179–195.

Schmitt, D. P. (2008). Attachment matters: Patterns of romantic attachment across gender, geography, and cultural forms. In J. P. Forgas & J. Fitness (Eds.), *Social relationships: Cognitive, affective, and motivational processes* (pp. 75–100). New York: Psychology Press.

Schwartz, S. H. (1992). Universals in the content and structure of values: Theoretical advances and empirical tests in 20 countries. In M. Zanna (Ed.), *Advances in Experimental Social Psychology* (Vol. 25, pp. 1–65). San Diego: Academic Press.

Shaver, P. R., & Hazan, C. (1993). Adult romantic attachment: Theory and empirical evidence. In D. Perlman & W. Jones (Eds.), *Advances in personal relationships* (Vol. 4, pp. 29–70). Greenwich, CT: JAI Press.

Singelis, T., Choo, P., & Hatfield, E. (1995). Love schemas and romantic love. *Journal of Social Behavior and Personality, 10*, 15–36.

Soon, H., & Malley-Morrison, K. (2000). Young adult attachment styles and intimate relationships with close friends. A cross-cultural study of Koreans and Caucasian Americans. *Journal of Cross-Cultural Psychology, 31*, 528–534.

Sprecher, S., Aron, A., Hatfield, E., Cortese, A., Potapova, E., & Levitskaya, A. (1994). Love: American style, Russian style, and Japanese style. *Personal Relationships, 1*, 349–369.

Stephan, C. W., & Bachman, G. F. (1999). What's sex got to do with it? Attachment, love schemas, and sexuality. *Personal Relationships, 6*, 111–123.

Stephan, C. W., Singelis, T., Bachman, G. F., & Choo, P. A. (1999). *Adult attachment styles: Measurement according to the unified theory of love schemas.* Unpublished manuscript, New Mexico State University.

Stone, L. (1977). *The family, sex, and marriage: In England 1500–1800.* New York: Harper & Row.

Stone, L. (1990). *Road to divorce: England 1530–1987.* New York: Oxford University Press.

Triandis, H. C. (1992). *Individualism and collectivism manual.* Unpublished manuscript. (Available from Prof. Harry C. Triandis, 603 E. Daniel St., Champaign, IL 60820)

Triandis, H. C., McCusker, C., & Hui, C. H. (1990). Multimethod probes of individualism and collectivism. *Journal of Personality and Social Psychology, 59*, 106–120.

van IJzendoorn, M. H., & Sagi, A. (1999). Cross-cultural patterns of attachment: Universal and contextual dimensions. In J. Cassidy & P. R. Shaver (Eds.), *Handbook of attachment: Theory, research, and clinical applications* (pp. 713–734). New York: Guilford Press.

Wang, D. C., & Mallinckrodt, B. S. (2006). Differences between Taiwanese and U.S. cultural beliefs about ideal adult attachment. *Journal of Counseling Psychology, 53*, 192–204.

15

Mothering From the Margins
The Mother–Daughter Relationship in a Culture of Son Preference

RACHANA JOHRI

CONTENTS

The study of human attachment has acquired paradigmatic status with immense explanatory potential. It is this enormous power of attachment theory that also provokes some anxiety regarding its cross-cultural validity. In this chapter the question of attachment is considered through a somewhat unconventional trajectory by examining the narratives of mothers of daughters living in India, a culture marked by son preference. The two issues raised in the chapter are (a) that Hinduism provides an alternative rendering of attachment from that prevalent in mainstream psychology (Saraswathi, 2005), and (b) that the two partners, the mother and the child, involved in the attachment process have well-specified constructions in the Indian context (Dube, 2001; Kakar, 1981). The central concern presented in this chapter is whether attachment theory in its current form can satisfactorily address the problems that potentially arise from these issues.

A word on India may help to create the context for the reflections that follow. A complex society with various communities that differ along the lines of caste, class, religion, and urban and rural location, Hindus form the largest religious group in India. In addition, Indian society is transitional with modernity and globalization emerging as significant influences. The impact of this is felt most strongly in urban areas. Although Hindus are only one of the significant communities in India, aspects of Hindu thought are relevant for the present discussion for two reasons. First, the participants of the study reported in the following are Hindu women. Second, as the subsequent parts of this chapter show, Hindu thought specifically provides a well-developed and nuanced critique of human attachment, fostering instead the goal of detachment. The concern in this chapter is not to create a stereotype of an unchanging Indian clinging to traditional ideas but to pose a challenge to the unexamined assumptions that guide the discipline of contemporary psychology. The moot question is whether alternative conceptualizations such as those of non-Western and nonindustrialized cultures require rethinking about the nature of human attachment.

This question has been approached from broadly two perspectives. The dominant paradigm in attachment research assumes cross-cultural universality (Schmitt et al., 2004; van IJzendoorn & Sagi, 2002). This view has been increasingly contested in recent years (Carlson & Harwood, 2003; Keller, 2008; Levine, 2002; Rothbaum & Morelli, 2005; Rothbaum, Weisz, Pott, Miyake, & Morelli, 2000). Although most critics of the theory accord attachment a central place in human relatedness, they differ on the extent to which this must develop along similar pathways across different cultures (Keller, 2008). The central argument is that children acquire an understanding of self and relationality within cultures with varied value systems (Kağitiçibaşi, 2007) that create alternative ideologies of child rearing with radically different goals (Levine, 2002; Rothbaum et al., 2000). The cultural critique of attachment theory is at a nascent stage. Yet, their arguments about the ideological roots of attachment theory are also likely to be applicable to the study of adult attachment.

Attachment theory assumes that early experiences of attachment result in the formation of an internal working model that predisposes the individual to experience relationships in a predictable manner (Bowlby, 1988). However, the fact that the relationship between early and later attachment is uncertain (Thompson, 2002) may leave room for many mediating influences including those coming from distinct cultural pathways. Similarly, questions of adult attachment, specifically romantic relationships, need rethinking in the context of non-Western cultures.

However, it may also be necessary to examine variations, particularly of those at the margins of society. This is a glaring lack in much cultural psychology. Kakar (1981) notes that in India, motherhood provides a woman with "a purpose and identity that nothing else in her culture can" (p. 56). However, this status is contingent on her giving birth to a son. Mothers with daughters are sometimes viewed as no better than barren. The patriarchal nature of Indian communities makes an analytic separation between patriarchy and culture difficult (Uberoi, 2003). Ideals such as detachment may therefore be used in the service of patriarchy.

This chapter is based on findings from a previous study (Johri, 1999), in which we analyzed mothers' narratives to suggest that the nature of the mother's attachment toward daughters is determined by the elaborate social constructions of gender present in Indian society. Mother–daughter relationships provide a unique vantage point to examine attachment within a culture of detachment from the experiential reality of marginalization. Unfortunately, there is little research in India on either infant attachment (Sharma, 2003) or the manner in which Hindu concepts are manifested in interpersonal and intergenerational relationships, particularly in a society with a marked idealization of sons (Chakkarath, 2005). This chapter attempts to address this gap.

THE HINDU WORLDVIEW

The growing concern with the rootedness of psychology in Western thought has prompted explorations of other epistemological traditions for alternative ethnotheories of development (Keller, 2008). The Hindu worldview provides one such theory that poses a significant challenge to the Euro-American view of attachment. Regardless of the truth of these assumptions, this has immense psychological significance as a belief system with a code of conduct for living life (Kakar, 1981; Kurtz, 1992; Saraswathi & Ganapathy, 2002).

The core beliefs of Hinduism are found in the Vedas and the Upanishads (Chakkarath, 2005; Kakar, 1981; Saraswathi, 2005). These texts emphasize the inherent suffering of human life and the cycle of birth, death, and rebirth through which the *atman* (soul) crosses from one life to another. Liberation (*moksha*) from the cycle of birth and rebirth involves realization of the ultimate oneness of the phenomenal self (*Atman*) with the cosmic self (*Brahman*). The concept of *karma*, the accumulation of good and bad deeds, provides another important coordinate within which the Hindu worldview functions. Although the ultimate goal of life is to attain moksha, the individual is expected to live as a social being through the paths of *dharma* (individual, social, and religious duties), *artha* (economic attainment), and *kama* (experience of desire and pleasure). The purpose of life is to attain these goals within the overarching framework of moksha. Notwithstanding the ideal of moksha, attachments are deeply valued and sought after in India. Cultural and cross-cultural psychologists have described India as a collectivist society that values interdependence over independence (Chaudhary & Bhargava, 2006). Thus Hindu personhood is framed within a complex interplay of relationality and detachment (Roland, 2005). As Lamb (2000) shows, the term *maya* can signify either attachment and affection or illusion. In Hindi the term *mayajaal* refers to the illusory web of relationships. Hindu texts speak of attachment as an affliction, the cause of clinging and yearning. It is an undesirable state that may be destroyed through the true knowledge of the self. A pervasive message for Hindus is that moksha is attainable if they cultivate a spirit of detachment toward all worldly attachments. While several texts mention a son as one of the objects of attachments, daughters are rarely mentioned (Sinha, 1986).

The paradox between relationality and detachment is partially resolved through the elaborate ethnotheory of life stages that structures daily life. Infancy is marked by care and limited discipline. An analysis of the remaining life stages shows that an individual is expected to move several times between close relatedness and disconnection within his life. The *brahamcharya* (student) is expected to be committed to the acquisition of knowledge. In contrast the *grihastha* (householder) lives a life of intimacy and investment in family life. As family obligations cease the individual is expected to move toward an ascetic path leading to gradual renunciation *vanaprastha* (ascetic) and finally, *sanyas* (renunciation; Chaudhary & Bhargava, 2006). The study of childhood in India provides us with a glimpse of socialization processes embedded in the ideology of detachment and renunciation.

Reflections in Child Rearing

For the Hindu worldview to be of ontogenetic significance it must play some part in child rearing. This has evoked considerable interest within anthropology and psychoanalysis (Carstairs, 1957; Kakar, 1981; Kurtz, 1992; Roland, 2005; Sharma, 2003; Trawick, 1992). However, the general paucity of research, the range of subcultural variations within India, and the diversity in theoretical frameworks from which the questions have been addressed have resulted in few definitive answers. The limited research within the paradigm of attachment in India is partially compensated for by some research on mother–infant interaction.

A review of the recent research on mother–infant interaction is available in Sharma (2003). Taken together, these studies yield some answers and raise several questions. There is general agreement about the prevalence of multiple mothering. However, the role of the biological mother is debated. Carstairs (1957) and Kakar (1981) believe that children are indulged during the first 5 years particularly sons. Babies are kept physically close to mothers, sleep regularly with them, and are fed promptly and for long periods of time. On the basis of a study of myths, popular cinema, clinical cases, and psychohistorical analysis, Kakar (1981) believes that there is an intense attachment between the mother and in particular the male child. Adult Indians too retain a "nostalgic wish for a benevolent presence" (Kakar, 1981, p. 85) and the death of an aged parent may be mourned without any self-consciousness. On the other hand, Roland (2005) argues that multiple mothering creates a "we-self," a highly relational and interdependent core of intense well-being within the self. At the same time, Roland also posits an autonomous spiritual self in Hindus that balances the narcissistic we-self and prevents it from becoming pathological.

Kakar (1981) and Kurtz (1992) share some assumptions about psychological development in India (Nagpal, 2000). Both emphasize the theme of liberation from the cycle of life in the psychic constellations of Hindus and the belief that maturity implies the renunciation of emotional ties. They also emphasize the initial significance of the mother–infant dyad, the presence of multiple caretakers, and the ultimate movement of the child toward a larger group. Kurtz's disagreement with Kakar and Roland (2005) stems from the interpretation of physical closeness between mother and child. According to Kurtz, Hindu child rearing aims at moving the child away from an exclusive attachment to the mother toward identification with the larger family and community. The mother prevents mirroring even when she is physically close to the infant. The purpose of offering her breast promptly is to "placate the child and free the mother for work" (p. 44). Care is arranged so that the child "voluntarily renounces infantile ties to the mother" (p. 61). The mother seems to want to teach the child that "his life will not come to an end" without her (p. 75). Kurtz believes that research on the self in India has been hampered by the inability of psychologists "to take seriously the Hindu idea that individuality is an illusion" (p. 6). The gentle push away from the mother to other mothers generates the Hindu emphasis on detachment as well as the discovery of ultimate unity.

Unfortunately Kurtz (1992) remains silent on the question of gender. On the basis of his writing it would seem that the daughter is pushed further than the son, given the ultimate renunciation that she will be required to make. Kakar (1981) argues instead that the initial difficulties are greater for the son whose mother first depends upon him for gratification and later severs the bond somewhat abruptly around the age of 8. This creates a split within the male construction of femininity. The experience of daughters is by comparison smooth. They are provided with basic care by their mothers and gradually acquire the caretaking function of younger siblings upon themselves, thus identifying with the mother. From cultural patterns it seems that the split within daughters is manifested in their idealization of mothers, and fear and hatred toward mothers-in-law.

Although mothers spend time in close proximity to infants, they are expected to minimize the display of affection toward the infant and rarely demonstrate signs of intense emotional involvement. The foregrounding of biological relationships is discouraged, as this would spell danger for the joint family. The concept of the *evil eye* is a pervasive belief that gazing at the child or expressing warmth can cause harm. Seymour (1999) describes the pattern in India as "mother's reluctant and interrupted physical response and minimal overt emotional involvement" (p. 76). Minturn and Hitchcock (1966) describe the baby as "the passive observer of the busy courtyard life. He is never alone, never the centre of attention" (p. 112). Child-rearing practices seem to work toward toning down *ahamkara* (individual pride) and accepting fate and destiny (Saraswathi, 2005).

THE SOCIAL CONSTRUCTION OF WOMANHOOD IN INDIA

A brief verse from an ancient text written around 1000 B.C. distinguishes between the position of the son and the daughter among Hindus:

> The pleasure
> A father has in his own son exceeds
> All other pleasures …, a daughter
> An object of compassion, but a son
> Is like the light sent from the highest heaven.

This verse from the Rigveda (as quoted in Gerber, 1991, p. 3) highlights the different emotional qualities that are associated with sons and daughters. The contrast between the son as pleasure and the daughter as compassion associates daughters with images of nurturance and suffering, and sons with pleasure and dignity. Wadley (1988) points out that femaleness in Hinduism has a dual character. The roles of mother and wife are significant here with the wife associated with goodness, and the mother with fertility but also with a certain power. This dual character in defining femaleness is manifested in the role prescriptions and lives of women in India.

The first of these expectations *"pativratadharma* may be … translated as those morally significant actions, duties, and attitudes that are appropriate to the status of a married woman, the central focus of which is the welfare of her husband" (Courtwright, 1995, p. 186). The goal of *pativratadharma* is to transfer the wife's *shakti* (energy) to preserve the husband. To fulfill this ideal, the woman must be given away in marriage by the father through *kanyadaan*, a set of rituals through which the daughter is transformed from *apni* (one's own) to *parayi* (belonging to another). The ideology of *kanyadaan* sets limits on a parent's entitlement over a married daughter and her claim over her parental home except to visit them on ritual occasions.

Societal prescriptions define a woman first as a daughter, then a wife and daughter-in-law, and finally as a mother (Kakar, 1981). Of these it is the role of mother, particularly of a son, that confers status upon her. Sons have ritual significance for performing the last rites of the father, maintaining the family lineage, and providing support in old age, and their birth is celebrated. Because her sexuality is a potential source of shame to the family and her marriage an expense, it is not unusual to mourn the birth of a daughter. Firstborn daughters, or a daughter whose birth is followed by the birth of a son, may be considered auspicious but daughters lower in the birth order experience considerable rejection.

Despite the elevation of status that comes with the birth of a son, mothers experience an unconscious understanding of shared fate with their daughters. The resultant warmth predisposes the daughter toward accepting the cultural norms of femininity (Kakar, 1981). At the same time the daughter may feel some unconscious ambivalence toward her mother for her preference for sons or her mother's inability to value the daughter sufficiently. Sons are usually given preference over material resources, including food and are allowed greater freedom of movement.

Girls grow up with the knowledge communicated both implicitly and explicitly that they are temporary members of the natal family. By puberty, references to marriage become more explicit and access to the outer world is restricted. Within the home, relationships with men, including the father, change, and there are frequent references to covering the body, and the possibility of danger and shame. The process of training the daughter to become a good wife and daughter-in-law is enhanced (Dube, 2001; Saraswathi & Dutta, 1990). Kakar (1981) believes that mothers and daughters become closer as the mother is aware of the impending departure of the daughter and the uncertainty of her future. However, the mother is also acutely conscious of the contingency of her reputation on the good behavior of the daughter now and after marriage, and deviations from appropriate behavior can be treated with harsh punishment.

Arranged marriages are the norm in India. Kakar's (1981) account of the transition from *beti* (daughter) to *bahu* (daughter-in-law) emphasizes the difficulties in renouncing ties with the mother and establishing an often dissatisfying encounter with sexuality. In stark contrast to her husband who is surrounded by his natal kin, the wife is among strangers. The bond between the husband and his mother also creates rivalry between the mother-in-law and the daughter-in-law. Drawing from object relations theory it is possible to argue that when daughters idealize mothers they also split off negative experiences of the mother and project them onto their mothers-in-law. The prevalence of stereotypes of the good mother and the bad mother-in-law may facilitate this process. In this context the birth of a son becomes the primary source of gratification for the woman. A vicious cycle of a fused mother–son relationship with ensuing difficulties in forming a sexual intimate bond between husband and wife is thus created.

The belief in the revered status of the Indian mother is so pervasive that little attention is paid to the fact that most cultural representations of mothers refer to mothers of sons (Johri, 1999). A cursory analysis of Indian myths indicates the relative absence of mothers of daughters (Beck, 1986). In folk songs, where mother–daughter themes appear prominently, the most frequently occurring themes are of the birth and marriage of daughters. The intertwining of the experience of the birth of the daughter with her departure is exemplified next:

> Ten months and ten days
> The mother dreams on ever,
> I'll have a son, I'll see him grow
> Now she's a daughter's mother. …
> It was the mother's dearest wish
> To keep the daughter near her …
> But a daughter stays as long as a dream,
> So grieves the daughter's mother. …

The song (as quoted in Tharu & Lalita, 1993, p. 134) portrays an empathic identification contextualized by the sorrow of imminent loss. This results in an apparently contradictory picture where mothers express a desire for sons and a love for daughters (Johri, 1999; Minturn & Lambert, 1964; Rohner & Chaki-Sircar, 1987). Lamb (2000) notes the "precious but ephemeral" quality of the mother–daughter bond as she quotes a mother from Bengal, "You just keep them with you for a few days and then give them away to another's house" (p. 53). The daughter's separation from the mother is depicted as cutting a vine, and the daughter's marriage depicted like the death of the mother (Trawick, 1992). The theme of the daughter's departure gains significance within the context of joint families where sons stay on and bring a wife as a daughter-in-law into the family (Chanana, 2003; Uberoi, 2003).

There have been many changes in levels of education, age at marriage, and employment of Indian women in the past few decades. Family structure has also changed with fewer joint families than ever before (Sharma, 2003). Despite these, the preference for sons remains one of the significant cultural ideals within which motherhood is experienced. The contradictory nature of this change is evident. A leading newspaper of Delhi has reported a drop in the sex ratio in one of the elite suburbs of Delhi ("Sex Ratio," 2008). Thus, while some couples are content to have only a daughter, evidence indicates that the acceptance of the small family is associated with greater use of sex-selective abortions to ensure creating a family with two sons (Mallik, 2003).

This preference for gender is evident despite the Prenatal Diagnostic Techniques (Regulation and Prevention of Misuse) Act passed in 1994 (Mallik, 2003). Census data of 2001 reveals a sex ratio of 933 women to 1,000 men in the age range of 0 to 5 in India (Office of the Registrar General & Census Commissioner, India, 2001). Another form of discrimination against women lies in the culture's expectation that a woman makes an unquestioning adaptation into her husband's home, adopts her parents-in-law as her parents, and relinquishes the emotional ties with her natal home. From the perspective of mothers, each of these requires relinquishing the relationship with the daughter in marked contrast to seeking after and maintaining the relationship with sons.

MOTHER LOVE FOR DAUGHTERS: NARRATIVES FROM HINDU WOMEN

The following narratives are from a previous study on mother love for daughters in a society marked by son preference (Johri, 1999). The narratives of 20 upper-middle-class women in Delhi who only had daughters (three or more) and no sons are presented. The participants who were selected for the study were middle-aged women who had experienced two crucial moments in the lives of mothers and daughters: the birth and marriage of daughters. The narratives were obtained through semi-structured interviews conducted in the homes of the women and analyzed using the method of critical discourse analysis as discussed in Hollway (1989). The focus of the analysis was to locate the available discourses within which narratives of mother love were located. The three dominant discursive themes, as described in the following sections, within which the individual narratives were constructed were: the daughter as a guest, the dispensability of daughters, and the resistance to cultural patterns. The narratives highlight an excessive preoccupation with performing one's duties, the positioning of the daughter as "belonging to another," and the cultural ideal of impermanence and how it contributes to the possibility of detached love for the daughter that may be inimical to her well-being.

The Daughter as a Guest

Vibha (all names are pseudonyms), responding to the question about the difference between having sons and daughters, gave the following explanation:

> When a son is born we build up a web of expectations. He'll grow up, support us in our old age …. And if he turns out to be different, it is very traumatic for the parents. When a daughter is born, there is no such anxiety. She belongs to another home. I have to separate from her someday. I believe you should give her as much love as you can because ultimately she is not going to stay on with us. Then there is no expectation from her that she should earn for us. There is no give and take which is the greatest source of enmity between people. We love her, give her everything possible, educate her and generate all sorts of capabilities in her. There are no expectations from her …. We won't blame her. This is why I believe that there is no need to be upset if you have a daughter, although I too was a bit. (Johri, 1999, p. 186)

It is apparent from her explanation that love for the daughter is constructed within the frame of temporary membership. The mother is aware of the cultural significance of marriage for daughters. She is also anxious that this experience may be oppressive and that as a mother, she will no longer be in a position to nurture her daughter. As Gayatri, another mother of three daughters, put it, "once she goes there it's her luck, it is scary when you have to give away something which is your own" (Johri, 1999, p. 191). Although mothers miss their daughters they are driven by an understanding that they no longer have a "claim" on her. The desire to be with her daughter is thought to be selfish, a fantasy that a mother can never actualize. Gayatri refers to tradition and says, "Well, even kings haven't kept their daughters, not amongst Hindus" (Johri, 1999, p. 191).

Apart from separation and loss, two significant issues here pertain to the centrality of fate and the need for detachment. However, mothers also suggest that this relationship creates the possibility of detachment. This was articulated by Vibha, "I have become quite spiritual now. Ultimately everything has to be left behind" (Johri, 1999, p. 208).

The Dispensable Daughter

A more pernicious theme in the mothers' narratives was of the dispensability of the daughter. The participants were aware of the social construction of mothers without sons as barren women. Almost all acknowledged that they had planned their last pregnancy hoping to have a son. The desire for the son was sometimes personal, but at other times in response to the significant others in their lives. The participants acknowledged the use of methods ranging from indigenous medicines to wearing a lucky charm to facilitate the birth of a son. Medical techniques of prenatal sex determination were available but not prevalent during their reproductive years. Although all the participants were aware of prenatal sex determination, only a few made tacit references to prenatal testing by expressing regret that they had not "planned better." Of the 20 mothers in the study, one used a prenatal ultrasound, and after discovering that it was a daughter gave her away for adoption. Two of the 20 women did attempt to have the tests conducted but failed for various reasons. The subsequent ban on sex-selective abortion has made research on the psychological implications of this practice difficult. The scant research that exists indicates that sex-selective abortion after giving birth to several daughters is condoned by the family (Visaria, Ramachandran, Ganatra, & Kalyanwala, 2004).

Archna recounted the rejection she felt by her mother-in-law as follows:

> She behaved as if I had committed a crime. When the nurses asked for a reward she commented, "you are asking for a gift. We are bereft. She may as well have not survived." I felt very bad. Today, if I had a son everyone would have gathered around me, celebrations would have taken place, and they have not even brought me food. (Johri, 1999, p. 182)

With the birth of the third daughter, the mother-in-law stopped eating for 3 days. Many years later the larger community continues to refer to her as the "poor woman who had three daughters, none of whom died" (Johri, 1999, p. 182).

Subtle messages that they had failed in their duties were common. The participants recounted that their own mothers worried that the daughter's marriage would suffer. Shobha remembered being reprimanded by her mother as she was not praying for a son. According to Shobha, "She used to say, 'Ask God. You've a very big ego. You don't even ask God'" (Johri, 1999, p. 199). The internalization of the cultural construction is evident in the greater frequency of postnatal depression amongst Indian women who have had a second daughter (Patel, Rodrigues, & DeSouza, 2002). Yet, mothers report that the feeling of depression converts to compassion for the daughter. Reena spoke of the birth of her second daughter, stating:

> When the second one was born, I felt bad. People were coming (to see me) no congratulations nothing. Just shows how bad they must have been feeling for me. Another daughter, no son! ... my sister in- law (even now I laugh), she said, "I thought if I congratulate you, you may feel bad, it's a second daughter, ..." Suddenly it was a very funny feeling. I was also disappointed. I suddenly just fell in love with the child so totally. My God! This poor child in the world, so unwelcome! So my whole feeling towards her changed. (Johri, 1999, p. 186)

A somewhat similar account comes from Seema, another mother of four daughters:

> When the first one was born, I was happy. I was a little disappointed with the second one but once the child is in your lap you feel happy. When the third one was born, I cried a lot. God has given me three daughters. But as she grew older the feeling went away. (Johri, 1999, p. 144)

One mother had tried to get the sex of her child determined to decide if she would continue with the pregnancy. The test could not be completed and the couple decided to go ahead with the pregnancy. When a daughter was born there was a tremendous guilt worsened by the willingness of relatives to adopt her.

The widespread process of rejection of daughters is likely to play a significant role in the nature of the mother–daughter attachment. The mothers in the study did report crying, anxiety that their husbands would leave them, and a sense of inadequacy. Yet they also described a moment of transformation from sadness to empathy that happens soon after birth, sometimes referring to the moment of seeing the baby or holding her in her lap. Unfortunately, there is no research available to unravel whether the transformation is successful in providing the daughter with a positive sense of self. Popular songs and myths suggest the prevalence of trust, longing, and ambivalence toward the mother who gave birth to her. The trust and longing are reflected in the prevalence of the term *maika*, the mother's home to which the daughter longs to return. Visits to the mother's home are occasions for celebration for many women. There is also a great desire to nurture the mother when she is ill, and one of the regrets of being a woman is that the space is controlled by the husband and sometimes the brother and his wife.

The consequences for daughters when the mother remains distressed are apparent in Bharati's narrative. The only participant who described her life as a mother of four daughters as useless, she complained both of the treatment meted out to her by her husband and mother-in-law and the lack of empathy she experienced in her daughters' attitude toward her. Bharati's narrative was marked by the death of her brother when she was still a child. Throughout her childhood her utmost desire was to take care of her mother. She was clear that the four pregnancies were motivated by the desire for a son that stemmed as much from a wish to provide her husband with an heir as to fulfill her mother's desire for the lost son. In terms of attachment processes, Bharati seemed preoccupied with her own childhood, perhaps idealizing her identification with her mother's sorrow. This, accompanied by the rejection she experienced from her husband and mother-in-law, seems to have impacted the mother–daughter relationship and the daughters' inability to empathize.

Bharati's narrative was not typical of most mothers who reported feelings of mutual care between mothers and daughters. Although the research did not include an assessment of attachment patterns in the daughters, mothers' narratives suggest that the cultural push is not towards the creation of autonomy in daughters. Rather, the knowledge of enforced separation results in a mutually felt yearning to maintain their connection. It is not clear whether this yearning indicated an early secure bond that resulted in accepting cultural expectations, or if it was a response to the ambivalence seen in mothers' narratives as they spoke of their initial disappointment followed by reparation toward their baby daughters.

Resistance to Cultural Processes

Although the themes discussed thus far remain significant in the lives of women in India, the society is also showing rapid change. With more nuclear families and increased urbanization, the position of daughters has changed dramatically in urban, educated Indian families. These examples are statistically rare but education, modernity, and the economic independence of women have somewhat enhanced the space to welcome a daughter back into the natal family. At the same time this parental support is usually available when daughters are under severe stress. In ordinary circumstances, daughters are expected to make adjustments and rarely share their difficulties with their mothers. One mother whose daughter faced a very oppressive marriage spoke of why she brought her back home. In evoking the bodily relationship with her daughter, the mother seemed to be questioning the morality of detachment and privileging her attachment to her daughter.

> If she is in any kind of danger, she must be brought back home by her parents. She is also a part of the body. Can we cut a finger and throw it away? ... It's a child of flesh and blood, not a piece of rubbish. (Johri, 1999, p. 140)

ATTACHMENT, DETACHMENT, FATE, AND MOTHER–DAUGHTER RELATIONSHIPS

Hindu mothers desire sons, but desire is the cause of all suffering in Hinduism (Sinha, 1986). Daughters are loved but lost. The traditional relationship with the daughter connotes suffering and loss, creating within the mother–daughter relationship a paradigm for experiencing *maya*—the illusory nature of relationships. Given the Hindu worldview that the source of suffering lies in attachments (Lamb, 2000; Sinha, 1986), mothers attempt to negotiate distance from their daughters by reference to the impermanence of all relationships. However, cultural ideals do not translate easily into personal qualities, and many mothers who have only daughters metaphorically equate the time when all their daughters will be married with death. Daughters too pine for their mothers and if given the choice, relate to them as frequently as possible. Evidence from the mothers' narratives suggests that daughters internalize the message that they are guests in the home. They frequently hide unhappiness from their mothers in a bid to protect them from pain and social ostracism. At the same time women in India do "choose" sex-selective abortion to create a family with a son (Johri, 2001).

Taken together with child-rearing patterns in India, these raise several issues pertaining to the four core hypotheses of attachment theory. First, how does multiple mothering impact attachment? Holmes (2001) suggests that the community may become the secure base for people living in an interdependent culture. Rothbaum and Morelli (2005) believe the outcomes of secure attachment will differ according to cultural conceptions of competence. In a collectivist culture security is likely to be manifested in accommodation and maintenance of harmony. With regard to adult mother–daughter attachment it seems that the fact that daughters are sent away does not create resentment toward the mother. Rather secure attachment and a sense of a shared fate enables daughters to follow paths suggested by parents. This security accompanied by the celebration and idealization of marriage may in turn enable the formation of new relationships despite the absence of a romantic relationship.

Many daughters do experience their maternal home (*maika*) as the secure base in the early years of marriage although it shifts to the husband and his kin network. Rothbaum et al. (2000) argue that romance and marriage are experienced differently across cultures and may not serve the same attachment functions as in the West. In India the daughter's marriage combines celebration with grief. Some of the themes recounted by the participants in our study bear resemblance to the three stages of grief (i.e., protest, despair, and detachment) that take the form of yearning, despair, and recovery in adulthood. Daughters create new bonds over time and attempt to negotiate spaces within the patriarchal system to retain the ties with the *maika*. When these attempts fail they abandon hopes of accessing the maternal home. Although mothers and daughters have prepared themselves for this loss from the moment of the daughter's birth, mothers experience a greater sense of loss. The ideology of the impermanence of relationships provides the framework within which the loss is lived.

The need for detachment between adult daughters and mothers has decreased in recent years and many young educated daughters maintain a trusting and communicative relationship with their mothers (Rastogi & Wampler, 1999). However, the practice of sex-selective abortion has grown. The mental health implications of repeated abortions of potential daughters have not been studied. However, while this is certainly not the intended ideal of detachment, it may provide defensive justification for aborting female fetuses. Indeed before the advent of technologies of sex determination, women could detach themselves from the culture's accusation of barrenness by making reference to destiny. The belief that much in life is preordained played a protective role for mothers, enabling them to carry on with pregnancies and resisting interventions to abort daughters. By contrast, with the recent availability of tests for sex determination of fetuses, it is no longer possible for mothers to speak of fate. Earlier explanations do not work in a culture where contemporary technologies of sex determination work in favor of patriarchy (Johri, 2001).

Sons are expected to maintain ties with the mother and continue to live in their natal home after marriage. Recent changes in age of marriage and levels of education of the daughter-in-law (Sharma, 2003), and greater acceptance of sexual intimacy (John, 1998) have complicated the erstwhile patterns of power relations where the mother-in-law had total control over her daughter-in-law's life and intimacy was denied (Kakar, 1989). Social change notwithstanding, a period of detachment from the narcissistic involvement with sons is required once they get married (Lamb, 2000). Yet this struggle differs from the sudden rupture that continues to characterize mother–daughter relations in many parts of India.

The issues raised in the chapter point to the many unanswered questions on the place of attachment theory across cultures. One question concerns the interpretation of avoidant attachment in a culture characterized by multiple mothering. Avoidant attachment has been associated with the idealization of attachment figures (Rholes, Simpson, & Friedman, 2006) a characteristic of most interdependent cultures (Schmitt et al., 2004). However, it is difficult to visualize the possibility of interdependence in a culture with a predominance of avoidance. Another significant concern comes from the centrality of two concepts—separation and autonomy—in the context of interdependent cultures. Similarly, although there may be some overlap between the concept of detachment in Hindu thought and attachment theory, neither the extent of this overlap nor the significance of the differences between the two frameworks has been adequately addressed. A more complex issue is whether patterns that manifest as avoidant attachments have different intrapsychic significance in a culture with an ideology of detachment. Finally, the study of mothers of daughters points to the need for an analysis of the relationship between culture, gender, and attachment theory. In India, given the preference for sons, are daughters likely to be more insecurely attached? Further, might insecure attachments in mothers have different consequences for sons and daughters? In this respect attachment theory may benefit from the reflections in feminist object relations theory in conceptualizing the child as necessarily gendered (Chodorow, 1978).

The analysis of the narratives of mothers of daughters indicates the enmeshed nature of the metaphysical with the psychological. There seems to be an urgent requirement for psychological research in differing contexts to locate local ethnotheories of attachment and study new questions within emic frameworks (Rothbaum & Morelli, 2005).

REFERENCES

Beck, B. E. F. (1986). Social dyads in Indian folktales. In S. H. Blackburn & A. K. Ramanujam (Eds.), *Another harmony: New essays on folklore of India* (pp. 76–102). Berkeley: University of California Press.

Bowlby, J. (1988). *A secure base: Parent-child attachment and healthy human development.* New York: Basic Books.

Carlson, V. J., & Harwood, R. I. (2003). Attachment, culture and the caregiving system: The cultural patterning of everyday experiences among Anglo and Puerto Rican mother-infant pairs. *Infant Mental Health Journal, 24*(1), 53–73.

Carstairs, G. M. (1957). *The twice-born.* London: Hogarth Press.

Chakkarath, P. (2005). What can Western psychology learn from indigenous psychology? In W. Friedlmeier, P. Chakkarath, & B. Schwarz (Eds.), *Culture and human development: The importance of cross-cultural research to the social sciences* (pp. 31–52). New York: Psychology Press.

Chanana, K. (2003). Female sexuality and education of Hindu girls in India. In S. Rege (Ed.), *Sociology of gender: The challenge of feminist sociological knowledge* (pp. 287–317). New Delhi, IN: Sage.

Chaudhary, N., & Bhargava, P. (2006). Mamta: The transformation of meaning in everyday usage. *Contributions to Indian Sociology, 40*(3), 343–373.

Chodorow, N. J. (1978). *The reproduction of mothering: Psychoanalysis and the sociology of gender.* Berkeley: University of California Press.

Courtwright, P. B. (1995). Sati, sacrifice and marriage: The modernity of tradition. In L. Harlan & P. B. Courtwright (Eds.), *From the margins of Hindu marriage: Essays on gender, religion and culture* (pp. 184–203). Oxford: Oxford University Press.

Dube, L. (2001). On the construction of gender: Socialization of Hindu girls in patrilineal India. In L. Dube (Ed.), *Anthropological explorations in gender: Intersecting field* (pp. 87–116). New Delhi, IN: Sage.

Gerber, W. (1991). *The mind of India.* Delhi, IN: Rupa & Co.

Hollway, W. (1989). *Subjectivity and method in psychology: Gender, meaning and science.* London: Sage.

Holmes, J. (2001). *The search for the secure base: Attachment theory and psychotherapy.* New York: Psychology Press.

John, M. (1998). Globalization, sexuality and the visual field: Issues and non-issues for cultural critique. In M. John & J. Nair (Eds.), *A question of silence? The sexual economies of modern India* (pp. 368–395). New Delhi, IN: Kali for Women.

Johri, R. (1999). *Cultural conceptions of maternal attachment: The case of the girl child* (Unpublished doctoral dissertation). University of Delhi, India.

Johri, R. (2001). The "freedom" of choices: A discursive analysis of mothers' narratives. *Psychological Studies, 46*(3), 192–201.

Kağitçibaşi, C. (2007). *Family, self, and human development across cultures.* New York: Psychology Press.

Kakar, S. (1981). *The inner world: A psycho-analytic study of childhood and society in India.* Delhi, IN: Oxford University Press.

Kakar, S. (1989). *Intimate relations: Exploring Indian sexuality.* Delhi, IN: Viking Press.

Keller, H. (2008). Culture and biology: The foundation of pathways of development. *Social and Personality Compass, 2*(2), 668–681.

Kurtz, S. N. (1992). *All the mothers are one: Hindu India and the cultural reshaping of psychoanalysis.* New York: Columbia University Press.

Lamb, S. (2000). *White saris and sweet mangoes: Aging, gender, and body in North India.* Berkeley: University of California Press.

Levine, R. A. (2002). *Attachment research as an ideological movement: Preliminary statement.* Revised from a presentation at the ISSBD, 2002, Ottawa. Retrieved February 18, 2009, from http://www.bec.ucla.edu/papers/levine.pdf

Mallik, R. (2003). Negative choice. *Seminar, 532.* Retrieved February 18, 2009, from http://www.india-seminar.com/2003/532.htm

Minturn, L., & Hitchcock, J. (1966). *The Rajputs of Khalapur.* New York: Wiley.

Minturn, L., & Lambert, W. W. (1964). *Mothers of six cultures: Antecedents of child rearing.* New York: John Wiley.

Nagpal, A. (2000). Cultural continuity and change in Kakar's works: Some reflections. *International Journal of Group Tensions, 29,* 285–322.

Office of the Registrar General & Census Commissioner, India. (2001). Census of India. Retrieved from www.censusindia.gov.in

Patel, V., Rodrigues, M., & DeSouza, N. (2002). Gender, poverty and post-natal depression: A study of mothers in Goa, India. *American Journal of Psychiatry, 159,* 43–47.

Rastogi, M., & Wampler, K. S. (1999). Adult daughters' perceptions of the mother-daughter relationship: A cross-cultural comparison. *Family Relations, 48,* 327–336.

Rholes, W. S., Simpson, J. A., & Friedman, M. (2006). Avoidant attachment and the experience of parenting. *Personality and Social Psychology Bulletin, 32*(3), 275–285.

Rohner, R. P., & Chaki-Sircar, M. (1987). *Women and children in a Bengali village.* Hanover, MD: University Press of New England.

Roland, A. (2005). Multiple mothering and the familial self. In S. Akhtar (Ed.), *Freud along the Ganges: Psychoanalytic reflections on the people and culture of India* (pp. 79–90). New York: Other Press.

Rothbaum, F., & Morelli, G. (2005). Attachment and culture: Bridging relativism and universalism. In W. Friedlmeier, P. Chakkarath, & B. Schwarz (Eds.), *Culture and human development: The importance of cross-cultural research to the social sciences* (pp. 92–113). New York: Psychology Press.

Rothbaum, F., Weisz, J., Pott, M., Miyake, K., & Morelli, G. (2000). Attachment and culture: Security in the United States and Japan. *American Psychologist, 55,* 1093-1104.

Saraswathi, T. S. (2005). Hindu worldview in the development of self ways: The "atman" as the real self. *New Directions for Child and Adolescent Development, 109,* 43–50.

Saraswathi, T. S., & Dutta, R. (1990). Poverty and human development: Socialization of girls among the urban and rural poor. In G. Misra (Ed.), *Applied social psychology in India* (pp. 141–169). New Delhi, IN: India.

Saraswathi, T. S., & Ganapathy, H. (2002). Indian parents' ethnotheories as reflections of the Hindu scheme of child and human development. In H. Keller, Y. H. Poortinga, & A. Scholmerich (Eds.), *Between culture and biology: Perspectives on ontogenetic development* (pp. 79–88). New York: Cambridge University Press.

Schmitt, D. P., Alcalay, L., Allensworth, M., Allik, J., Ault, L., Austers, I., ... Zupanèiè, A. (2004). Patterns and universals of adult romantic attachment across 62 cultural regions: Are models of self and of other pancultural constructs? *Journal of Cross-Cultural Psychology, 35,* 367–402.

Seymour, S. C. (1999). *Women, family and childcare in India: A world in transition.* New York: Cambridge University Press.

Sharma, D. (2003). *Childhood, family, and sociocultural change in India: Reinterpreting the Inner World.* New Delhi, IN: Oxford University Press.

Sinha, J. (1986). *Indian psychology.* Delhi: Motilal Banarasidas.

Tharu, S., & Lalita, K. (1993). *Women writing in India* (Vol. I). Delhi, IN: Oxford University Press.

Thompson, R. A. (2002). Early attachment and later development. In J. Cassidy & P. R. Shaver (Eds.), *Handbook of attachment: Theory, research, and clinical applications* (pp. 265–286). New York: Guilford Press.

Sex ratio dismal in swanky Gurgaon. (2008, November 28). *Times of India*, p. 369.

Trawick, M. (1992). *Notes on love in a Tamil family*. Berkeley: University of California Press.

Uberoi, P. (2003). Problems with patriarchy: Conceptual issues in anthropology and feminism. In S. Rege (Ed.), *Sociology of gender: The challenge of feminist sociological knowledge* (pp. 88–126). New Delhi, IN: Sage.

van IJzendoorn, M. H., & Sagi, A. (2002). Cross-cultural patterns of attachment: Universal and contextual dimensions. In J. Cassidy & P. R. Shaver (Eds.), *Handbook of attachment: Theory, research, and clinical applications* (pp. 713–734). New York: Guilford Press.

Visaria, L., Ramachandran, V., Ganatra, B., & Kalyanwala, S. (2004). Abortion in India. Emerging issues from qualitative studies. *Economic and Political Weekly*, 5044–5052.

Wadley, S. (1988). Women in the Hindu tradition. In R. Ghadially (Ed.), *Women in Indian society* (pp. 23–43). New Delhi, IN: Sage.

16

Adult Attachment Patterns and Their Consequences in Romantic Relationships
A Comparison Between China and the United States

LIN SHI

CONTENTS

*O*ne cannot help but wonder if Ainsworth, when she set out to empirically test attachment theory in Uganda, was inspired by anticipating the unveiling of the universality of attachment relationships coupled with a consideration of cultural contexts. Her pioneering spirit was not appreciated and followed up on by the next generation of researchers. Thus, attachment research has been conveniently conceptualized and conducted in the West and has mainly remained a Western phenomenon until recently. Today, however, the field is mature and confident enough to look beyond the Western culture and is ready to once again test the validity of attachment theory in much greater and more complex territories. Proof of such organized efforts are the Strange Situation Procedure being applied to young children from the West to the East, as well as from rural to urban areas (Carlson & Harwood, 2003; Tomlinson, 2001), and an increase in cross-cultural adult attachment studies (i.e., Ng, Trutsy, & Crawford, 2005; Schmitt et al., 2004; Wang & Mallinckrodt, 2006; You & Malley-Morrison, 2000).

Along with cross-cultural validation of attachment relationships there is also evidence of cultural variation. For example, in northern Germany the avoidant pattern was overrepresented (Grossmann, Grossmann, Spangler, Suess, & Unzner, 1985) among young children, whereas in Japan the preoccupied pattern was observed in greater frequency (Cassidy & Berlin, 1994). These variations undoubtedly are influenced by the cultural contexts in which children interact with attachment figures. In northern Germany the cultural norm is to make a child obedient by discipline (Grossmann et al., 1985). In Japan encouraging *amae*, a relationship that involves both bond and dependence (Doi, 1992; Yamaguchi, 2004), is the cultural norm. Any great research question is bound to attract and intrigue various, even polarized, perspectives, as is the interpretation of these data.

Most attachment researchers today do not deny the role of culture but recognize that culture may influence specific behaviors (Cassidy & Shaver, 1999; Rothbaum & Morelli, 2005; van IJzendoorn, Bakermans-Kranenburg, & Sagi-Schwartz, 2006; Yamaguchi, 2004). However, they stress that the core of attachment is independent of cultural influence and that the available research supports cross-cultural validity of attachment theory (van IJzendoorn & Sagi, 1999). Yet, some researchers question the universality of the core of attachment theory and argue that it is first and foremost imbedded in Western values and practices (e.g., Rothbaum, Weisz, Pott, Miyake, & Morelli, 2000). Secure attachment and its consequences may be defined and observed differently in another cultural context. In other words, so-called secure attachment is the product of biology and Western culture working together. Parental sensitivity in Japan is defined and practiced differently in the United States. If, for example, U.S. parents adopted Japanese sensitivity, insecurely attached children judged by the Strange Situation Procedure might be the outcome (Rothbaum et al., 2000).

Either commonalities of secure attachment are the themes across cultures, or secure attachment calls for its definition in specific cultures. The ongoing debate makes it more intriguing to explore adult attachment in different cultural contexts. Adult attachment is more complex to study because of the complexity of the social environment to which a growing individual is increasingly exposed. Bowlby (1980) was confident about the long-lasting influence of the initial attachment relationship on later life. Bowlby argued that the internal working model, once formed, tends to be stable, and that there are three possible reasons for this stability. First, an internal working model develops and operates in the context of the relatively stable family environment. Second, it becomes habitual and automatic over time and functions unconsciously. Finally and most important, since the internal working model is applied to interpersonal relationships, it tends to be self-fulfilling and creates consequences that reinforce the current relationship model. The internal working model, therefore, has a strong potential for affecting the individual across the life cycle, especially the way in which close relationships are maintained. Bowlby (1977) concluded that "attachment behavior is held to characterize human beings from the cradle to the grave" (p. 201), and that attachment behaviors continue to be "manifested throughout life, especially when distressed, ill, or afraid" (p. 201). Bowlby did not, however, theorize if and how the proportion of attachment factors change as an individual is increasingly exposed to more varied cultural influences from different aspects during the developing process.

As the most influential theory in relatedness, attachment theory must provide a means to address the intricate relationship between cultural expectation and attachment consequences. "Cross-cultural research on key issues in attachment theory is one of the most exciting prospects for the next generation of attachment research" (Waters & Cummings, 2000, p. 169). While the exploration and debate of universality and cross-cultural patterns continue for child attachment, a more accurate and extensive understanding of cross-cultural patterns of adult attachment also calls for further research. Two key issues in adult attachment await further exploration and confirmation. One is whether adults raised in different cultures share commonalities in attachment pattern and its consequences. The other one is whether observed variations in behavior are due to attachment or to cultural expectations.

Although adult attachment shares components of child attachment, it is different from infant attachment in several important ways (Weiss, 1982). First, the infant–parent attachment is a complementary relationship where the infant receives care and the parent provides it; whereas adult attachment is usually formed with peers and involves a two-way interaction between two equals (West & Sheldon-Keller, 1994). Second, the attachment behavioral system in infancy is not yet well integrated with other behavioral systems (West & Sheldon-Keller, 1994). In contrast, adults are able to survive and function to a certain extent even if the attachment relationship is under threat. Third, adult attachment relationships are usually formed by or develop into, but are not limited to, sexual relationships. These differences make it inappropriate to attempt to translate the consistent or inconsistent findings of cross-cultural child attachment directly into the adult domain. Nevertheless, the findings can and should serve as a starting point to explore a relatively new territory such as cross-cultural adult attachment research. Van IJzendoorn and Sagi (1999) proposed four findings that can be hypotheses for cross-cultural studies based on studies conducted in the West. The *universality hypothesis* is based on the conclusion that all infants without neurophysiological impairment become attached to a single or to multiple caregivers. Within the Western cultural contexts, 60% of infants are securely attached and 40% are insecurely attached, lending rationale for the *normativity hypothesis*. Furthermore, the confirmed link between sensitivity of parents and attachment security in children is referred to as the *sensitivity hypothesis*. Finally, the conclusion that attachment security leads to greater competence and affect regulation is referred to as the *competence hypothesis*. The four core hypotheses provided a guideline for the current study.

By surveying college students living and studying in Chinese and U.S. cultural contexts, the current study presented in this chapter examined the existence and distribution of attachment patterns (the universality and normativity hypothesis), the link between reported retrospective parental sensitivity and current adult attachment pattern (the sensitivity hypothesis), and if and how attachment patterns are related to conflict resolution behavior in romantic relationships (the competence hypothesis).

CONFLICT RESOLUTION: ONE AREA OF COMPETENCY IN ROMANTIC RELATIONSHIP

Internal working models are most likely to be activated in stressful situations such as conflictual interaction in romantic relationships, which accentuates the importance of maintaining a cooperative partnership and the need for psychological support from partners (Kobak & Duemmler, 1994). During conflict resolution, partners may bring their early childhood and current relationship models to the present and slip into certain attachment behavior patterns without their full awareness. Conflict resolution in romantic relationships has received ample attention mainly in the West due to its long-established strong relation to relationship satisfaction (Bodenmann, Kaiser, Hahlweg, & Fehm-Wolfsdorf, 1998; Heavey, Christensen, & Malamuth, 1995; Klinetob & Smith, 1996; Roberts, 2000). Effective problem solving has been repeatedly confirmed as an important contributor to and an indicator for relationship satisfaction at early, middle, and later stages of relationships (Belsky & Kelly, 1994; Carstensen, Gottman, & Levenson, 1995; Cohan & Bradbury, 1997; Gottman, Coan, Carrere, & Swanson, 1998; Roberts, 2000). Conflict resolution is an ultimate test for competency in romantic relationships in the Western cultural context.

There have been no studies identified that examined conflict resolution behavior and its link to attachment in the Chinese cultural context. Empirical evidence from studies conducted in the West indicates that attachment style is related to conflict resolution behaviors. Individuals classified as secure engage in higher levels of verbal engagement (Collins & Read, 1990), self-disclosure (Collins & Read, 1990; Mikulincer & Nachshon, 1991; Pistole, 1993), and mutual discussion and understanding (Feeney, Noller, & Callan, 1994). They rely more on integrating and compromising strategies (Corcoran & Mallinckrodt, 2000; Pistole, 1989), and are less likely to engage in withdrawal and verbal aggression (Creasey, Kershaw, & Boston, 1999; Senchak & Leonard, 1992). Those with an anxious/ambivalent attachment style have a strong tendency to exercise pressure on their partners, dominate conflict resolution processes (Corcoran & Mallinckrodt, 2000) and display greater hostility (Simpson, Rholes, & Phillips, 1996). Anxiety over abandonment is likely to lead to disengagement from conflict resolution, attempts to dominate the interaction, feelings of guilt and hurt after conflict, and lack of mutual discussion and understanding. It is also related to the use of blame, threats, physical and verbal aggression, patterns of demand–withdraw and pressure–resistant (Feeney et al., 1994). Partners with an avoidant attachment style tend to withdraw from conflict resolution and are less confident about regulating negative moods (Creasey et al., 1999). They are least likely to engage in compromising and integrating behaviors (Corcoran & Mallinckrodt, 2000), and are more likely to engage in inadequate support seeking under stress (Collins & Feeney, 2000).

The link between attachment and conflict resolution remains largely unclear in the Chinese context due to lack of research in this area. As stated earlier, the current study intended to examine cross-cultural adult attachment using the four core hypotheses (van IJzendoorn & Sagi, 1999) as a guideline. By comparing college students living and studying in the Chinese and the U.S. cultural contexts, the study addressed the following issues: (a) if and how attachment patterns and their distribution among Chinese college students were different from those of their U.S. counterparts, (b) whether perceptions of availability of parental (attachment) figures before entering adulthood are associated with later attachment patterns in adulthood and competencies in the area of conflict resolution in romantic relationships, and (c) whether attachment feelings and experiences in romantic relationship are associated with competencies in the form of conflict resolution.

In addition, earlier attachment studies found mixed results on gender differences (e.g., Bartholomew & Horowitz, 1991; Scharfe & Bartholomew, 1994; Shi, 2003). Therefore, the current study also examined gender differences in attachment patterns and conflict resolution behaviors.

METHOD

Participants

The sample of the study consisted of college students in the United States and mainland China who were or had been in a serious romantic relationship. The U.S. participants were recruited from a large university in the Southwest. The Chinese participants were recruited from two large universities in a southern province that has played a leading role in China's economic boom. Participants in both countries were recruited from different academic departments with broad varieties of majors. The author personally collected the responses by going to classes. An agreement was made between the author and instructors to give special assignments to students who were not willing to participate or who were not eligible for the study, to enable them to obtain equal extra credit. Virtually all eligible students contacted by the author agreed to participate. All questionnaires were presented to the Chinese participants in English considering that a much higher English proficiency among current college students is the norm rather than an exception. The sample for analysis consisted of 397 U.S. college students (185 males, 212 females) and 132 Chinese college students (57 male, 75 female). The mean age for both groups was 21.

Measures

Inventory of Parent–Peer Attachment (IPPA) Attachment experiences with parents before age 18 were measured by the Inventory of Parent–Peer Attachment (IPPA; Armsden & Greenberg, 1987). The current study included only the Mother and Father scales. Participants were asked to think about their relationships with their mothers and fathers (or parental figures if parents were not available) before they reached 18. Therefore, the 50 items in these scales were modified to the past tense. Participants rated each item on a 5-point Likert scale (1 = almost always or always true, 3 = sometimes true, 5 = almost never or never true). An overall score of positive relationship with each parent was calculated. The sums were labeled Closeness with Mother and Closeness with Father. In the current sample, Cronbach alphas for Closeness with Mother and Closeness with Father were .95 and .96, respectively, for the U.S. group, and .93 and .94, respectively, for the Chinese group.

To fully explore attachment patterns in the two cultural contexts, two assessments for attachment were utilized.

Attachment Style Prototypes (ASP) The Attachment Style Prototypes (ASP; Hazan & Shaver, 1987) is the first self-report adult attachment measure that is derived directly from the infant attachment typology of Bowlby (1969, 1977, 1980) and Ainsworth, Blehar, Waters, and Wall (1978). It consists of three paragraphs corresponding to secure, avoidant, and anxious/ambivalent attachment styles. Participants were required to choose one of three paragraphs that best described their feelings of comfort in romantic relationships. The reliability of the scale has been demonstrated by similar results in terms of distribution of attachment styles obtained internationally (e.g., Collins & Read, 1990, in the United States; Feeney & Noller, 1990, in Australia; Mikulincer & Nachshon, 1991, in Israel).

Experiences in Close Relationships Scale (ECRS) The Experiences in Close Relationships Scale (ECRS; Brennan, Clark, & Shaver, 1998) is a two-dimensional, four-category conceptualization based on the model of self and the model of others (Bartholomew & Horowitz, 1991). It has been utilized widely in adult attachment research. The 36-item measure assesses how individuals feel in romantic relationships. Each item on the ECRS was answered on a 7-point Likert scale ranging from 1 (disagree strongly) to 7 (agree strongly), with a middle score of 4 (neutral/mixed). The measure consists of two 18-item subscales, Avoidance and Anxiety. The Avoidance subscale reflects levels of avoidance to intimacy, discomfort with closeness, and self-reliance. The Anxiety subscale reflects jealousy, fear of abandonment, and fear of rejection. Participants were asked how they felt in their current romantic relationships or how they felt in their most significant relationship if they were not romantically involved with anyone at the time. The Cronbach alphas in the current sample for anxiety and avoidance were .90 and .94, respectively, in the U.S. group, and .81 and .88, respectively, in the Chinese group.

Both hierarchical and nonhierarchical cluster analyses have revealed four distinctive groups whose scores on the avoidance and anxiety subscales matched the four groups Bartholomew and Horowitz (1991) had identified. These groups are *secure*, *dismissing*, *fearful*, and *preoccupied* (known as *anxious/ambivalent* in the three-category attachment measure). Participants in the secure cluster score low on both avoidance and anxiety. Those in the fearful cluster score high on both avoidance and anxiety. Participants in the preoccupied (anxious/ambivalent) cluster score low on avoidance and high on anxiety. Finally, those in the dismissing cluster score high on avoidance and low on anxiety (Brennan et al., 1998).

Rahim Organizational Conflict Inventory-II (ROCI-II)   Like adult attachment assessed by ECRS, styles of handling interpersonal conflict can be conceptualized on two dimensions: the dimension of attempting to satisfy his or her own concerns (high or low) and the dimension of a person wanting to satisfy the concerns of others (high or low). The combination of the two dimensions results in five conflict resolution styles (Rahim, 1983): *integrating* (high on self, high on others), *dominating* (high on self, low on others), *obliging* (low on self, high on others), *avoiding* (low on self, low on others), and *compromising* (medium on self, medium on others). Integrating assesses the degree one can be open with the other and come up with solutions that satisfy both partners. Dominating describes the tendency to force one's opinion on the other. Obliging focuses on the tendency of other-pleasing behaviors at the cost of sacrificing the concern for self. Avoiding assesses the degree one stays away from disagreement with the partner. Compromising evaluates one's ability to propose a middle ground when facing a difficult issue. It is less favorable than integrating because the proposal requires both partners to give up a certain benefit. The behaviors of compromising and integrating satisfy needs of both the self and others, and are more likely to generate win–win solutions. The reliabilities in the current sample for the conflict resolution behavior of integrating, avoiding conflict, dominating, obliging, and compromising were .90, .85, .81, .81, and .74, respectively, in the U.S. group; they were .84, .70, .62, .72, and .71, respectively, in the Chinese group.

RESULTS

Preliminary Analyses

Gender difference in attachment dimensions, conflict resolution behaviors, relationship satisfaction, and perception of parental availability were examined. In the U.S. group, gender differences were detected on the conflict resolution behaviors of avoiding (males = 4.11, females = 3.59; $p < .001$) and obliging (males = 5.16, females = 4.89; $p < .01$). In the Chinese group, however, gender differences did not exist. Between the two cultural groups, significant differences were present in all but one variable, the conflict resolution behavior of dominating (Table 16.1). The Chinese group reported higher scores in the two adult attachment dimensions (i.e., anxiety and avoidance) and lower scores on closeness with parents. These scores indicated higher levels of anxiety and avoidance, and perception of lower parent availability when compared to the U.S. participants. Among the four conflict resolution behaviors on which the two groups differ, the scores of the Chinese group

TABLE 16.1   Preliminary Comparisons Between the Two Cultural Groups

		N	Mean	Standard Deviation	t
Adult Attachment Dimensions					
Anxiety	Chinese	133	3.87	.81	4.04°°
	American	396	3.46	1.07	
Avoidance	Chinese	133	3.18	.958	6.33°°
	American	396	2.50	1.10	
Attachment Experiences With Parents					
Closeness with mother	Chinese	134	2.93	.22	−17.98°°
	American	389	4.07	.72	
Closeness with father	Chinese	133	2.94	.28	−9.99°°
	American	385	3.70	.87	
Conflict Resolution Behaviors					
Integrating	Chinese	132	5.17	.95	16.23°°
	American	397	3.46	1.07	
Avoiding	Chinese	132	4.20	.94	3.06°
	American	397	3.83	1.25	
	Chinese	132	4.04	.78	−1.83
Dominating	American	397	4.22	1.06	
Obliging	Chinese	132	4.79	.79	−2.61°
	American	397	5.01	.89	
Compromising	Chinese	132	4.65	.83	−5.40°°
	American	397	5.11	.86	

°°$p < .001$. °$p < .01$.

also indicated a greater likelihood for using integrating, avoiding, and obliging behaviors but a lesser likelihood for compromising behaviors.

Attachment Patterns

The distribution of the three attachment styles assessed by ASP was the same in the two groups (Table 16.2). Cluster analysis (k-means) was performed using the two attachment dimensions, anxiety and avoidance, to define the clusters. The solution was restricted to four clusters. In both cultural groups four distinctive attachment styles emerged. The results were consistent with the four-category model of Brennan et al. (1998): secure (low on anxiety and avoidance), fearful (high on anxiety and

TABLE 16.2   Distributions of Attachment Patterns

	Chinese (n = 133)		U.S. (n = 396)	
	Frequency	Percent	Frequency	Percent
ASP				
Secure	78	60.5%	227	59.3%
Avoidant	39	30.2%	116	30.3%
Anxious/Ambivalent	12	9.3%	40	10.4%
ECRS				
Secure	39	30%	134	34%
Dismissing	32	21%	74	19%
Preoccupied	30	24%	128	32%
Fearful	32	24%	61	15%

avoidance), dismissing (low on anxiety and high on avoidance), and preoccupied (high on anxiety and low on avoidance). The distributions are displayed in Table 16.2.

Perceptions of Closeness to Parents and Current Attachment Pattern

Multiple regressions showed that perceptions of closeness with both parental figures were not associated with current attachment patterns in romantic relationships in the Chinese group (F = .342, p > .05 for anxiety; F = .274, p > .05 for avoidance), but associated in the American group (F = 12.595, p < .001 for anxiety; F = .6.215, p < .005 for avoidance) but with low R^2 (.057 and .027 for anxiety and avoidance, respectively).

Competency in Conflict Resolution

To examine whether perceptions of availability of parental figures before entering adulthood are associated with competencies in the area of conflict resolution in romantic relationships, and whether attachment feelings and experiences in romantic relationships are associated with competencies in the form of conflict resolution, hierarchical multiple regressions were performed with perception of closeness with parental figures entered first as a block followed by adult attachment dimensions (Table 16.3). Results showed that perception of closeness with parental figures did not predict any conflict resolution behavior in the Chinese group. For the U.S. group they predicted conflict resolution behavior of dominating and integration but explained variances in them only minimally (R^2 = .023, p < .01; R^2 = .029, p < .001).

Integrating, the most favorable conflict resolution behavior, was predicted by both attachment dimensions in both cultural groups with very similar amounts of variances explained. The second favorable conflict resolution behavior, compromising, was also predicted by a combination of attachment dimensions in both cultural groups. Obliging, the behavior to please the other at the cost of self, was predicted by a combination of attachment dimensions in both cultural groups with a fairly close amount of variances explained. The remaining negative conflict resolution behaviors of avoiding and dominating were predicted by a combination of

TABLE 16.3   Hierarchical Multiple Regression Analyses of Conflict Resolution Behaviors

	Chinese (n = 132)			U.S. (n = 397)		
	Beta	F	R^2	Beta	F	R^2
Avoiding Conflict						
Step 1: Early attachment		1.551	0.008		2.744	0.009
With mother	−0.038			−0.055		
With father	−0.136			0.092		
Step 2: Adult attachment		1.655	0.020		15.504	0.132°°
Anxiety	0.161			0.334°°		
Avoidance	0.007			0.092		
Compromising						
Step 1: Early attachment		2.053	0.016		3.386	0.012
With mother	−0.063			0.072		
With father	−0.151			0.024		
Step 2: Adult attachment		3.642	0.075°°		18.156	0.153°°
Anxiety	−0.043			−0.392°°		
Avoidance	−0.257°			0.104		
Dominating						
Step 1: Early attachment		0.439	−0.009		5.491	0.023°
With mother	−0.102			0.017		
With father	0.045			−0.109		
Step 2: Adult attachment		1.063	0.002		8.707	0.075°°
Anxiety	0.127			0.139°		
Avoidance	0.076			0.175°°		
Integrating						
Step 1: Early attachment		3.659	0.039		6.704	0.029°°
With mother	−0.132			0.047		
With father	−0.148			0.029		
Step 2: Adult attachment		17.884	0.342°°		60.196	0.383°°
Anxiety	−0.223°			−0.586°°		
Avoidance	−0.464°°			−0.081°		
Obliging						
Step 1: Early attachment		0.770	−0.004		0.155	−0.004
With mother	0.066			−0.042		
With father	−0.148			0.042		
Step 2: Adult attachment		8.422	0.186°°		17.390	0.147°°
Anxiety	0.019			−0.378°°		
Avoidance	−0.451°°			0.225°°		

°$p < 0.01$. °°$p < 0.001$.

attachment dimensions only in the U.S. group. For both cultural groups lower levels of anxiety and avoidance were associated with more positive conflict resolution behaviors than they predicted.

Among the three conflict resolution behaviors that the combination of the attachment dimension successfully predicted in the Chinese group, avoidance was the only predictor for compromising and obliging. While both dimensions were significant predictors for integration, avoidance was significant at the .001 level and anxiety was at the .01 level. In the U.S. group there was no such clear pattern. Anxiety was the only predictor for avoiding conflict and compromising, yet both anxiety and avoidance predicted dominating, integrating, and obliging. For dominating, anxiety was significant at the .01 level; however, the combination of the dimensions only explained approximately 8% of the variance.

DISCUSSION

Attachment Patterns

The ASP revealed the same attachment pattern distribution between the two cultural groups. A similar distribution was found in earlier studies. In the Hazan and Shaver (1987) study, the distribution of the three attachment styles is consistent between two samples, the nonstudent sample and the undergraduate student sample, with both samples consisting of significantly more females than males. The frequencies are secure, 56% and 56% (nonstudent and student, respectively); avoidant, 25% and 23%; and anxious/ambivalent, 19% and 20%. Other studies conducted in the United States using samples from undergraduate populations yield similar results. For example, Keelan, Dion, and Dion (1994) using Hazan and Shaver's (1987) single-item questionnaire found the proportion of the three attachment styles to be 58% secure, 29% avoidant, and 14% anxious/ambivalent This proportion is similar to that reported in American studies of infant–mother attachment (Hazan & Shaver, 1987). A strikingly similar proportion is obtained in other countries using undergraduate student samples with more females than males. Feeney and Noller (1990) in Australia obtained proportions of 55% secure, 30% avoidant, and 15% anxious/ambivalent, measured by Hazan and Shaver's single-item attachment questionnaire. Mikulincer and Nachshon (1991) in Israel obtained a similar proportion of 63% secure, 22% avoidant, and 15% anxious/ambivalent measured by Hazan and Shaver's (1988) continuous measure. The Chinese data has also revealed a very similar distribution of attachment pattern when assessed by the ASP.

Although the two groups scored differently on the attachment dimensions of anxiety and avoidance measured by ECRS, four attachment styles clearly emerged in both groups. This suggests that both the two-dimension (anxiety and avoidance) and the four-category (secure, dismissing, fearful, and preoccupied) adult attachment conceptualizations are as applicable to the Chinese participants as they are to the U.S. participants. It is important to point out that the means of the Chinese participants (Anxiety = 3.88, Avoidance = 3.19) were virtually the same as those reported by Wang and Mallinckrodt (2006) when they surveyed Chinese and Taiwanese international students from two public universities in the Midwest (anxiety = 3.81, avoidance = 3.14). This provides validation of the reliability of ECRS when utilized in Chinese college students raised in the Chinese cultural context both in the home country and overseas.

Attachment studies conducted in the West have revealed different distributions when assessed by the ASP and ECRS (Bartholomew & Shaver, 1998). This is mainly due to the two different conceptualizations on which they were based (Bartholomew, 1990). The distributions of preoccupied and fearful are quite different between the Chinese and the U.S. groups with the Chinese group revealing a higher percentage. However, the distributions in the Chinese group in the current sample are very close to those found by Brennan et al. (1998) in a large sample of American college students (30% secure, 24% preoccupied, 21% dismissing, 24% fearful), including the distributions of preoccupied and fearful. Therefore, it is inconclusive whether the higher percentage in the Chinese group is due to the collectivistic cultural influence as suggested by Schmitt et al. (2004). More cross-cultural studies are needed to examine this issue further.

The presence of all attachment styles was confirmed and similar distributions were revealed by categorical and continuous measures in the two groups. The attachment pictures in the two distinctive cultural contexts are more alike than different. It is now necessary to return to the cross-cultural child attachment literature. It has been pointed out that parents in East Asia tend to anticipate their infants' needs, whereas parents in the West tend to respond to their infants' signals for need (Rothbaum & Morelli, 2005). Researchers propose that parent–child attachment created and maintained within cultural expectations leads to different outcomes or competencies preferred within a specific culture (Grossmann, Grossmann, & Keppler, 2005). For example, a desirable outcome of secure attachment in the West is autonomy and independence; in the East, it is interdependence and concerns for group well-being (Trommsdorff & Friedlmeier, 1993). Regardless of how attachment security may be defined and achieved, and how its consequences may be different among children, very similar if not the same outcomes seem to have been achieved in young adulthood. Security of attachment is reflected by the value of and trust in the self and others, and insecurity is reflected by the lack of either or both.

This confirmation fills the blank of cross-cultural adult attachment pattern and distribution, but at the same time, raises a more intriguing question: Do young children, raised in cultures with differences, some of which are concrete enough to be captured by words and others too subtle to be described, tend to eventually develop toward a similar outcome? In this study, perception of earlier parental availability failed to predict adult attachment dimensions in the Chinese group and only minimally accounted for the variances in the U.S. group. This is contrary to Bowlby's (1980) theoretical speculation that adult attachment style should be associated with an internal working model formed at an earlier stage of life. Lopez, Melendez, and Rice (2000) found a significant association between perceived parental bond and adult attachment pattern; however, parental bond accounted for over twice as much variance in adult attachment anxiety in college students from divorced families than those from intact families (15% versus 6%). The current study did not look into parents' marital status during participants' childhood so it is not possible to determine if the influence of parental bond was moderated by a large percentage of intact parental marriages. A possible explanation for a lack of association in the Chinese group can be that due to cultural practices, stronger or more significant attachment may have been formed with figures other than parents, for example, grandparents. It is inconclusive, based on this study, if and how early attachment experiences are connected to later attachment patterns, and it remains a critical question to be answered.

The finding that there is not a direct or a strong link between perceived parental availability (or sensitivity) and later attachment security raised more questions. What happens in the black box of development between early childhood and young adulthood? Are the same or similar goals achieved by different means because humans, for the sake of evolution, work toward a goal that may look culturally different but contains the same core, and that if one does not value and trust the self and others, one cannot be a competent person in any society?

Attachment Patterns and Competency in Conflict Resolution

The study of attachment patterns is only meaningful when the patterns are examined in relation to competency in various social and life aspects. Despite significant differences between the two cultural groups on attachment dimensions, lower levels of anxiety and avoidance, indicators for an internal working model of secure attachment, predicted competency in conflict resolution in romantic relationships in both groups. The best example is the examination of integration, the most favorable choice of conflict resolution behavior; 34% and 38% of the variances in the Chinese and the U.S. groups, respectively, were attributed to the adult attachment dimensions. A deep sense of self-worth and a high trust in the significant other's availability shine in time of distress and help generate the most mutually beneficial strategy. On the contrary, low sense of self-worth and confidence in others are likely to lead to a negative conflict resolution behavior. An example in this sample is obliging behavior, a tendency to engage in pleasing others at the cost of the self.

Cultural Variation in Prediction of Competency in Conflict Resolution

Despite more commonalities than differences between the two cultural groups, two interesting cultural variations deserve special attention. First, in the Chinese group, among all three negative conflict resolution behaviors, attachment dimensions predicted only obliging and failed to predict conflict resolution behavior of avoiding and dominating. In other words, insecure attachment was not associated with conflict resolution behavior of avoiding and dominating, but it was related to conflict resolution behavior of obliging. In the U.S. group, however, the dimensions predicted all three negative conflict resolution behaviors. These variations may find explanations in the different socializations. The traditional emphasis in the Chinese culture on group harmony leads to a routine practice of taking a step back from disagreement and shying away from placing individual opinion over consensus or other people's feelings (Shi & Wang, 2008). These beliefs and philosophies may have been so wired into the people's psyche that they are followed as creed by many, rather than as a consequence of insecure attachment. It may even work its way into responses to the instrument items without awareness through the work of social desirability. The selection of an obliging behavior is a reflection of a lack of confidence in the self and others, and, therefore, is likely to be predicted by attachment patterns. In the United States children are rarely taught to withdraw from a disagreement or conflict and are encouraged to express their unique perspectives. As a result, these strategies are likely to have remained in the pool of options to choose from when disagreements arise. This variation suggests that cultural expectation may override what attachment might have set out to predict in social and relational competency. It further indicates that the role of attachment and its social consequences such as competency should be discussed in the cultural context in which cultural norms and expectations are defined. It is beyond the scope of this study to further examine how specific attachment styles and their consequences may be moderated or reinforced by collectivistic and individualistic cultural norms. It is, however, a critical aspect in cross-cultural attachment research.

A second variation has to do with the function of individual attachment dimensions. The attachment dimension of avoidance proved a stronger predictor for conflict resolution behavior in the Chinese group, whereas anxiety was a stronger predictor in the U.S. group. For the Chinese participants, levels in avoidance of intimacy, discomfort with closeness, and self-reliance were more responsible for the conflict resolution behaviors adopted. Higher scores of avoidance were associated with obliging and lower scores were associated with integrating and compromising. For the U.S. group, although there was not a clear pattern as in the Chinese group, jealousy, fear of abandonment, and fear of rejection played a somewhat more significant role and predicted all five conflict resolution behaviors (avoidance predicted three). Higher levels of jealousy and fear were related to avoiding conflict, dominating, and obliging, while lower levels were related to compromising and integrating. The reasons for this variation may again lie in socialization and cultural expectations. With the influence of traditional Chinese values, a parent is more or less an authority figure: at best a coach or a mentor to provide discipline and guidance that will help the child achieve academic and career goals. In such a relationship, communication concerning feelings and emotions is scarce, if not absent. Children may have learned not to value their feelings but instead to focus on concrete life goals such as succeeding on the College Entrance Examination. This relational pattern is likely to be brought into romantic relationships as part of an internal working model. In the U.S. cultural context, the emphasis on independence and competence may have increased the uncertainty that parental love is based on personal quality rather than on deeds and achievements. This concern, of course, can be built into the internal working model.

It is premature to conclude, based on a single study, whether the between-group variations are due to cultural beliefs, the function of attachment, or the dynamic relations of the two. Satisfactory explanations call for a close examination of the intricate and, at times, subtle relationship between attachment and culture, about which the field is trying to obtain a more accurate and comprehensive understanding. More cross-cultural research needs to be conducted to confirm if and how cultural variations exist and, more important, to provide answers to whether culture is a greater defining factor than attachment.

CLINICAL IMPLICATIONS

This study validates universality of adult attachment with expected cultural variations, which further highlights the complexity when approaching attachment-ridden issues in long-term romantic relationships. Although not entirely separable, recognizing the work of cultural influences on attachment process and outcome is a challenging yet necessary component for a competent clinical conceptualization and effective clinical interventions. The following case illustrates the process of trying to understand a Chinese couple's dynamics within a cultural context.

Ping, who suffered from chronic depression, had been married to Yong for 10 years and together they had an adorable 7-year-old son. Yong enjoyed a very successful career and was very family oriented. Ping had no complaint about him and sincerely considered him an excellent father and husband, but she was puzzled as to why she could not simply enjoy the good life that she saw in many of her female friends. She was convinced that there had to be something wrong with herself. After some time in therapy, the therapist finally gained a cultural understanding of the issues. The clue was Ping's casual indication of a lack of emotional and sexual intimacy in their marriage, which she attributed to Yong's efforts to give her space. The therapist concluded that Yong, with an avoidant attachment style, had been maintaining his avoidance through culturally acceptable behavioral choices including praising Ping as a good mother and wife, providing for her and the family financially, helping with chores and child rearing, and following her wishes indiscriminately on many family issues. In other words, through his obliging behaviors toward Ping, he kept her from complaining about his emotional unavailability. Ping, following cultural expectations, convinced herself that she was to blame for her depression. Without the therapist recognizing Yong's disguised avoidance within this cultural context, the course of therapy would have been sidetracked.

LIMITATIONS AND FUTURE DIRECTIONS

This was an exploratory study examining the relationship between cultural influence and attachment through comparisons between an Eastern and a Western cultural group. One obvious limitation is the sole inclusion of college students in the sample. Due to age, life experience, and contextual factors, college students may bear certain unique characteristics where relationships are concerned. This is probably even truer for Chinese college students. Despite a huge increase of college students during the past decade, they are a very special group compared to the general population, even when comparing them to the urban population. This group is psychologically more comfortable with Western influences and may have adopted these influences more than they are aware of. In other words, college students may not be the best representation of the Chinese population. This study provides insight to the attachment picture during a time of rapid change, a time not typical to the Chinese cultural context. To accurately address the interaction between culture and attachment, adult attachment research needs to be conducted in inland rural areas where the traditional values still dominate daily life.

The use of conflict resolution behavior as a partial indicator of relational competency in romantic relationships is arguably a limitation. Conflict resolution behavior is likely to be affected by cultural norms (Cingoz-Ulu & Lalonde, 2007), making it difficult to separate the influence of attachment experiences and patterns from cultural expectations with the current research design. Future studies relying on more sophisticated design and statistical analyses such as path analysis should be conducted.

The third and greatest limitation of the study lies in an adoption of an *etic* approach, a practice to apply theories and assessment developed in one society to a culturally different society, to test their cross-cultural validity (van IJzendoorn & Sagi, 1999). This conceptualization and practice may lead to exclusion and rejection of phenomena that do not match the system. The *emic* approach attempts to understand a culture from within, thereby developing a conceptualization and trajectory that are cultural specific (van IJzendoorn & Sagi, 1999). If the etic approach is a convenient one, the emic approach is more challenging, but it is greatly needed if the field wants to solve the remaining puzzles in attachment theory. In a sense, attachment research is not winding down, but has just started. Studies of young children, adolescents, young adults, and mature adults using an emic approach need to be diligently conducted in various typical cultural settings and compared to the results using an etic approach. Such a process will lend a new level of understanding of complex human emotions and relationships.

REFERENCES

Ainsworth, M. D. S., Blehar, M. C., Waters, E., & Wall, S. (1978). *Patterns of attachment: A psychological study of the strange situation*. Hillsdale, NJ: Lawrence Erlbaum Associates.

Armsden, G. C., & Greenberg, M. T. (1987). The Inventory of Parent and Peer Attachment: Individual differences and their relationship to psychological well-being in adolescence. *Journal of Youth and Adolescence, 16*, 427–454.

Bartholomew, K. (1990). Avoidance of intimacy: An attachment perspective. *Journal of Social and Personal Relationships, 7*, 147–178.

Bartholomew, K., & Horowitz, L. (1991). Attachment styles among young adults: A test of a four-category model. *Journal of Personality and Social Psychology, 61*, 226–244.

Bartholomew, K. & Shaver, P. R. (1998). Methods of assessing adult attachment: Do they converge? In J. A. Simpson, & W. S. Rholes (Eds.), *Attachment theory and close relationships* (pp. 25–45). New York: Guilford Press.

Belsky, J., & Kelly, J. (1994). *The transition to parenthood*. New York: Dell.

Bodenmann, G., Kaiser, A., Hahlweg, K., & Fehm-Wolfsdorf, G. (1998). Communication patterns during marital conflict: A cross-cultural replication. *Personal Relationships, 5*, 343–356.

Bowlby, J. (1969). *Attachment and loss: Vol. 1. Attachment*. New York: Basic Books.

Bowlby, J. (1977). The making and breaking of affectional bonds. *British Journal of Psychiatry, 130*, 201–210, 421–431.

Bowlby, J. (1980). *Attachment and loss: Vol. 3. Loss*. New York: Basic Books.

Brennan, K., Clark, C., & Shaver, P. (1998). Self-report measurement of adult attachment. In J. A. Simpson & W. S. Rholes (Eds.), *Attachment theory and close relationships* (pp. 46–76). New York: Guilford Press.

Carlson, V., & Harwood, R. (2003). Attachment, culture, and the caregiving system: The cultural patterning of everyday experiences among Anglo and Puerto Rican mother-infant pairs. *Infant Mental Health Journal, 24*, 53–73.

Carstensen, L. L., Gottman, J. M., & Levenson, R. W. (1995). Emotional behavior in long-term marriage. *Psychology and Aging, 10*, 140–149.

Cassidy, J., & Berlin, L. (1994). The insecure/ambivalent pattern of attachment: Theory and research. *Child Development, 65*, 971–991.

Cassidy, J., & Shaver, P. R. (1999). *Handbook of attachment: Theory, research, and clinical application.* New York: Guilford Press.

Cingoz-Ulu, B., & Lalonde, R. N. (2007). The role of culture and relational context in inter-personal conflict: Do Turks and Canadians use different conflict management strate-gies? *International Journal of Intercultural Relations, 31*, 443–458.

Cohan, C. L., & Bradbury, T. N. (1997). Negative life events, marital interaction, and the longitudinal course of newlywed marriages. *Journal of Personality and Social Psychology, 73*, 114–128.

Collins, N., & Read, S. (1990). Adult attachment, working models, and relationship quality in dating couples. *Journal of Personality and Social Psychology, 58*, 644–663.

Collins, N. L., & Feeney, B. C. (2000). A safe haven: An attachment theory perspective on support seeking and caregiving in intimate relationships. *Journal of Personality and Social Psychology, 78*, 1053–1073.

Corcoran, K., & Mallinckrodt, B. (2000). Adult attachment, self-efficacy, perspective taking, and conflict resolution. *Journal of Counseling & Development, 78*, 473–483.

Creasey, G., Kershaw, K., & Boston, A. (1999). Conflict management with friends and romantic partners: The role of attachment and negative mood regulation expectan-cies. *Journal of Youth and Adolescence, 28*, 523–543.

Doi, T. (1992). On the concept of amae. *Infant Mental Health Journal, 13*, 7–11.

Feeney, J., Noller, P., & Callan, V. (1994). Attachment style, communication and satisfaction in the early years of marriage. *Advances in Personal Relationships, 5*, 269–308.

Feeney, J. & Noller, P. (1990). Attachment style as a predictor of adult romantic relation-ships. *Journal of Personality and Social Psychology, 58*, 281–291.

Gottman, J. M., Coan, J., Carrere, S., & Swanson, C. (1998). Predicting marital happi-ness and stability from newlywed interactions. *Journal of Marriage and the Family, 60*, 5–22.

Grossmann, K., Grossmann, K. E., Spangler, G., Suess, G., & Unzner, L. (1985). Maternal sensi-tivity and newborns' orientation responses as related to quality of attachment in northern Germany. In I. Bretherton & E. Waters (Eds.), Growing points in attachment theory and research. *Monographs of the Society for Research in Child Development, 50*, 233–256.

Grossmann, K. E., Grossmann, K., & Keppler, A. (2005). Universal and culture-specific aspects of human behavior: The case of attachment. In W. Friedlmeier, P. Chakkarath, & B. Schwarz (Eds.), *Culture and human development: The importance of cross-cultural research for the social sciences* (pp. 75–98). New York: Psychology Press.

Hazan, C., & Shaver, P. (1987). Romantic love conceptualized as an attachment process. *Journal of Personality and Social Psychology, 52*, 511–524.

Hazan, C., & Shaver, P. (1988). *Adult Attachment Questionnaire.* Unpublished scale, University of Denver, CO.

Heavey, C. L., Christensen, A., & Malamuth, N. M. (1995). The longitudinal impact of demand and withdrawal during marital conflict. *Journal of Consulting and Clinical Psychology, 63*, 797–801.

Keelan, J. P., Dion, K. L., & Dion, K. K. (1994). Attachment style and heterosexual relation-ships among young adults: A short term panel study. *Journal of Social and Personal Relationships, 11*, 201–214.

Klinetob, N. A., & Smith, D. A. (1996). Demand-withdraw communication in marital interaction: Tests of interpersonal contingency and gender role hypotheses. *Journal of Marriage and the Family, 58*, 945–957.

Kobak, R. R., & Duemmler, S. (1994). Attachment and conversation: Toward a discourse analysis of adolescent and adult security. In K. Bartholomew & D. Perlman (Eds.), *Attachment process in adulthood* (pp. 121–149). London: Jessica Kingsley.

Lopez, F., Melendez, M., & Rice, K. (2000). Parental divorce, parent-child bond, and adult attachment orientations among college students: A comparison of three racial/ethnic groups. *Journal of Counseling Psychology, 47*, 177–186.

Mikulincer, M., & Nachshon, O. (1991). Attachment style and patterns of self-disclosure. *Journal of Personality and Social Psychology, 61*, 321–331.

Ng, K., Trusty, J., & Crawford, R. (2005). A cross-cultural validation of the attachment style questionnaire: A Malaysian pilot study. *The Family Journal: Counseling and Therapy for Couples and Families, 13*, 416–426.

Pistole, M. C. (1989). Attachment in adult romantic relationships: Style of conflict resolution and relationship satisfaction. *Journal of Social and Personal Relationship, 16*, 505–510.

Pistole, M. C. (1993). Attachment relationships: Self-disclosure and trust. *Journal of Mental Health Counseling, 15*, 94–106.

Rahim, F. (1983). A measure of styles of handling interpersonal conflict. *Academy of Management Journal, 26*, 368–376.

Roberts, L. (2000). Fire and ice in marital communication: Hostile and distancing behaviors as predictors of marital distress. *Journal of Marriage and the Family, 62*, 693–707.

Rothbaum, F., & Morelli, G. (2005). Attachment and culture: Bridging relativism and universalism. In W. Friedlmeier, P. Chakkarath, & B. Schwarz (Eds.), *Culture and human development: The importance of cross-cultural research for the social sciences* (pp. 92–113). New York: Psychology Press.

Rothbaum, F., Weisz, J., Pott, M., Miyake, K., & Morelli, G. (2000). Attachment and culture: Security in the United States and Japan. *American Psychologist, 55*, 1093–1104.

Scharfe, E., & Bartholomew, K. (1994). Reliability and stability of adult attachment patterns. *Personal Relationships, 1*, 23–43.

Schmitt, D. P., Alcalay, L., Allensworth, M., Allik, J., Ault, L., & Austers, I., … Zupanèiè, A. (2004). Patterns of universals of adult romantic attachment across 62 cultural regions: Are models of self and of other pancultural constructs? *Journal of Cross-Cultural Psychology, 35*, 367-402.

Senchak, M., & Leonard, K. (1992). Attachment styles and marital adjustment among newlywed couples. *Journal of Social and Personal Relationships, 9*, 51–64.

Shi, L. (2003). The association between adult attachment styles and conflict resolution in romantic relationships. *The American Journal of Family Therapy, 31*, 143–157.

Shi, L., & Wang, L. (2008). A multilevel contextual model for couples from mainland China. In M. Rastogi & V. Thomas (Eds.), *Multicultural couple therapy* (pp. 297–316). Thousand Oaks, CA: Sage Publications.

Simpson, J., Rholes, W. S., & Phillips, D. (1996). Conflict in close relationships: An attachment perspective. *Journal of Personality and Social Psychology, 71*, 899–914.

Tomlinson, M. (2001). Mother-infant attachment, culture and research: A pilot study. *Southern African Journal of Child and Adolescent Mental Health, 13*, 41–54.

Trommsdorff, G., & Friedlmeier, W. (1993). Control and responsiveness in Japanese and German mother-child interactions. *Early Development and Parenting, 2*, 65–78.

van IJzendoorn, M. H., Bakermans-Kranenburg, M. J., & Sagi-Schwartz, A. (2006). Attachment across diverse sociocultural contexts: The limits of universality. In K. H. Rubin & O. B. Chung (Eds.), *Parenting beliefs, behaviors, and parent-child relations: A cross-cultural perspective* (pp. 107–142). New York: Taylor & Francis.

van IJzendoorn, M. H., & Sagi, A. (1999). Cross-cultural patterns of attachment: Universal and contextual dimensions. In J. Cassidy & P. R. Shaver (Eds.), *Handbook of attachment: Theory, research, and clinical applications* (pp. 713–734). New York: Guilford Press.

Wang, C., & Mallinckrodt, B. (2006). Acculturation, attachment, and psychological adjustment of Chinese/Taiwanese international students. *Journal of Counseling Psychology, 53*, 422–433.

Waters, E., & Cummings, E. M. (2000). A secure base from which to explore the environment. *Child Development, 71*, 164–172.

Weiss, R. (1982). Attachment in adult life. In C. M. Parkes & J. Stevenson-Hinde (Eds.), *The place of attachment in human behavior* (pp. 171–183). New York: Basic Books.

West, M. L., & Sheldon-Keller, A. E. (1994). *Patterns of relating: An adult attachment perspective*. New York: Guilford Press.

Yamaguchi, S. (2004). Further clarifications of the concept of Amae in relation to dependence and attachment. *Human Development, 47*, 28–33.

You, H. S, & Malley-Morrison, K. (2000). Young adult attachment styles and intimate relationships with close friends: A cross-cultural study of Koreans and Caucasian Americans. *Journal of Cross-Cultural Psychology, 31*, 528–534.

Section V

Clinical Applications

17

Attachment Dynamics and Latin Cultures
Areas of Convergence and Divergence

PAUL R. PELUSO, ALEXIS O. MIRANDA,
MIRIAM FIRPO-JIMENEZ, and MYLINH T. PHAM

CONTENTS

A ttachment is the emotional bond that develops between a child and a caregiver. According to Bowlby (1969, 1973, 1988), these attachment relationships are universal to human child rearing and provide a secure base for the child in times of real or perceived threat where the child can return for physical and emotional comfort. In addition, the security of the attachment relationship influences the extent to which the child feels comfortable exploring the world.

The more secure these relationships are, the better able children are to meet their needs and more confidently explore their environment (Bowlby, 1988).

Researchers have examined the nature and function of attachment in infancy and have documented the importance of secure attachments in childhood for emotional adjustment, social competence, and eventually self-esteem and attachment in adults (see Peluso, Peluso, White, & Kern, 2004, for a review). Attachment plays a vital role in building the foundation of an individual's model of relating to others, which helps to fulfill his or her emotional needs. These early experiences are incorporated into the child's working model of self and others, and form the basis for a person's later adult relational style (Ainsworth, Blehar, Waters, & Wall, 1978; Bowlby, 1988; Fraley & Shaver, 2000; Griffin & Bartholomew, 1994; Peluso, Peluso, Buckner, Kern, & Curlette, 2009; Peluso et al., 2004; Sroufe, 1988).

When the quality of the attachment relationship is poor, children are more susceptible to a variety of cognitive and affective disorders. This is due, in part, to the persistent disregard of the child's basic emotional needs for comfort, stimulation, and affection, regardless of a child's basic physical needs. Frequent change in the primary caregiver may prevent the child from forming a stable attachment. The result can have long lasting consequences for individuals' performance in schools, with peers, and with romantic partners (Bowlby, 1988; Fraley & Shaver, 2000; Peluso et al., 2004; Sroufe, 1988).

While these assertions about attachment relationships have stood up well to the empirical scrutiny of decades of research, many individual differences exist that have not been well defined (Bowlby, 1988). This is especially true in investigating the moderating and mediating influence of an individual's culture on the formation of attachment relationships, and the development of working models of self and others.

The Latin cultures from Central America, the Caribbean, or South America share a heritage of colonial rule from Spain that contains many unique cultural factors. In addition, there is a vast array of subcultures that have distinct indigenous elements to them. Within these subcultures is an overarching theme of centrality and closeness of the family (*familismo*), the importance of the extended family on child rearing, and traditional views of gender roles (*machismo* and *marianismo*). Each of these has a direct impact on the development of attachment relationships, as well as the internal working models of self and others (Miranda, Bilot, Peluso, Berman, & Van Meek, 2006). Indeed, in other cultural contexts— such as a culture that favors independence rather than interdependence within the community and family—these cultural "norms" might look like (and produce) insecurity. Specifically, in Latino cultures, the close attention that is paid to family members may seem like "enmeshment" and a lack of "appropriate" detachment from the family of origin. However, findings from several recent, cross-cultural studies indicate that there are no differences in the percentages of securely attached children (Greenfield, Keller, Fuligni, & Maynard, 2003; Keller et al., 2004). There are some findings that show some culturally influenced elements, such as independence versus interdependence, produce variations in attachment dynamics (Schmitt et al., 2004). As a result, there are several areas of interest that may provide attachment theorists and counselors alike with information that can shape interventions as well as future investigations. Thus, the purpose of our chapter is to discuss both the converging and diverging areas of attachment within Latin cultures using the latest research and to illustrate this more fully with a case study.

OVERVIEW OF LATIN/HISPANIC CULTURES

The terms *Hispanic* and *Latino* are both labels used to describe people who come from a variety of countries and cultural backgrounds. Although there may be different connotations to either Hispanic or Latino, to facilitate consistency throughout this chapter, we will use the word Latino. Latinos are not a homogeneous or monolithic group, as there is great genetic diversity as well as socioeconomic, educational, and demographic variation both between and within Latino ethnic groups. The term Latino describes a population with a common cultural heritage and most often a common language; but, it does not refer to race or a common ancestry.

The indigenous people of what is today considered Mexico, Central and South America, the Caribbean, and the American Southwest were overpowered by the conquistadores and the religious persuasion of the Catholic missionaries who accompanied them. Intermarriage led to the evolution of mixed races and cultures with the union of European and American Indian and African that resulted in the *criollo* or *mulatto* (Santiago-Rivera, Arredondo, & Gallardo-Cooper, 2002). As a result, although Latinos have been considered to be first and foremost an ethnic group, they represent a heterogeneous mix of Native American, European, and African ancestries.

Traditional Latinos can be characterized as interdependent, collectivistic, and family-oriented compared to Americans who are viewed as independent, individualistic, and self-focused. Conflicting Latino versus American cultural values have been used to explain Latino Americans' failure to use mental health services, attitudes toward mental health services, counseling, and coping strategies. The American notions of individual counseling often conflict with Latinos' values or preferences for seeking help from family, friends, and other social networks (Carter, Yeh, & Mazulla, 2008). This presents a need for cultural sensitivity and oftentimes involvement of families with treatment.

The collective world of Latinos can be described by several cultural concepts. *Familismo* and the familial self represent the Latino value of close family relationships. This self-family construction is useful in understanding Latinos' dedication to children, parents, family unity, and family honor (Falicov, 1998). Family in Latino culture can refer to either blood or extended family members. Nonblood relatives, such as godparents (*madrinas* and *padrinos*) are considered key family members with associated strong feelings of interconnectedness. Again, considering this collectivist cultural perspective, the family unit's reputation takes primacy over the needs of the individual. Building on this concept, there is great emphasis on the importance of children (including adult children) to show respect (*respeto*) and to be respectable (*bien educado*) by adhering to family and cultural values, as well as to avoid situations that may create shame (*verguenza*). Tied into this is the idea of *marianismo,* encompassing the expectation that women emulate the self-sacrificing virtues of the Virgin Mary (Arredondo, 2005). As a result, contemporary women sometimes struggle with the cultural expectation that they "put up with" (*aguantar*) undesirable family and gender role situations.

Within the concept of *marianismo,* Latino mothers have a great deal of influence and power in the family. The role of the mother is revered in the culture. She is considered the most important figure of the family, and other members of the family are both devoted to her (Mealy, Stephan, Abalakina-Paap, 2006). As such, mothers' opinions greatly influence the behavior, attitudes, and values of their children. Devotion comprises attachment, affection, dedication, and loyalty. This devotion to mother is generally produced by a combination of cultural characteristics. As children learn to show or express love and respect to their family (parents, aunts, uncles, elders, etc.) they are expected to be obedient and to practice good behavior. This focus on mother (and subsequent focus on others) may behaviorally appear to be similar to the preoccupied attachment style. Again, as with children who keep thoughts and feelings to themselves and who are securely attached, these individuals who devote considerable attention to others may seem insecurely attached, but they are acting in a culturally congruent fashion (Greenfield et al., 2003). This, in turn, provides the individual with a more secure attachment, therefore, positive models of self and others.

Differences in parental relationship and family closeness in individualistic versus collectivistic cultures is especially evident in the transition from adolescence to adulthood. Traditionally, in the North American individualistic culture "adulthood" is conferred when a child hits the legal age of 18, during which time most complete a high school degree, anticipate legal independence, move out of the family home, and are introduced to the world as an official adult.

In other collectivist communities and cultures, such as the Latino culture, the focus is less on the individual and more on the extended family unit. The transition to adulthood involves a longer process; and, customs and traditions support adolescents to remain in the home and in close interaction with their family. When interpreted from a North American perspective, this extended connectedness is sometimes viewed as delayed development, and the inability to detach from parents is seen as a weakness (Mealy et al., 2006).

Arrias and Hernández (2007) state that in Spain and Mexico the notion of being family-oriented relates to protecting individuals, which "implies a strong ideological and practical involvement of family and kinship networks in protecting their members against economic and social risk" (p. 477). One manifestation of this is the transition of becoming an adult. In these cultures, entrance into adulthood encompasses a extended developmental time period that may be marked by many different life events, such as finishing educational (college) degrees, entering the workforce, becoming financially responsible, getting married, becoming a parent, and so forth (Arrias & Hernández, 2007), rather than a fixed age (18 or 21 years old).

EXPERIENCE OF IMMIGRATION TO THE UNITED STATES ON LATINO IMMIGRANTS

For many Latinos, coming to the United States is experienced as coming to the "promised land." Arriving in the United States means the ability to have employment, better educational opportunities for children, and the possibility of home ownership. The degree to which cultural influences are maintained varies considerably among Latino groups and is associated with national origin. Immigration to the United States can represent a significant, and many times negative, transition in life that taps into such attachment issues as security, exploration, and interacting with others. In an attempt to explain this further and detail the impact on individual behavior, we will discuss the unique pressures of immigration on Latinos.

Most Latinos living in the United States share a common language (Spanish), immigration experience, and cultural attitudes and values that differ from those of the mainstream White, English-speaking non-Latinos (Burchard et al., 2005). This can create a series of shared experiences that are important to understand when working with Latino clients. One of these shared experiences is the maintenance of a connection to their native country. Many Latinos often use a label that describes their country of origin or ethnic group identification, such as Cubans, Mexicans, Puerto Ricans, Argentineans, Colombians, Dominicans, Nicaraguans, Salvadorians, and all other nationalities that make up South American, Central America, and the Caribbean. Historically, immigrants maintained connection to the home country by sending remittances (money and American-made goods) back to relatives in the homeland. In addition, many Latino immigrants also maintained contact by traveling back or telephoning relatives. The extent of these activities varied considerably, depending on financial and often political status. Today, easy travel to Central or South America, ability to receive broadcasts from the region, and the use of the Internet are also facilitating connection with one's home country.

The extent to which Latino immigrants maintain active connections is an important marker of their attitudes toward the United States, their native country, and their own lives as immigrants. For most, the native country is an essential part of their personal identity. While they are optimistic about their future in the United States, they also continue to see much that is positive in the countries where they were born, and their core identity is linked to the country of birth. A large proportion (94%) describes themselves as nationals of their native land (Waldinger, 2007), regardless of how long they have been in the United States. Overall, Latino immigrants to the United States who either arrived as children or have been in the United States for decades are less connected to their native country than those who arrived more recently or immigrated as adults.

Latino immigrants generally have a positive outlook regarding their children's well-being in the United States, but are divided when they consider moral values. According to Waldinger (2007), 28% of Latino respondents believed that moral values are better in the United States while 31% believe the moral values are better in their country of origin. Immigrants are seeking a middle road, trying to find a solution that will reconcile their new U.S. lives and attachments to their relatives, and friends in the areas where they lived previously. These deep cultural connections also have a clear and defined impact on how immigrants think of themselves, and influence the form of attachment relationships they adopt in adolescence and adulthood (Waldinger, 2007). We will discuss some of these elements next.

Attachment in the Latin Cultures

In this section, we will present some of the relevant literature that outlines the similarities and the unique subtleties of attachment theory, as well as the expression of these attachment dynamics within Latino cultures.

Similarities With Traditional Attachment Theory   Researchers investigating attachment theory (see Fraley & Shaver, 2000) have found strong confirmation for the lifelong stability of the core elements of attachment styles and the internal working models of self and others. Bowlby (1969, 1973, 1988) argued for the cross-cultural or universal nature of attachment, and conducted cross-cultural observations in support of the universality of attachment. Recently, Schmitt and colleagues (2004) used a worldwide database to look at attachment styles from over 62 different cultures. They found that two underlying dimensions of attachment (view of others and view of self) were consistently valid across the different cultures, suggesting, as predicted by Bowlby, that attachment is a universal human process beginning in infancy and having a lifelong impact on our relationship styles. In addition, they were able to determine that attachment styles tended to follow the predicted "secure" and "insecure" patterns, though the expressions of attachment (i.e., what constituted fearful versus preoccupied) were culture specific. The truly worldwide scale of their work has provided solid validation for attachment. They conclude: "At both the individual cultural level and at the world-regional level, two factors were appropriate for explaining variation among the romantic attachment scales … By this measure, the two-dimensional structure of romantic attachment is a true cultural universal" (Schmitt et al., 2004, p. 386). Attachment researchers prefer this dimensional conceptualization to categorical conceptualizations of attachment (Fraley & Shaver, 2000; Fraley & Waller, 1998).

Researchers also discovered some interesting differences regarding the manifestations of the various attachment styles. This suggests that there might be cultural differences that influence or impact attachment behaviors. We will detail some cultural phenomenon associated with Latino cultures and discuss the impact of these on the development of attachment styles.

Unique Subtleties and Issues: Different Cultures + Parenting Styles = Different Attachments   According to Keller et al. (2004) parenting is an important factor in the transmission of culture and cultural values to children. Strategies of parenting are oriented towards one of two general goals: the goal of independence or interdependence. Independence emphasizes personal accomplishment and achievement, whereas interdependence places greater value on communal goals and experiences. Keller et al. (2004) discussed how the values

that shape the development of people from individualistic (independent) societies compared to collectivistic (communal) societies thusly:

> The independent agent is supposed to be adjusted to modern and postmodern information-based societies in which individual performance and competition among individuals are necessary requirements for a successful life. The communal agent is supposed to be adjusted to agrarian subsistence-based communities in which cooperation among individuals pertaining primarily to social roles is crucial for survival. (p. 26)

Different cultural and developmental contexts will create different parenting styles, which, in turn, will create differences in the expressions of attachment or attachment styles.

In a recent cross-cultural study, Keller et al. (2004) observed Costa Rican mothers and infants (representing Latino cultures) and compared them to samples from Africa, India, Northern Europe, and Southern Europe. The authors hypothesized that Costa Ricans' observable parenting systems would contain a mix of the "traditional" elements of Latino heritage and parenting systems influenced by the U.S. media. When compared to other groups, researchers observed that Costa Rican mothers had higher percentages of body contact and body stimulation, lower percentages of object stimulation, and higher percentages of face-to-face contact with infants. When statistically clustered along these parenting systems, Costa Rican parents were grouped with the African and Indian parenting groups. The Northern and Southern European groups were also clustered together. This was clearly contrary to the researchers' hypotheses regarding the "mixed" cultural parenting that they expected in the Costa Rican sample and suggests that "for the understanding of the socialization processes, the content cannot be separated either from behavior or culture. The family environment constitutes the context in which the child adopts, participates, and appropriates the local culture" (pp. 41–42). In this Costa Rican sample, the cluster (coined the "proximal style" for the high percentage of body contact and body stimulation) is consistent with a parenting style that would emphasize the cultural values of interdependence common to Latino, and other collectivist cultures, rather than the United States.

Consistent with the intractability of the cultural impact on parenting, and subsequently attachment, Cote and Bornstein (2003) compared Latin Americans mothers who rated themselves as collectivist and traditional European Americans who rated themselves as individualists. They found that the parental cognitions that affect parenting behaviors were specific to culture and directly related to the child's development in attachment. In addition, they found that there were no cultural differences between South American mothers in the United States and mothers in their native home country (Cote & Bornstein, 2003). They concluded that the key component that was involved was the mental representations of what an ideal parent would be. They found that this representation directed parents' behaviors toward their children (Carlson & Harwood, 2003).

Greenfield et al. (2003) provided additional context regarding the unique elements of Latino development (and subsequent attachment styles) distinguishing them from Western or North American cultures. They discuss how culture affects the development of children's thinking and worldview. Greenfield et al. related how Mayan collectivist cultures express their understanding of knowledge differently than Western societies. They state that "the Tzoil word *na*, meaning 'to know' has a more person-centered meaning than the English word *know*. ... Whereas 'to know' in English always involves the mind, *na* often involves the heart and soul" (p. 472). Closely related to this is the Spanish word *educación*. Although very similar to the English word "education," the translation is not wholly accurate. Rather, *educación* refers to the "inculcation of proper and respectful social behavior ... the connotation is that learning does not suffice to make a person educated" (Greenfield et al., 2003, p. 473). These differences are reflected in the way that Latino parents teach their children to value social interaction and proper behavior. These in turn, affect how children conceptualize the world around them and influence their behavior.

RESEARCH FINDINGS ON ATTACHMENT THEORY AND LATIN CULTURES

In addition to the aforementioned points of similarity across cultures, Schmitt et al. (2004) addressed two additional points that are noteworthy. Specifically, they were the role of stressors on the development of attachment and the unique behavioral expressions of attachment styles, particularly in Latin cultures. These points will be addressed next.

Schmitt et al. (2004) found that cultures where there were higher levels of fearful and dismissing attachment styles also had higher levels of economic hardship and harsh physical environments. In fact, cultures with a higher gross domestic product had higher rates of secure attachment. This led the researchers to conclude: "The sociohistorical forces that presumably cause certain people to exhibit more interdependent or collectivist interpersonal orientations across cultures may similarly impact their basic romantic attachment orientations" (p. 398). In other words, the long-term economic and physical context, which directly impact culture, also seems to impact parenting strategies and attachment. In fact, regardless of exposure to economic or cultural changes, as Keller et al. (2004) speculated in their research with Costa Rican mothers, traditional cultural influences seem to be generational and deep rooted.

It would be an oversimplification to equate good economy and comfortable living with secure attachment. Schmitt et al. (2004) found that in

> nearly all cultures people possess basic cognitive-emotional attitudes that constitute romantic attachment Models of Self and Other. These internal working models likely exist as pancultural constructs, forming independent dimensions that underlie romantic attachment types across cultures. However, the four categories or types of romantic attachment outlined by Griffin and Bartholomew (1994)—secure, dismissing, preoccupied, and fearful—seem not to reside within this two-dimensional space in precisely the same way across all regions of the world. It is unclear why cultures would vary in romantic attachment structure, especially given the strong theoretical rationale for thinking that internal working Models of Self and Other are elemental components of human psychology. (p. 397)

In the South American sample, Schmitt et al. found that the preoccupied and dismissing attachment styles did not align along the two-dimensional space (positive or negative models of self and others) as predicted by attachment theorists. What this means is that although individuals may look preoccupied or dismissing, indicative of insecure attachment and either negative models of self or others, in actuality, they were securely attached. This supports the strong influence that cultures exert on the variability of how secure attachments are expressed. In addition, there are implications for how to treat these individuals clinically.

In an exploratory study Becerra (2007) observed Latina mothers and the effect of their interactions with their children. They found that Latinos express warmth through their actions, rather than through verbal expressions of affection directly to the individual or child. At times, particularly when expressing dissatisfaction, a family member may restrain his or her feelings and withhold affection for long periods of time. Behaviorally this may look like an inconsistent or dismissing attachment style, though the behavior is culturally normative and reflects a secure attachment.

There are a number of treatment issues that counselors face when working with Latino clients. By considering the implications of attachment dynamics within the Latino culture, counselors will be better able to understand and help these clients. We will discuss some of these relevant clinical issues next.

TREATMENT CONSIDERATIONS

Cabassa (2007) reported that the underuse of mental health services appears to be greater among Latino immigrants compared to individuals from other racial and ethnic minority groups. There is very little research on this area, but what does exist reveals negative attitudes toward mental illness like depression and seeking mental health treatment among Latinos. Instead, those individuals who were surveyed believed in self-reliance, keeping talk about emotional problems within the family, feeling shamed when talking to a clinician, and viewing drugs such as antidepressants as addictive (Arredondo, 2005). For clinicians working in the 21st century, this is a pressing need that must be addressed in a comprehensive and culturally sensitive manner.

The key to successful counseling of individuals from Latino cultures is for the counselor to be adaptive and flexible when applying particular counseling models. The relationship between counselor and client takes on added importance with this population, as getting along with others is a key cultural value (*personalismo*) for them. Individuals, and by extension the family, may be viewed negatively in the greater community when social values are transgressed. Knowing the individual's familial, social, and environmental contexts are also important and promote a multicultural orientation to counseling that includes an understanding of the context of the individual (Arredondo, 2005). We will now present a case to illustrate this further.

CASE STUDY

The following case involves individual counseling of a 27-year-old, married Latina woman. Maria,° a young woman in her early 20s, came to the United States from Colombia in the late 1990s. Maria attained a bachelor's degree in business administration from a university in Colombia. However, in the United States, she worked as a clerk at a women's lingerie store as she did not have documentation to obtain legal employment in the business world.

Presenting Concerns

Maria was self-referred to counseling. Her presenting concern was her inability to develop trusting relationships and an inability to remain monogamous while in a romantic relationship. During intake, Maria reported that she lived with her husband who also lived in the United States illegally. However, she began to grow distant from him and eventually succumbed to an extramarital affair that ultimately drove a final blow to the couple's marital relationship. Maria reported she has a history of "flirting" with men and that it is a "game." Throughout the assessment and development of the therapeutic relationship, Maria came to terms with her realization that she did not know how to feel secure in relationships. She denied a history of suicidal, self-mutilating behaviors or drug/alcohol abuse. However, she reported symptoms of extreme emotionality, hypervigilance, anxiety, and eating disturbance. In terms of physical health, Maria reported that she gained 20 pounds in the 10 months prior to initiating counseling.

History

Maria reported she was the only child of a widowed woman from a small town in Colombia. She did not have memories of her father, as he reportedly died when Maria was 2 years old. Through the course of therapy, Maria revealed that she had a history of incest by her maternal grandfather and a maternal uncle. Maria related the sexual abuse began when she was 5 years old and lasted until she was 12 years old. Maria reported that she disclosed the abuse to her mother, who was not supportive of Maria and accused her of lying about her grandfather's and uncle's affection toward her. The sexual abuse ended when Maria and her mother moved from their town and went to live in Bogota. When Maria saw her grandfather again for a family reunion, she was 15 years old and avoided being alone with him for fear that he would start the abuse again. The uncle married and never approached Maria again.

In counseling, Maria reported that she and her mother did not talk about the sexual abuse after Maria's initial disclosure at the age of 5 and her mother's inability to be supportive and protective of Maria. It was Maria's perception that as a widow

---

° To protect client confidentiality, the pseudonym Maria is used during the discussion of the case. In addition, the case is an amalgamation of several individual cases, and no identifying information is included.

in Colombia her mother was financially dependent on her father and was thus emotionally unable to protect Maria from the sexual abuse for fear of the financial repercussions of confronting him and her older brother. As an adult, Maria reported an estranged relationship with her mother, who still lived in Colombia. Maria reported she missed her mother and wished they could have a closer relationship. True to her cultural identity, Maria telephones her mother on a weekly basis and sends her money to support her.

Case Formulation Based on Bowlby's Five Therapeutic Tasks

The current case presents the use of Bowlby's (1988) five therapeutic tasks of a therapist: (a) provision of a secure base; (b) exploring current relationships; (c) exploring of the therapist–client relationship; (d) exploring how the past is alive and active in the present; and (e) enabling the client to recognize various working models of self, others, and meanings. Each of these tasks is focused on utilizing the therapeutic relationship to address the attachment disruptions or inconsistencies that impact current functioning.

A Secure Base   For Maria, the therapeutic relationship resembled the parent–child relationship as she was able to make deep human connections and establish intimacy within a safe, nurturing, and consistent environment where she was totally accepted and felt supported while exploring the impact of childhood trauma on adult behavior. The therapy established the secure base on which Maria could further explore her development and the pain experienced from lacking an appropriate father figure, and having abusive male role models and an emotionally absent mother. The therapist's task, in this case, was to set the tone of verbal and nonverbal attunement and develop an alternate attachment in which to explore and repair the original attachment.

In the present case, the secure base was facilitated by the counselor's speaking Spanish. However, in cases where this is not possible, remaining sensitive to the struggle that Latino clients have with language would also be important. For many Latinos who use Spanish as their primary language, being able to accurately translate their experiences into English can be a constant frustration. Clinicians need to be aware of their clients' effort to communicate bilingually and provide encouragement for the effort. For example, when a client apologizes because her "English isn't so good," an encouraging remark such as "Communicating in a language other than your primary language is not easy, and requires a lot of concentration and ability" can facilitate creating a secure base.

Current Relationships   Within the safety of the therapeutic relationship, Maria began to explore how her use of men and sex was ways to connect to others, but also helped her remain distant from true intimacy. When framed in the cultural context of being close, both proximally and emotionally, with others, Maria realized that when that was violated by her grandfather and uncle, she concluded that the only way to have closeness without being violated or losing control was to be the aggressor. The therapist helped her to recognize the dissonant feelings of pride about her ability to manipulate men and shame for not being able to genuinely connect with someone on an intimate level.

Therapist–Client Relationship   In the safety of the therapeutic relationship, Maria experienced verbal and nonverbal communication regarding the therapist's unconditional acceptance of her as she related feelings of disgust, shame, and blame toward herself as well as toward her mother, spouse, grandfather, uncle, and other males. She was able to experience the therapist's attunement to her expressions and feelings in a similar process to that of the mutual regulation that occurs between parent and child. The fact that the therapist followed Maria's lead in her request to have the counseling sessions in Spanish further enhanced Maria's sense of acceptance and feeling "in sync" with the therapist in the relationship.

Exploring How the Past Is Alive and Active in the Present   During the counseling process, Maria was able to uncover past patterns in current behaviors, finding meaning in those behaviors, and begin to explore other relationships beyond the secure base of the therapeutic alliance. Specifically, she was able to grasp that her negative interactions with others were, in part, re-creations of her anger and disappointment with her mother, grandfather, and uncle. In addition, her fear of intimacy and hypersexuality was a recapitulation of her desire to remain connected and in control at the same time.

Supporting Client Recognition of Various Working Models of Self, Others, and Meanings   Eventually, Maria developed a coherent autobiographical narrative that integrated the trauma and helped her develop a balanced view and sense of self and others, especially her biological family. This helped her enhance her ability to self-regulate and engage in nurturing safe, secure, and comforting relationships in a nonsexual manner. She recognized how her internal negative model of others had been expressed in sexual or interpersonal relationships and was an expression of her internalized anger.

Cultural Treatment Considerations

In addition to the aforementioned considerations, there are several important points for the therapist to consider as it related to Maria's Latina cultural heritage:

- Being mindful and respectful of the linguistic variances of the Spanish language.
- Recognizing the important aspects of Latino culture, including family, religion, and discipline.
- Exploring ways that the sexual abuse was at the heart of her relationship problems with men.
- Examining how her behavior toward others, primarily men, was distrustful and could be possibly a dismissing attachment style and a negative model of others, symptomatic of the insecurity that she was feeling, and patterned after her abuse experiences with uncle and grandfather.

- Addressing her anger toward her mother while simultaneously addressing the ambivalence and the cultural aspect of confronting her mother about not protecting her and denying the abuse.
- Exploring how the sexual abuse affected her feelings about belonging and fitting into the family.
- Promoting opportunities for the development of nonsexual supportive relationships.

Course of Treatment

At Maria's request, all counseling sessions were carried out in Spanish. Sessions were held weekly for 6 months. Maria addressed the distress that she felt because she was not able to have the close and secure relationship with her mother that she desired. She was able to see how her attachment relationship with her mother was influenced by anger for not protecting her from the sexual abuse, and the cultural norm of closeness and admiration of her mother. She was able to see how these were confusing for her because of the anger and loss of security. As a result, this was translated into difficulties in her relationships with men and a feeling of emptiness inside.

At the time of termination, Maria was not able to express her dissatisfaction to her mother, but understood her unwillingness to do so as part of her desire to care for her relationship with her mother. As a result, Maria found a way to "protect" her mother from her traumatic feelings in a way that her mother was not able to protect her from her uncle and grandfather. This felt congruent to Maria, and she understood the need to prevent damage to relationships from the viewpoint of her cultural heritage. In addition, Maria began to explore how she might be able to interact with men without sexualizing the relationship. She understood that she was confusing many cultural elements of outward expressions of warmth and close contact with intimacy, sex, and meeting her attachment needs. However, at termination she was not in a relationship and did not want to become involved in a relationship.

This case highlights how the therapeutic relationship can be enhanced by client–therapist attunement within an attachment framework with a potentially anxious dismissing attachment-style client. Treatment focused on providing Maria a safe and secure relationship from which to explore past trauma while bringing to her attention the different patterns of relationships, reevaluation of the functionality of those patterns, and learning new ways to regulate affect.

CONCLUSION

It is a universal and essential need of a child to develop a secure and healthy attachment style. Although this is a universal human phenomenon, the expression of attachment security is influenced by cultural norms. Consequently, it is important for clinicians from different cultures to understand the impact of these cultural norms (e.g., collectivism, familism, etc.) on secure attachment behaviors.

It is projected by the U.S. Census Bureau (1993, 2007) that Latinos will make up 25% of American citizens by 2050, making them one of the largest ethnic groups the United States. Unique factors, such as immigration and acculturation, as well as common presenting concerns such as depression or anxiety, will be the hallmarks of practice in the 21st century. Understanding child-rearing beliefs and parenting practices, as well as other culturally ensconced practices will be of critical importance for future practitioners as they assess, diagnose, and treat Latino clients. In this chapter, we have presented the most relevant research and clinical data related to Latino cultures and attachment dynamics. However, there is clearly a need for more extensive basic and applied research in this area.

REFERENCES

Ainsworth, M. D., S., Blehar, M. C., Waters, E., & Wall, S. (1978). *Patterns of attachment: A psychological study of the strange situation*. Hillsdale, NJ: Lawrence Erlbaum Associates.

Arredondo, P. (2005). Latinas/Latinos in counseling: A cultural, strengths-based approach: A review of the video. *PsycCritique*, reviewed by Yvette N. Tazeau. American Psychological Association Psychotherapy Videotape Series V, Item no. 4310617.

Arrias, D. F., & Hernández, A. M. (2007). Emerging adulthood in Spanish and Mexican youth: Theories and realities. *Journal of Adolescent Research, 22*, 476–503.

Becerra, P. (2007). *Latina mothers: An exploratory study on their attachment with their children* (Unpublished master's thesis). Smith College School for Social Work, Northampton, MA.

Bowlby, J. (1969). *Attachment and loss: Vol. 1. Attachment*. London: Hogarth Press.

Bowlby, J. (1973). *Attachment and loss: Vol. 2. Separation*. New York: Basic Books.

Bowlby, J. (1988). *A secure base*. New York: Basic Books.

Burchard, E. G., Borrel, L. N., Choudry, S., Naqvi, M., Hui-Ju, T., Rodriguez-Santana, J. R., … Risch, N. (2005). Latino populations: A unique opportunity for the study of race, genetics, and social environment in epidemiological research. *American Journal of Public Health, 95*, 2161–2168.

Cabassa, L. (2007). Latino immigrant men's perceptions of depression and attitudes toward help seeking. *Hispanic Journal of Behavioral Sciences, 29*, 492–509.

Carlson, V. J., & Harwood, R. L. (2003). Attachment, culture, and the caregiving system: The cultural patterning of everyday experiences among Anglo and Puerto Rican mother-infants. *Infant Mental Health Journal, 24*, 53–73.

Carter, R. T., Yeh, C. J., & Mazulla, S. L. (2008). Cultural values and racial identity statuses among Latino students: An exploratory investigation. *Hispanic Journal of Behavioral Sciences, 30*, 5–23.

Cote, L. R., & Bornstein, M. H. (2003). Cultural and parenting cognitions in acculturating cultures. *Journal of Cross-Cultural Psychology, 34*, 323–349.

Falicov, C. J. (1998). Mexican families. In M. McGoldrick, J. Giordano, & J. K. Pearce (Eds.), *Ethnicity and family therapy* (pp. 169–182). New York: Guilford Press.

Fraley, R. C., & Shaver, P. R. (2000). Adult romantic attachment: Theoretical developments, emerging controversies, and unanswered questions. *Review of General Psychology, 4*, 132–154.

Fraley, R. C., & Waller, N. G. (1998). Adult attachment patterns: A test of the typological model. In J. A. Simpson & W. S. Rholes (Eds.), *Attachment theory and close relationships* (pp. 77–114). New York: Guilford Press.

Greenfield, P. M., Keller, H., Fuligni, A., & Maynard, A. (2003). Cultural pathways through universal development. *Annual Review of Psychology, 54*, 461–490.

Griffin, D. W., & Bartholomew, K. (1994). Models of self and other: Fundamental dimensions underlying measures of adult attachment. *Journal of Personality and Social Psychology, 67*, 430-445.

Keller, H., Lohaus, A., Kuensemueller, P., Abels, M., Yovsi, R., Voelker, S., … Mohite, P. (2004). The bio-culture of parenting: Evidence from five cultural communities. *Parenting, Science and Practice, 4*, 25–50.

Mealy, M., Stephan, W. G., & Abalakina-Paap, M. (2006). Reverence for mothers in Ecuadorian & Euro-American culture. *Journal of Cross-Cultural Psychology, 37*, 465–484.

Miranda, A. O., Bilot, J. M., Peluso P. R., Berman, K., & Van Meek, L. (2006). Latino families: The relevance of the connection among acculturation, family dynamics, and health for family counseling research and practice. *The Family Journal: Counseling and Therapy for Couples and Families, 14*, 268–273.

Peluso, P. R., Peluso, J. P., Buckner, J. P., Kern, R. M., & Curlette, W. L. (2009). Measuring lifestyle and attachment: An empirical investigation linking individual psychology and attachment theory. *Journal of Counseling and Development, 87*(4), 394–403.

Peluso, P. R., Peluso, J. P., White, J. F., & Kern, R. M. (2004). A comparison of attachment theory and individual psychology: A review of the literature. *Journal of Counseling and Development, 82*, 139–145.

Santiago-Rivera, A. L., Arredondo, P., & Gallardo-Cooper, M. (2002). *Counseling Latinos and la familia: A practical guide.* Thousand Oaks, CA: Sage.

Schmitt, D. P., Alcalay, L., Allensworth, M. Allik, J., Alut, L., Austers, I., … Zupanèiè, A. (2004). Patterns and universals of adult romantic attachment across 62 cultural regions: Are models of self and of other pancultural constructs? *Journal of Cross-Cultural Psychology, 35*, 367–402.

Sroufe, L. A. (1988). The role of infant-caregiver attachment in development. In J. Belsky & T. Nezworski (Eds.), *Clinical implications of attachment* (pp. 18–38). Hillsdale, NJ: Lawrence Erlbaum Associates.

U. S. Census Bureau. (1993). *Introduction to census data.* Washington, DC: Author.

U. S. Census Bureau. (2007). *The American community—Hispanics: 2004-2006.* Washington, DC: Author.

Waldinger, R. (2007). *Between here and there: How attached are Latino immigrants to their native country?* Retrieved February 4, 2009, from http://www.pewhispanic.org/reports/report.php?ReportID=80

18

Contextual Thinking in Attachment
Implications for Clinical Assessment and Interventions in Cultural Contexts

LIN SHI

CONTENTS

*M*any societies have legends about successful individuals who originate from humble but loving environments, as well as stories about individuals who fail despite having been born in circumstances of material abundance but lacking love. These legends reflect the belief in emotional bonds. Deep emotional bonds between children and their parental figures, as well as between adults, are universally valued (Grossmann, Grossmann, & Keppler, 2005; Rothbaum, & Morelli, 2005; van IJzendoorn, Bakermans-Kranenburg, &

Sagi-Schwartz, 2006) as depicted by attachment theory and adult attachment research. While attachment theory highlights the common theme across cultures and generations, variations should and do exist in making and maintaining bonds to achieve desired consequences (Rothbaum, Weisz, Pott, Miyake, & Morelli, 2000; Weisner, 2005). Put differently, there can be different, albeit slightly different, versions of secure attachments and corresponding ways of achieving them. In the traditional Chinese family, for example, the model of a "strict (and distant) father and a loving (and enmeshed) mother" was regarded as ideal in raising competent children. Whereas in the West, the ideal is for children to grow up with two equally sensitive and responsive parents (Belsky, 1999; Bowlby, 1988). Existing variations inevitably lead to acknowledgment of cultural influences on attachment practices (Carlson & Harwood, 2003; Doherty, Hatfield, Thompson, & Choo, 1994; Rothbaum & Morelli, 2005) when applying principles of attachment theory to clinical practice. This acknowledgment demands that attachment phenomena be examined within the relevant cultural context.

Fully acknowledging universality of attachment, in this chapter I will analyze and explore cultural variations of secure attachment, the desired outcomes, and ways to achieve security, on which a clinical assessment incorporating cultural consideration will be introduced and illustrated.

UNIT OF ANALYSIS IN CULTURAL CONTEXT: DYAD AND BEYOND

The focus of attachment theory, since its origin, has been the dyad (Byng-Hall, 1999). A paradigm shift from a narrow focus on individuals to the attachment theory perspective has allowed us to witness how the interaction within the dyad influences, if not determines, the outcome of attachment formation and outcome. A good attachment interaction is a well-choreographed dance between the mother and the child (West & Sheldon-Keller, 1994) that satisfies both, but more important, plants seeds to foster the growth of an autonomous individual. Three basic infant attachment styles, one secure and two insecure, were identified as being closely related to the mother's sensitivity and consistency in her responses to the infant's needs (Ainsworth, Blehar, Waters, & Wall, 1978; Main, 1991). Mothers who are sensitive to signals for physical and emotional needs and are consistent in responding tend to raise securely attached children. Mothers who are insensitive, intrusive, and inconsistent when interacting with their children are likely to raise insecurely attached children, being avoidant or anxious/ambivalent with attachment (Main, 1991).

The dyadic focus was accepted widely, with appreciation, in the West. The dyadic conceptualization innately matches the culture's gravitation toward the nuclear family constellation. The most important initial influence on the infant is a dyad and most likely the mother–infant dyad. The analysis of the dyad in the West has added a unique dimension to understanding relationship dynamics that traditional individual-based psychotherapy failed to provide. However, the sole focus on the dyad may fall short for the East, as well as for other subcultural groups that may include ethnic minorities, gay/lesbian families, and other within-culture varia-tions common to the West where the dyad may not be the norm. For example, it is a common practice in certain cultures for the grandparents to move in, or closer to, the nuclear family to actively participate in caregiving as additional and sometimes even primary parental figures. Furthermore, in Eastern cultures as well as in some ethnic minority groups in the West, the boundary between a nuclear family and an extended family is defined differently or completely absent, as the definition of family is often stretched to include extended families. An infant son is viewed, not as just the son of his parents, but also as a grandson in a role equally significant, if not more significant, than that of the son.

As a result, two culturally defined variations are present in the East when compared to the traditional Western practice. First, interactions with multiple caregivers across two generations lead to multiple attachment figures and possibly different attachment styles toward them. Second, the attachment practice adopted by the mother does not only reflect her preference and history, but also the values and traditions from the extended family passed down through generations, in the form of advice, suggestions, or even direct interventions (as they are no less impor-tant than parents). A social consequence of such practice is that the infant learns to navigate a more complex, interpersonal web early in life. The adoption of this attachment exposure and experience is consistent with the desired socialization outcome in Eastern and other non-Western cultural contexts, to create an interde-pendent social being with great concern for group harmony.

ATTACHMENT PRACTICE AND CONSEQUENCE IN CULTURAL CONTEXT

Attachment theory has brought awareness of and appreciation for a universal prac-tice in making and maintaining emotional bonds. Now the field calls for the study of cultural variation (Waters & Cummings, 2000) to gain a more comprehensive understanding of the role and function of attachment in human development. Caretakers provide physical and emotional needs in order for an infant to sur-vive. While the most basic biological needs are nonnegotiable conditions for the survival of all human infants, include being fed, clothed, and sheltered, emotional needs and the extent to which they should be met, tend to be influenced by culture (Carlson & Harwood, 2003). This brings out the issue of how secure attachment is defined and promoted in various cultural contexts.

The internal working model of secure attachment as defined in the West con-tains three elements: the worthiness of self; the availability of attachment figures; and, based on the above, the utilization of attachment figures as a secure base to explore the unfamiliar (Bowlby, 1980). An infant is viewed as a vulnerable, yet independent being who is capable of determining if help is needed and capable of giving signals to request help. The goal of successful upbringing is to nurture and maximize the development of independence that will help shape the child into a highly autonomous and independent adult. It is easy to note that attachment theory matches Western society's expectations.

Whereas the goal of secure attachment in the West is autonomy, the goal is interdependence in the East (Rothbaum et al., 2000). Compared to the good attachment practice in the West, where parents stay sensitive to the infant's signals for needs, a good mother in the East tries to anticipate and provide the needs before the child gives signals (van IJzendoorn & Sagi, 1999). For example, in many Eastern cultures an infant is accompanied by an adult day and night as it is believed that the infant may be severely distressed seeing no protective adults upon awakening. A common practice in the West is to arrange for infants to sleep in their own room, or at least in their own bed, as a necessary step toward autonomy. For another example, when a toddler stumbles and falls to the ground and starts to cry for help, a typical response observed in the East is for the adult to rush to pick up the toddler and provide immediate comfort, whereas a common response in the West is to encourage the toddler to get up and give praises for such an effort. The chosen response reflects a deeply rooted cultural belief in relationships that the parents try to instill in their children. It shapes the care-seeking–caregiving interaction and defines roles and expectations for the child entering adulthood. The typical practice in the East conveys to the infant that it is the constant concern of its caregivers and that the essence of close interpersonal relationships involves proactive mutual consideration and caretaking. Being able to maintain a harmonious relationship, not autonomy, is the ultimate competence for which Eastern caregivers strive.

Enmeshment is regarded as dysfunctional, not only in attachment theory, but also in Minuchin's structural family therapy (Minuchin & Fishman, 1981) and Bowen's family systems theory (Kerr & Bowen, 1988). When comparing and judging Eastern attachment styles with those of the West, there are indications that attachment practices in the East promote less secure attachment styles among infants, as Eastern caregivers seem overprotective or even intrusive by Western standards. These infants in the East are more likely to be classified as anxious/ambivalent in the Strange Situation Procedure (Rothhaum et al., 2000), and the family relationships are perceived as enmeshed. However, in the East, secure attachments may be evidenced by maintaining proximity to the caregiver in the Strange Situation. When taking the goal of the attachment practice into consideration, that is, to shape the child into an interdependent social being, the relationship pattern is functional and productive. Therefore, the judging criterion is whether emotional needs, defined and determined by a particular culture, are satisfied.

Due to varied attachment practices and desired outcomes, adults in distinctively different cultures may value varied competence and relational models. This may mean that a competent individual in one culture may not feel or be considered as competent, and a desirable relational model may not be the most functional in another. In the Western context a competent individual is assertive and autonomous, whereas in the East such a person may be regarded as immature and not well raised (Rothbaum et al., 2000). An ideal marital relationship in the West is relatively symmetrical with each partner providing and receiving love (Shaver, Hazan, & Bradshaw, 1988), but a preferred middle-class marital relationship in Japan is asymmetrical with the wife providing physical and emotional care to the husband (Onishi & Gjerde, 2002). The existence of such differences reflects and validates the cultural values in which they reside.

ONE MORE DIMENSION: EVOLVING CULTURE

Cultures, as all things in an open system (Whitchurch & Constantine, 1993), are not static but evolving. Globalization has brought so far the greatest interchanges between cultures and set the stage for people to examine and modify their own cultural practices. A developing economy inevitably brings necessary modifications to cultural beliefs and practices. In developing countries in the East more young couples choose or are forced into living in a separate household from their parents, which facilitates the growth of the autonomy of nuclear families. Exposure to urban lifestyles and Western influences has brought silent changes to marital relationships and parenting practices. Western societies are also increasingly open to Eastern philosophies. During times of such changes, it is all the more important to put attachment practice into the cultural, social, and economic context.

CONTEXTUAL THINKING IN ASSESSMENT AND INTERVENTION

Attachment theory addresses the most fundamental emotional experiences affecting humans from "the cradle to grave" (Bowlby, 1977). Every people and culture has formed its own unique way, in the geographic environment and historical context, of loving and protecting the young, ways that have been considered beneficial to the well-being and future of the community and to the survival of the culture. Each version of attachment practice has been effective in its own way in reaching its goal or it would not have survived (Grossmann et al., 2005). The implication of the richness of, and the distinction between, attachment practices is twofold. The diversity of attachment practice enriches and furthers attachment theory and research. The importance of this knowledge gives us reasons to promote diversity and to remain nonjudgmental of non-Western practices. On the other hand, in today's rapidly changing society, existing attachment practices are inevitably challenged to various degrees. Different groups, or even different family members, may have different reactions and responses to new input, thus bringing forward disagreements and even conflicts between parents and children and/or between parental figures (Minuchin, 2002). From this angle, attachment practice must go through some forms of negotiation, or adjustment, to serve its purpose.

Contextual thinking in an attachment framework is a practice of placing attachment phenomenon into the cultural conditions in which it occurs. It does not equate to indiscriminately endorsing any practice in the name of cultural diversity. Either extreme enmeshment or disengagement eventually leads to pathology (Kerr & Bowen, 1988; Minuchin & Fishman, 1981; Rothbaum, Rosen, Ujiie, & Uchida, 2002). Variations within a reasonable limit, however, enrich the human heritage.

Attachment Assessment Within Cultural Contexts

The central premises of clinical applications of attachment theory are the provisions of a safe haven and of a secure base for the client (Bowlby, 1988; Byng-Hall, 1999); therefore, it is essential to understand cultural norms surrounding close relationships, giving and receiving love, expectations of each other, and rules of reciprocity. In addition, one must bear in mind that an attachment relationship model that has been an excellent fit in one cultural condition or developmental stage, may not work as effectively in another, unless necessary adjustments are applied. To determine if the attachment system functions adequately, the therapist needs to listen to the client and the family to gather attachment history and desired attachment outcomes.

Based on this analysis, an attachment assessment that includes four domains is presented next. The four domains are consistent with the spirit of Bowlby's five therapeutic tasks (1988), but new dimensions are added to emphasize the consideration of cultural context and the inclusion of triad analysis. These four domains are not steps or procedures to be followed strictly in a specific order; rather, they serve as guidelines for understanding each individual's unique attachment experience in a complex emotional world that may or may not resemble what the therapist is comfortable or familiar with.

Domain 1   The therapist should obtain knowledge about the culture(s) to which the client was exposed while growing up and after entering adulthood. The cultures include not only the macrocultures, such as the overarching Chinese culture, but also microcultures, such as a regional culture, which stands as a unique version of the macroculture. Regional cultures can play an unusually significant role in certain countries and in rural or even suburban areas. Also included in the consideration is the within-group variation in the same cultural group. For example, although living in the same country during the current era, couples in Shanghai, the largest city in China, are known for their equality, especially for males' active participation in household chores and child rearing, whereas men in inland areas would consider such participation a disgrace. The difference can affect the child's attachment expectations and experiences directly or indirectly as well as marital interaction and satisfaction. Finally, in most open societies where new developments are constantly presented, established traditions and ideas including subtle cultural assumptions can be challenged and even violated. This either leads to periods of confusion, frustration, and anger, or difficult and at times painful adjustments in behavior.

The therapist must understand how multiple layers of cultures influence particular attachment practice and experiences as well as the evolving nature of culture. One way to avoid making stereotypical inferences regarding attachment experiences and expectations is to take the stance of not knowing (Anderson & Goolishian, 1988). While being aware of one's own cultural assumptions and beliefs, the therapist must be willing to explore and understand others' beliefs and practices in full cultural contexts. Kalyanpur and Harry (1997) refer to this ability as cultural reciprocity. The goal of this domain of the assessment, figuratively speaking, is to understand a particular school of fish and the water in which they live. Sample questions that a therapist might ask include the following:

1. I understand you grew up in _____ country within _____ culture. I learned over the years through my reading of your culture and my inter- action with people from your culture that the following are your basic cultural beliefs. … Did I begin to get an accurate idea of your culture?
2. I see that you grew up in this particular region. How culturally unique is your region compared to the rest of the country, and what are the differ- ences in terms of maintaining close relationships?
3. Was your experience of being raised similar or different from those of your peers? What historical factors or family dynamics contributed to the difference?
4. Was there a significant or gradual change in the environment in which you grew up? What was the change and how do you think it affected the way you were parented?

The case involving a female client, Mrs. Yang, who entered therapy for the treatment of her depressive symptoms illustrates Domain 1. Born and raised in mainland China, Mrs. Yang immigrated to the United States in her mid-20s as a graduate student. She reported that she had been "blindly positive" about her own upbringing until she observed how loving American parents could be toward their children. Being in a strained marital relationship had made her feel even more strongly that the seeds of unhappiness were planted by her emotionally unexpres- sive parents while she was young. When inquired about how love was typically expressed in China when she was growing up, she was able to see that her parents followed the cultural norm allowed in the particular political environment, the provision of food and clothes to their best abilities. She even recalled for the first time that her mother gave her a quick kiss when they were alone and realized how much love her mother must have felt toward her to be so openly affectionate. Coming to realize that she had been loved by her parents in a culturally appropri- ate, despite a less ideal way by her current standards, was a relief and liberation. She also realized that she had never been openly affectionate toward her parents and decided that when visiting them next time she would tell them how much she appreciates the hardship they had to go through to raise her and that she loves them.

Domain 2   The therapist should invite the client to share if he or she felt loved while growing up and ask for specific examples. It is important to inquire how attachment figures expressed their love toward the client and the channel through which the client perceived the love. The therapist should explore what the client would do when he or she was in need of the attachment figure(s) emotionally, and what the differences were between the expected and actual responses. The Adult Attachment Interview (AAI; George, Kaplan, & Main, 1996) may be used as a reference for appropriate questions. Sample questions that a therapist might ask include the following:

1. Was your childhood a happy one? What made it happy or unhappy or neutral?
2. I understand in your culture the word "love" may not be used frequently, or at all, but how did your parental figures/parents expressed their love toward you while you were growing up? Could you give a few specific incidents?
3. Did you feel loved or special while growing up? Could you share with me specific times when you felt that way? How often did you feel that way?
4. What would happen when you were in need of your parental figures emotionally and/or physically (i.e., you were emotionally upset, you got hurt)? Did you normally receive what you needed from them? What would you do if you did not receive what you expected?

Domain 2 is illustrated by the case of Mr. and Mrs. Smith, a Caucasian couple. They came in for couple therapy under the insistence of Mrs. Smith who had been increasingly unhappy with her husband's emotional unavailability. Mr. Smith argued that it was only due to his temporary work demand and suggested that his wife was inconsiderate of his situation and was being too needy. When inquired about his childhood attachment experiences, he said with an unquestionable tone that his mother was very loving toward him but he was unable to provide any specific examples to support his claim. He blamed stress for his failure to recall loving interactions with his mother and insisted that he knew his mother was supportive of him. When inquired about what he would do when he was emotionally upset, he replied that he would solve the problem by himself, which his mother had successfully trained him to do. However, when further inquired about whether his mother would notice his emotional ups and downs, he became visibly upset with the therapist and said that he would appreciate having no more questions about his childhood because it had nothing to do with his current marital relationship. The therapist decided that reevaluating and reprocessing his childhood emotional needs should precede the resolution of the presenting complaint.

Domain 3   The therapist should assess and build insight in attachment relationships and interactions. A set of therapeutic questions leading the client or the family to reevaluate attachment experiences and expectations can be utilized to assist the process. Sample questions that a therapist might ask include the following:

1. What did you before as well as currently consider to be good attachment practices?
2. What should be an ideal relationship between a child and an attachment figure?
3. What do you expect your child or spouse to perceive from his or her attachment interactions with you?

The case of Mr. Yamaguchi, an immigrant from Japan to the United States, illustrates Domain 3. Mr. Yamaguchi credited his success to his parents' effective discipline when he was a boy. He was confident that the same parenting against which his 14-year-old son rebelled would eventually produce the same positive results he had experienced. The therapist led Mr. Yamaguchi to revisit and analyze his own attachment interactions with his parents in the socioeconomic context in which he grew up and compared them to the context his son was in. Through the exploration Mr. Yamaguchi realized that his son might need more and varied attention than he had been providing and concluded that he would maintain the core values he had held dearly but add new dimensions in his parenting to meet his son's emotional needs.

Domain 4   While examining the attachment dynamic, the therapist needs to expand the unit of analysis to include various triads. Integrating the analysis with systems theory seems to be a solution to the limitations of the dyad focus as systems theory innately focuses on the triad and its effect on current functioning (see Rothbaum et al., 2002, for more details). Integrating an analysis of current interaction dynamics with a profound understanding of the internal driving force pushing family members into the existing interaction pattern presents a more comprehensive clinical conceptualization. The therapist should ask the client who served as attachment figures while he or she was growing up and the characteristics of the relationships with and between the attachment figures. When young children experience emotional and behavioral difficulties it is important to explore the impact of current relationship dynamics on their adjustment. Sample questions that a therapist might ask include:

1. Who played the important roles in raising you? How was your life arranged between these adults?
2. How did the adults who participated in raising you get along? Was one particular person's opinion more significant than those of the others'? What was it like for you to interact with multiple parental figures?
3. Did you receive different values/ideas/relationship models from different parental figures? Did you and do you feel that different input from them made it harder for you to form your own identity? Have you been able to integrate them? What was the process like?
4. What messages do you suspect that your young child has been receiving from multiple parental figures in terms of emotional availability? What important messages do you wish your child to receive consistently from the parental figures?

The case of Miss Lopez, a client in her early 20s, illustrates Domain 4. Miss Lopez sought individual therapy because she had been distressed by her relationship with her father who she felt had been critical and distant. After a few individual sessions the therapist invited her parents to a family session to conjointly explore her early attachment experience and its influence on her as well as on her parents. Miss Lopez was raised with three parental figures. She interacted almost on a daily basis with her biological parents and her maternal grandmother who moved into their neighborhood soon after her birth. Miss Lopez's father came from a lower socioeconomic family and the grandmother openly criticized his "lack of class." Although frequently expressing her affection for Miss Lopez, the grandmother was also overly critical of her thinking and behavior, trying to make sure that she would not disgrace the "good family genes" from her side. The mother would often refuse to be triangulated by her mother against her husband, but she did not openly support her husband either to avoid family disputes. Caught between three parental figures, Miss Lopez experienced her grandmother's love as conditioned upon her compliance with her strong will, and her parents love as inconsistent and unreliable. She resented her father's withdrawal and regarded his inability to protect her from grandmother's intrusiveness as proof of lack of love. Consequently, she failed to develop a deep trust in her attachment figures' emotional availability and support in times of need. After her grandmother passed away, she withdrew further from her father yet was unable to resolve her disappointment in him, thus frequently running into conflictual interactions with him. After leading the family through a thorough exploration of the triads in which the relational dynamics were formed and maintained, the therapist was able to help Miss Lopez express her emotional needs to her parents without fear of rejection.

THERAPIST AS A SECURE BASE: A BACKGROUND CONCEPT

The therapist also utilizes the assessment process to build insight and expand the territory of a client, serving as a secure base (Byng-Hall, 1999). For example, in couples therapy, no two spouses will have the exact attachment experiences that shape expectations of each other, which, when coupled with challenges and stresses, is likely to induce disputes about meeting one another's needs. Reflections on respective attachment experiences and feelings, facilitated by the therapist, can help a couple build empathy for each other (Shi, 2006) and reach a common ground regarding giving and receiving love, further strengthening their attachment. Thus, the couple establishes a new secure base for each other.

In individual therapy, a common challenge is to define one's identity (Rogers, 1961) when surroundings change. For example, if one who was raised to be an interdependent person moves to an individualist society, where maintaining harmony in a group is seldom the primary concern, one has to determine, first, whether an adjustment is called for and justified; and second, whether the adjustment is a betrayal to the native or original culture (Shi & Wang, 2008). One then has to relearn how to relate to others and how to navigate the interpersonal web in a new cultural context. This process involves examining one's past life and relevant coping skills and then looking into the uncertain future to determine the changes needed. This process can expand one's sense of identity, resulting in a stronger and wiser self. There are many attachment-theory-informed interventions (i.e., Bowlby's five therapeutic tasks, 1988) that a competent therapist can offer a client for such an exploration.

WORKING WITH IMMIGRANT FAMILIES IN THE UNITED STATES: ANALYSIS AND RECOMMENDATIONS

More immigrant families in the United States are seeking therapeutic help to assist them through various challenges. These families are not only faced with economic and employment hardships, but also confusions and frustrations of raising their children in an environment with different rules and values. How to help immigrant children whose attachment to their parents can be severely challenged or compromised is a great task that no mental health professional should overlook. For this reason the following culture-informed clinical analysis and recommendations are presented to illustrate how to conceptualize and intervene in attachment issues within cultural contexts.

Attachment Experiences in Cultural Contexts: A Contextual Analysis

Love takes a central place in children's development. In Western, especially American, culture parents express their love for their children by openly displaying affection. Parents speak positively to and about them, initiate and exchange physical contact such as kisses and hugs, and regard them as independent individuals. Children are encouraged to be assertive, and they are made to feel that their personal feelings and opinions matter. In other cultures, including Asian cultures and subcultures in the West, love may be displayed mainly through concerns and plans for the specific goal-oriented future of the child. Love is not expressed overtly and emotions are minimized if discussed at all. Children are taught to regard themselves as members within complicated extended family systems and the community. Daily efforts are made to mold children into a cooperative element of a harmonious society. Any attempt to think only of themselves is considered selfish. Parents seldom praise their children for fear of spoiling them: expressing comments such as "They may end up feeling they are bigger than they really are if I praise them for every little achievement." Instead, parents painstakingly point out areas in which the children need to grow. Very rarely do they give high praise to their children, even if they are truly deserving of it. When parents talk to others about their children, they make considerable effort not to give the impression of bragging about their children, for fear of disturbing the existing harmonious balance.

In addition, perceptions and interpretations of attachment interactions are culturally defined. For example, within certain cultural groups in the East, parental concern for their children's success results in the parents frequently pointing out areas where they need to improve. These parental efforts are often interpreted as being critical, intrusive, and indicating a lack of respect for the child's autonomy. This may be perceived as profound love in another culture. It is an absence of demand for betterment, on the contrary, that may be interpreted by the child as the withdrawal of love. A change of environment can make cultural subtleties like this one appear ambiguous, even though it would appear reasonable in the original native context.

Parents who immigrate to a new culture experience abrupt and major changes in every aspect of life. In addition to meeting the challenges of making a living in a society with different game rules, they experience confusion in how to be loving parents. What were common and sound parenting practices in their native land may become somewhat unpopular or questionable in the new world. It is expected that when traditions clash, some parents try to look for strength and wisdom from their centuries-old parenting practices. Meanwhile, immigrant children go through a confusing stage trying to understand what constitutes love. With less of a language barrier and easy access to peer influence these children have discovered the existence of new patterns of parent–child relationships where children are given considerable autonomy and their milestones are celebrated with open displays of affection. Comparisons children make between themselves and their new peers cause them to feel sad and inferior, and they are stuck with the conviction that their parents' behavior is old-fashioned and disrespectful. They may take the old style of parenting as evidence that their parents are not as loving as they could be. The pull between different cultures deteriorates the parent–child bonding and communication. The safe haven and secure base are severely compromised. Leaving other attachment figures, such as grandparents behind, also intensifies the sense of loss felt by a child.

Recommendations for Clinical Intervention

To free family members from this emotional lockup, the therapist, first, should facilitate productive communication by helping the child express the emotional needs that may have developed in the new cultural environment. The therapist should focus on struggles the child is going through and what emotional support is desired, rather than focusing on handling specific demands, such as suggestions that parents buy material things for their children to show their love.

Second, parents are an important element in the attachment process, and the therapist needs to help them make necessary adjustments. Often when parents are struggling themselves, they become less available to their child, which may cause the child to perceive them as less loving. Sometimes there is an unfortunate role reversal due to the language barrier the parents face, and they might rely on the child to take care of many aspects of family functioning, and subsequently restrict them from enjoying a normal life. To respond to this, it is recommended that the therapist try to learn how parenting is typically practiced in the home country. It is also helpful to discuss how love was typically expressed in the family before their immigration to the United States and what the parents' attachment experiences were (Liddle & Schwartz, 2002). Having such discussions will enable the parents to be more appreciative of their children's emotional struggles and to be more aware of their emotional needs.

Third, the attachment dance between the parents and the child can be "off" while both are busy adapting to the new environment. In the process of integrating into a new society, children tend to be a few steps ahead of their parents. They may have incorporated new elements into their definition of love and hope to modify the attachment dance, figuratively speaking, from a waltz to a quick step. The therapist's role is essential in tuning the attachment dance. Children should be encouraged to share their experiences in the new environment with the parents, and the parents should be coached to explore new ways of meeting their children's emotional needs. For example, "you are doing okay" may be the highest praise given to a child in the home country and its meaning is well understood in that context. Yet having lived in the United States and hearing "you are doing great!" so many times, the child may start feeling a lack of warm encouragement from the parents. In this case, the parents can be more generous in their compliments than their culture normally allows, or they can keep the old expressions but elaborate on how the child is "doing okay."

Finally, for parents there is a danger in completely abandoning the old way of relating when pressured to prove their love to the child. This may lead the child to question or deny previous attachment experiences with his or her parents, resulting in more confusion during his or her emotional exploration. It is recommended that therapists help parents maintain the core of their own established methods for emotional connection and help them to learn how to add more elements when necessary.

CONCLUDING REMARKS

Attachment theory focuses on the dyad. The well-being of the infant is dependent upon the physical and emotional availability of the surrounding parental figures. The parental figures' well-being and their ability to be available to the infant, without question, depend on the support and understanding received from the extended family, the community, and ultimately the established cultural norm. It is fair to say that attachment theory infers contextual thinking. This chapter promotes the inclusion of triads when examining attachment-related clinical issues. It also emphasizes an evaluation of attachment and its consequences within cultural contexts. Given the current speed with which we are presented new developments in technology and the social realms, parts of old norms will be challenged and new norms will be introduced and tested. Examining the adequacy or goodness of attachment practices can only occur in the context in which they occur. Otherwise, we fall into the trap of making value judgments.

The exploration application of attachment theory in cultural contexts helps demonstrate that there are similarities to share and uniqueness to offer. Regardless of race, gender, or religious and cultural backgrounds, humans across the globe believe that emotional bonds are essential. Humans want and need to be loved, cared for, comforted, talked with, listened to, touched, and embraced. Humans also think highly of establishing and maintaining meaningful relationships with others, whether they are parents, romantic partners, siblings, friends, or counselors. Humans as a collective group have come up with many ways to establish and maintain emotional bonds, and it is comforting to realize that humans are capable of more than one means of creating quality connections. Most important in this rapidly changing world, individuals from all ethnic groups should be proud knowing they have the ability to adapt to the most fundamental emotional experiences that are essential to every nation and people.

REFERENCES

Ainsworth, M. D. S., Blehar, M. C., Waters, E., & Wall, S. (1978). *Patterns of attachment: A psychological study of the strange situation.* Hillsdale, NJ: Lawrence Erlbaum Associates.

Anderson, H., & Goolishian, H. (1988). Human systems as linguistic systems: Preliminary and evolving ideas about the implications for clinical theory. *Family Process, 27,* 371–394.

Belsky, J. (1999). Interactional and contextual determinants of attachment security. In J. Cassidy & P. R. Shaver (Eds.), *Handbook of attachment: Theory, research, and clinical applications* (pp. 249–264). New York: Guilford Press.

Bowlby, J. (1977). The making and breaking of affectional bonds. *British Journal of Psychiatry, 130,* 201–210, 421–431.

Bowlby, J. (1980). *Attachment and loss: Vol. 3. Loss.* New York: Basic Books.

Bowlby, J. (1988). *A secure base: Parent-child attachment and healthy human development.* Routledge: London.

Byng-Hall, J. (1999). Family and couple therapy: Toward greater security. In J. Cassidy & P. R. Shaver (Eds.), *Handbook of attachment: Theory, research, and clinical applications* (pp. 625–645). New York: Guilford Press.

Carlson, V., & Harwood, R. (2003). Alternate pathways to competence: Culture and early attachment relationships. In S. M. Johnson & V. E. Whiffen (Eds.), *Attachment process in couple and family therapy.* New York: Guilford Press.

Doherty, W., Hatfield, E., Thompson, K., & Choo, P. (1994). Cultural and ethnic influences on love and attachment. *Personal Relationships, 1,* 391–398.

George, C., Kaplan, N., & Main, M. (1996). *The adult attachment interview.* Unpublished manuscript, Department of Psychology, University of California at Berkeley.

Grossmann, K. E., Grossmann, K., & Keppler, A. (2005). Universal and culture-specific aspects of human behavior: The case of attachment. In W. Friedlmeier, P. Chakkarath, & B. Schwarz (Eds.), *Culture and human development: The importance of cross-cultural research for the social sciences* (pp. 75–98). New York: Psychology Press.

Kalyanpur, M., & Harry, B. (1997). A posture of reciprocity: A practical approach to collaboration between professionals and parents of culturally diverse backgrounds. *Journal of Child and Family Studies, 6,* 485–509.

Kerr, M. E., & Bowen, M. (1988). *Family evaluation: An approach based on Bowen theory.* New York: W. W. Norton & Company.

Liddle, H., & Schwartz, S. (2002). Attachment and family therapy: Clinical utility of adolescent-family attachment research. *Family Process, 41,* 455–476.

Main, M. (1991). Metacognitive knowledge, metacognitive monitoring, and singular (coherent) vs. multiple (incoherent) model of attachment: Findings and directions for future research. In C. M. Parkes, J. Stevenson-Hinde, & P. Marris (Eds.), *Attachment across the life cycle* (pp. 127–159). Routledge: London.

Minuchin, P. (2002). Cross-cultural perspectives: Implications for attachment theory and family therapy. *Family Process, 41,* 546–550.

Minuchin, S., & Fishman, H. C. (1981). *Family therapy techniques.* Boston: Harvard University Press.

Onishi, M., & Gjerde, P. (2002). Attachment strategies in Japanese urban middle-class couples: A cultural theme analysis of asymmetry in marital relationships. *Personal Relationships, 9,* 435–455.

Rogers, C. R. (1961). *On becoming a person.* Boston: Houghton Mifflin.

Rothbaum, F., & Morelli, G. (2005). Attachment and culture: Bridging relativism and universalism. In W. Friedlmeier, P. Chakkarath, & B. Schwarz (Eds.), *Culture and human development: The importance of cross-cultural research for the social sciences* (pp. 92–113). New York: Psychology Press.

Rothbaum, F., Rosen, K., Ujiie, T., & Uchida, N. (2002). Family systems theory, attachment theory, and culture. *Family Process, 41*, 328–350.

Rothbaum, F., Weisz, J., Pott, M., Miyake, K., & Morelli, G. (2000). Attachment and culture: Security in the United States and Japan. *American Psychologist, 55*, 1093–1104.

Shaver, P., Hazan, C., & Bradshaw, D. (1988). Love as attachment: The integration of three behavioral systems. In R. J. Sternberg & M. L. Barnes (Eds.), *The psychology of love* (pp. 68–99). New Haven, CT: Yale University Press.

Shi, L. (2006). Promoting empathy in couple therapy using the one-way mirror. *Journal of Family Psychotherapy, 17*(3/4), 175–180.

Shi, L., & Wang, L. (2008). A multi-level contextual model for couples from mainland China. In M. Rastogi & V. Thomas (Eds.), *Couple therapy with ethnic minorities*. Thousand Oaks, CA: Sage.

van IJzendoorn, M., Bakermans-Kranenburg, M., & Sagi-Schwartz, A. (2006). Attachment across diverse sociocultural contexts: The limits of universality. In K. Rubin & O. B. Chung (Eds.), *Parenting beliefs, behaviors, and parent-child relations: A cross-cultural perspective* (pp. 107–142). New York: Psychology Press.

van IJzendoorn, M. H., & Sagi, A. (1999). Cross-cultural patters of attachment: Universal and contextual dimensions. In J. Cassidy & P. R. Shaver (Eds.), *Handbook of attachment: Theory, research, and clinical applications* (pp. 713–734). New York: Guilford Press.

Waters, E., & Cummings, E. M. (2000). A secure base from which to explore the environment. *Child Development, 71*, 164–172.

Weisner, T. (2005). Attachment as a cultural and ecological problem with pluralistic solutions. *Human Development, 48*, 89–94.

West, M. L., & Sheldon-Keller, A. E. (1994). *Patterns of relating: An adult attachment perspective*. New York: Guilford Press.

Whitchurch, G., & Constantine, L. (1993). Systems theory. In P. Boss, W. J. Doherty, R. LaRossa, W. R. Schumm, & S. K. Steinmetz (Eds.), *Sourcebook of family theories and methods: A contextual approach* (325–352). New York: Plenum Press.

Index

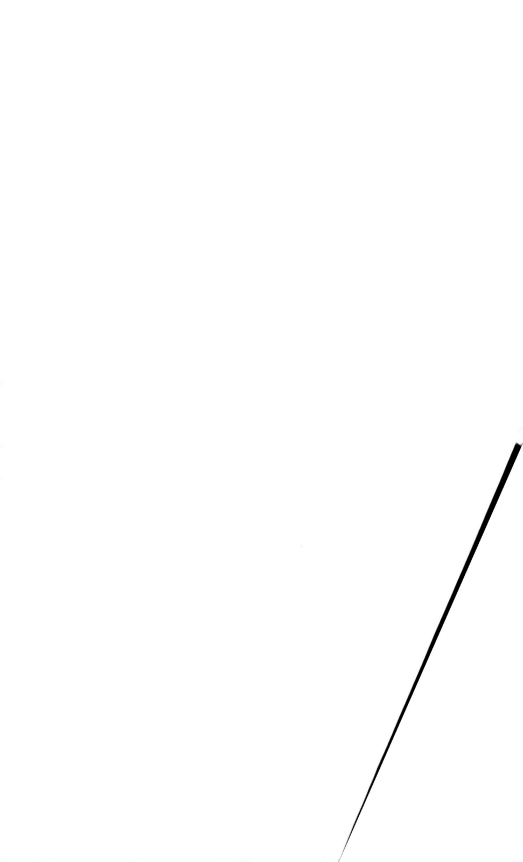

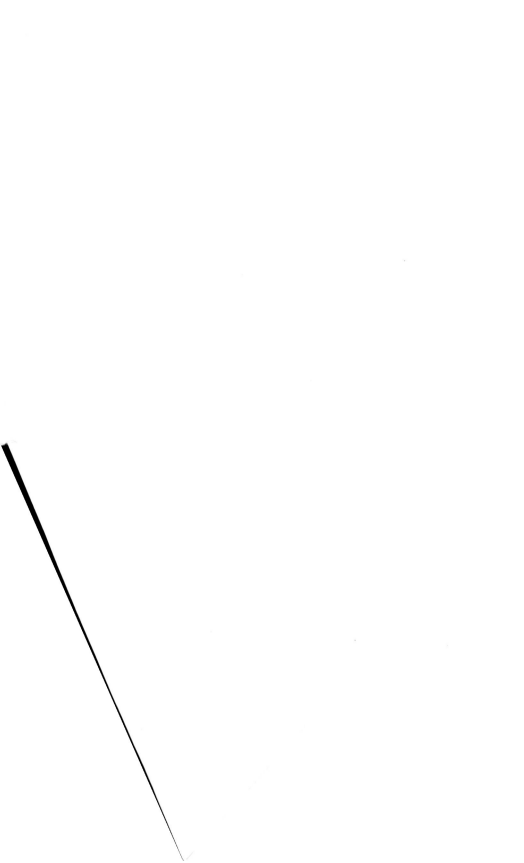